An Introduction to Persons with Severe Disabilities

An Introduction to Persons with Severe Disabilities

Educational and Social Issues

John J. McDonnell

Michael L. Hardman

Andrea P. McDonnell

Richard Kiefer-O'Donnell
University of Utah

Allyn and Bacon
Boston • London • Toronto • Sydney • Tokyo • Singapore

Series Editor: Ray Short
Marketing Manager: Ellen Mann
Production Administrator: Marjorie Payne
Editorial Assistant: Christine Shaw
Cover Administrator: Suzanne Harbison
Composition/Prepress Buyer: Linda Cox
Manufacturing Buyer: Megan Cochran
Editorial-Production Service: Chestnut Hill Enterprises, Inc.

Copyright © 1995 by Allyn & Bacon
A Simon & Schuster Company
Needham Heights, Massachusetts 02194

Library of Congress Cataloging-in-Publication Data

An introduction to persons with severe disabilities : educational and
    social issues / authors, John McDonnell . . . [et al.].
        p.   cm.
    Includes bibliographical references and index.
    ISBN 0–205–15090–X
    1. Handicapped—Services for—United States.   2. Handicapped—
Education—United States.   I. McDonnell, John J. (John Joseph),
1931–   .
HV1553.I59   1995
362.4'048'0973—dc20   94–32871
                                                                             CIP

Printed in the United States of America

10 9 8 7 6 5 4 3 2 1   00 99 98 97 96 95

Contents

Preface

In the last two decades, significant changes have occurred in society's perceptions about people with severe disabilities. Historically, "difference" or "deviance" has been something to be shunned by our society. People's differences were often used as a rationale for denying them their basic civil rights and segregating them from the "mainstream" of society (Dusault, 1989, Minnow, 1990). Many groups have suffered as a result of this oppressive social policy, including ethnic minorities, women, and people with disabilities. Although such discrimination continues to occur in many communities, public policy regarding people who are "different" has gone through a subtle but important transformation (Minnow, 1990). We have, at least at the institutional level, come to realize that the only thing that human beings have in common is that we are all different from one another. Equally important, the extent to which someone is different from you depends totally on your perspective. If you are seven feet tall, nearly everyone is shorter than you; if you are five feet tall, then only some people are shorter than you. Furthermore, whether these differences are important or not depends entirely on the context. Being seven feet tall is an advantage if you want to play basketball for a living, but it is a disadvantage if you own a compact car.

Our society's increasing openness to differences among people has created the conditions necessary to improve the quality of life experienced by people with severe disabilities. Less than thirty years ago these individuals were routinely placed in large institutions. This practice continued in spite of growing evidence that institutional programs were not effective in meeting the habilitative needs of people with severe disabilities and routinely exposed them to abuse and mistreatment. In contrast, today many individuals with severe disabilities attend their neighborhood schools, work in local businesses, live in their own homes, and participate as full members of our communities.

Society's increasing acceptance of people with disabilities has occurred with concurrent and dramatic improvements in the effectiveness of educational and community service programs. Our understanding of how to support persons with severe disabilities in school, home, and community settings has grown at a rapid pace. The research literature is replete with demonstrations of persons with severe disabilities learning to perform skills and activities that would have been dismissed as impossible just ten years ago. Advances in technology have revolutionized the way that advocates, researchers, and policy makers think about service programs for this group of people.

In spite of the changing social context and improvements in our technology, people with severe disabilities still face significant challenges in becoming part of our communities. This book is designed as an introduction to people with severe disabilities, focusing on the significant educational and social issues that still must be addressed in designing school and community programs to meet individual needs. *An Introduction to Persons with Severe Disabilities: Educational and Social Issues* is written using a life-span approach (birth through aging) so that professionals will understand the challenges faced by individuals of all ages.

Chapter 1 explores the various definitions of severe disabilities and describes the influences that these definitions have on the design of educational and community service programs. Chapter 2 reviews the history of service programs for people with severe disabilities in this century and outlines the emerging values and principles undergirding the development of current programs. Chapter 3 discusses the role of families, friends, and society in supporting the inclusion of persons with severe disabilities in our communities. It emphasizes the need for service programs to supplement rather than supplant the natural supports that people have available to them. Chapter 4 examines some of the most critical ethical issues facing society in its treatment of people with severe disabilities. This chapter provides an ethical framework for exploring topics such as genetic screening, abortion, and withholding of medical treatment. Chapters 5 through 10 describe the current status of service programs for people with severe disabilities, beginning with infants and continuing through the aging and elderly. Each of these chapters reviews effective practice and describes the critical operational components of service programs at each age level.

We would like to acknowledge the support of our colleagues Julie Hightower, Vicky Hoagland, Shelly Kiefer-O'Donnell, Connie Mathot-Buckner, Van Padjen, and Nadine Thorson during this project. They showed admirable levels of patience, even when our preoccupation made their lives miserable. We cannot thank them enough.

We also acknowledge the helpful comments of the following reviewers: Michael P. Brady, University of Houston; Felix Billingsley, University of Washington; Mary A. McEvoy, University of Minnesota; John Schuster, University of Kentucky; Margaret Penn Hutchins, University of Illinois; and Earle Knowlton, University of Kansas.

Dussault, W. L. E. (1989). Is a policy of exclusion based upon severity of disability legally defensible? In F. Brown & D. H. Lehr (Eds.), Persons with Profound Disabilities: Issues and Practices (pp. 43–60). Baltimore: Paul H. Brookes Publishing Company.

Minnow, M. (1990). Making all the difference: Inclusion, exclusion, and American law. Ithaca, NY: Cornell Univeristy Press.

About the Authors

John McDonnell is a Professor and Chair of the Department of Special Education at the University of Utah. Dr. McDonnell completed his doctorate at the University of Oregon in 1984. He has published numerous journal articles, chapters, and books in the area of severe disabilities. He has directed a number of state and federally funded research and model development grant projects. His primary research interests focus on effective instructional practices in school and community settings and the transition of students from school to community life. Dr. McDonnell has been actively involved in a number of state and national committees that have shaped policies governing service programs for persons with severe disabilities.

Michael L. Hardman is Associate Dean for Research in the Graduate School of Education, and Professor of Special Education at the University of Utah. Dr. Hardman, who completed his doctorate in educational administration at the University of Utah, has published 11 college textbooks and numerous national journal articles within the field of education. He has also directed several national demonstration projects on inclusive education and transition from school to adult life. Michael Hardman has been the recipient of a Joseph P. Kennedy, Jr. Foundation Public Policy Fellowship, and served as a staff member in the United States Senate, where he drafted legislation in the areas of vocational rehabilitation and the education of students with disabilities. He is very active in both professional and advocacy organizations, having served on national boards and committees for the Association for Persons with Severe Handicaps, Council for Exceptional Children, the ARC, and the Kennedy Foundation. He is currently the national president of the Higher Education Consortium for Special Education.

Andrea McDonnell is an Assistant Professor and Early Childhood Program Coordinator in the Department of Special Education at the University of Utah. She received a B.S. in Elementary Education from Western Oregon State College, a M.S. in Special Education and Rehabilitation from the University of Oregon, and a Ph.D. in Special Education from the University of Utah. Dr. McDonnell has been a special education teacher and has served as a Principal Investigator or Project Director on numerous model development, model dissemination, research, and training grants from the U.S. Department of Education and the Utah State Office of Education. She has presented papers at a number of national conferences and has published journal articles in the areas of early childhood special education, integrated programs for young children with severe disabilities, and behavior management.

Richard Kiefer-O'Donnell currently holds adjunct faculty appointments with the Departments of Special Education of the University of Utah and Utah State University. He directs a consortium project for the two institutions that prepares teachers of students with dual sensory impairments. He is currently finishing his Ph.D. in the area of severe disabilities, and has specific interests in effective inclusionary practices, functional communication, research methodology, and distance education. Prior to serving in his current role, he coordinated several state and federal personal training and technical assistance projects for students with severe disabilities, and taught in Georgia and Illinois.

Understanding People with Severe Disabilities

This book is about *people* with severe disabilities. Although often defined and characterized as a "disability population," each individual brings a unique set of needs, characteristics, and life experiences to this world. As we begin our discussion of the various definitions and characteristics associated with severe disabilities, we hope to maintain

---

WINDOW 1-1   Anita

Anita is nine years old, and lives with her mother and two brothers in a small town on the western plains of Nebraska. She attends Edgemont Elementary School with her younger brother, John, and friends from the neighborhood. Each morning at 7:00 a.m., John and Anita's mother help her into the family van, and along with her wheelchair, drive to a street corner a mile away to wait for the school bus. After a 45-minute ride, Anita settles in for a day at school with her 4th grade classmates, her teacher, and the special education support team.

Anita is in a setting with "typical" students, each bringing their own individual needs and experiences to the class and school. She is one of 26 kids, with her own unique personality, a beautiful smile, and a somewhat short temper when it comes to wanting something she can't have. Did we also mention that Anita has **mental retardation**, is blind, and unable to walk?

So, what is Anita, a child with **severe disabilities**, doing in a regular education setting? No, the instructional goals and strategies used to foster her learning aren't necessarily the same as her 25 "typical" classmates, but the overall intended outcomes are very much the same—access to, and participation in, a complex and often ambivalent society.

Throughout her school day, the classroom teacher, special education support team, and her peers work with Anita on individualized goals that range from increasing her communication skills to learning how to be more independent when eating. All of this takes place in the context of the regular school and classroom using strategies such as a **transdisciplinary approach** to instruction and **cooperative learning**. All of this takes place in a classroom that promotes learning for all children.

A POINT OF INTEREST! 1-1   Definitions Tell Us Very Little about People
with Severe Disabilities

If you have a severe disability, the very first thing that others would most likely be told about you would be a summary of your "deficits." Chances are, whatever they were, there would be a file containing a lengthy description of your intellectual shortcomings, your physical impairments, and your behavior problems, Even the most rudimentary personal information included on a driver's license—your eye color, hair color, height, and weight—remain a mystery throughout hundreds of pages of written records. Nowhere would someone learn that you had a lovely smile, a strong sense of identity, and a family that cared about you. Instead, we might read about your "inappropriate affect," your "noncompliance," and the "overprotectiveness" of your "difficult" parents. And although you might like to think of yourself as an active teenager interested in the "top 40" hits and the latest fashion in dress, hairstyle, and make-up, you may find yourself listening to nursery rhymes, dressed in a shapeless sweatsuit, your hair cropped short and straight, and with no access to even acne medication much less makeup. Why? Because an assumption has been made that your *disability* tells all there is no know about you, and from the moment you were diagnosed (or even *dually* diagnosed), you ceased being regarded as a person and became a "subject," a "client," or—worse yet—a "case." Your personality, your identity, and your lifestyle have become minor and even hidden details in a clinical history that tells the world about your weaknesses, faults, and deficits.

Source: Meyer, L. H., Peck, C. A. & Brown, L. (1991a). Definitions and diagnoses. In L. H. Meyer, C. A. Peck, and L. Brown (Eds.), *Critical Issues in the Lives of People with Disabilities* (pp. 17). Baltimore: Paul H. Brookes Publishing Company.

a clear separation of the person, as an individual, from the "disability" label. Anita from our opening window is a nine-year old child, who also happens to have severe disabilities. Instead of initially describing Anita as a child with green eyes and a beautiful smile who loves to listen to Bon Jovi with her brothers, she may be defined solely by her deficits: severely multiply disabled with profound retardation, blindness, and physical impairments.

The failure to separate the person from the label can be taken even further when people's names are actually replaced by "disability" labels. Anita, Devyn, and Thomas may be grouped together as "the severely disabled," or "the retarded." In this book, regardless of whether we are talking about definitions, characteristics or causation, the language will be "people first." As in our opening window, the focus is on Anita, *a child with severe disabilities.* The individual's name is always first, and the nature of their disability is mentioned second.

Definitions of Severe Disabilities

When the term *severe disabilities* is broken down into its two component parts, there is a stark revelation about what labels communicate. Severe is defined in the dictionary as extreme, bleak, harsh, inflexible, and uncompromising. Disability is described as lacking ability, debilitated, incapacitated, mutilated, or crippled. To say the least, these are ominous descriptors with a foreboding sense of hopelessness and despair. Possible combinations of dictionary terms for severe disability could then include: extremely debilitating, inflexibly incapacitated, or uncompromisingly crippled. This sense of hopelessness is often reflected in historical definitions of severe disabilities.

Traditional Approaches

> **Focus 1:**
>
> Distinguish between definitions of severe disabilities that are based on negative behavioral descriptors and those emphasizing individual instructional needs.

Abt Associates (1974) described the "severely handicapped[1] individual" as mentally retarded, emotionally disturbed, deaf-blind, or multiply handicapped. They are unable ". . . to attend to even the most pronounced social stimuli, including failure to respond to invitations from peers or adults, or loss of contact with reality" (p.v). This definition uses such terms as self-mutilation (head banging, body scratching, hair pulling), ritualistic behaviors (rocking, pacing), and self-stimulation (masturbation, stroking, patting) as descriptors of behavior exhibited by individuals with severe disabilities. The focus is on the individual's deficits. All the possible conditions that could be considered a severe disability are listed first, and then the accompanying characteristics are described.

Justen (1976) proposed a definition that moved away from negative behavioral descriptors to one that described individuals with severe disabilities as having a developmental disability with learning and behavior problems that required extensive modification in their instructional program.

> *The "severely handicapped" refers to those individuals age 21 and younger who are functioning at a general development level of half or less than the level which would be expected on the basis of chronological age and who manifest learning and/or behavior problems of such magnitude and significance that they require extensive structure in learning situations if their education needs are to be well served (Justen, p. 5).*

The Justen definition defines severe disabilities on the basis of the discrepancy between what is "normal" development for an individual of a certain chronological age, and the manifestation of significant learning and behavior problems that require extensive modifications in educational services. Both criteria must be met for the individual to be considered severely disabled. As such, a child with a severe disability would not only have to be at one-half the developmental level of their

---

[1] The terms *handicapped* and *disability* are often used interchangeably in definitions. The authors use the term *disability* throughout this book except when citing directly from a source where *handicapped* is part of a quotation.

peers who are not disabled (for example, an IQ of 50 or less where 100 is the average, or a language age of less than five for a ten-year-old child), but would also require alterations in their educational program due to extensive learning and behavior problems.

Sailor and Haring (1977) abandoned Justen's emphasis on establishing a discrepancy between normal and atypical development, and proposed a definition that was oriented solely to the instructional needs of the individual.

> *A child should be assigned to a program for the severely/multiply handicapped according to whether the primary service needs of the child are* basic *or academic. . . . If the diagnosis and assessment process determines that a child with multiple handicaps needs* academic *instruction, the child should not be referred to the severely handicapped program. If the child's service need is basic skill development, the referral to the severely/multiply handicapped program is appropriate (p. 68).*

Sailor and Haring do not include any behavioral descriptors in their definition, developmental or otherwise, but focus solely on the differences in educational need (basic or academic). Furthermore, the child is defined by the program they would attend, rather than the nature of their disability.

This emphasis on program requirements rather than negative descriptors is evident in the definition of severely handicapped children used by the U.S. Department of Education. This definition emphasizes the need to provide an appropriate educational program that includes related services (such as medical support) for every student regardless of the nature or extent of the disabling condition.

> *Severely handicapped children are those who because of the intensity of their physical, mental, or emotional problems, or a combination of such problems need educational, social, psychological, and medical services beyond those which are traditionally offered by regular and special education programs, in order to maximize their potential for useful and meaningful preparation in society and for self-fulfillment (*Federal Register, 1988, p. 118).

Snell (1987, 1991) expanded on the concept of defining individuals with severe disabilities according to instructional need, and suggested that the focus be on meeting educational needs in inclusive classroom settings. "Currently, among researchers and practitioners of integrated programs serving students with severe disabilities there is a general consensus that the concept of integrated schools is essential to an appropriate education. . ." (Snell, 1991). For Anita, this would mean structuring an educational program that is intended to decrease her dependence on others and create opportunities for her to be included in home, school, and neighborhood settings. In defining severe disabilities then, the emphasis moves to developing instructional outcomes that promote independence, rather than identifying a set of general characteristics that attempt to describe the individual.

The TASH Definition

Focus 2:

Identify the three components of the TASH definition of severe disabilities.

The movement toward defining individuals with severe disabilities on the basis of instructional need has continued to gain momentum with an increasing emphasis on identifying the supports necessary to promote access and opportunity in inclusive settings. The drawback of the definitions centered on instructional support (Sailor & Haring, 1977; Snell, 1991) is the emphasis on meeting the needs of school-age children. The Association for Persons with Severe Handicaps (TASH) dealt with this issue by proposing a definition of severe disabilities that includes "individuals of all ages," and maintains an emphasis on "extensive ongoing support."

> *These people include individuals of all ages who require extensive ongoing support in more than one major life activity in order to participate in integrated community settings and to enjoy a quality of life that is available to citizens with fewer or more disabilities. Support may be required for life activities such as mobility, communication, self-care, and learning as necessary for independent living, employment, and self-sufficiency (Meyer, Peck, & Brown, 1991b, p. 19).*

The TASH definition defines severe disabilities in terms of an adaptive fit between the individual and the environment. Adaptive fit is the degree to which an individual is able to cope with the requirements of a family, school, or community environment, and the extent to which the environment recognizes and accommodates individual diversity. The process of creating an adaptive fit is always dynamic with continuous adjustments between the individual and the environment in order to foster a mutually supportive coexistence. The TASH definition suggests that to create an adaptive fit for persons with severe disabilities there is a need to develop "extensive ongoing support" in a variety of life activities that could include getting around from place to place, interacting with people who are not disabled, taking care of one's own needs, and learning about lifestyle choices and economic self-sufficiency.

Definitions and Classification By Category of Disability

The evolution of the definition of severe disabilities as a specific condition has been primarily cross-categorical, and directed at the support necessary for the individual to participate in inclusive community and school settings. This cross-categorical approach has run parallel to the use of numerous categorical definitions of disability (such as mental retardation and hearing impairments). The categorical approach first defines the condition on the basis of specific criteria such as intelligence, adaptive behavior, achievement, or physical characteristics that separate one specific condition from another. For example, mental retardation is characterized by low intelligence and adaptive behavior deficits, whereas learning disabilities is characterized by average or high intelligence and low achievement in school. Once the specific criteria has been established for a category, individuals within that category can be classified according to the severity of the condition. For example, a person with mental retardation may be described as having significant intellectual and adaptive behavior limitations that can be classified as mild or severe in nature. A person with a hearing impairment may described as having a hearing loss that is mild (hard-of-hearing) or severe (deaf). In this section, we will examine some of the individual disability categories and classification systems that are based on severity of the condition. Table 1-1 provides a summary of disability categories and classification systems.

Focus 3:

How is severity determined in the disability categories of mental retardation, behavior disorders, autism, learning disabilities, sensory impairments, and physical and health impairments?

Mental Retardation

Definition
In 1992, the Association on Mental Retardation (AAMR[2]) revised its definition for the fourth time in 30 years. Mental retardation, according to AAMR is a condition characterized by:

> *. . . significantly subaverage intellectual functioning, existing concurrently with related limitations in two or more of the following applicable adaptive skill areas: communication, self-care, home living, social skills, community use, self-direction, health and safety, functional academics, leisure and work. Mental retardation manifests before age 18. (Luckasson et al., 1992)*

This revision maintained the basic elements of the AAMR definition adopted in 1983, which included significantly subaverage intellectual functioning, impairments in adaptive behavior, and manifestation prior to age 18 (Grossman, 1983). However, there is an expanded description of the adaptive skill areas which is not a part of the earlier AAMR definition, and the approach to classification is completely revised.

Classification
Mental retardation has traditionally been associated with classification by *severity* of the condition. The extent to which intellectual functioning and adaptive skills deviate from the average can be described in terms of mild, moderate, severe, and profound mental retardation. The 1983 AAMR definition uses a symptom severity approach to

---

[2] AAMR was formerly known as the Association for Mental Deficiency (AAMD). The acronym AAMD may be used periodically in this chapter in a historical context, such as the AAMD Adaptive Behavior Scales of 1969.

Table 1-1   Disability Categories and Classification by Severity

Disability Category	Description	Severity Classification

Mental Retardation	*Intellectual functioning (IQ) is below 70–75
	*Significant disabilities in two or more adaptive skill areas
		*Based on IQ and Level of Supports
		  • *Severe* mental retardation includes individuals with 25–40 IQs and adaptive skill deficits, which may include: fine and gross motor difficulties, speech and language delays, difficulty taking care of personal needs and developing interpersonal relationships
		  • Individual requires *extensive or pervasive* supports in environmental settings

Behavior Disorders	*The following characteristics are exhibited over a long period of time and to a marked degree:
	  • inability to have satisfactory relationships
	  • inappropriate behaviors or feelings under normal circumstances
	  • pervasive mood of unhappiness or depression
	  • develops physical symptoms or fears associated with personal or school problems
		*Based on frequency and extent of behavior exhibited
		*Terminology associated with severe behavior problems may include:
		  • *severe emotional disturbance*
		  • *psychosis*
		*Behavior exhibited may include:
		  • lack of contact with reality (such as withdrawal)
		  • behavior excesses (aggression; vandalism)
		  • low achievement in school
		  • hyperactivity and impulsivity

Autism	*Significant difficulties with verbal and nonverbal communication, as well as social interactions	*Although extent of communication difficulties vary from person to person, autism is generally considered a *severe* disability
		*Behavior exhibited may include:
		  • irregular and impaired communication
		  • repetitive activities and stereotypical movements
		  • resistance to change in daily routines or environmental conditions
		  • unusual responses to sensory experiences

Learning Disabilities	*Deficits in understanding or using language (spoken or written) which may be manifested in problems with listening, thinking, speaking, reading, writing, spelling, and mathematics
	*The definition of learning disabilities excludes students with sensory impairments, mental retardation, emotional disturbance, motor handicaps, or who are culturally, economically, or environmentally disadvantaged
		*Classification is not generally by severity-Learning disabilities is often referred to as a mildly handicapping condition
		*However, U.S. Department of Education rules and regulations indicate a *severe discrepancy* must exist between capacity (intelligence) and achievement in school. Severe discrepancy must be in one or more of the following:
		  • oral expression
		  • listening comprehension
		  • written expression

(continued)

Table 1-1   *Continued*

Disability Category	Description	Severity Classification
		• reading skills and/or comprehension • mathematical calculation and/or reasoning
Hearing Impairments	*Includes hearing losses ranging from the ability to process information from sound with an aid to losses so severe that hearing cannot be used as means to acquire information	*Classification by *severity* of loss includes hard-of-hearing and deaf • hard-of-hearing: generally described as a more mild hearing loss where residual hearing is sufficient to process information from sound with an aid • Deaf: a *severe hearing loss* of 90 db or more—Even with aids the individual is unable to use hearing as primary way to acquire information
Visual Impairments	*Includes visual losses ranging from the ability to process information through sight with an aid to losses so severe that sight cannot be used as means to acquire information	*Classification by *severity* includes partially-sighted and blindness • partial sight: having enough vision remaining with an aid to acquire information through the eyes • blindness: unable to use sight, and must rely on other senses to acquire information
Physical and Health Disorders	*Physical disorders: interfere with mobility and coordination, and may also have secondary effect on communication, learning, and emotional adjustment *Health disorders: chronic or acute health problems that result in limited strength, vitality and alertness, and may also adversely effect school performance	*Physical and health disorders are not generally classified by severity, although various conditions can result in mild through *severe* problems (such as cerebral palsy, traumatic brain injury, seizure disorders, or AIDS)

classify individuals with mental retardation on the basis of intelligence quotient (IQ) and adaptive behavior. IQ levels include mild (IQ 55–70), moderate (IQ 40–55), *severe* (IQ 25–40), and profound (IQ 25 or lower). Impairments in adaptive behavior are broken down into mild through profound descriptors as well. As defined by Grossman, "Adaptive behavior refers to what people do to take care of themselves and to relate to others in daily living rather than the abstract potential implied by intelligence" (p. 42). In the school setting, adaptive behavior can be described in terms of how well the student applies skills learned in a classroom setting to home and community environments. Adaptive behavior deficits then can be described in terms of the degree to which an individual's behavior differs from what is expected according to his or her chronological age. Differences are then described in terms of mild, moderate, *severe*, and profound adaptive behavior deficits. The AAMR severity approach to classification runs parallel to one used by the public schools based on expected achievement in school-related situations in conjunction with the individual's score on an intelligence test. Educability classification descriptors include educable, trainable, and custodial retardation. The IQ and expected achievement for both the AAMR and public school classification systems may be found in Table 1-2.

The 1992 definition of mental retardation (Luckasson et al., 1992) abandoned the symptom severity approach to classification and adopted a system that concentrated on the *supports* needed for the individual to have optimal growth and development in family, school, and community settings. These supports include both human and material resources. Human supports can be both natural (family, friends, neighbors, co-workers) and formalized (teachers, job coaches, physicians). Material supports may range from access to barrier-free buildings for individuals who are in a wheelchair to the use of electronic devices to assist communication.

The AAMR classification system describes the steps necessary to identify the appropriate supports for each individual:

1. Describe the person's strengths and weaknesses in reference to psychological/emotional considerations.
2. Describe the person's overall physical health and indicate the condition's cause.
3. Describe the person's current environmental placement and the optimal environment that would facilitate the person's growth and development (Luckasson et al., 1992).

Once the description of the individual's *adaptive fit* with the environment has been completed, the next step is to identify the level of supports that would be required to facilitate optimal growth and development. AAMR breaks down these supports into four levels: intermittent, limited, extensive, and pervasive. See Table 1-3.

TABLE 1-2 Severity and Educability Classification Approaches in Mental Retardation According to IQ Level

IQ Level	Severity of Condition	Educability	Expectation
55–70	Mild	Educable	Achievement in school may range from second to fifth grade level; may achieve total or partial independence in the community, including competitive employment
40–55	Moderate	Trainable	Learning primarily in functional skill areas (such as self-help); may acquire some primary academic skills in reading and math; may achieve partial independence in the community, including competitive employment with supports
25–40	*Severe*	Custodial	Individual may need extensive and on-going supports (social, educational and medical) to adapt to home and community living
Below 25	Profound	Custodial	

TABLE 1-3   AAMR Levels of Support for People with Mental Retardation

Level	Intensity
Intermittent	Supports are provided as needed and may be episodic (supports not always necessary) or short-term (job loss or medical crisis). Intermittent supports may be high or low intensity.
Limited	Supports are characterized by consistency. Time may be limited but is not intermittent. In comparison to more intensive supports, fewer staff may be required and costs may be lower (for example, time-limited employment training or transitional supports from school to adult life).
Extensive	Supports are characterized by regular involvement (such as daily) in some environments, but are not time-limited (for example, long-term job and home-living support).
Pervasive	Supports are characterized by constancy and high intensity across all environments; may be potentially life-sustaining in nature. Pervasive supports typically involve more staff and are more intrusive than extensive or time-limited supports.

Source: Luckasson, R., Coulter, D., Polloway, E., Reiss, S., Schalock, R., Snell, M., Spitalnik, D., & Stark, J. (1992). *Mental retardation: Definitions, classification, and systems of supports* (9th ed.). Washington, D.C.: American Association on Mental Retardation.

Behavior Disorders

Definition
People with behavior disorders experience problems relating to others in a variety of ways, and across multiple environments. The term is often used synonymously with "emotional disturbance," and to a lesser extent "mental illness." One of the more widely adopted definitions of behavior disorders is included in the *Individuals with Disabilities Education Act (IDEA)*. It relies heavily on negative behavior descriptors:

> (i) *The term means a condition exhibiting one or more of the following characteristics over a long period of time and to a marked degree, which adversely affects educational performance:*
> (A) *An inability to learn which cannot be explained by intellectual, sensory or health factors;*
> (B) *An inability to build or maintain satisfactory interpersonal relationships with peers and teachers;*
> (C) *Inappropriate types of behavior or feelings under normal circumstances;*
> (D) *A general pervasive mood of unhappiness or depression;*
> (E) *A tendency to develop physical symptoms or fears associated with personal or school problems.*
> (ii) *The term includes children who are schizophrenic. The term does not include children who are socially maladjusted, unless it is determined that they are seriously emotionally disturbed. (34 C.F.R. 300.5(b)(8)(1990)*

Although this definition includes multiple behavioral descriptors, the most important determinants of the condition are that the behaviors are significant in nature (to a marked degree) and occur over a long period of time. The condition is characterized by poor interpersonal relationships, inappropriate behavior, a pervasive sense of unhappiness, and physical symptoms associated with the problems.

Classification

There are several different systems used to classify behavior disorders, one of which is based on the *severity* of the condition. Stainback and Stainback (1980) developed a classification paradigm that contrasts mild with severe behavior disorders across intellectual, social, academic, and behavioral domains. They viewed the individual with *severe emotional disturbance* as: (1) having a lower average IQ; (2) functioning in the below average range in academic achievement across most content areas; (3) exhibiting hyperactive and impulsive behavior; (4) losing contact with reality; (5) more likely to display aggressive behaviors of a serious nature; and (6) highly dependent on others (may be unable to perform basic life skills). Teachers of students who have been identified as *severely disturbed* describe their students as showing no social interest in relating to others, and often have multiple handicapping conditions (Olson, Algozzine, & Schmid, 1980).

Autism

Autism has traditionally been characterized as a *severe behavior disorder*. When first identified (Kanner, 1943), autism was thought to be the result of parental rejection and hostility toward the child. Today, however, autism is characterized more as a severe language disorder resulting from brain dysfunction. In the 1990 amendments to the Education of the Handicapped Act, *IDEA*, the U.S. Congress defined autism as a separate category under the law, no longer considering the condition as a type of severe behavior disorder.

> *Autism means a developmental disability significantly affecting verbal and nonverbal communication and social interaction, generally evident before age three, that adversely affects educational performance. Characteristics of autism include- irregularities and impairments in communication, engagement in repetitive activities and stereotyped movements, resistance to environmental change or change in daily routines, and unusual responses to sensory experiences.*

The primary determinants of autism are that onset occurs prior to the age of three, and that communication and social interaction problems affect educational performance.

The American Psychiatric Association has also developed a diagnostic criteria for autism based on time of onset and the manifestation of behavioral problems that are atypical for the individual's developmental level and chronological age. A summary of this diagnostic criteria is presented in Table 1-4.

TABLE 1-4 American Psychiatric Association Diagnostic Criteria for Autism

At least eight of the following sixteen items are present, these to include at least two items from A, one from B, and one from C. **Note:** Consider a criterion to be met *only* if the behavior is abnormal for the person's developmental level.

A. Qualitative impairment in reciprocal social interaction as manifested by the following:

(The examples within parentheses are arranged so that those first mentioned are more likely to apply to younger or more handicapped, and the later ones, to older or less handicapped, persons with this disorder.)

 (1) marked lack of awareness of the existence or feelings of others (e.g., treats a person as if he or she were a piece of furniture; does not notice another person's distress; apparently has no concept of the need of others for privacy)
 (2) no or abnormal seeking of comfort at times of distress (e.g., does not come for comfort even when ill, hurt, or tired; seeks comfort in a stereotyped way, e.g., says "cheese, cheese, cheese" whenever hurt)
 (3) no or impaired imitation (e.g., does not wave bye-bye; does not copy mother's domestic activities; mechanical imitation of others' actions out of context)
 (4) no or abnormal social play (e.g., does not actively participate in simple games; prefers solitary play activities; involves other children in play only as "mechanical aids")
 (5) gross impairment in ability to make friendships (e.g., no interest in making peer friendships; despite interest in making friends, demonstrates lack of understanding of conventions of social interaction, for example, reads phone book to uninterested peer)

B. Qualitative impairment in verbal and nonverbal communication, and in imaginative activity, as manifested by the following:

(The numbered items are arranged so that those first listed are more likely to apply to younger or more handicapped, and the later ones, to older or less handicapped, persons with this disorder.)

 (1) no mode of communication, such as communicative babbling, facial expression, gesture, mime, or spoken language
 (2) markedly abnormal nonverbal communication, as in the use of eye-to-eye gaze, facial expression, body posture, or gesture to initiate or modulate social interaction (e.g., does not anticipate being held, stiffens when held, does not look at the person or smile when making a social approach, does not greet parents or visitors, has a fixed stare in social situations)
 (3) absence of imaginative activity, such as playacting of adult roles, fantasy characters, or animals; lack of interest in stories about imaginary events
 (4) marked abnormalities in the production of speech, including volume, pitch, stress, rate, rhythm, and intonation (e.g., monotonous tone, questionlike melody, or high pitch)
 (5) marked abnormalities in the form or content of speech, including stereotyped and repetitive use of speech (e.g., immediate echolalia or mechanical repetition of television commercial); use of "you" when "I" is meant (e.g., using "You want cookie?" to mean "I want a cookie"); idiosyncratic use of words or phrases (e.g., "Go to green riding" to mean "I want to go on the swing"); or frequent irrelevant remarks (e.g., starts talking about train schedules during a conversation about sports)
 (6) marked impairment in the ability to initiate or sustain a conversation with others, despite adequate speech (e.g., indulging in lengthy monologues on one subject regardless of interjections from others)

C. Markedly restricted repertoire of activities and interests, as manifested by the following:

TABLE 1-4 *Continued*

(1) stereotyped body movements, e.g., hand-flicking, or -twisting, spinning, head-banging, complex whole-body movements
(2) persistent preoccupation with parts of objects (e.g., sniffing or smelling objects, repetitive feeling of texture of materials, spinning wheels of toy cars) or attachment of unusual objects (e.g., insists on carrying around a piece of string)
(3) marked distress over changes in trivial aspects of environment, e.g., when a vase is moved from usual position
(4) unreasonable insistence on following routines in precise detail, e.g., insisting that exactly the same route always be followed when shopping
(5) markedly restricted range of interests and preoccupation with one narrow interest, e.g., interested only in lining up objects, in amassing facts about meteorology, or in pretending to be a fantasy character

D. Onset during infancy or childhood

Specify if childhood onset (after 36 months of age).

Source: American Psychiatric Association. (1987). *Diagnostic and Statistical Manual of Mental Disorders, Third Edition, Revised*. Washington, DC: Author.

Learning Disabilities

Whereas autism is a condition often associated with severe problems, learning disabilities has been more traditionally described as a mild disability. The view that learning disabilities is a mild condition originates from the fact that these individuals are by definition normal or near normal in intelligence, and experience learning problems primarily in academic content areas. However, as pointed out by Hardman, Drew, Egan, and Wolf (1993), ". . . learning disabilities is a generic label representing a very heterogeneous group of disabilities, ranging from mild to severe" (p. 172). They further suggest that "no other disability label has generated more controversy, confusion, and polarization among contemporary professionals" (p. 173).

The National Joint Committee for Learning Disabilities defines learning disabilities as:

> *. . . a general term that refers to a heterogeneous group of disorders manifested by significant difficulties in the acquisition and use of listening, speaking, writing, reasoning, or mathematical abilities. These disorders are intrinsic to the individual, presumed to be due to central nervous system dysfunction, and may occur across the lifespan. Problems in self-regulatory behaviors, social perception, and social interaction may exist with learning disabilities but do not by themselves constitute a learning disability. Although learning disabilities may occur concomitantly with other handicapping conditions (for example, sensory impairments, mental retardation, serious emotional disturbance) or with extrinsic influences (such as cultural differences, insufficient or inappropriate instruction), they are not the result of those conditions or influences. (1988, p. 1)*

This definition addresses the heterogeneous nature of the condition, and emphasizes that the individual with learning disabilities must have "significant difficulties" in learning. This further stresses the point that the condition is not necessarily mild in nature.

Classification

Although learning disabilities is usually not classified according to the severity of the condition, the federal rules under *IDEA* require that any criterion for classifying a student with learning disabilities must be based on an already *severe* discrepancy between capacity (intelligence) and achievement across seven areas relating to communication skills and mathematical abilities (See Table 1-1). The exact nature of this *severe* discrepancy is often open to interpretation and differs from state to state.

Sensory Impairments

Definitions

Hearing and visual impairments are both defined by the type and degree of sensory loss. The terms describe the entire range of auditory and visual loss from mild through severe conditions. People with hearing impairments are usually divided into two groups: hard-of-hearing and deafness. For the person who is hard-of-hearing, audition is deficient but the individual has enough residual hearing with an aid to acquire information through the auditory channel. Deafness, on the other hand is typified by a hearing loss so great that the person does not have any functional hearing even with the use of a hearing aid.

People with visual impairments have losses ranging from partial to total blindness. As described by Warren (1989), people with visual impairments include those who:

> *have never had any visual function, those who had normal vision for some years before becoming gradually or suddenly partially or totally blind, those with [disabilities] in addition to the visual loss, those with selective impairments of parts of the visual field, and those with a general degradation of acuity across the visual field. (p. 155)*

Classification

Hearing and visual impairments are most often classified by the *severity* of the condition. Hard-of-hearing and partially-sighted represent the more mild end of the severity spectrum; deafness and blindness are both considered *severe* disabilities. Deafness is usually defined by a loss of 90 decibels (dbs) or greater. Even with the assistance of hearing aids or other amplification, communication skills are primarily developed through the visual channel. Blindness is the counterpart of deafness in the visual channel. A person who is blind has a visual acuity of 20/200 or worse in the best eye with correction. A person who is blind will use the auditory channel as the primary avenue for acquiring information.

Physical and Health Impairments

Definitions
The range of physical and health impairments is extremely diverse, and includes conditions that interfere with mobility and coordination, as well as those that limit strength, vitality, and alertness. Physical impairments, described in *IDEA* as orthopedic impairments, include such conditions as traumatic brain injury, cerebral palsy, spina bifida, amputations, spinal cord injuries, and muscular dystrophy. Health impairments, which result from chronic or acute health problems, involve such conditions as AIDS, tuberculosis, heart disease, rheumatic fever, leukemia, diabetes, and lead poisoning. In order for a student with a physical or health impairment to be considered as eligible for special education services under *IDEA*, the condition must adversely affect educational performance.

Classification
Physical and health impairments are most often classified by the type and nature of the condition, such as problems resulting from genetic anomalies, trauma, cancer, heart disease, or virus. Although physical and health problems are not generally classified according to severity, many of these conditions result in serious impairments that not only affect an individual's educational performance and community living, but are life-threatening.

Severe Multiple Disabilities

From our previous discussions on cross-categorical and categorical definitions, it is obvious that severe disabilities embraces a very diverse group of individuals. Most will have multiple conditions that may include intellectual, learning, behavior, and physical differences. As such, severe disabilities may also be characterized by the *multiplicity* of conditions associated with these individuals. It is possible for severe multiple disabilities to include any combination of two or more individual disability conditions that result in outcomes such as poor educational performance, or the need for additional supports to access home or community living environments.

In a number of cases associated with severe multiple disabilities, mental retardation is the primary condition (Hardman et al., 1993). For example, approximately 60 percent of people with cerebral palsy are mentally retarded (Batshaw & Perret, 1986). A significant percentage of persons labeled as mentally retarded have seizure disorders or spina bifida (Brimer, 1990). In fact, nearly half of all people with seizure disorders also have an intellectual impairment (Rodin, Shapiro, & Lennox, 1976). Several researchers have also suggested a strong relationship between mental retardation and behavior disorders. Individuals with both conditions are referred to as **dually diagnosed**.

Dual Diagnosis: Mental Retardation and Behavior Disorders

Focus 4:

Identify two concerns in applying the term *dual diagnosis* to persons with severe disabilities.

The relationship between mental retardation and behavior disorders has received considerable attention in recent years. The occurrence of serious behavioral problems (specifically psychiatric disorders) in people with mental retardation is higher than average (Bruininks, Hill, & Morreau, 1988). Estimates range from one in every four to approximately 90 percent of the population (Matson & Barrett, 1982; Senatore, Matson, & Kazdin, 1985). Reiss (1990a), in a study of community-based day programs for individuals with mental retardation, found that more than 39 percent of people participating were "dually diagnosed." However, Reiss (1990b) suggests that, in actuality, there has been little research on the condition, and that definitions and valid measures are still in the early stages of development.

The Association for Persons with Severe Handicaps (TASH), while recognizing that mental illness may occur in conjunction with mental retardation, expressed its apprehension regarding the growing use of the term *dual diagnosis*. In a resolution to its membership, the association expressed concern that the term could be misapplied in order to improperly institutionalize people who are "dually diagnosed, as well as promote the use of aversive behavioral procedures, psychotropic medications, and punishment through the judicial system." TASH indicated strong support for:

- *The development of standards for the diagnosis of mental illness for people with mental retardation that are as stringent for people who are not disabled;*
- *Programming principles that support individualized, personalized services, and non-aversive methods;*
- *Additional research to determine the influence of environmental factors affecting the increase in behaviors associated with mental illness;*
- *Support and assistance based on individual need rather than labels. (Meyer, Peck, & Brown, 1991c)*

Focus 5:

Define deaf-blindness

Dual Sensory Impairments

A severe multiple disability that involves concomitant loss of both vision and hearing is known as deaf-blindness, a dual-sensory impairment. Persons defined as deaf-blind have severe learning and communication problems that require extensive support from

---

WINDOW 1-2   The Dual Diagnosed Dilemma of Morris Mason

The state of Virginia electrocuted 32-year-old Morris Mason on June 25, 1985, in spite of his dual diagnosis of mental retardation and mental illness. Mason grew up on the sparsely populated Eastern shore. Folks knew him as a school dropout, a loner, and the butt of other kids' pranks.

He spent time in three mental hospitals, where he was diagnosed as having an "IQ of 66, and schizophrenic reactions." At age 22, he lost control, committed an act of arson, and went to prison.

Two and a half years later, he left the prison, but he couldn't adjust to the outside world. Feeling himself rapidly losing control, he called his parole officer twice, asking for help. On May 12, 1978, he called again, asking that he be placed in a "halfway house" or some kind of supervised environment. The parole officer set a meeting for later that week.

That appointment was never kept because the next day Mason went on an alcoholic rampage, killing a 72-year-old woman and burning her house. On May 14, he attacked two girls, ages 12 and 13, leaving one with paraplegia.

He pleaded guilty and waived his right to a trial. Sentenced to death, he left the courtroom "talking crazy" about being "the killer for the Eastern shore" and making "the Eastern shore popular."

The Eastern shore's demand for revenge, understandably, never ceased. On the other hand,

the judges never stopped the legal machinery long enough to determine whether it was proper to electrocute a person so retarded and mentally ill. Virginia law requires the transfer of any prisoner diagnosed as insane to a mental-health facility. The prison warden, however, is solely responsible for initiating a sanity hearing in the case of a condemned prisoner (VA Code, 1975). As for the man's mental retardation, it was ignored. . . .

After Mason's execution, Joseph Giarratano, a fellow inmate on death row, wrote a touching memoir:

When they executed Morris they didn't kill a consciously responsible individual: they executed a child in a man's body. To this day I do not believe that Morris knew right from wrong, or left from right for that matter. He just didn't want anyone to be angry with him. That includes the guards who worked the unit. The guards were always his best listeners: They had to be here for eight hours a shift anyway. And Morris would stand there and babble for as long as they would sit and listen. Back then, conditions on the row were pretty harsh, but nothing seemed to phase him. No one here, prisoner or guard, saw Morris as a threat. If he were here today, he would still be chattering on about sports, and trying to please people in his own out-of-touch-with-reality way. (Ingle, 1990, p. 251.)

Source: Perske, R. (1991). *Unequal justice?* Nashville: Abingdon Press.

many professional disciplines. Bullis and Otos (1988) suggest that there is ". . . no condition as disabling as deaf-blindness, the loss of part or all of one's vision and hearing" (p. 110). Given the complexity of this condition, it is not surprising that there is confusion regarding what is an appropriate support structure to meet the educational and social needs of this population. The traditional concept of deaf-blind is that these individuals are of average intelligence, and lost their hearing and sight after having acquired language. However, another view is that these individuals are severely retarded ". . . to the extent that sensory function in vision and hearing was also severely impaired" (Hammer, 1989, p. 177). Whether these individuals are mentally retarded or not is up for debate. From a functional standpoint, Downing and Eichinger (1990) describe individuals who are deaf-blind as not being able to initiate or respond to ". . . appropriate interactions with others and often exhibit behavior that is considered socially inappropriate" (p. 99). As Hammer points out, in order to better understand deaf-blindness, there is a very real need to develop a systematic method to identify these individuals, and then describe them through appropriate assessment procedures.

In addition to individuals who are deaf-blind and those who are dually diagnosed as mentally retarded and behavior disordered, there are other possible combinations of severe multiple disabilities. For example, a severe multiple disability may involve mental retardation with physical impairments, or severe behavior disorders with a dual sensory loss. What is important to remember, however, is that definitions are at best only very rough approximations of characteristics, and at worst stereotypical labels that can result in unintended negative outcomes for those who are "labeled." We will examine issues of labeling and assessment as they impact the lives of people with severe disabilities later in this chapter.

Prevalence

> **Focus 6:**
>
> What are the estimated prevalence and causes of severe disabilities?

Individuals with severe disabilities constitute a relatively small percentage of the general population. However, the actual number of individuals with severe disabilities is elusive because prevalence is relative to the definition used. As Brimer (1990) indicates, "the broader the definition, the higher the prevalence figures" (p. 17). If we use a cross-categorical definition of severe disabilities, estimates range from 0.1 to 1.0 percent of the total population (Hardman et al., 1993; Ludlow & Sobsey, 1984). Brown (1991), referring to individuals defined by TASH as severely disabled, suggested that this group constitutes the lowest one percent of the general population.

Categorical definitions of severe disabilities result in a somewhat different view of prevalence. It is estimated that individuals with severe mental retardation constitute about .5 percent of the general population or about one million people. There are approximately 4 out of every 1,000 individuals with severe disabilities where the primary symptom is mental retardation.

There is disagreement regarding the prevalence of severe behavior disorders. Some estimates (Bower, 1982; Knoblock, 1983) are in the range of 1 to 2 percent of the general population, while Brimer suggests that .4 percent is probably a more accurate figure. It is also estimated that about 80 percent of all individuals with severe behavior disorders are male (Paluszny, 1979).

Prevalence estimates for individuals with severe multiple disabilities also vary. The U.S. Department of Education (1991) estimates that about 88,000 students were served in the public schools under the label multiple disabilities during the 1989–90 school year, or about 2 percent of the four million students considered as eligible for special education services under *IDEA*. This figure does not include the 1,700 students labeled as deaf-blind. It is estimated that there are no more than about 14,000 people of all ages who are deaf-blind, or about 754 per 100,000 people.

Causation

People with severe disabilities are a heterogenous group of individuals, and the causes associated with their condition are equally diverse. The nature of the disability(ies) is most often present at birth, whether it be problems resulting from a genetic origin (such as chromosomal abnormalities), or difficulties that are the result of inadequate prenatal care, poor maternal nutrition, birth trauma, infectious diseases, radiation exposure, or sexually transmitted diseases. However, it is also possible for severe disabilities to occur later in life as a result of abuse and neglect, poisoning, disease, malnutrition, or trauma.

Assessment and Labeling Issues

Definitions and classification systems result from an assessment process intended to differentiate the characteristics of one individual from another. Once a common set of characteristics has been established for a specific group of people, then a definition is developed, and a labeled applied. One fundamental purpose of definitions and labels is to determine who is eligible for services (social, medical, or educational) and who is not. For example, Anita, from our opening window, is a child with characteristics that are consistent with the definitions and labels associated with *mental retardation* or *severe multiple disabilities*. If she is to receive specialized services, she must be labeled by law as mentally retarded and/or severely multiply disabled. Labels evolve out of definitions, and definitions evolve from the process of assessment.

The purposes for assessment are primarily to compare one person's performance to another, or to compare performance with a desired goal. Although assessment and testing are often used synonymously, they are not the same. Testing is one element of the assessment process, which may also include observations, interviews, or behavior sampling. Salvia and Ysseldyke (1991) define testing as a means to expose ". . . a person to a particular set of questions in order to obtain a score" (p.3). Testing can be either standardized or informal in nature. Whereas informal or criterion-referenced tests focus on how the individual performs relative to a set objective or goal (the criterion), the purpose of standardized tests is to provide a comparison of one person to another. Everyone who takes a standardized test gets the same set of questions, using the same administration procedures. The answers to these questions form "a score" for the individual that is relative to everyone else who has taken the test. More than 250 million standardized tests are given each year to school-age children in the United States for purposes ranging from eligibility for special education services in the public schools to establishing college entrance requirements.

Definitions and Use of Standardized Tests

> **Focus 7:**
>
> Why do many professionals prefer the functional approach over the use of standardized tests in assessing individuals with severe disabilities?

Traditionally, most definitions of disability categories have relied on standardized tests as the means to assess whether or not an individual's characteristics are consistent with the established criteria. The most obvious example of reliance on standardized tests is the AAMR's definition of mental retardation. "Significantly subaverage intellectual functioning" is determined by an intelligence test that results in an IQ score. In order for an individual to be considered retarded, the IQ score must fall below 70 to 75 where the norm is 100 (Luckasson et al., 1992). Even in the measurement of adaptive behavior, where there is more opportunity for a broader assessment using observations or behavior sampling, the move has been toward the development of standardized tests, such as the AAMD Adaptive Behavior Scale (Nihira et al., 1969), the Revised Vineland Social Maturity Scale (Sparrow, Balla & Cicchetti, 1984) and the Scales of Independent Behavior (Bruininks, Woodcock, Weatherman, & Hill, 1984).

The reliance on standardized tests is also evident in other disability definitions. Definitions of learning disabilities rely on a standardized assessment of severe discrepancy between intelligence and academic achievement; hearing and visual impairments are based on a standard measure of sight or hearing loss; and behavior disorders relies heavily on standardized behavior scales or checklists to identify characteristics consistent with the definition.

The validity of standardized assessments, particularly the IQ test, to define and describe individuals with severe disabilities has been seriously questioned. Some professionals suggest that IQ testing is of no use whatsoever in defining severe disabilities (Evans, 1991; Heward & Orlansky, 1992; Meyer et al., 1991b). Evans suggest that "IQ tests, as currently constituted, have no place in the assessment of individuals with severe intellectual disabilities" (p. 40).

The Functional Assessment Approach

Whether it be establishing a definition, determining eligibility for services, or developing an instructional program for students with severe disabilities, the use of standardized testing has been strongly criticized as invalid. The alternative is a functional assessment approach. As described by Gaylord-Ross and Browder (1991), functional assessment:

- *Focuses on practical* independent living skills *that enable the person to survive and succeed in the real world.*
- *Has an* ecological *emphasis that looks at the individual functioning in his or her surrounding environment.*

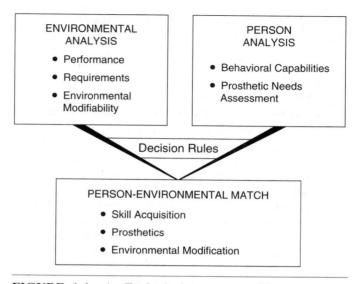

FIGURE 1-1   An Ecological Assessment-Placement Approach

Source: Schalock, R. (1986). *Transitions from school to work.* Washington, DC: National Association of Rehabilitation Facilities.

- *Examines the* process *of learning and performance.*
- *Suggests* intervention *techniques that may be successful.*
- *Specifies ongoing monitoring procedures that can evaluate treatment progress. (p. 45)*

Functional assessments concentrate on the actual skills necessary for an individual to access and participate in natural settings, such as the home, the regular school or classroom, and the community at-large. The *ecological* aspect of functional assessments is an important element in meeting the needs of individuals with severe disabilities. The ecological approach is concerned with a match between environmental demands and individual needs, experiences, and abilities. This notion of an adaptive fit between the individual and the environment is consistent with the definition of severe disabilities proposed by the Association for Persons with Severe Handicaps (TASH), discussed earlier in this chapter. The outcomes for the individual are related to an assessment process that results in the availability of the *supports* necessary for the individual to participate in natural settings. As described by McDonnell, Wilcox, and Hardman (1991):

> *Skills are never taught in isolation from actual performance demands. Additionally, the individual does not 'get ready' to participate in the community through a sequence of readiness stages as in the developmental model, but learns and uses skills in the setting where the behavior is expected to occur. (p. 23)*

The specific assumptions and elements of the ecological model are discussed in more depth in Chapter 2.

Conclusion

This chapter has examined the myriad definitions associated with severe disabilities. The more traditional definitions use negative behavioral descriptors and rely on standardized tests to assess and describe people with severe disabilities. Concerns regarding the validity of this approach have resulted in more recent definitions (such as the TASH definition of severe disabilities and the 1992 AAMR definition of mental retardation) that concentrate on functionally assessing the relationship between the individual and the demands of the environment. These definitions address the supports necessary for the individual to access and participate in inclusive school and community settings.

If the purpose of human services is to prepare people with severe disabilities for an inclusive lifestyle, then it follows that the definitions used to characterize these indi-

****

POINT AND COUNTERPOINT 1-1   To Standardize or Not to Standardize
That is the Question

The debate regarding standardized vs. functional approaches to assessment for people with severe disabilities is important to our understanding of the diverse needs and characteristics of these individuals. Here are two points of view on the use of standardized intelligence tests for people with severe disabilities.

Point:

It is generally too expensive and inconvenient to observe people's daily behavior sufficiently in school and work to obtain a dependable measure of intelligence. One problem with observation is that it is all but impossible to standardize the conditions of everyday life to permit fair comparisons. Intelligence tests, however, do contain standardized series of tasks or work samples that provide for the efficient assessment of intelligence. Such intelligence tests or scales are administered under highly controlled conditions so that an individual's score may be appropriately compared with the norms secured for other people.[3]

Counterpoint:

Traditional methods of intelligence testing . . . are virtually useless with many children who have severe handicaps [disabilities]. If tested they tend to be assigned IQ scores at the extreme lower end of the continuum. Knowing that a particular student has an IQ of 25, however, is of no value in designing an appropriate educational program. Educators . . . tend to focus on the specific skills a child needs to learn, rather than on intellectual level.[4]

****

[3] Source: Grossman, H. J. (Ed.) (1983). *Classification in mental retardation*. Washington, D.C.: American Association on Mental Deficiency.

[4] Source: Heward, W. L., & Orlansky, M. D. (1992). *Exceptional Children* (4th ed.). New York: Merrill Publishing Co.

viduals should be consistent with that objective. Definitions and classification systems that are more concerned with information that is " . . . of direct benefit to the individual" (Gaylord-Ross & Browder, 1991, p. 45) will result in a social and educational support structure that leads to greater independence, choice, autonomy, and economic self-sufficiency.

Focus Review

Focus 1: Distinguish between definitions of severe disabilities that are based on negative behavioral descriptors and those emphasizing individual instructional needs.

- The more traditional definitions of severe disabilities described the individual in terms of their negative behavioral characteristics. Characteristics, such as self-mutilation and stimulation, loss of contact with reality, or failure to respond to social stimuli were included in these definitions.
- Whereas some definitions focus on individual deficits, others are oriented to the instructional needs of each individual. Definitions based on instructional need emphasize the importance of an appropriate educational program for every student regardless of the nature or extent of the disabling condition.

Focus 2: Identify the three components of the TASH definition of severe disabilities.

- The definition includes people with severe disabilities of all ages.
- Extensive ongoing support is required for people with severe disabilities.
- Individuals with severe disabilities need support in life activities that will facilitate their participation in inclusive settings.

Focus 3: How is severity determined in the disability categories of mental retardation, behavior disorders, autism, learning disabilities, sensory impairments, and physical and health impairments?

- Mental retardation: The severity of the condition is the extent to which intellectual functioning and adaptive skills deviate from the average. Individuals with severe mental retardation are usually described as having IQs below 40.
- Behavior disorders: Individuals described as severely emotionally disturbed generally (1) have a lower than average IQ, (2) function in the below average range in academic achievement, (3) exhibit hyperactive and impulsive behavior, (4) lose contact with reality, and (5) are highly dependent on others.
- Autism: This condition is generally considered a severe disability, and includes (1) irregular and impaired communication, (2) repetitive activities and stereotypical movements, (3) resistance to change in daily routines or environmental conditions, and (4) unusual responses to sensory experiences.

- Learning disabilities: Classification for this condition is not generally based on severity. However, learning disabilities may be described in terms of a *severe* discrepancy between capacity (intelligence) and academic achievement.
- Sensory impairments: Classification by severity is based on the type and extent of hearing or visual loss. Deafness is a severe hearing loss where, even with aids, the individual is unable to use hearing as a primary avenue to acquire information. Blindness is a severe visual loss where the individual is unable to use sight, and must rely on other senses to acquire information.
- Physical and health impairments: Although not generally classified by severity, these conditions may result in mild through severe problems.

Focus 4: Identify two concerns in applying the term *dual diagnosis* to persons with severe disabilities.

- *Dual diagnosis* could be misapplied in order to improperly institutionalize people.
- *Dual diagnosis* could promote the use of aversive behavioral procedures, psychotropic medications, and punishment.

Focus 5: Define deaf-blindness.

- Individuals have concomitant loss of both vision and hearing with severe learning and communication problems.
- There are opposing viewpoints as to whether individuals who are deaf-blind are also severely retarded.

Focus 6: What are the estimated prevalence and causes of severe disabilities?

- Prevalence estimates for severe disabilities vary, but are usually in the range of .1 to 1.0 percent of the general population.
- Approximately 4 out of every 1,000 individuals are severely disabled where the primary symptom is mental retardation.
- Severe disabilities are most often present at birth. Severe disabilities can result from numerous causes which can be either genetic or associated with such factors as: inadequate prenatal care, poor maternal nutrition, birth trauma, infectious diseases, radiation exposure, sexually transmitted diseases, or advanced maternal age.

Focus 7: Why do many professionals prefer the functional approach over the use of standardized tests, specifically the IQ test, in assessing individuals with severe disabilities?

- IQ tests may have no validity whatsoever in defining severe disabilities.
- Functional assessments concentrate on the actual skills necessary for an individual to access and participate in natural settings, including the home, school, or community at-large.

References

34 C.F.R. 300.5(b)(8)(1990).

Abt Associates (1974). *Assessments of selected resources for severely handicapped children and youth. Vol I: A state-of-the-art paper.* Cambridge, MA: Author (ERIC Document Reproduction Service No. ED 134 614).

American Psychiatric Association. (1987). *Diagnostic and Statistical Manual of Mental Disorders* (3rd ed., revised). Washington, DC: Author.

Batshaw, M., & Perret, Y. (1986). *Children with handicaps: A medical primer* (2nd ed.). Baltimore: Paul H. Brookes.

Bower, E. (1982). Defining emotional disturbances: Public policy and research. *Psychology in the Schools, 19,* 55–60.

Brimer, R. W. (1990). *Students with severe disabilities: Current perspectives and practices.* Mountain View, CA: Mayfield Publishing Co.

Brown, L. (1991). Who are they and what do they want? In L. H. Meyer, C. A. Peck, & L. Brown (Eds.), *Critical issues in the lives of people with severe disabilities* (pp. xxv). Baltimore: Paul H. Brookes.

Bruininks, R. H., Hill, B. K., & Morreau, L. E. (1988). Prevalence and implications of maladaptive behaviors and dual diagnosis in residential and other service programs. In J. A. Stark, F. J. Menolascino, M. H. Albarelli, & V. C. Gray (Eds.), *Mental retardation and mental health: Classification, diagnosis, treatment, services* (pp. 3–29). New York: Springer-Verlag.

Bruininks, R. H., Woodcock, R., Weatherman, R., & Hill, B. (1984). *Scales of Independent Behavior: Woodcock-Johnson Psycho-Educational Battery, Part 4.* Allen, TX: DLM/Teaching Resources.

Bullis, M., & Otos, M. (1988). Characteristics of programs for children with deaf-blindness: Results of a national survey. *The Journal of the Association for Persons with Severe Handicaps, 13,* 110–115.

Downing, J., & Eichinger, J. (1990). Instructional strategies for learners with dual sensory impairments in integrated settings. *The Journal of the Association for Persons with Severe Handicaps, 15,* 98–105.

Evans, I. M. (1991). Testing and diagnosis: A review and evaluation. In L. H. Meyer, C. A. Peck, & L. Brown (Eds.), *Critical issues in the lives of people with severe disabilities* (pp. 25–44). Baltimore: Paul H. Brookes.

Federal Register. (1988). Code of federal regulations. 34: Education: Parts 300–399, revised as of July 1, 1988. Washington, D.C.: U.S. Government Printing Office.

Gaylord-Ross, R., & Browder, D. (1991). Functional assessment: Dynamic and domain properties. In L. H. Meyer, C. A. Peck, & L. Brown (Eds.), *Critical issues in the lives of people with severe disabilities* (pp. 45–66). Baltimore: Paul H. Brookes.

Grossman, J. J. (Ed.) (1983). *Manual on terminology and classification in mental retardation.* Washington, D.C.: American Association on Mental Deficiency.

Hammer, E. K. (1989). Research issues in educating visually handicapped persons with multiple impairments. In M. C. Wang, M. C. Reynolds, & H. J. Walberg (Eds.), *Handbook of special education: Research and Practice Vol 3 Low incidence conditions* (pp. 173–188), Oxford, England: Pergamon Press.

Hardman, M. L., Drew, C. J., Egan, M. W., & Wolf, B. (1993). *Human exceptionality: Society, school, and family* (4th ed.). Boston: Allyn & Bacon.

Heward, W. L., & Orlansky, D. (1992). *Exceptional children.* New York: Merrill Publishing Co.

Ingle, J. B. (1990). *Last rights: 13 fatal encounters with the state's justice.* Nashville: Abingdon Press.

Justen, J. (1976). Who are the severely handicapped? A problem in definition. *AAESPH Review, 1*(5), 1–11.

Kanner, L. (1943). Autistic disturbances of affective contact. *Nervous Child, 3,* 217–250.

Knoblock, P. (1983). *Teaching emotionally disturbed children.* Boston: Houghton Mifflin.

Luckasson, R., Coulter, D., Polloway, E., Reiss, S., Schalock, R., Snell, M., Spitalnik, d., & Stark, J. (1992). *Mental retardation: Definitions, classification, and systems of supports* (9th ed.). Washington, D.C.: American Association on Mental Retardation.

Ludlow, B. L., & Sobsey, R. (1984). *The school's role in educating severely handicapped students.* Bloomington, IN: Phi Delta Kappa Educational Foundation.

Matson, J. L., & Barrett, R. P. (1982). *Psychopathology in the mentally retarded.* New York: Grune & Stratton.

McDonnell, J., Wilcox, B., & Hardman, M. (1991). *Secondary programs for students with developmental disabilities.* Boston: Allyn & Bacon.

Meyer, L. H., Peck, C. A. & Brown, L. (1991a). Definitions and diagnoses. In L. H. Meyer, C. A. Peck, and L. Brown (Eds.), *Critical Issues in the Lives of People with Disabilities* (p. 17). Baltimore: Paul H. Brookes.

Meyer, L. H., Peck, C. A., & Brown, L. (1991b). Definition of the people TASH serves. In L. H. Meyer, C. A. Peck, & L. Brown (Eds.), *Critical issues in the lives of people with severe disabilities* (p. 19). Baltimore: Paul H. Brookes.

Meyer, L. H., Peck, C. A., & Brown (1991c). Resolution on people with mental retardation who are also diagnosed as mentally ill. In L. H. Meyer, C. A. Peck, & L. Brown (Eds.), *Critical issues in the lives of people with severe disabilities* (p. 20). Baltimore: Paul H. Brookes.

National Joint Committee on Learning Disabilities. (1988). [Letter to NJCLD member organizations].

Nihira, K., Foster, R., Shellhaas, M., & Leland, H. (1969). *AAMD Adaptive Behavior Scale.* Washington, D.C.: American Association on Mental Deficiency.

Olson, J., Algozzine, B., & Schmid, R. E. (1980). Mild, moderate, and severe: An empty distinction. *Behavior Disorders, 5*(2), 96–101.

Paluszny, M. (1979). *Autism: A practical guide for parents and professionals.* Syracuse, NY: Syracuse University Press.

Perske, R. (1991). *Unequal justice?* Nashville: Abingdon Press.

Reiss, S. (1990a). Prevalence of dual diagnosis in community-based day programs in the Chicago metropolitan area. *American Journal on Mental Retardation, 94*(6), 578–585.

Reiss, S. (1990b). Introduction to special section on dual diagnosis. *American Journal on Mental Retardation, 94*(6), 577.

Rodin, E., Shapiro, H., & Lennox, K. (1976). *Epilepsy and life performance.* Detroit: Lafayette Clinic.

Sailor, W., & Haring, N. (1977). Some current directions in the education of the severely/multiply handicapped. *AAESPH Review, 2*, 67–86.

Salvia, J., & Ysseldyke, J. E. (1991). *Assessment* (5th ed.). Boston: Houghton Mifflin. Schalock, R. (1986). *Transitions from school to work.* Washington, D.C.: National Association of Rehabilitation Facilities.

Senatore, V., Matson, J., & Kazdin, A. (1985). An inventory to assess psychopathology of mentally retarded adults. *American Journal of Mental Deficiency, 82*, 459–466.

Snell, M. E. (1987). What does an "appropriate" education mean? In M. E. Snell (Ed.), *Systematic instruction of persons with severe handicaps* (pp. 1–6). Columbus, OH: Merrill Co.

Snell, M. E. (1991). Schools are for all kids: The importance of integration for students with severe disabilities and their peers. In J. Lloyd, N. N. Singh, & A. C. Repp (Eds.), *The regular education initiative: Alternative perspectives on concepts, issues, and models* (pp. 133–148). Sycamore, IL: Sycamore Publishing.

Sparrow, S., Balla, D., & Cicchetti, D. (1984). *Manual for the Vineland Adaptive Behavior Scales.* Circle Pines, MN: American Guidance Service.

Stainback, S., & Stainback, W. (1980). *Educating children with severe maladaptive behaviors.* New York: Grune & Stratton.

U.S. Department of Education. (1991). To assure a free and appropriate public education of all handicapped children. *Thirteenth annual report to Congress on the implementation of the Education of the Handicapped Act.* Washington, D.C.: U.S. Government Printing Office.

Warren, D. H. (1989). Implications of visual impairments for child development. In M. C. Wang, M. C. Reynolds, & H. J. Walberg (Eds.), *Handbook of special education: Research and practice. Vol. 3 Low incidence conditions* (pp. 155–172). Oxford, England: Pergamon Press.

Chapter 2

Valuing People with Severe Disabilities: Toward Effective Education and Community Service Systems

Service programs for people with severe disabilities have improved dramatically during the last century. The development of these programs has mirrored society's changing views about this group of people. During the early 1900s, it was believed that individuals with severe disabilities were incapable of learning or making a meaningful contribution to the community. In response, many states established large institutions which were designed simply to provide long-term physical and medical care. During this period many people with severe disabilities lived their entire lives in institutions separated from persons without disabilities and the community.

During the 1960s and 1970s, the public began to question some of the basic assumptions upon which institutional programs were based. Research suggested that with systematic training persons with severe disabilities could learn a variety of complex vocational and self-care skills, and with adequate support could work and live in the community (Switzky, Dudzinski, Van Acker & Gambor, 1988). Empirical evidence also indicated that rather than providing nurturing environments, institutions actually limited and decreased the development of persons with disabilities (Dennis & Sayegh, 1965; Kaplan, 1943; Skeels, 1966; Sloane & Harmon, 1947). Most troubling were the frequent reports of mistreatment and abuse of people living in institutions (Blatt, Biklen, & Bogdan, 1977; Blatt & Kaplan, 1966). In all too many cases, the basic human rights of these people were simply ignored.

WINDOW 2-1   Getting to Know Craig

Craig's life is very much like yours and mine. He gets up in the morning, goes to work, cleans his apartment, does errands on the weekends, and tries to find time to have fun with his friends. While these things seem rather mundane to many of us, for Craig they are part of a completely new life. Just over three years ago Craig was released from a large state institution. He had spent nearly 20 years of his life there. While living in the institution, Craig worked on the grounds as part of a work crew. He would sometimes get very angry when someone asked him to do something and when he got mad he would hit other people or himself. And even though he could take care of himself, he often wouldn't change his clothes or shower unless someone forced him to do it. Craig's "release" from the institution occurred because of increasing pressure by advocacy groups on the state agency which operated the institution to develop community-based living and work alternatives for people with severe disabilities.

Craig moved out of the institution and into an apartment program with two other young men who had also lived in the institution. These three men got help in learning how to take care of their home from several people who worked for a local non-profit agency set up to provide residential services to persons with disabilities. During the day Craig went to a employment agency and he eventually got a job in a large hotel working as a maintenance man. He gets support from a job coach who is hired by the employment agency. Craig is learning to deal with his anger in more appropriate ways and hasn't hit anyone else or himself for over a year. He also takes a shower and puts on clean clothes every day without anyone telling him to do it.

Critics of institutions began to question the moral and ethical fiber of a society that could treat such a vulnerable group of individuals in this way. Ultimately, these questions led to a shift in our society's view of persons with disabilities. This new philosophy was based on the assumption that all human beings have inherent value and should be given the opportunity to meet their fullest potential. The result of this shift in philosophy was the deinstitutionalization movement. States began to develop community-based educational, employment, and residential service programs. The principle objective of these alternative service programs was to promote the participation of individuals with disabilities in the normal routines of community life.

This chapter provides an overview of the changing societal values that have driven services for persons with severe disabilities over the last century. The primary service models developed during this century will be reviewed and discussed. Finally, the emerging values that will undergird educational and community service programs for persons with severe disabilities in the future will be outlined.

History of Educational and Community Services

During this century three different program models have been used to provide services to persons with disabilities. These models are: (1) the institutional model, (2) the developmental model, and (3) the ecological model. The emergence of each of these program models reflects significant changes in society's view of and assumptions about persons with disabilities.

The Institutional Model

For the better part of the twentieth century the expected outcomes of service programs for people with disabilities focused simply on providing care and protection. The primary intervention used to achieve such outcomes was to place individuals in state institutions. Although institutions have been downsized substantially since the late 1960s, a large number of people with disabilities still live in these settings. The institutional model is based on three broad assumptions about people with disabilities.

Focus 1:

Identify the three assumptions underlying the institutional model.

Individuals with Disabilities Are "Sick"

Institutions are structured largely on a "medical model" of service delivery, which assumes that, if provided effective "treatment," individuals with disabilities can be cured. People who are placed in institutions are often referred to as patients, living areas are called "wards," and the staff are attendants, nurses, and physicians. Service is based on a diagnosis of the individual's pathology and a treatment regimen that is designed to return the person to a normal "healthy" state. When a "cure" cannot be expected the prescribed treatment is long-term invalid care designed to meet the individual's basic physical needs.

Individuals with Disabilities Cannot Learn

A second assumption of the institutional model is that persons with severe disabilities, especially those with severe and profound mental retardation, are incapable of benefiting from education and training:

> . . . the severely and profoundly retarded cannot be expected to profit from a program of normalization that emphasizes the traditional goals of education, nor can they be expected to take on a self-directed role in society. (Burton & Hirshoren, 1979; p. 599).

Critics also argued that attempts to teach persons with severe disabilities basic academic and personal care skills were not only unrealistic but could also be perceived as a particularly perverse form of mistreatment by forcing these individuals to participate in training with no hope of mastering targeted skills. As such, comprehensive attempts at education and training were often deemed unnecessary.

Individuals with Disabilities Are a Menace to Society

While institutions are designed to provide care and protection to individuals with disabilities, they are also structured in part to protect society from persons with disabilities. In the early 1900s individuals with disabilities were held responsible for a whole host of social evils including corruption, crime, sexual immorality, venereal diseases, and prostitution and degeneracy (Wolfensberger, 1972). As such, many states initiated systematic programs of compulsory commitment to institutions for people with mental retardation, with "parole" being allowed only after the person demonstrated no further threat to the community. Many of these misperceptions about people with disabilities persist even today.

Focus 2:

What factors prompted the deinstitutionalization movement of the late 1960s and 1970s?

During the 1960s and 70s, the institutional model was challenged by parents, advocates, and professionals. This challenge stemmed from the growing evidence that not only were institutions ineffective in "treating" persons with disabilities, but that their structure and organization often lead to significant abuse and mistreatment by staff. Questions were raised about the values of a society which allows anyone to be placed in such nontherapeutic environments:

> *Our concern reflects our belief that institutions are products primarily of society, not of individuals, and that the effects of institutionalization can best be understood as originating from social rather than individual forces. . . . It would be easy to lay the blame for wrongdoing with the attendants who manage these wards, but that would be rather like prosecuting the soldier for firing his gun after sending him to do battle. While individuals occasionally may make institutional life intolerable, institutions are primarily the products of societies, not individuals. (Blatt et al., 1977; p. 35–36)*

Additional challenges to institutions came from the courts (Henderson & Vitello, 1988). An increasing number of judicial actions questioned the rights of states to commit individuals with disabilities to environments which (a) frequently violated their basic constitutional rights and (b) provided no consistent educational or habilitative benefit. Ultimately, the findings of the courts forced many states to initiate "deinstitutionalization" programs and develop community-based alternatives for persons with disabilities.

While the deinstitutionalization movement did result in a significant reduction in the total number of persons with disabilities served in institutions, research suggests that there are still as many as 100,000 individuals living in these settings nationally (Braddock, 1987; Braddock, Hemp, & Howes, 1985; Epple, Jacobsen, & Janiki, 1985). Although the overall population of institutions has decreased, the number of persons with severe and profound disabilities in these settings has increased (Lakin, Hill, & Bruinicks, 1985). In many states, institutions have become little more than "holding tanks" for persons with the most intense education and training needs. Heated debates continue in many states about the closure of institutions. Proponents of institutional programs continue to use society's past assumptions about persons with disabilities as the primary arguments for keeping institutions open (see Newsworthy 2-1). This occurs

Denial of disability

Rationale for public schools: to produce useful citizens

The disappointment of most parents who find they have a child with a congenital disability of the brain or the nervous system is human. It is also human that many parents would try to deny or minimize the extent of such disability.

We all are tempted to turn our backs on unpleasant reality. There are also more practical reasons for claiming that an afflicted child can be "mainstreamed," i.e., sent to school with normal children. It feeds the pretense that there is nothing really wrong, and it relieves the mother or guardian of the duty for caring for the child during school hours.

The old idea of simply locking away from society those whom we used to call "feeble-minded" has, fortunately, been greatly changed in recent years. We now know that many persons of abysmally low intelligence can be trained for routine and repetitive jobs. Their happiness at feeling themselves useful is wonderful to see.

But defensive parents who insist that a public school system run, in effect, a mental hospital for their disturbed children are asking too much. Federal judges have carried the idea of de-institutionalizing children to absurdity. Hissom-like facilities are being padlocked all over America and those children with mental or nervous problems are being dumped on the public schools.

In larger cities, where such children can be segregated in "special education" classes, the disruption may be minimal. But in small school systems, children subject to frequent seizures or spectacular outbursts have nowhere else to go but regular class. The effect on the learning environment for normal students of children given to hyperactive wandering, outbursts of shouting and spells of eccentric behavior can be devastating.

And the situation is going to grow worse. We now have increasing numbers of children whose brains were fried before birth by mothers on crack and other drugs. We'll soon have to do more than deplore the human irresponsibility that manufactures defective children.

Let us accept one basic principle: The essential mission of a public school system is to educate the normal. It is not to serve as a sanitarium for the abnormal. Where afflicted children can be melded into a classroom situation without diminishing the ability of the teacher to teach, that's fine. But let's not forget that the rationale for a public school system is to produce useful citizens for a more effective society in the future. That is not possible in a chaotic classroom.

We are passing through a period of unworkable social theories enforced by judicial decisions based on sentimentality. Let's pray that it will be a short period.

NEWSWORTHY 2-1

despite the overwhelming evidence that community-based service alternatives are superior to institutions on a number of different measures of effectiveness. For example, research has demonstrated:

1. Individuals living in community residences make more gains in general adaptive behavior than those individuals living in institutions (Haney, 1988).
2. The quality of life enjoyed by persons living in community settings is better than that of individuals living in institutional programs (Nisbet, Clark, & Covert, 1991).
3. Institutions are the most expensive service alternative for persons with severe disabilities and nationally absorb the majority of the funds appropriated for service programs for all persons with disabilities (Braddock, 1987). Consequently not only do institutions cost more, their very existence often prevents states from expanding community-based alternatives.

The Developmental Model

The developmental model of services for persons with disabilities emerged as the need to move beyond institutional programs became more widely accepted by policy-makers and the public at large. Switzky, Dudzinski, Van Acker, & Gambro (1988) state that:

> The "developmental model" conceives of handicapped persons as individuals who can benefit from training and educational instruction...and that the same principles of learning and development apply to both handicapped and nonhandicapped persons. (p. 32).

Focus 3:

What are the primary assumptions underlying the developmental model?

A critical assumption underlying the developmental model is that persons with and without disabilities develop cognitive, communication, social, motor, and self-care skills in the same way, except that, persons with disabilities require more intense levels of training and support to develop these skills. This assumption led to the emergence of comprehensive developmental curricula designed to promote the acquisition of skills that would allow "normal" performance by persons with disabilities in home, school, work, and other community settings. The instructional objectives in these curricula were organized around the developmental milestones exhibited by persons without disabilities. In general it was believed, that if people with disabilities had access to these curriculum and systematic instruction they would learn the skills necessary to function independently in the community.

A second, but equally important movement during this phase of program development was the articulation of the "Principle of Normalization" (Nirje, 1969; Wolfensberger, 1972). The Principle of Normalization is based on the assumption that persons with disabilities have a right to a lifestyle that is as close as possible to that of individuals without disabilities. The principle of normalization states that individuals with disabilities should participate equally in the normal routines of community life including having a home to live in, access to school or a job, self-selected and self-directed leisure time, and the opportunity to establish social networks which include individuals without disabilities. Based on the principle of normalization, service programs were designed to promote the participation of individuals with disabilities in all aspects of community life.

These two concepts provided the framework for the development of an elaborate system of community-based educational, residential, and employment programs which are still intact today. To achieve the goals of developmental learning and normalization, these service systems adopted a structure known as the "continuum of services" (Taylor, 1988). The "continuum" was conceived as a hierarchy of service programs (Figure 2-1). It is designed to teach persons with disabilities increasingly more complex skills and to incrementally move them toward a more "normal" lifestyle. Service programs at the first level in the continuum were designed to provide the most intense service support and focus training efforts on basic developmental milestones. As individuals learned these skills they would graduate to the next program in the continuum. It was believed that this structure would ultimately result in the re-entry of persons with disabilities into the mainstream of the community.

Focus 4:

Identify the factors that prevented the developmental model from achieving its primary goals and objectives.

Despite the more positive view of persons with disabilities inherent in the development model, it has only achieved full community participation for some individuals with disabilities. Many people with disabilities find themselves continually getting ready for their re-entry into the mainstream of the community with little hope of ever actually achieving this outcome. This occurs because their disability often prevents them from mastering the "pre-requisite developmental skills" necessary to graduate to the next level in the continuum.

For example, Bellamy, Rhodes, Borbeau, & Mank (1986) using data from the U. S. Department of Labor examined the average length of time that individuals with disabilities required to move from one program to another in the employment continuum. Based on this information, they found that if a person with severe disabilities was placed in a work activity center (the first step in the continuum) at age 22 they would not reach competitive employment in the community (the last step in the continuum) until age 64. Researchers have reported similarly dismal findings in the residential (Hill, Lakin, & Bruinicks, 1988) and educational service systems (Rostetter et al., 1984).

Beyond the ineffectiveness of the developmental model in achieving full community participation for persons with severe disabilities, other research suggests that many of the programs have done little to improve the quality of life of persons with disabilities. For example research has shown that:

1. A significant number of adults with disabilities are unemployed (Harris & Associates, 1986; Hasazi, Gordon, & Roe, 1985; Wagner, 1989; Wehman, Kregel, & Seyfarth, 1985).
2. Many adults with disabilities who are employed do not work in jobs that take full advantage of their skills or potential productivity. In general, they are trapped in unrewarding positions with little opportunity for advancement or in extremely restrictive service programs that inhibit interaction with nondisabled peers (Bellamy, Rhodes, Borbeau, & Mank, 1986; Harris and Associates, 1985).
3. The wages of adults with disabilities who do work is far below the poverty line (Buckley & Bellamy, 1985; Harris and Associates, 1985; Whitehead, 1981).

The School Continuum

FULL-TIME REGULAR CLASS PLACEMENT

Participation in age-appropriate grade-level or content area classes.

↑

REGULAR CLASS WITH RESOURCE SUPPORT

Participation in age-appropriate grade-level or content area classes. Students are pulled-out of regular classes for instruction on specific educational goals.

↑

PART TIME SPECIAL CLASS PLACEMENT

Student is served in a separate class only for children with disabilities for instruction in the primary curriculum domains. They participate in regular grade-level or content-area classes for "non-academic" or "elective" courses.

↑

SPECIAL CLASS PLACEMENT

Student is served in separate classes only for children with disabilities for instruction on all curriculum domains.

↑

SPECIAL SCHOOLS

Student is served in a separate school only for children with disabilities.

↑

HOMEBOUND INSTRUCTION

Student receives educational services at home.

↑

RESIDENTIAL SCHOOL

Student is placed and lives in a private school structured to provide services to a specific group of children with disabilities.

↑

PUBLIC INSTITUTION

Student is placed and lives in publically operated institution for persons with disabilities.

The Vocational Continuum

COMPETITIVE EMPLOYMENT

Employed in an integrated community business.

↑

TRANSITIONAL EMPLOYMENT SERVICES

Individual is provided training in a specific job in a community business. Once trained, the individual is placed in competitive employment.

↑

SHELTERED WORKSHOPS

Individual is placed in a separate facility only for adults with disabilities located in the community. The habilitative program is designed to provide therapeutic and tolerance activities designed to foster work readiness. The individual must be provided renumerative work at no less than 50% of minimum wage.

↑

WORK ACTIVITY CENTERS

Individual is placed in a separate facility only for adults with disabilities located in the community. The program is focused on personal and social adjustment, and work readiness skills.

↑

DAY TREATMENT CENTER

Individual is placed in a separate facility only for adults with disabilities located in the community. The program is focused on basic academic motor communication, and self-help skills.

The Residential Continuum

INDEPENDENT LIVING

Individual lives in their own home.

↑

SEMI-INDEPENDENT LIVING

Individual lives in community with a small number of persons with disabilities, the habilitative program is focused on training personal and household management skills necessary for independent living.

↑

FOSTER CARE

Individual lives with a nondisabled person or family. The individual or family may serve more than one person with disabilities. The program focuses primarily on care, may include some skill training.

↑

GROUP HOMES

Individual lives in a home with several other adults with disabilities. Paid staff provide support to the residents in meeting basic personal needs. The habilitative program focuses on personal and household management skills.

↑

INTERMEDIATE CARE FACILITIES

Individual is placed in a facility with a large number of individuals with disabilities. The program is structured to provide on-going medical services to the person.

↑

PUBLIC INSTITUTION

Individual is placed and lives in publically operated institution for persons with disabilities.

FIGURE 2-1   Continuums of Service

4. Most individuals with disabilities do not have friends outside of their residential program (Gollay, Freedman, Wyngaarden, & Kurtz, 1978; Bercovici, 1981).
5. The majority of adults with disabilities do not have friends without disabilities (Gollay et al., 1978; Reiter & Levi, 1980; Schalock, Harper, & Genung, 1981).
6. Most adults with disabilities do not date or have intimate relationships (Gollay et al., 1978).
7. Adults with disabilities spend most of their leisure time engaged in passive activities like watching T. V. rather than in activities that increase their presence and participation in the community (Gollay et al., 1978; Kregel, Wehman, & Seyfarth, 1985; Salzberg & Langford, 1981; Wehman, Schleien, & Kiernan, 1980).
8. Adults with disabilities generally have little independence and autonomy in making lifestyle choices for themselves (Baker, Seltzer, & Seltzer, 1977; Gollay et al., 1978; Sheerenberger & Felsentahl, 1977).

The failure of the developmental model to achieve its primary objectives, has prompted a reevaluation of the underlying assumptions of the service programs operating today. Increasingly people with disabilities, parents, advocates, professionals, and policymakers are recognizing the need for a system of service delivery which is not based on the assumption that persons with disabilities must "earn" access to the community. Rather, services should be redesigned to provide the support necessary to allow these individuals to be successful in home, school, work, and other community settings.

The Ecological Model

The ecological model is also based on the assumption that people with disabilities should have the opportunity to participate in the social, economic, and recreational life of the community. The ecological model differs from the developmental model in that it assumes that achieving these outcomes will not only require developing the skills of the individual but providing adequate support in home, school, work, and community settings. In addition, the ecological model does not require individuals with disabilities to "earn" their way into the community.

Focus 5:

What are the primary assumptions underlying the ecological model?

As described by Schalock (1986), the model "stresses that successful adjustment to the environment depends less on individual characteristics per se and more on the match between person and environmental attributes" (p. 2). The intended outcomes of service programs are to support a person-environmental fit. In order to achieve this fit, training focuses on activities that are performed in a natural setting (grocery shopping, eating in a restaurant, work, home, etc.) and the expected level of independent performance is adjusted to match the individual's capabilities. In other words, training is focused on achieving the maximum level of participation possible for the person, not necessarily on achieving "normal" performance. For some people, this may mean total independence and for others it may mean partial participation in activities. In each case, the intervention provided by the service program is tailored to the individual's needs.

The ecological model uses a three-phase process to maximize the fit between the person and the environment (Schalock, 1986). First, each person's behavioral capabilities are assessed in relationship to specific demands of the activity and environment. Second, the "goodness of fit" between the person's capabilities and the environmental demands is determined, specifically focused on the barriers which prevent the individual's successful performance in the setting. Finally, an intervention is designed to overcome these barriers. The intervention may include skill training, adaptation of activity or physical environment, or the provision of support.

Focus 6:

What current service delivery programs for persons with severe disabilities incorporate the critical features of the ecological model?

The ecological model has provided the basis for the development of a number of educational and community service programs for persons with disabilities. These include supported education, supported employment, and supported living (c.f., Meyer, Peck, & Brown, 1991). The primary focus of these programs is to identify life options for each individual that meet his or her personal needs and interests, and then to provide the training and support necessary to ensure their success. In such programs, services are brought to the persons with disabilities and designed around their needs rather than placing a particular individual in a service program. For example, supported employment is designed to assist the individual to find a job which matches personal interests and needs, to promote the acquisition of necessary work and work related skills, and to provide ongoing support in the job site to ensure his or her success (Window 2-2). Research indicates that in comparison to those people served in the continuum of employment services, people enrolled in supported employment programs earn significantly higher wages, engage in more remunerative work, have more frequent social interactions with nondisabled co-workers during the work day, have more frequent social interactions with nondisabled individuals after the work day, and utilize community services to a greater extent (Rusch, Chadsey-Rusch, & Johnson, 1991). Similar results have been found in both supported living (Nisbet et al., 1991) and supported education programs (Giangreco & Putnam, 1991).

The ecological model and the notion of supported education, work, and living have opened new doors for persons with severe disabilities. Indeed, these programs have created the first real opportunities for persons with severe disabilities to become an integral part of our communities.

WINDOW 2-2   A Real Job To Go To!

Martha is 24 years old and works at A Child's Place, a day care center for preschool age children. She has always liked children. When she was in high school she would baby sit for her younger brother and sister and would occasionally stay with the kids of some of her next door neighbors. When she left high school she was placed in a sheltered workshop program in the community in which she lived. Although she liked the staff and the people she worked with she was never very happy about the job that she was doing. The workshop had a contract with a national airlines to clean and package the ear phones that passengers used to listen to music or watch movies on the plane. She worked about 3 hours a day. The rest of the time was spent working on skills that she had learned while she was in school. She made about 25 to 30 dollars per week. She would frequently complain to her mother and father that she really did not like her job and she felt like she spent most of her time doing nothing.

After about a year, Martha was given the opportunity to participate in the supported employment program operated by the agency. Before she got involved, the staff in the supported employment program talked with Martha and her parents about what she would like to do. The first thing that she said was that she would like to take care of kids. Both her mom and dad told the staff that she had done sitting for them and for neighbors and had done a great job. After some discussion, Martha, her parents, and the staff in the supported employment program agreed to look for a job in a child care center. The staff from the supported employment program scoured the newspaper and contacted the local job service office to see if any positions were open. A Child's Place was advertising for a 30-hour per week aide. A staff person from the supported employment program contacted Marge Smith who was the director of A Child's Place and asked her if she would consider hiring a person with a disability. At first she was hesitant but agreed to meet with the staff person to discuss the possibility.

During the meeting the staff person explained the supported employment program to Marge and told her a little bit about Martha. Marge agree to meet Martha and talk with her about the job. On the day of the interview Martha was nervous. She and the staff person from the supported employment program went to A Child's Place and Martha spent about 30 minutes talking with Marge about her experience with children and what she liked to do with them. Marge told Martha and the staff persons that she wanted a day or so to think about it and she would get back to them. The next day Marge call Martha to let her know that she had gotten the job.

Before Martha went to work, staff from the supported employment program went out to A Child's Place and analyzed the steps of the job that Martha would be expected to do. They worked closely with Marge to make sure that they had accurately identified the demands of the job. Once the analysis was completed Martha came to work with one of the staff people. The staff person worked with Martha to learn the jobs she was responsible for and to ensure that the jobs got done to Marge's satisfaction. As Martha got better at the job the staff person began to reduce the amount of assistance she provided. She also worked with Marge and with the other aides in the program on when and how to give Martha help when she needed it. In addition, she helped Martha make arrangements to come to weekly staff meetings and to participate in the after-school social outings that the staff had every Friday. Eventually, the staff person reduced her assistance to weekly visits. When Martha needed help, Marge or the other aides would give it to her, when she needed to learn a new job, they would help her with it. The staff person continued to follow-up with Martha to make sure she was doing her job right and that Marge was satisfied with her work. Martha now earns about $100 dollars a week after taxes. Martha has become an important part of A Child's Place staff. Marge has told both Martha and her parents that she is one of the best employees that she has ever had. Best of all Martha is very happy with her new job, she recently told her Mom that she liked work because she had "a real job to go to"!

Emerging Values in Service Programs

Focus 7:

What values will drive the development of educational and community service programs for persons with severe disabilities during the next decade?

Each step in the evolution of service programs for persons with disabilities has been initiated and bolstered by changing societal values. Individuals with disabilities, parents, professionals, and policymakers are now beginning to articulate a new set of values that will guide the development of educational and community service programs over the next decade. These values expand upon many of the assumptions underlying the Developmental and Ecological models. However, they also stress the need for increased individualization of service and reliance on other community members, rather than service programs, to support the participation of people with disabilities in community life. This emerging set of values are: (1) full inclusion, (2) natural supports, and (3) choice and autonomy.

Full Inclusion

Since the late 1960s, service programs have sought to increase the involvement of children and adults with severe disabilities in community life. Despite the intentions of these programs their actual success in achieving this outcome has been marginal. For many persons with severe disabilities community life remains a protracted story of segregation. They live, work, and go to school only with other individuals who have disabilities and access community resources only when the program staff paid to serve them schedules "community activities." While the development of supported work, living, and educational programs have the potential to open many doors for persons with severe disabilities, only a limited number of these people have access these programs (c.f., Buckley & Bellamy, 1985). In many states, these programs are simply "add-ons" to the existing service delivery system. Furthermore they are perceived by many professionals as just one more step in the continuum of service. Just as people with severe disabilities have been traditionally required to "earn" their way into competitive employment, independent living, and the educational mainstream, they are now being required to demonstrate that they are "ready" to benefit from supported employment, living, and education programs. In this way, the current service system continues to function as a gatekeeper to, rather than a promoter of community integration for persons with severe disabilities.

Many persons with disabilities, parents, and advocates now argue that full inclusion must not simply be a philosophical ideal, but rather must become an integral component of all educational, employment, and living programs. Achieving this outcome will require two fundamental changes in the way in which service programs are designed and implemented.

First, many of the specialized services now provided to persons with disabilities exist simply because the generic services and resources available to persons without disabilities have not been structured to accommodate diversity (Skrtic, 1991; Taylor, Biklen, & Knoll, 1987). If people with severe disabilities are going to be fully included in the community, then service and resource programs for people without disabilities must be restructured to meet the needs of all people. Discussions about how to create service and resource programs that can accommodate all community members has already begun. For example, the recent debate on the Regular Education Initiative (REI) in the field of special education is focused specifically on how the regular education system must be changed to accommodate all children with disabilities and the role of special education service programs in this restructuring process (Kauffman, 1989; Lipski & Gartner, 1989; Stainback & Stainback, 1992). In some cases, policymakers have already acted to create legislation that will ensure the inclusion of persons with disabilities in the basic elements of community life. For instance, Congress recently enacted ADA, the Americans with Disabilities Act (Federal Register, 1991). This bill mandates that businesses provide equal consideration to individuals with disabilities for employment and must provide needed modifications in the work environment to allow individuals with disabilities to be successful in their job.

The second fundamental change which must occur if full inclusion is to be achieved is the replacement of the current "continuum of service" with a "menu of services." Functionally, the continuum of service is designed to "plug" individuals into service programs. The result is that the living, work, and educational opportunities available to persons with severe disabilities are limited to the service programs offered by the system.

In contrast, a "menu of service" approach would be structured to allow individuals to select the types and intensity of service they need to be successful in home, school, work, or community settings. The mix of services actually provided to individuals would vary significantly and would be tailored to the person. The supported living, work, and educational programs of today are the initial prototypes of this kind of service structure. However, the type and intensity of services provided through these programs are also often restricted by the philosophical orientation and administrative organization of the agencies which provide these services. Furthermore, the limited availability of these programs in local communities often restricts the options available to people with severe disabilities. For example, the only supported employment program available in a small rural community may be organized to provide support to those individuals interested in employment in the agricultural industry. Obviously, in this situation, the choices available to people with severe disabilities who live in this community are going to be limited by the options provided by the local service program. Ultimately, achieving full inclusion of people with disabilities in the community will require a flexible system that can provide not only specific services but can create new services as necessary to meet the needs of individuals with severe disabilities.

Natural Supports

Individuals without disabilities derive a significant amount of support in coping with the demands of daily life from friends, family, neighbors, and co-workers. This support can range from getting a ride to the grocery store when our car is in the shop to just having someone around to listen to us when we have had a tough day at work. The support that we receive from these various people is not only critical to successful community living, it influences our quality of life. Sociologists have long recognized the interdependence of individual members of any community (Unger & Powell, 1980; Unger & Wandersman, 1985). In one way or another each member of the community is dependent on all other members to successfully deal with day-to-day life.

While this is a widely accepted truism for people without disabilities, it is far from reality for most people with severe disabilities. The design and structure of most educational, living, and employment programs inhibit the development of these natural sources of support for persons with disabilities. Not only are persons with severe disabilities segregated from other community members, often the only time they access community settings is when they participate in a specially organized activity. Furthermore, particularly as adults, these people are often cut off from their family because they are forced to live in communities where services are located rather than where their parents or siblings live. The bottom line is that for most people with disabilities who no longer live with their families the primary source of support in the community comes from individuals who are paid to provide services. Without questioning the commitment of professionals who work in these programs, the very nature of this relationship creates conditions that will inevitably lead to the intrusion of paid staff into the lives of persons with severe disabilities. The level of community inclusion that persons with severe disabilities enjoy often revolves around the skills, resources, and values of paid staff.

Not surprisingly, individuals with severe disabilities, parents, advocates, professionals, and policymakers are calling for the development of service programs that rely more heavily on the natural supports available in schools, businesses, and neighborhoods (Froland, Pancoast, Chapman, & Kimboko, 1981; O'Brien, 1987; Nisbet, 1992; Nisbet & Callahan, 1987; Rusch & Hughes, 1988). Such service programs would attempt to (a) foster support by individuals who live, work, or go to school with the person with severe disabilities and (b) reduce the frequency and intensity of support provided by paid staff. While this approach at first seems unfeasible there are an increasing number of demonstrations that these natural supports can be successfully fostered in living, work, and school settings for persons with severe disabilities (Giangreco & Putnam, 1991; Nisbet, Clarke, & Covert, 1991; Rusch, Chadsey-Rusch, & Johnson, 1991).

It is unlikely that significant progress toward full inclusion of persons with severe disabilities in the community will be made until other community members acknowledge their social responsibility in supporting this group of individuals. The reliance on paid staff by educational and community service programs is likely to continue to reinforce attitudes of segregation by the community at large, and reliance on specialized services for persons with disabilities.

Choice and Autonomy

While the values of full inclusion and natural support are critical to enhancing the quality of life of persons with severe disabilities, these concepts hold very little weight if the decisions about how they are operationalized are not driven by individual needs and preferences. There is no single answer for what constitutes an acceptable quality of life. Each of us has different hopes and dreams, different ways of thinking about work, and different ways of meeting the demands of community living. Through the long evolution of service programs for people with severe disabilities, society has made serious errors in judgment about what this group of people are capable of and what they might want or need. In our attempts to humanely deal with persons with severe disabilities we have often ignored one of the most basic human rights: the right to choose.

Supporting choice for persons with severe disabilities is a complex matter. It is often assumed that people with severe disabilities lack the cognitive and communication skills necessary to indicate choices about where they live, where they work, who they spend time with, and so on. However, for many persons with severe disabilities it is equally likely that their lack of choice simply reflects (a) the unresponsiveness of caretakers to nontraditional strategies of communication used to indicate preference, (b) a lack of training on more effective ways of communicating choices, and (c) a lack of opportunity in many educational and community service programs to make choices (Parsons & Reid, 1990; Reichle, Sigafoos, & Piche, 1989; Rice & Nelson, 1988). Although the research base in this area is small, it is clear that nearly all persons with severe disabilities can assume some role in the decisions that are made about their lives.

Consequently, people with disabilities and their advocates are demanding that educational and community service programs adopt strategies that maximize the participation of people with severe disabilities in decisions that affect their lives. These strategies include procedures for making major life decisions such as where a person works and lives (O'Brien, 1987; Vandercook, York, & Forrest, 1989) to involving the individual in deciding the activities they complete on a day-to-day basis (Parsons & Reid, 1990; Rice & Nelson, 1988). It is unlikely that people with severe disabilities will achieve full inclusion in the community unless they are empowered to make choices for themselves and given the resources and tools necessary to act upon those choices.

Conclusion

Historically, society has not valued people with severe disabilities. These individuals were often viewed as being incapable of making a meaningful contribution to the economic and social fabric of the community and further as having little capacity to improve that situation. In response, society developed service delivery systems that were designed to remove people from the mainstream of society and to meet their basic physical needs. Since the 1960s and 70s the focus on care and protection in educational and community service programs have been replaced by an emphasis on personal development, inclusion in the community, and self-determination. While much progress has been made since then, the quality of life of individuals with and without disabilities is still extremely discrepant. However, the new set of values that are being articulated by persons with severe disabilities and their advocates will hopefully begin to shape public policy and professional practice in ways that will close this gap. The subsequent chapters in this book will describe program models at each age level which reflect this emerging set of values and will describe the roles of professionals in supporting people with severe disabilities in the community.

Focus Review

Focus 1: Identify the three assumptions underlying the institutional model.

- Individuals with disabilities are sick.
- Individuals with disabilities cannot learn.
- Individuals with disabilities are a menace to society.

Focus 2: What factors prompted the deinstitutionalization movement of the late 1960s and 1970s?

- Research demonstrated that persons with disabilities, even persons with the most severe disabilities could learn to function in the community.
- Research demonstrated that institutional programs often inhibited rather than promoted the development of persons with disabilities.
- There were frequent reports of mistreatment and abuse.

Focus 3: What are the primary assumptions underlying the developmental model?

- Individuals with disabilities learn in the same way as people without disabilities but require more time to master basic skills.
- Individuals with disabilities have the right to participate in the normal routines of community life and to establish a lifestyle comparable to that of persons without disabilities.

Focus 4: Identify the factors that prevented the developmental model from achieving its primary goals and objectives.

- The structure of the continuum of services required individuals with disabilities to "earn" their way into the community.
- Poor outcomes for people with disabilities.

Focus 5: What are the primary assumptions underlying the ecological model?

- People with disabilities have the right to participate in economic and social aspects of the community.
- Service programs should be designed to provide support to people with disabilities in natural home, school, work, and community settings.

Focus 6: What current service delivery programs for persons with severe disabilities incorporate the critical features of the ecological model?

- *Supported education*—providing training and support to students with disabilities in regular education settings.
- *Supported work*—providing training and support to adults with disabilities in competitive employment settings.
- *Supported living*—providing training and support to people with disabilities in their own homes.

Focus 7: What values will drive the development of educational and community service programs for persons with severe disabilities during the next decade?

- Full inclusion in all aspects of community life.
- Increased reliance on natural supports to promote the success of persons with disabilities in the community.
- Maximizing personal choice and autonomy.

References

Baker, B. L., Seltzer, G., & Seltzer, M. (1977). *As close as possible*. Boston: Little, Brown, and Co.

Bellamy, G. T., Rhodes, L. E., Borbeau, P., & Mank, D. M. (1986). Mental retardation services in sheltered workshops and day activity programs: Consumer outcomes and policy alternatives. In F. R. Rusch (Ed.), *Competitive employment: Issues and strategies* (pp. 257–272). Baltimore: Paul H. Brookes.

Blatt, B., Biklen, D., & Bogdan, R. (1977). *An Alternative Textbook in Special Education: People, Schools and Other Institutions*. Denver, CO: Love Publishing Company.

Blatt, B., & Kaplan, F. (1966). *Christmas in Purgatory: A Photographic Essay in Mental Retardation*. Newton, MA: Allyn & Bacon.

Boles, S., Horner, R. H., & Bellamy, G. T. (1988). Implementing transition: Programs for supported living. In B. L. Ludlow, A. P. Turnbull, & R. Luckason (Eds.), *Transition to Adult Life for People with Mental Retardation—Principles and Practices* (pp. 85–100). Baltimore: Paul H. Brookes.

Braddock, D. (1987). *Federal policy toward mental retardation and developmental disabilities*. Baltimore: Paul H. Brookes.

Braddock, D. Hemp, R., & Howes, R. (1985). *Public expenditures for mental retardation and developmental disabilities in the United States: Analytical Summary*. Chicago, IL: University of Chicago, Institute for the Study of Developmental Disabilities, Evaluation and Public Policy Analysis Program.

Buckley, J., & Bellamy, G. T. (1985). National survey of day and vocational programs for adults with severe disabilities: A 1984 profile. In P. Ferguson (ed.), *Issues in transition research: Economic and social outcomes* (pp. 1–12. Eugene, OR: Specialized Training Program, University of Oregon.

Burton, T. A., & Hirshoren, A. (1979). The education of severely and profoundly retarded children: Are we sacrificing the child to the concept? *Exceptional Children*, 618–623.

Dennis, W. & Sayegh, Y. (1965). The effect of supplementary experiences upon the behavioral development of infants in institutions. *Child Development*, 36, 81–90.

Epple, W. A., Jacobsen, J. W., & Janicki, M. P. (1985). Staffing ratios in public institutions for persons with mental retardation in the United States. *Mental Retardation*, 23, 115–124.

Froland, C., Pancoast, D., Chapman, N., & Kimboko, P. (1981). *Helping networks and human services*. Beverly Hills: Sage Publications.

Giangreco, J. F., & Putnam, J. W. (1991). Supporting the education of students with severe disabilities in regular education environments. In L. H. Meyer, C. A. Peck, & L. Brown (Eds.), *Critical Issues in the Lives of People with Severe Disabilities* (pp. 245–270). Baltimore: Paul H. Brookes.

Gollay, E., Freedman, R., Wyngaarden, M., & Kurtz, N. R. (1978). *Coming Back*. Cambridge, MA: Abt Associates, Inc.

Haney, J. I. (1988). Empirical support for deinstitutionalization. In L. W. Heal, J. I. Haney, and A. R. Novak Amado (Eds.), *Integration of Developmental Disabled Individuals into the Community* (pp. 37–58). Baltimore: Paul H. Brookes.

Harris, L., and Associates, Inc. (1986). *International Center for the Disabled Survey of Disabled Americans: Bring Disabled Americans into the Mainstream*. New York: Author.

Hasazi, S. B., Gordon, L. R., & Roe, C. A. (1985). Factors associated with the employment status of handicapped youth exiting high school from 1975 to 1983. *Exceptional Children, 51*, 455–469.

Hasazi, S., Johnson, R. E., Hasazi, J., Gordon, L. R., & Hull, M. (in press). Employment of youth with and without handicaps following school: Outcomes and correlates. *Journal of Special Education*.

Henderson, R. A., & Vitello, S. J. (1988). Litigation related to community integration. In L. W. Heal, J. I. Haney, and A. R. Novak Amado (Eds.), *Integration of Developmental Disabled Individuals into the Community* (pp. 273–282). Baltimore: Paul H. Brookes.

Hill, B. K., Lakin, K. C., & Bruininks, R. H. (1988). Characteristics of residential facilities. In L. W. Heal, J. I. Haney, and A. R. Novak Amado (Eds.), *Integration of Developmental Disabled Individuals into the Community* (pp. 89–124). Baltimore: Paul H. Brookes.

Hill, M., Wehman, P., Banks, D., & Metzler, H. M. D. (1988). Employment outcomes of people with moderate and severe disabilities provided supported competitive employment after eight years. In P. Wehman, J. Kregel, M. S. Shafer, & M. L. Hill (Eds.), *Competitive employment for persons with mental retardation: From research

to practice (Volume II). Richmond, VA: Rehabilitation Research and Training Center, School of Education, Virginia Commonwealth University.

Horner, R. H., McDonnell, J. J., & Bellamy, G. T. (1986). Teaching generalized skills: general case Instruction in simulation and community settings. In R. H. Horner, L. H. Meyer, H. D. Fredericks (Eds.), *Education of learners with severe handicaps: Exemplary service strategies* (pp. 289–214). Baltimore: Paul H. Brookes.

Kaplan, O. L. (1943). Mental decline in older morons. *American Journal of Mental Deficiency, 47*, 277–285.

Kauffman, J. M. (1989). The regular education initiative as Reagan-Bush education policy: A trickle-down theory of education of the hard to teach. *Journal of Special Education, 21*, 6–11.

Lakin, K. C., Hill, B. K., & Bruininks, R. H. (Eds.). (1985). *An Analysis of Medicaid's Intermediate Care Facility for the Mentally Retarded (ICF-MR) Program*. Minneapolis, MN: Center for Residential and Community Services.

Lipski, D. K., & Gartner, A. (1989). *Beyond Separate Education: Quality Education for All*. Baltimore: Paul H. Brookes.

Mank, D. M., Rhodes, L. E., & Bellamy, G. T. (1986). Four supported employment alternatives. In W. E. Kiernan & J. A. Stark (Eds.), *Pathways to employment for adults with developmental disabilities* (pp. 139–154). Baltimore: Paul H. Brookes.

Meyer, L. H., Peck, C. A., & Brown, L. (1991). *Critical Issues in the Lives of People with Severe Disabilities*. Baltimore: Paul H. Brookes.

Nirje, B. (1969). The normalization principle and its human management implications. In R. Kugel & W. Wolfensberger (Eds.), *Changing Patterns in Residential Services for the Mentally Retarded* (pp. 231–240). Washington, D. C.: President's Committee on Mental Retardation.

Nisbet, J. & Callahan, M. (1987). Achieving success in integrated workplaces: Critical elements in assisting persons with severe disabilities. In S. J. Taylor, D. Biklen, & J. Knoll (Eds.), *Community Integration for people with Severe Disabilities* (pp. 184–201). New York: Teachers College Press.

Nisbet, J., Clark, M., & Covert, S. (1991). Living it up! An analysis of research on community living. In L. H. Meyer, C. A. Peck, & L. Brown

(Eds.), *Critical Issues in the Lives of People with Severe Disabilities* (pp. 115–144). Baltimore: Paul H. Brookes.

O'Brien, J. (1987). A guide to life-style planning: Using the Activities Catalog to integrate services and a natural support systems. In B. Wilcox & G. T. Bellamy (Eds.). *A Comprehensive Guide to the Activities Catalog: An Alternative Curriculum for Youth and Adults with Severe Disabilities* (pp. 175–189). Baltimore: Paul H. Brookes.

Parsons, M. B., & Reid, D. H. (1990). Assessing food preferences among persons with profound mental retardation: Providing opportunities to make choices. *Journal of Applied Behavior Analysis, 23,* 183–195.

Reichle, J., Sigafoos, J., & Piche, L. (1989). Teaching an adolescent with blindness and severe disabilities a correspondence between requesting and selecting preferred objects. *The Journal of The Association for Persons with Severe Handicaps, 14,* 74–80.

Reiter, S., & Levi, A. M. (1980). Factors affecting social integration of noninstitutionalized mentally retarded adults. *American Journal of Mental Deficiency, 85,* 25–30.

Rice, M. S., & Nelson, D. L. (1988). Effect of choice-making on a self-care activity in mentally retarded adult and adolescent males. *The Occupation Therapy Journal of Research, 8,* 75–83.

Rostetter, D., Kowalski, R., & Hunter, D. (1984). Implementing the integration principle of PL 94-142. In N. Certo, N. Haring, & R. York (Eds.), *Public School Integration of Severely Handicapped Students: Rational Issues and Progressive Alternatives* (pp. 277–292). Baltimore: Paul H. Brookes.

Rusch, F. R., Chadsey-Rusch, J., & Johnson, J. R. (1991). Supported Employment: Emerging Opportunities for Employment Integration. In L. H. Meyer, C. A. Peck, & L. Brown (Eds.), *Critical Issues in the Lives of People with Severe Disabilities* (pp. 145–170). Baltimore: Paul H. Brookes.

Rusch, F. R., & Hughes, C. (1988). Supported employment: Promoting employee independence. *Mental Retardation, 26,* 351–356.

Schalock, R. (1986). *Transitions from school to work.* Washington, D.C.: National Association of Rehabilitation Facilities.

Schalock, R. L., Harper, R. S., & Genung. T.(1981). Community integration of the developmentally disabled: Variables affecting community placement and program success. *The American Journal of Mental Deficiency, 85*(5), 478–488.

Sheerenberger, R. C., & Felsenthal, D. (1977). Community settings for mentally retarded persons: Satisfaction and activities. *Mental Retardation, 15*(4), 3–7.

Switzky, H. N., Dudzinski, M., Van Acker, R., & Gambro, J. (1988). Historical foundations of out-of home residential alternatives for mentally retarded persons. In L. W. Heal, J. I. Haney, & A. R. Novak Amado (Eds.), *Integration of Developmental Disabled Individuals into the Community* (pp. 19–36). Baltimore: Paul H. Brookes.

Skeels, H. M. (1966). Adult status of children with contrasting early life experiences. *Monographs of the Society for Research in Child Development, 31(3),* 1–65.

Skrtic, T. M. (1991). *Behind Special Education: A Critical Analysis of Professional Culture and School Organization.* Denver, CO: Love Publishing Company.

Sloane, W., & Harmon, H. H. (1947). Constancy of IQ in mental defective. *Journal of Genetic Psychology, 71,* 177–185.

Stainback, S., & Stainback, W. (1992). *Curriculum Considerations in Inclusion Classrooms: Facilitating Learning for All Students.* Baltimore: Paul H. Brookes.

Taylor, S. J. (1988). Caught in the continuum: A critical analysis of the principle of the Least Restrictive Environment. *The Journal of The Association for Persons with Severe Handicaps, 13,* 41–53.

Taylor, S. J., Biklen, D., & Knoll, J. (1987). *Community Integration for People with Severe Disabilities.* Baltimore: Paul H. Brookes.

Unger, D. G., & Powell, D. R. (1980). Supporting families under stress: The role of social networks. *Family Relations, 29,* 566–574.

Unger, D. G., & Wandersman, A. (1985). The importance of neighbors: The social, cognitive, and affective components of neighboring. *American Journal of Community Psychology, 13,* 139–169.

Vandercook, T., York, J., & Forest, M., (1989). The McGill Action Planning System (MAPS): A Strategy for Building the Vision. *The Journal of the Association for Persons with Severe Handicaps, 14,* 205–215.

Wagner, M. (1989). *Report on the National Longitudinal Study of Secondary Students with Handicaps.* Washington, D. C.: The Project Directors' Fifth Annual Meeting, Office of Special Education and Rehabilitative Services.

Wehman, P., Moon, M. S., Everson, J. M., Wood, W., & Barcus, J. M. (1988). *Transition from school to work: New challenges for youth with severe disabilities.* Baltimore: Paul H. Brookes.

Whitehead, C. (1981). *Final report: Training and employment services for handicapped individuals in sheltered workshops.* Washington, D. C.: Office of Social Services Policy, Office of the Assistant Secretary for Planning and Evaluation, U. S. Department of Health and Human Services.

Wolfensberger, W. (1972). *Normalization: The Principle of Normalization in Human Services.* Washington, D. C.: National Institute on Mental Retardation.

Chapter 3

Family, Friends, and Society: Supporting People with Severe Disabilities

---

Focus 1:

Distinguish between formal and natural supports for people with severe disabilities.

The need to support and be supported is an integral part of who we are in this world. Whether it be the love of a family member, the strength of a friend, the encouragement of a teacher, or the sustenance provided by an employer, everyone is part of a support network. For the young child, this network is most often the family unit, which in today's society may be constituted in many different ways. As this child grows up, supports expand to the neighborhood, the school, and eventually to a larger heterogeneous group we call "community."

Is the need for a support network of family, friends, and community any different for a person with severe disabilities? Obviously, the answer is "no," although the nature and extent of the support necessary may vary for individuals with severe disabilities. As explained by Sailor and Guess (1983), it is doubtful that people with severe disabilities could actively participate in the life of a community without ". . . a formalized support system to identify and coordinate the variety of needed services" (p. 329). Historically, formalized support systems have been more oriented to socially isolating people with severe disabilities in order to protect them from an uncaring society, and to protect the society from the individual. One manifestation of this social isolation was institutions for people defined as deviant. Institutions are an example of a societal support structure that, while attempting to provide care for the individual, actually promote dependence and

WINDOW 3-1   Larry

Sixteen-year-old Larry O'Brien's friends at St. Marys' High School had just finished getting to know him when I visited their room. They had taped large sheets of paper on the wall, and many student-inspired ideas had been written on them with a magic marker:

What Are Your Dreams for Larry?

- To have a social life
- To have a meaningful job he is happy doing
- To share a house or apartment with others his own age
- To have friends

What Could Be Larry's Nightmares?

- No real friends
- No meaningful job
- To live with paid staff or in an institution

Who Is Larry?

- Friendly
- Charming
- Aggressive
- Romantic
- Cheerful
- Generous
- Fun
- Frustrated
- Stubborn
- Nonverbal
- Grabby

Larry's Needs

- To learn to behave properly in the cafeteria
- To not grab people and things
- To get off the bus properly
- To communicate effectively
- To sit still and listen
- More guys

- To learn to match numbers
- To learn to count
- To be part of classes (gym, English, typing, art, math, drama, computers)

Possible Jobs

In the Community	In School
mailman	cut grass
bag boy in grocery store	put cards in library books
garbageman	coat room at school dances
take tickets at movie theater	pick up paper on school grounds
coat check man	work with janitor
bellboy at hotel	clean
put food trays on wagon in hospital	sweep
snack bar	in cafeteria
packaging/unpacking	put food out
work with younger children	clean tables
work at nursing home	in office
	deliver messages
	staple papers
	put mail in slot
	fill pop machines

The students participate in regular planning sessions to produce charts on Larry's behalf. According to faculty members at St. Mary's, each session becomes more sophisticated, focused and relevant to Larry, the friend the students are getting to know better and better.

Source: Perske, R. (1988). *Circles of friends*. Nashville: Abingdon Press, p. 43.

highlight differences between people. More recently, the concept of support for people with severe disabilities has moved away from isolating the individual in programs and services that are separate from people with severe disabilities to providing both formal, as well as *natural supports* within the home, regular school, and community.

The purpose of a *formal support* system is to bring together the services necessary in assisting the individual with severe disabilities to more actively participate in community and family life. Formal support systems may be funded through the government in areas such as income maintenance, health care, education, housing, or employment. Examples of these formalized government supports include Social Security, Medicaid, mandated special education services, and vocational rehabilitation.

Another type of formal support network is the **advocacy organization**. Advocacy groups may lobby the Congress, state legislatures, and government agencies on behalf of people with severe disabilities for improved and expanded services. They may also provide family members a place to interact and support one another.

Whereas formal supports are structured through agencies and organizations, natural supports may be provided directly by the nuclear and extended family members, friends, or neighbors. Natural supports are often more effective than formal systems in assisting individuals and their family members to not only cope with the barriers imposed by a severe disability, but to learn and succeed in family, school, or community settings. An example of the importance of natural supports may be found in the employment of people with severe disabilities following school. Adults who are successfully employed after leaving school find *more* jobs through their network of family and friends than through formalized support systems (Hasazi, Johnson, Hasazi, Gordon, & Hull, 1989).

In this chapter, we will examine both natural and formal support networks for people with severe disabilities. We will look at the nature of the supports provided to and by family members, the importance of building friendships in community settings, and the diversity of formalized societal support networks.

The Family

The family is an evolving, dynamic system characterized by a set of a unique purposes, roles, and expectations for its various members depending on the basic organization of the unit. Traditionally, families have been defined as a group of individuals, all of whom have biological bonds, and live under one roof with a mother and a father. In the most traditional sense, we may think of a working father and a mother who stays at home to take care of the children and manage the house. However, we see a much more diverse picture of this evolving social system in the 1990s. Only forty years ago about 60 percent of all U.S. households consisted of a working father, a mother who stayed at home, and about two school-age children. Today about 25 percent of all children are living in single-parent families with the mother as the head of the household in 90 percent of the cases. About 60 percent of mothers whose youngest child is over two years of age are in the workforce (National Association of State Directors, 1991). The reality of the 1990s is that the traditional family consisting of a mother, father, and children all under one roof is now only one of many different family constellations that may range from single-parent households to formal family support systems (such as foster care).

NEWSWORTHY 3-1   **Innovative Approaches to Family Support: Chicago Pilot Program for Home Care**

In a northern suburb of Chicago, Illinois, one family with a child with a developmental disability has successfully fought for the resources to care for that family member at home. By receiving state and federal reimbursement equal to what it would cost to care for their daughter in a group home, Ellen and Ed M. have been able to hire respite caregivers for Laura, who is fourteen, and to keep her at home.

Laura had been placed in a group home at the age of ten. Non-ambulatory and non-verbal, Laura required extensive assistance. . . . But the M.'s were not happy with placing Laura away from home. Ellen M. said: "It just didn't make sense that a child would leave the family at 10 years. There was this emptiness that something wasn't the way it should be."

With the help of Community Alternatives Unlimited, a case management services provider, the M.'s and their friends formed Community Living Inc. (CLI), a nonprofit group dedicated to aiding the families of children with disabilities in Chicago's northern suburbs. CLI asked the state to authorize a pilot project for Laura; the proposal was approved. In March 1989, Laura returned home.

The state agreed to provide the same level of funding that it was providing for Laura in the group home, which is about half of what it would

have cost to move her to a state-run institution, and to assist the M.'s in home adaptations, including installation of outdoor and indoor chairlifts. Two other resources were the Social Security Administration's SSI program and the state's respite care program. The state funds actually go to CLI, which, with no administrative expenses, use all of the available resources to pay for the caregivers. Laura is home now because the M.'s have caregivers for 47 hours in a typical week—from 3 p.m. to 8 p.m. during the week and eleven hours a day on Saturdays and Sundays. During the week, Laura attends Wilmette Junior High School for half the day where she has a busy schedule assisted by three other seventh grade girls who have volunteered their services, and an aide. She helps catalogue materials in the library as part of her schedule, and also takes a computer class with the help of assistive technology.

Ellen M. is hopeful that Laura's community integration will continue to grow as everyone involved recognizes its value to both her and to her community. Although the M.'s acknowledge that a home-care program may not be the best alternative for every family with a child with a disability, they believe that, in Laura's case, "As long as she's a child, this is where she belongs, under our roof."

Source: "Innovative Approaches to Family Support: Chicago Pilot Program for Home Care," Fall, 1990, *Family Support Bulletin*, p. 9. Published by United Cerebral Palsy Associations, Inc.

The family, which is more divergent than ever and already under considerable stress in today's world, often faces an even greater challenge with the advent of a child with severe disabilities. This child may throw the family into further crisis, weakening emotional bonds, and imposing severe financial problems (Shelton, Jeppson, & Johnson, 1987). However, it is also possible that family members ". . . may see this child as a source of unity that bonds them and actually strengthens relationships" (Hardman, Drew, Egan, & Wolf, 1993, p. 412). How the family responds to the member with severe disabilities depends on a number of internal factors, as well as the formal and natural supports available to its members.

Formal Family Support Services

> **Focus 2:**
>
> What is the purpose of formal family supports, and how do they prevent or delay "out-of-home" placements for children with severe disabilities?

For the better part of the twentieth century, families of children with severe disabilities confronted a human services system that provided little, if any, direct family support. Many families were unable to receive medical, financial, or educational assistance unless the child was removed from the home and placed in a separate facility or hospital, usually a large institution. The national mandate to provide a free and appropriate public education to all students with disabilities didn't occur until 1975, and has paralleled the **deinstitutionalization** movement of the past two decades. With the passage of **Public Law 94-142** (now the **Individuals with Disabilities Education Act**), and the movement of people with severe disabilities out of institutions and into community settings, the need for formalized family support programs has become critical.

Formal family support programs are designed to assist families in meeting the needs of the child or adult with disabilities within the context of the home. Such programs attempt to prevent or at least delay "out-of-home" placements (Herman & Hazel, 1991; Krause, 1986). The most obvious formal supports include any one or more of government-supported programs for people with disabilities, such as special education services, health-care, income maintenance, employment training and placement, or housing. Programs that are less obvious, but nevertheless important to families, include respite care, in-home assistance, family counseling, and skill training. The purpose of respite care and in-home assistance is to provide some additional relief and help for family members attempting to cope with everyday stresses that may seem overwhelming at times. In-home respite care may involve a companion or sitter spending some time with the individual with severe disabilities. Out-of-home respite care may be provided by families who are licensed to take individuals with severe disabilities into their home for a limited period of time, or parent cooperatives, day-care centers, and community recreational services (Levy & Levy, 1986). Nisbet, Clark, and Covert (1991) suggest that respite care services may ". . . enable family members to become more socially active and in turn reduce their feelings of social isolation" (p. 135). An example of in-home assistance is help from a professional homemaker to reduce the family's time in dealing with household management tasks.

In addition to respite care and in-home assistance, families may also receive counseling services and training to help them meet the challenges and stress associated with living with a child who is severely disabled. It is important that both counseling services and family training programs focus on the relationships and interactions between and among the members, and not just on the individual with severe disabilities. Such an approach, referred to as a "family systems perspective" is based on the premise that ". . . all parts of the family are interrelated; furthermore, each family has unique properties, understood only through careful observation of the relationships and interactions among all members" (Bronicki & Turnbull, 1987, p. 22).

As described by Turnbull and Turnbull (1990), the family systems approach has four components: family characteristics, family interaction, family functions, and family life cycle. The *family characteristics* component is concerned with identifying the basic descriptors of the family unit, such as size, cultural background, socioeconomic status, individual coping styles and skills, health, and geographic location. This information is factored in with the characteristics (type and severity) of the member who is disabled. Understanding the family's cohesiveness and adaptability in coping with the challenges of a member with disabilities is the major element of the *family interaction's* component. Essentially, the more cohesive and adaptable each family member is to living with an individual with severe disabilities, the healthier the family. *Family functions* are those activities that the family engages in to meet its needs. These functions include socialization, self-definition, affection, daily care, recreation, economics, and educational endeavors. The *family life cycle* component analyzes the impact of the child's disability on each member of the family over time. The impact will vary, as it does for all families, during different phases and transitions of the lifecycle. For example, a three-year-old child, who has a strong need for parental attention, may express more jealousy and resentment toward their sibling with disabilities than a teen who is less concerned with parents and more oriented to peers outside the family.

Family training programs that are consistent with a systems approach pay particular attention to (a) facilitating positive intra-family interactions, (b) developing instructional skills for teaching the child with a disability that can be effectively used by all family members, and (c) the importance of the family working together when interacting with professionals. Specific training programs may focus on divergent areas of need, such as coping with emotional and financial stress, locating appropriate resources in the community, effective behavioral interventions in the home, or strengthening the family's network of natural supports.

Strengthening Natural Family Supports

Focus 3:

What are natural family supports, and why are they an important part of an effective support network for people with severe disabilities?

The family support network also extends beyond the services sponsored by government programs and provided by trained professionals to an informal system of assistance: natural supports provided by extended family members, friends, and neighbors. The importance of a natural family support network cannot be overstated. It is through this network that family members may find a personal bonding with others who will listen, understand, and support them as they attempt to cope with the many challenges of a family member with severe disabilities. Lehman, Ellard, and Wortman (1986), in a study of people who had recently lost a close relative, identified the natural supports

POINT OF INTEREST 3-1   Statement in Support of Families and Their Children

THESE PRINCIPLES SHOULD GUIDE PUBLIC POLICY TOWARD FAMILIES OF CHIL-
DREN WITH DEVELOPMENTAL DISABILITIES . . . AND THE ACTIONS OF STATES
AND AGENCIES WHEN THEY BECOME INVOLVED WITH FAMILIES:

All children, regardless of disability, belong with families and need enduring relationships with
adults.

> When states or agencies become involved with families, permanency planning should be a
> guideline philosophy. As a philosophy, permanency planning endorses children's rights to a
> nurturing home and consistent relationships with adults. As a guide to state and agency
> practice, permanency planning requires family support, encouragement of a family's rela-
> tionship with the child, family reunification for children placed out of home, and the pursuit
> of adoption for children when family reunification is not possible. Families should receive the
> supports necessary to maintain their children at home.

Family support services must be based on the principle "whatever it takes."

> In short, family support services should be flexible, individualized, and designed to meet the
> diverse needs of families.

Family supports should build on existing social networks and natural sources of support.

> As a guiding principle, natural sources of support, including neighbors, extended families,
> friends, and community associations, should be preferred over agency programs and profes-
> sional services. When states or agencies become involved with families, they should sup-
> port existing social networks, strengthen natural sources, and help build connections to
> existing community resources. When natural sources of support cannot meet the needs of
> families, professional or agency-operated support services should be available.

Family supports should maximize the family's control over the services and supports they
receive.

> Family support services must be based on the assumption that families, rather than states
> and agencies, are in the best position to determine their needs.

Family supports should support the entire family.

> Family support services should be defined broadly in terms of the needs of the entire family,
> including children with disabilities, parents, and siblings.

Family support services should encourage the integration of children with disabilities into the
community.

> Family support services should be designed to maximize integration and participation in
> community life for children with disabilities.

When children cannot remain with their families for whatever reason, out-of-home placement
should be viewed initially as a temporary arrangement and efforts should be directed toward
reuniting the family.

> Consistent with the philosophy of permanency planning, children should live with their
> families whenever possible. When, due to family crisis or other circumstances, children must

(continued)

POINT OF INTEREST 3-1   *Continued*

leave their families, efforts should be directed at encouraging and enabling families to be reunited.

When families cannot be reunited and when active parental involvement is absent, adoption should be aggressively pursued.

In fulfillment of each child's right to a stable family and an enduring relationship with one or more adults, adoption should be pursued for children whose ties with their families have been broken. Whenever possible, families should be involved in adoption planning and, in all cases, should be treated with sensitivity and respect. When adoption is pursued, the possibility of "open adoption," whereby families maintain involvement with a child, should be seriously considered.

While a preferred alternative to any group setting or out-of-home placement, foster care should only be pursued when children cannot live with their families or with adoptive families.

After families and adoptive families, children should have the opportunity to live with foster families. Foster family care can provide children with a home atmosphere and warm relationships and is preferable to group settings and other placements. As a state or agency sponsored program, however, foster care seldom provides children the continuity and stability they need in their lives. While foster families may be called upon to assist, support, and occasionally fill in for families, foster care is not likely to be an acceptable alternative to fulfilling each child's right to a stable home and enduring relationships.

From Center on Human Policy. (1987b). Statement in support of families and their children. Syracuse, NY: Author.

that were most helpful to families under stress. These individuals benefited from ongoing contact with others who were in similar circumstances, and could relate directly to their feelings of loss. Additionally, they were able to cope more with their loss when they could express their feelings openly to others, and receive expressions of concern. Support-giving that was least helpful included providing advice on what to do and how to cope, trying to minimize the feelings of loss, and expressing forced cheerfulness. As Singer and Irvin (1991) point out, the feelings of isolation for parents of children with disabilities may be ". . . aggravated by well-meaning but painfully superficial statements of support from others" (p. 300).

Natural family supports may include the extended family unit, as well as close friends, colleagues, and neighbors. Extended family members are those individuals who do not necessarily live in the same household, but have ongoing contact with the members of the nuclear family. They might include grandparents, uncles, cousins, etc. These extended family members are often an important base of support to the primary family unit. For example, grandparents may be the only source of respite care for the parents (Seligman & Darling, 1989). Extended family members may also provide in-home assistance by periodically helping with meals, cleaning the house, providing transportation, or just listening when everyone is overwhelmed. Hardman et al. (1993) suggest that grandparents and other extended family members are a critical resource network, especially if they are willing to provide assistance before the primary family unit has depleted all its emotional and financial resources in coping with the child with severe disabilities. However, the effectiveness of extended family members as a resource will be dependent upon their willingness to help, as well as how prepared and informed they are about the child with severe disabilities. These extended family members must be able to openly "voice their questions, feelings, and concerns" about the child with disabilities, and the emotional impact he or she is having on family members. In turn, parents must be willing to help extended family members to learn as much as possible by sharing their own feelings, as well as by providing written information (as suggested by professionals) on the nature and impact of the child's condition on the family unit (Hardman et al., 1993).

Many of the issues regarding whether or not extended family members are in a position to serve as a support network also apply to friends and neighbors. However, parents of a child with a severe disability may be less likely to reach out to friends and neighbors than to extended family members for several reasons. They may want to keep the family's personal business private, or not burden a friend with their problems. They may fear rejection from friends or neighbors who don't understand their emotional needs and concerns. Thoits (1986) suggests that people in general are more comfortable seeking help from others who have had similar experiences, and whose reactions to difficulties are comparable to their own. Nevertheless, it is possible for

---

WINDOW 3-2   Richard: A Grandmother's Point of View

When I discovered that our grandson, Richard, was retarded, I wasn't sure how I should respond. You must remember that, in my day, children who were retarded weren't talked about a lot. They were actually hidden or sent away to a state hospital or something like that. My husband was particularly perplexed by the birth of our new grandson. He really didn't know what to say or how to respond. Of course, I wasn't much better. We decided that we needed to educate ourselves. Our daughter was kind enough to give us a few pamphlets that helped us learn about our new grandson's condition. We also talked with some other friends of ours who have a granddaughter with Down syndrome. They didn't know a whole lot more than we did, but the talking did us both some good.

Since that time, we've tried to be supportive of our daughter and her situation. We try to volunteer whatever assistance we can when she seems to be pressed or to need a reprieve for a couple of hours. We're glad that we live somewhat close to her.

I remember our first contacts with Richard. We weren't sure how different he would be. Actually, it took very little time for us to realize that Richard wasn't all that different. We found that he does things a little bit more slowly, but other than that, he's pretty much normal.

We think our daughter and her husband, John, have handled this situation extremely well. In fact, we're very proud of them. And we realize that this could happen to anyone.

We enjoy Richard a lot. Yes, we worry a little about his future and what he'll do when he's older, but we've learned from John and Marilyn that sometimes, it's better to take things one day at a time.

Betty, a grandmother

Source: Hardman, M. L. Drew, C. J., Egan, M. W., & Wolf, B. (1993) *Human exceptionality: Society, school, and family* (4th edition). Boston: Allyn and Bacon, Inc., p. 429.

friends and neighbors to be part of a natural support network for the family. The nature and type of support will be unique to the individuals involved, and be dependent on a mutual level of comfort in both seeking and providing assistance. Clear communication regarding what friends or neighbors are willing to do, and how that matches with the needs of the family, is essential if this support is to be meaningful to the child with a severe disability and their family members.

Building Friendships

> *All children need to learn with and from other children . . . All children need to belong and feel wanted and loved . . . All children need to have fun and enjoy noise and laughter in their lives . . . And fall and cry and get hurt . . . All children need to be in real families and real schools and real neighborhoods. (Forest, 1991, p. 403)*

Friendship is a bond between individuals, favored companions who are emotionally connected to each other by mutual affection or esteem. Friendships develop as an evolutionary process. First, there is an awareness of common values, interests, concerns, or backgrounds. Then, individuals must have the opportunity to interact with one another to discover and explore these similarities. During this exploration process, ". . . friendships are more likely to develop when individuals are competent at making social discriminations and initiating and maintaining social interactions" (McDonnell, Wilcox, and Hardman, 1991, p. 186).

If common abilities and interests are the basis for friendship development, one might conclude that individuals with severe disabilities would only have friends who are also disabled. Certainly, friendships between people with disabilities do occur, and are an integral part of each person's social network. However, Voeltz (1984) suggests that although current friendship patterns among children and adults in our society promote homogeneous relationships between friends who are similar in their abilities, it is possible to ". . . value and experience mutually rewarding, 'heterogenous' friendships—with people who are somehow different than our usual friends" (p.180). There are compelling reasons why friendships between people with and without disabilities benefit everyone involved.

Benefits to People with Severe Disabilities

> **Focus 4:**
>
> What are the mutual benefits of building friendships between people with and without disabilities?

Friendships with people who are not disabled will contribute directly to a "social, emotional, and practical" support base for people with severe disabilities that will facilitate active participation in the life of a community (Traustadottir, 1993). It is through

POINT OF INTEREST 3-2   Why Friends Are Important

Friendships are such an everyday thing, we just take them for granted. They are like electricity, telephone, clothing, and three meals a day—we anguish only when we are deprived of them.

And yet we have just begun to sense the pain experienced by people with disabilities when they are deprived of mutually satisfying friendships with ordinary people. We suddenly see that family support, regular schooling, and community living programs are not enough. Those people need friends just as we do. Consider the following:

Friendship is a familiar but elusive term. Alfred North Whitehead, in *Science and the Modern World*, shows that familiar things—like friendships—are the hardest to research (p. 6). Researchers, of course, reduce their focus to specific *relationships* or *social interactions*, classifying, counting, and analyzing. But the rest of us need to view a good friendship the way we look at a sunrise, seeing it in all its radiance. Otherwise, as Whitehead believes, research will degenerate into a medley of ad hoc hypotheses, truncated findings without a philosophic base (p. 25).

Families provide things that friends can't. We need childhood nurturing, a place in a family history, strong birth-to-death ties.

But friends help us stretch beyond our families. In *Just Friends*, social scientist Lillian Rubin illustrates vividly that young people turn more to friends than to family when they seek to be affirmed as adults (pp.15–33).

Human-service workers do things that friends can't. When such a team is at its best, it can focus on a specific problem and draw up an orchestrated plan. Then, in unison, the workers try to help a person achieve a specific healthy outcome.

But friends help us move beyond human-service goals. Friends provide us with myriad options that never could be programmed.

Friends help us rehearse adult roles. You and I are the way we are largely because we rehearse our actions and attitudes with friends—things we wouldn't think of saying or doing with family or human-service workers.

Friends serve as fresh role models. We often choose certain friends because we see something in them that we wish for ourselves.

Good friendships are a mystery. There's no ritual or program for starting them. Sometimes they thrive and sometimes they fade. And they may end without celebration, certificate, plague, funeral, or divorce decree.

Good friendships are attractive. Others watch interactions between friends with great interest. As Letty Pogrebin, in *Among Friends*, says, "Friendship is like sex: We always suspect there's some secret technique we don't know about" (p. 5).

Friendships generate their own energy. Quite often, when two people do things together, their zest and success equal much more than the sum of two people's efforts.

Friendships become a haven from stress. When things get tough, many of us have good friends "on call."

Spouses and committed couples can be good friends. When two people can't, they are in trouble.

Friendships are reciprocal. Both parties receive enrichment from the relationship.

People in authority often frown on friendships. In *The Four Loves*, C. S. Lewis says, "Men who have real friends are less easy to manage or 'get at'; harder for good authorities to correct or for bad authorities to corrupt" (p. 115).

Friends can demystify strange behaviors. While I visited two friends in a print shop in Rockville, Maryland, one friend—during a moment of boredom—began to move his arms and fingers in patterns professionals call "autistic." When I asked the other friend what he thought

(continued)

POINT OF INTEREST 3-2   *Continued*

about such movements, he replied, "Hey man, if you think that's weird, you should come with me to my favorite tavern on Friday nights."

Human-service workers cannot program friendships. They can, however, set up frameworks in which friendships can happen.

Every friendship is unique and unrepeatable. What happens in each relationship sets it apart as vividly as a fingerprint. That's why each friendship described in this book differs vastly from the others.

One can learn much from good friendships. A good friendship can become a *living document.* With great interest, we can study the remarkable things friends do with each other. And it doesn't matter whether society has imaged us as a so-called normal or as a person with a disability, good friendships can inspire us to try refreshing new interpersonal activities in our own lives—things we've never done before.

Source: Perske, R. (1988). *Circles of friends*. Nashville: Abingdon Press, p. 12–13.

these one-to-one friendships that we see the long-term changes in behavior that promote the acceptance of differences, and move us closer to an inclusive society. Rees, Spreen, and Harnadek (1991) found that direct contact between people with mental retardation and their nondisabled peers resulted in improved attitudes for university undergraduate students over time. They further suggest that shifts in public policy (such as the passage of the *Americans with Disabilities Act*) and the movement toward community integration have also contributed significantly to the positive change in attitudes toward people with mental retardation.

Haring (1991) suggests five reasons why social relationships between people with and without disabilities should be considered a defining characteristic of an integrated service system:

1. *Social relationships contribute substantially to quality of life.*
2. *Social interaction skills, ideally produced within the context of an ongoing relationship with another person, are necessary for functional participation in many critical activities*
3. *Many critical skills are maintained over time by complex, remote schedules of reinforcement but are maintained on an immediate basis by the socially reinforcing aspects of interacting with people with whom you have a relationship.*
4. *There is a relationship between social skills use and the lessening of a need for programming based on behavioral control.*
5. *There is an increasing awareness that disability is more an attitude held by professionals and [people who are not disabled] than it is a property or defining characteristic of the person with disabilities. (p. 197)*

The benefits of friendship-building with nondisabled peers are receiving increased attention in the education of students with severe disabilities. Many educators and parents are demanding a greater emphasis on the development of socialization skills that will facilitate ongoing friendships (Lutfiyya, 1990; Taylor & Bogdan, 1987). Hamre-Nietupski, Nietupski, and Strathe (1992) indicate that parents are challenging the prevailing skills training approach, and are emphasizing to educators how important friendships are in supporting their children's integration into the community. In a survey of parents with severe and profound disabilities, these researchers found that friendship/social relationship development was considered equal in importance with functional skills (such as paying for meals in a restaurant or brushing teeth), but was significantly more important than academic skills.

Benefits to People Who Are Not Disabled

While much of the emphasis on the importance of friendships focuses on benefits to people with severe disabilities, there are some positive outcomes for people without disabilities as well. Biklen, Corrigan, and Quick (1989), in a study of students with severe disabilities and their nondisabled peers in an integrated elementary school classroom, reported that the experience had resulted in an enhanced understanding and caring about other people on the part of students who were not disabled. In a study of an inner-city high school, Murray-Seegert (1989) found that students without disabilities participated in a social integration program because they were challenged by the opportunity of working with people with disabilities, and had positive feelings about knowing that they were helping others.

Peck, Donaldsen, and Pezzoli (1990) examined the perceptions of 21 high-school-age students without disabilities to determine their perceptions of the benefits of developing relationships with students who are moderately and severely disabled. As Peck et al. reported, these high school students appeared to have benefited in a number of ways from their experiences, including ". . . improved self-concept, social-cognitive growth, reduced fear of human differences, increased tolerance of other people, development of principles of personal conduct, and enjoyment of relaxed and accepting friendships" (p. 248).

The mutual benefits that occur as a result of friendships between individuals with and without disabilities may be best summed up in the following scenario.

> . . . *On the first day of school a new student with severe disabilities arrived in one of our schools. Because of his appearance, and the fact that he was in a wheel chair, most students were reluctant to interact with him. One third-grade boy reacted quite negatively to the arrival of this student. As time passed, this boy observed how the teachers and students acted toward this student in a loving and caring manner. He noted how this student was "included," just like everyone else. One day the third grader asked to be the student's special helper during recess. As the days passed the two boys developed a real friendship. Both students came to feel liked and important. [Emphasis added] (Stephens & Engle, 1993, p. 11).*

Societal Support Networks

The inclusion of people with severe disabilities into the life of a community is framed in a philosophy that recognizes and accepts the range of human differences (Hardman et al., 1993). However, stating a philosophy is one thing, turning it into positive outcomes for persons with severe disabilities is quite another. As suggested by Gerry and McWhorter (1991), "persons with severe disabilities pursue the same personal goals as do persons without disabilities: a comfortable home, a meaningful job, and social network of family members and friends" (p. 509). When a philosophy of inclusion is backed up by social policies that translate words into action, people with disabilities have ". . . emerged as valuable members of the overall community" (Gerry & McWhorter, p. 509). The question is then how do we establish both formal and natural support networks within society that will foster the inclusion of people with severe disabilities? What are the barriers to participation, and how do we break them down? We will examine these issues from several perspectives: civil rights legislation, government-supported programs, and the role of advocacy in the lives of people with severe disabilities.

The Americans with Disabilities Act (ADA)

Focus 5:

Identify the major provisions of the *Americans with Disabilities Act* (*ADA*).

The Americans with Disabilities Act of 1990 (*Public Law 101-336*) is a national mandate to break down the barriers of discrimination against individuals with disabilities in private-sector employment, all public services, and public accommodations, transportation, and telecommunications. Under the *ADA*, businesses that serve the public must remove architectural barriers, such as curbs on sidewalks, narrow doorways, or shelving and desks that prevent access by a person with a disability. These same businesses must provide "reasonable accommodations" to people with disabilities in hiring or promotion practices, restructuring jobs, and modifying equipment. All new public transit facilities (such as buses or train stations) must be accessible, and transportation services must be available to people with disabilities who can't use fixed bus routes. The law also mandates against discrimination in public accommodations (restaurants, hotels, retail stores), and in state and local government agencies. Telecommunication devices for people who are deaf must be made available by all companies who offer telephone service to the general public.

The *ADA*, as social policy, is one way that government can ensure that the rights of citizens with disabilities are protected. It is an attempt to provide people with disabilities an "equal playing field" as they seek access to the same opportunities afforded those who are not disabled. Another way to assist people with disabilities is for the government to actually develop and fund programs and services that provide income, health care, adequate housing, employment, and education.

POINT OF INTEREST 3-3 The *Americans with Disabilities Act*: **Opening Doors**

In the past, individuals with disabilities have had to contend with the reality that learning to live independently did not guarantee access to all that society had to offer in terms of services and jobs. Although several states have long had laws that promised otherwise, access to places such as public rest-rooms and great restaurants and success in mainstream corporate America has often eluded those with disabilities, primarily because of architectural and attitudinal barriers.

The *Americans with Disabilities Act (ADA)*, phase 1 of which began January 26, 1992, has promised to change all that, giving 43 million Americans with disabilities new legal rights, at an estimate cost to businesses of $1 billion to $2 billion. All businesses that serve the public, such as laundromats, retail stores, hospitals, and banks, are required to remove architectural barriers. Included among those changes considered to be "readily achievable" and therefore required are:

- Making curb cuts in sidewalks
- Repositioning shelves, desks, and telephones
- Widening doors
- Removing or providing convenient alternatives to turnstiles

Employers are also required to make "reasonable efforts" to hire people with disabilities. Under the *ADA*, employers may not:

- Use hiring or firing practices to discriminate against a worker or applicant who has a disability
- Ask whether a person has a disability or has had prior medical treatments (employers may ask only about the applicant's ability to perform a particular job)
- Use tests or screen out an applicant or worker due to his or her disability
- Deny access to employment or advancement to someone living with or involved in a relationship with a person who has a disability
- Limit job classifications or promotion opportunities

American Telephone and Telegraph (AT&T) and local carriers are required to provide services that enable individuals with hearing and speech impairments to make and receive calls on telephones. Mass transit services must also be accessible to all people with disabilities.

Clearly, individuals with disabilities are a minority group that has been discriminated against regularly in the past. As a result, many such people either cannot get jobs or have stopped looking altogether, making the community of individuals with disabilities one of the poorest in the nation. According to the President's Committee on the Employment of People with Disabilities, two-thirds of these individuals of working age cannot get jobs, even in sound economic times.

Much as the Civil Rights Act of 1964 gave clout to the African-American struggle for equality, The *Americans with Disabilities Act* has promised to do the same for those with disabilities. The degree to which it will be successful in eliminating the fears and prejudices of the general community remains to be seen.

Source: Hardman, M. L., Drew, C. J., Egan, M. W. & Wolf, B. (1993). *Human exceptionality* (4th ed.). Boston: Allyn & Bacon, p. 16.

The Individuals with Disabilities Education Act

Focus 6:

Identify the major provisions of the *Individuals with Disabilities Education Act.*

Education is a basic value in the United States, reflecting the view that every individual should have access to schools that promote personal growth and development throughout life. School is a place to prepare people for life, as well as an environment in which one can engage in reflection and reasoning. Schools exist to promote literacy, personal autonomy, economic self-sufficiency, personal fulfillment, and citizenship. Whether the value be reason and reflection or practical knowledge for living and learning in a democratic society, the expectation is full participation for everyone regardless of race, cultural background, socioeconomic status, physical disabilities, or mental limitations (Resnick, 1987).

The translation of this value into actual practice for all students with disabilities began with the landmark case of *Brown v. Topeka, Kansas, Board of Education* in 1954. Although heralded as a mandate to end racial desegregation, the U.S. Supreme Court's decision that education must be made available to everyone on an equal basis also set a major precedent for students with disabilities. A unanimous Supreme Court stated, "In these days, it is doubtful that any child may reasonably be expected to succeed in life if is he is denied the opportunity of an education. Such an opportunity, where the state has undertaken to provide it, is a right which must be made available to all on equal terms" (*Brown v. Topeka*, 1954).

Nearly twenty years later, the Pennsylvania Association for Retarded Citizens filed a class-action suit on behalf of children with mental retardation who were excluded from public education on the basis of intellectual deficiency (*Pennsylvania Association for Retarded Citizens* v. *Commonwealth of Pennsylvania*, 1971). The issue was whether public school programs should be required to accommodate the students with significant intellectual differences. Under a court order, schools were to provide a free public education to all children with mental retardation, ages six to twenty-one consistent with their individual learning needs. Preschool-age children with mental retardation were also entitled to a free and appropriate public education if the local school district was providing it for other children. The *Pennsylvania* decision was expanded in the case of *Mills* v. *District of Columbia* (1972) to include all children with disabilities. The *Pennsylvania* and *Mills* cases served as catalysts for several court cases, and eventually the passage of *Public Law 94-142 (Part B of the Education of the Handicapped Act)* in 1975. This act was renamed the *Individuals with Disabilities Education Act (IDEA)* in 1990.

Basic Requirements of IDEA

The *IDEA* mandates that all eligible students regardless of the *extent or type* of disability are to receive at public expense the special education services necessary to meet their individual needs. Special education is defined as instruction in all settings, including the workplace and training centers. The law also requires the provision of any related services that are necessary to ensure that students benefit from their educational experience. Eligibility for educational services under the *IDEA* are determined by disability condition. There are several types of disability under the law, including mental retardation, serious emotional disturbance, learning disabilities, autism, sensory impairments, and physical (orthopedic) and other health impairments. The basic provisions of the *IDEA* provide for (a) nondiscriminatory and multidisciplinary assessment, (b) parental involvement in the development of the student's educational program, (c) placement in the least restrictive environment (LRE), and (d) an individualized education program.

Nondiscriminatory and multidisciplinary assessment involves testing students in their native or primary language whenever possible. Evaluation procedures must be selected and administered to prevent cultural or racial discrimination. A multidisciplinary team must conduct the assessment using several pieces of information to formulate a placement decision. All assessment tools used by this team must be validated for the purpose for which they are being used.

Under the *IDEA*, parents have the right to:

1. Consent in writing before the child is initially evaluated
2. Consent in writing before the child is initially placed in a special education program
3. Request an independent education evaluation if they feel the school's evaluation is inappropriate
4. Request an evaluation at public expense if a due-process hearing decision is that the public agency's evaluation was inappropriate
5. Participate on the committee that considers the evaluation, placement, and programming of the child
6. Inspect and review educational records and challenge information believed to be inaccurate, misleading, or in violation of the privacy or other rights of the child
7. Request a copy of information from their child's educational record
8. Request a hearing concerning the school's proposal or refusal to initiate or change the identification, evaluation, or placement of the child, or the provision of a free appropriate public education.

The least restrictive environment is defined as an educational setting that (a) is consistent with the academic, social, and physical needs of the student, and (b) educates students who are disabled with their nondisabled peers to the maximum extent appropriate. In order to comply with this requirement, federal regulations mandate the development of a continuum of placements, including regular classrooms with support services, resource rooms, special classes and schools, and homebound and hospital programs.

The individualized education program (IEP) is a set of goals and activities that are based on the needs of each student as determined by the multidisciplinary team. Each student's IEP must contain a statement on (a) present level of performance, (b) annual goals, (c) short-term instructional objectives, (d) related services, (e) percent of time in regular education, (f) beginning and ending dates for special education services, and (g) an annual evaluation. In addition to meeting individual student needs, the IEP is also intended to strengthen communication between school personnel and the family.

In 1990, a new requirement was added to the IEP. Beginning no later than age 16 and annually thereafter, the IEP must include a statement of the transition services needed for students as they leave school and enter adulthood. As suggested by McDonnell, Wilcox, and Hardman (1991), the statement should (a) identify the range of services needed by the individual to participate in the community, (b) identify activities that must occur during high school to facilitate the individual's access to an adult service program, and (c) establish timelines and responsibilities for completion of these services.

Early Intervention and Preschool Services under the IDEA

The *Education of the Handicapped Act* (now the *IDEA)* was amended in 1986 to include provisions for preschool-age students with disabilities. *Public Law 99-457* established a mandate to provide a free and appropriate education for all preschool-age children with disabilities (three through five years), and established a new early intervention program for infants, toddlers, and their families (The Infant and Toddlers with Disabilities Program [Part H]).

While programs for preschool-age students were mandated under *P.L. 99-457*, participation in *early intervention programs* under Part H was at the option of each individual state. States were eligible for federal funds if they chose to do so and agreed to meet federal implementation requirements after an initial five-year planning period. The Part H program included some unique requirements, not specified in the *Part B* preschool and school-age educational programs. These requirements were designed to recognize the unique needs of infants and toddlers and their families, and to support individualized family-centered intervention rather than creating school-like programs for younger children. For example, infants and toddlers become eligible for early intervention services based on the presence of a developmental delay or a condition which has a high probability of resulting in a developmental delay. This means that it is not necessary to establish the presence of a permanent disability or a type of disability (such as mental retardation) in order to provide early intervention services. Similarly, rather than an IEP, an individualized family service plan (IFSP) is developed for every eligible child and their family. The IFSP is very important because it reflects the goals, plan of action, services, and strategies that family members and multidisciplinary team members agree upon as the defined individualized early intervention most important for that child and family. A more in-depth discussion of IFSP's and other requirements for Part H early intervention programs is provided in Chapter five.

The original provisions in *P.L. 99-457* represent the same breakthrough for *preschool-age children* and their families that the 1975 passage of *P. L. 94-142* (now *IDEA)* had been for school age children. While *P. L. 94-142* provided some incentives for states to establish preschool programs for children with disabilities, they were not required to do so unless they also provided educational opportunities for all typically developing three-, four-, and five-year olds. Many states did provide kindergarten for five-year olds, but most did not routinely educate three- and four-year olds. As such, they were under no pressure to provide preschool special education services. *P. L. 99-457* eliminated this "loophole" and established a full service mandate for all preschoolers eligible to receive special education and related services. Additionally, it provided the same protections and rights for these children and their families that had previously existed for school-age children.

Preschool programs are governed by *Part B of IDEA*, as are services for school-age children. However, *Part B-Section 619* (the section addressing preschool programs) and the 1991 amendments to the *IDEA (P. L. 102-119)* make some important distinctions for preschool programs (Noonan & McCormick, 1993). These distinctions include:

1. Noncategorical eligibility for programs as "children with disabilities"
2. Increased emphasis on efforts to assist families and to strengthen the parents' role in the development and implementation of their child's IEP. In fact, planning for assistance to parents may be included as a part of the IEP if it is considered necessary to help the child benefit from special education.
3. Parental training activities may be included as support services on the IEP.
4. A longer school day or year is allowed for purposes of contracting with other programs or agencies if this is necessary to meet the requirements for provision of a full range of services. Examples of agencies or programs with which a school district might develop such contracts include Head Start, a private preschool program, or Children's Special Health Care Services.

All states receiving funds under the *IDEA* must assure that three- to five-year-old children were receiving a free appropriate public education by the 1990–1991 school year. One significant difference, however, between the requirements for school-age children and preschoolers is that states are not required to report preschool children by disability category (e.g., learning disabilities, mental retardation, deafness, etc.).

Public Law 99-457 is administered directly through the state and local education agencies. To support states in meeting the requirements of this law, several new initiatives were enacted, including the establishment of demonstration and outreach programs for preschool-age children with a disability, the authorization of early childhood institutes to generate and disseminate research findings on early childhood education, and projects to demonstrate cost effective methods of delivering educational services. A more in-depth discussion on other federal legislation influencing programs and services for preschool children may be found in Chapter 6 of this text.

Other Government-Supported Programs

Focus 7:

How do government-supported programs provide assistance to people with severe disabilities?

The overall purposes of government-supported programs range from providing basic economic support for people with disabilities (such as income maintenance, Medicaid, and Medicare) to education and training (such as vocational rehabilitation and special education services). Table 3-1 presents a summary of the key federally funded programs

TABLE 3-1   Key Federally Funded Programs for People with Disabilities

Program	Federal Legislation	Purpose	Services
Income maintenance:			
Supplemental Security Income (SSI)	*Social Security Amendments of 1972 (PL 92-603), Title XVI*	Basic economic support	Direct cash payments to eligible people with disabilities
	Employment Opportunities for Disabled Americans Act of 1986	Reduce disincentives to work under SSI	SSI payments reduced (but not terminated) by $1 for every $2 earned about $85 monthly income
Social Security Disability Insurance for Adult Disabled Children (ADC)	*Social Security Act of 1956, Title II*	Basic economic support	Direct cash payments for disabled children 18 and over of disabled workers eligible for Social Security
Health Care:			
Medicare	*Social Security Act, Title XVIII*	National insurance program for elderly and eligible people with disabilities	Short-term hospitalization; related care in nursing homes; home care, physician services; outpatient services; ambulance, medical supplies, and equipment
Medicaid	*Social Security Act, Title XIX*	Payments for health care services to eligible residents	Inpatient and outpatient hospital services; laboratory services; physician services; family planning; skilled nursing services; early screening; treatment and immunization; other medical services as established by states on an individual basis
Residential Alternative:			
Intermediate Care Facilities for the Mentally Retarded	*Social Security Act (PL 92-223) As Amended in 1971, Title XIX*	Fund residential living and other services to people with mental retardation needing 24-hour care	Reimbursement to states for costs of service in facilities that provide health care, rehabilitation, and active treatment to Medicaid-eligible clients
Home and community based waiver	*1981 Amendments to the Social Security Act*	Allow states to include community-based home care in Medicaid plans	Same services as above, but can be provided in non-institutional settings
Employment:			
Vocational Rehabilitation	*Vocational Rehabilitation Act*	To train and place people with	Vocational training and placement, career guidance, reim-

TABLE 3-1   *Continued*

Program	Federal Legislation	Purpose	Services
	of 1973 (PL 93-516)	disabilities in employment	bursement for prosthetic appliances (supported employment services added in 1986 amendments)
Coordinated Planning and service delivery	*Developmental Disabilities and Bill of Rights Act of 1970*	Incentives for states to establish coordinated planning and service activities	Planning councils to coordinate service of various government agencies; "bill of rights" that defined appropriate service in the least restrictive environment; protection and advocacy systems; university-affiliated programs
Education:			
Special Education Services	*The Individuals with Disabilities Act* (formerly *Public Law 94-142*)	To provide a free and appropriate public education to all students who are disabled.	Special education and support (related) services provided through an individual education program in the least restrictive environment; multidisciplinary and non-biased assessment; parent involvement and safeguards.

Source: Adapted from McDonnell, J., Wilcox, B., & Hardman, M. (1991). *Secondary programs for students with developmental disabilities*. Boston: Allyn and Bacon, p. 26–27.

that are intended to support people with disabilities in community settings. Government programs that provide basic economic support are sometimes criticized as a barrier to equal opportunity for people with disabilities, because they create disincentives to work. Braddock and Fujiura (1988) indicate that income maintenance programs, such as Supplemental Security Income (SSI), have made it ". . . economically advantageous for the individual with a disability to remain unemployed" (p. 265). Gerry and McWhorter (1991) suggest that income maintenance programs have been completely ineffective in helping people with severe disabilities enter and stay in the competitive labor force. They further recommend significant changes in the structure of federal programs providing support to people with severe disabilities. Specific changes would include:

1. Expansion of federal financial support for programs serving infants and toddlers.
2. The passage of new federal legislation to develop and implement public schools that would serve all children, including those with severe disabilities.
3. A new program in the U.S. Department of Health and Human Services that would focus on effective transition from school to adult life, expanded community employment opportunities, and support for independent living.

4. Elimination of work disincentives and other inequities within the income maintenance programs.

Current government programs send a mixed message to people with severe disabilities and their families. While one government program, such as education,
encourages these individuals to become contributing members of society, another
(Social Security) supports their continued dependence. It may be that the most effective role for the government is to coordinate those services that are most likely to
facilitate access and participation in inclusive settings (Sailor & Guess, 1983),
develop strategies that help change public attitudes about the capabilities of people
with severe disabilities (OECD, 1986), and disseminate information on model programs that are successful in promoting quality community living (Hardman et al.,
1993).

Advocacy Organizations

Focus 8:

How do advocacy organizations assist people with severe disabilities?

Advocacy is speaking for, or in behalf of, someone else. Advocacy may occur in many
ways for people with severe disabilities. Family members and friends may serve in
advocacy roles to ensure that the rights of the individuals with severe disabilities are not
ignored. There are also formal disability advocacy organizations, such as the Association for Persons with Severe Handicaps, the ARC—A National Organization on Mental Retardation (formerly the Association for Retarded Citizens), the Council for
Exceptional Children, the National Society for Autistic Citizens, and United Cerebral
Palsy. These organizations have successfully lobbied Congress, state, and local policy
makers for the improvement of formalized support systems for people with severe disabilities. Along with "mutual aid" groups from local hospitals and schools (parent-
teacher-student organizations), these disability advocacy organizations have also served
as an important contact point for information and assistance to families, and have
been influential with the general public in creating awareness of the needs of people
with severe disabilities (Singer & Irvin, 1991).

A major movement in this country is toward "self-advocacy": people with disabilities having more to say in their lives rather than having others always "do" and speak
for them. At the core of the self-advocacy movement is the power of choice. Even in
some of the "best" programs and services for people with severe disabilities, these individuals may have little choice in their lives about who their friends are, where they live,
what time they go to bed, when they eat, or what they do with their free time. As we
move more toward the reality of an inclusive society, it seems inconceivable that such
an ideal could ever be fully reached without people with severe disabilities being able
to participate in the choices that affect their lives.

Conclusion

This chapter has examined both formal and natural supports for people with disabilities in the context of the family, building friendships, and the establishment of a societal support network. Formal supports may result from government-funded programs, or come through advocacy organizations. Natural supports may be provided by the nuclear family, extended family members, friends, colleagues, or neighbors. Both formal and natural supports are necessary for the individual with severe disabilities to actively participate in the life of a community.

Formal family supports, which include respite care, in-home assistance, family counseling, and skill training are services intended to help family members meet the needs and challenges of a child or adult with severe disabilities living in the home. Natural family supports, provided by extended family members, friends, and neighbors provide a network of assistance that develops personal bonding between individuals to help cope with everyday stress and feelings of isolation.

Friendships between people with and without disabilities can be mutually beneficial for everyone involved. For people with disabilities, friendships provide a network of support that helps facilitate their active participation in community life. These friendships often result in long-term attitude and behavioral changes toward people

****

POINT AND COUNTERPOINT 3-1   Friends

Is it really possible for a person with severe disabilities to be "friends" with someone who is not disabled? While one approach to friendships emphasizes common abilities, interests, and backgrounds as a basis for a relationship, another is more concerned with people accepting and caring about each other regardless of individual abilities. Here are two points of view on friendships between people with and without disabilities.

Point:

Friendships between people with severe disabilities and those who are not disabled really don't make a lot of sense. People become friends because of their common intellect, backgrounds, and interests. If one individual is more intellectually capable than another, then the relationship is really one that is protective or caregiving. One person will be in a position of dominating the other. True friendships for individuals with severe disabilities are with others who are similar in their capabilities.

Counterpoint:

It is a very narrow viewpoint that focuses only on people being friends with "their own kind." Such a perspective disregards the individuality in each of us. We all establish friendships for many different reasons. Friendships may develop from the comfort of being with someone who accepts you for who you are, regardless of your "limitations." It may be that the person who is not disabled learns more about themselves through a friendship with a person with severe disabilities, or maybe it's just they enjoy a relaxed and accepting relationship. Perhaps, Robert Perske says it best: "Every friendship is unique and unrepeatable. What happens in each relationship sets it apart as vividly as a fingerprint" (1988, p. 13).

****

with disabilities. For people who are not disabled, a friendship with a person with severe disabilities may improve their self-concept, reduce their fear of people who are different, increase their tolerance of other people, and help them enjoy a relaxed and accepting relationship.

Societal support networks may result from civil rights legislation, government-supported programs, and involvement through advocacy organizations. The *Americans with Disabilities Act (ADA)* is civil rights legislation that attempts to break down the barriers of discrimination against people with disabilities. The major provisions of this Act ban discrimination in private-sector employment, public services and accommodations, transportation, and telecommunications. Government-supported programs for people with disabilities may include such services as direct financial assistance, health care, employment training and ongoing support, housing, and access to a free and appropriate public education. Advocacy organizations play an important role in lobbying the Congress and other policymakers for improved and expanded programs and services for people with severe disabilities. These organizations are also an important source of information and assistance to persons with disabilities and their families.

Focus Review

Focus 1: Distinguish between formal and natural supports for people with severe disabilities.

- Formal supports bring together the services necessary in assisting the individual with severe disabilities to more actively participate in community and family life.
- Formal supports may (a) be funded through the government in areas such as income maintenance, health care, education, housing, or employment, or (b) come through advocacy organizations which lobby on behalf of people with severe disabilities and provide family members a place to interact and support one another.
- Natural supports may be provided directly by the nuclear and extended family members, friends, or neighbors.

Focus 2: What is the purpose of formal family supports and how do they prevent or delay "out-of-home" placements for children with severe disabilities?

- Formal supports assist families in meeting the needs of the child or adult who is disabled within the context of the home.
- Services, such as respite care, in-home assistance, family counseling, and skill training are made available to the family to help members support the child with severe disabilities in a home environment.

Focus 3: What are natural family supports, and why are they an important part of an effective support network for people with severe disabilities?

- Natural family supports may include the extended family unit, as well as close friends, colleagues, and neighbors.
- Family members find a personal bonding with others who will listen, understand, and support them as they attempt to cope with the many challenges of a family member with severe disabilities.

Focus 4: What are the mutual benefits of building friendships between people with and without disabilities?

- Friendships with people who are not disabled will contribute directly to a support base for people with severe disabilities that will facilitate active participation in the life of a community.
- Friendships between people with and without disabilities result in long-term changes in behavior that promote the acceptance of differences.
- People without disabilities are challenged by the opportunity of working with people who are disabled, and have positive feelings about knowing that they were helping others.
- Friendships may result in improved self-concept, social-cognitive growth, reduced fear of human differences, increased tolerance of other people, development of principles of personal conduct, and enjoyment of relaxed and accepting friendships for people who are not disabled.

Focus 5: Identify the major provision of the *Americans with Disabilities Act (ADA)*.

- The *ADA* bans discrimination against individuals with disabilities in private-sector employment, all public services, and public accommodations, transportation, and telecommunications.

Focus 6: Identify the major provisions of the Individuals with Disabilities Education Act.

- The basic provisions of the *IDEA* provide for (a) nondiscriminatory and multidisciplinary assessment, (b) parental involvement in the development of the student's educational program, (c) placement in the least restrictive environment (LRE), and (d) an individualized education program.
- States have the option of establishing an early intervention programs for infants and toddlers under Part H that (a) provides services to infants and toddlers with developmental delays or who have a diagnosed physical or mental condition with a high probability of resulting in a developmental delay, and (b) establishes a written individualized family service plan for every eligible child and their family.
- States are required to meet the same requirements for preschool children as mandated in the *IDEA* for school-age children with the following exceptions: (a) eligibility is noncategorical, (b) increased emphasis on efforts to assist families and to strengthen the parents' role in the development and implementation of their

child's IEP, (c) parental training activities may be included as support services on the IEP, and (d) a longer school day or year is allowed.

Focus 7: How do government-supported programs provide assistance to people with severe disabilities?

- Government-supported programs may provide direct income (financial assistance), health care, employment training and on-going support, housing, as well as access to a free and appropriate public education for persons with severe disabilities.

Focus 8: How do advocacy organizations assist people with severe disabilities?

- Advocacy organizations may lobby Congress, state, and local policy makers for the improvement of formalized support systems for people with severe disabilities.
- Self-advocacy groups help people with disabilities speak up for themselves and make personal choices.

References

Biklen, D., Corrigan, C., & Quick, D. (1989). Beyond obligation: Students' relations with each other in integrated classes. In D. Lipsky & A. Gartner (Eds.), *Beyond special education: Quality education for all* (pp. 207–221). Baltimore: Paul H. Brookes.

Braddock, D., & Fujiura, G. (1988). Federal foundations for transitions to adulthood. In B. L. Ludlow, A. P. Turnbull, & R. Luckasson (Eds.), *Transitions to adult life for people with mental retardation: Principles and practices* (pp. 257–274). Baltimore: Paul H. Brookes.

Bronicki, G. J., & Turnbull, A. P. (1987) Family-professional interactions. In M. E. Snell (Ed.), *Systematic instruction of persons with severe handicaps* (pp. 9–35). Columbus, OH: Charles E. Merrill.

Brown v. Topeka, Kansas, Board of Education (1954). 347 U.S. 483.

Center on Human Policy. (1987b). Statement in support of families and their children. Syracuse, NY: Author.

Forest, M. (1991). It's about relationships. In L. H. Meyer, C. A. Peck, & L. Brown (Eds.), *Critical issues in the lives of people with severe disabilities* (pp. 399–407). Baltimore: Paul H. Brookes.

Gerry, M. H., & McWhorter, C. M. (1991). A comprehensive analysis of federal statues and programs for persons with severe disabilities. In L. H. Meyer, C. A. Peck, & L. Brown (Eds.), *Critical issues in the lives of people with severe disabilities* (pp. 495–525). Baltimore: Paul H. Brookes.

Hamre-Nietupski, S., Nietupski, J., & Strathe, M. (1992). Functional life skills, academic skills, and friendship/social relationship development: What do parents of students with moderate/ severe/profound disabilities value? *Journal of the Association for Persons with Severe Handicaps, 17*(1), 53–58.

Hardman, M. L., Drew, C. J., Egan, M. W., & Wolf, B. (1993). *Human exceptionality: Society, school, and family* (4th ed.). Boston: Allyn and Bacon, Inc.

Haring, T. (1991). Social relationships. In L. H. Meyer, C. A. Peck, & L. Brown (Eds.), *Critical issues in the lives of people with severe disabilities* (pp. 195–217). Baltimore: Paul H. Brookes.

Hasazi, S., Johnson, R. E., Hasazi, J., Gordon, L. R., & Hull, M. (1989). Employment of youth with and without handicaps following school: Outcomes and correlates. *Journal of Special Education, 23*, 243–255.

Herman, S. E., & Hazel, K. L. (1991). Evaluation of family support services: Changes in availability and accessibility. *Mental Retardation, 29*(6), 351–357.

Innovative approaches to family support: Chicago pilot program for home care. (1990, Fall). *Family Support Bulletin, 9.*

Krause, M. W. (1986). Patterns and trends in public services to families with a mentally retarded member. In J. J. Gallagher & P. M. Vietze (Eds.), *Families of handicapped persons: Research, programs, and policy issues* (pp. 237–248). Baltimore: Paul H. Brookes.

Lehman, D. R., Ellard, J. H., & Wortman, C. B. (1986). Social support for the bereaved: Recipients' and providers' perspectives on what is helpful. *Journal of Consulting and Clinical Psychology, 54,* 438–446.

Levy, J. M., & Levy, P. H. (1986). Issues and models in the delivery of respite services. In C. L. Salisbury & J. Intagliata (Eds.), *Respite care: Support for persons with developmental disabilities and their families* (pp. 99–116) Baltimore: Paul H. Brookes.

Lutifyya, Z. M. (1990, January). Affectionate bonds: What we learn. *TASH Newsletter, 9.*

McDonnell, J. J., Wilcox, B., & Hardman, M. L. (1991). *Secondary programs for students with developmental disabilities.* Boston: Allyn & Bacon.

Mills v. District of Columbia Board of Education (1972), 348 F.Supp. 866 (D.D.C.).

Murray-Seegert, C. (1989). *Nasty girls, thus, and humans like us: Social relations between severely disabled and nondisabled students in high school.* Baltimore: Paul H. Brookes

National Association of State Directors of Special Education (1991, March). Reference notes for speechmaking or understanding the forces at work which are driving social policy. Washington, D.C.: Author.

Nisbet, J., Clark, M., & Covert, S. (1991). Living it up! An analysis of research on community living. In L. H. Meyer, C. A. Peck, & L. Brown (Eds.), *Critical issues in the lives of people with severe disabilities* (pp. 115–144). Baltimore: Paul H. Brookes.

Noonan, M. J. & L. McCormick (1993). *Early intervention in natural environments: Methods and procedures.* Pacific Grove, CA: Brookes/Cole Publishing Co.

Organization for Economic Cooperation and Development (OECD). (1986). *Young people with handicaps: The road to adulthood.* Paris, France: Author.

Peck, C. A., Donaldson, J. & Pezzoli, M. (1990). Some benefits nonhandicapped adolescents perceive for themselves from their social relationships with peers who have severe handicaps. *Journal of the Association for Persons with Severe Handicaps, 15*(4), 241–249.

Pennsylvania Association for Retarded Citizens v. *Commonwealth of Pennsylvania* (1971). 334 F.Supp. 1257 (E.D.Pa. 1971).

Perske, R. (1988). *Circles of friends.* Nashville: Abingdon Press.

Rees, L. M., Spreen, O., & Harnadek, M. (1991). Do attitudes towards persons with handicaps really shift over time? Comparison between 1975 and 1988. *Mental Retardation, 29*(2), 81–86.

Resnick, L. B. (1987). Learning in school and out. *Educational Researcher, 53*(9), 13–20.

Sailor, W. & Guess, D. (1983). *Severely handicapped students.* Boston: Houghton Mifflin.

Seligman, M., & Darling, R. B. (1989). *Ordinary families, special children.* New York: Guilford Press.

Shelton, T. L., Jeppson, E. S., & Johnson, B. H. (1987). *Family-centered care for children with special health-care needs.* Washington, D.C.: Association for the Care of Children's Health.

Singer, G.H.S., & Irvin, L. K. (1991). Supporting families of persons with severe disabilities: Emerging findings, practices, and questions. In L. H. Meyer, C. A. Peck, & L. Brown (Eds.), *Critical issues in the lives of people with severe disabilities* (pp. 271–312). Baltimore: Paul H. Brookes.

Stephens, T., & Engle, S. (1993, January). Severely disabled clearly benefit from public school. *Washington County Schools Newsletter, 11.*

Taylor, S., & Bogdan, R. (1987). *On accepting relationships between people with mental retardation and nondisabled people.* Syracuse, NY: Center of Human Policy.

Thoits, P. A. (1986). Social support as coping assistance. *Journal of Consulting and Clinical Psychology, 54,* 416–423.

Traustadottir, R. (1993, January). Gender Patterns in friendships. *TASH Newsletter*, 8.

Turnbull, A. P., & Turnbull, H. R. (1990). *Families, professionals and exceptionality: A special partnership* (2nd ed.). Columbus, OH: Merrill Publishing Co.

Voeltz, L. M. (1984). Program and curriculum to prepare children for integration. In N. Certo, N. Haring, and R. York, *Public school integration of severely handicapped students* (155–183). Baltimore: Paul H. Brookes.

Chapter 4

Biomedical Issues

Twenty-five years ago, for every three children born with severe handicaps, one would be alive at the age of 21. Today, for every three children born with a severe defect, two are alive at the age of 21, and the prediction is that it will be two and one-half out of three by the year 2000 due to advances in medical technology. (National Association of State Directors, 1991, p. 1)

Every year more than 20,000 infants with severe disabilities are born in the United States (Cohen, 1990; Gerry, 1985). Approximately 3 to 15 percent of babies born alive in the United States have some type of birth defect. These infants are born prematurely with low birthweight (often less than 1,500 grams), congenital disorders, and any variety of other medical conditions, such as asphyxia (lack of oxygen), hyaline membrane disease (immature lung development), chromosomal abnormalities (Down syndrome, Fragile X Syndrome), heart problems, underdeveloped brains, drug and alcohol syndromes, or infections. Rapid advances in medical science have resulted in a growing number of these infants surviving at birth far beyond what was thought possible even a decade ago. The majority of critically ill newborns (nearly 75 percent) will survive the neonatal period. Approximately 16 percent of these survivors will have moderate or severe disabilities (U.S. Congress, 1987). While medical science continues to decrease infant mortality and increase the average lifespan, this same technology is also raising a number of serious ethical issues regarding decisions about prevention, care, and selective nontreatment of infants with severe disabilities. When do individual rights begin? Who should live and who should die? What is personhood? Who defines quality of life? What are the rights of the individual in relationship to the obligations of a society? Who shall make these difficult decisions? As suggested by Dunlop (1983), "no decision is more difficult than choosing life or death for another. As life-sustaining technology advances, families and doctors increasingly confront that decision, without easy answers" (p. 56).

In recent years, there has been an increasing awareness and interest in what is termed "bioethical" issues, particularly as they relate to serious illness and disabilities that occur both prior to and after birth. These issues range from concerns about the pur-

WINDOW 4-1   But I Wanted to Go to Italy?

When you're going to have a baby, it's like you're planning a vacation to Italy. You are all excited. Seeing the Coliseum . . . the Michelangelo . . . the gondolas of Venice. You get a whole bunch of guidebooks. You learn a few phrases in Italian so you can order in restaurants and get around. When it comes time, you excitedly pack your bags, head for the airport and take off for Italy . . . only when you land, the stewardess announces, "Welcome to Holland."

You look at one another in disbelief and shock saying, Holland? What are you talking about—Holland? I signed up for Italy!! But they explain that there's been a change of plans and the plane has landed in Holland—and there you must stay.

"But I don't know anything about Holland! I don't want to stay here," you say. "I never wanted to come to Holland!" "I don't know what to do in Holland and I don't want to learn!!" But, you do stay, you go out and buy some new guidebooks. You learn some new phrases in a whole new language and you meet people you never knew existed.

But the important thing is that you are not in a filthy, plague-infested slum full of pestilence and famine. You are simply in another place . . . a different place than you had planned. It's slower-paced than Italy; less flashy than Italy; but after you've been there a little while and have had a chance to catch your breath, you begin to discover that Holland has windmills . . . Holland has tulips . . . and Holland even has Rembrandts.

But everyone else you know is busy coming and going from Italy. And they're all bragging about what a great time they had there. And for the rest of your life you will say, "Yes, that's where I was going . . . that's where I was supposed to go . . . that's what I had planned." And the pain of that will never, ever go away.

And you have to accept that pain because the loss of that dream, the loss of that plan is a very, very significant loss. But . . . if you spend your life mourning the fact that you didn't get to Italy, you will never be free to enjoy the very special, the very lovely things about Holland.

Source: Kingsley, E. P. (cited in Crutcher, D. M., 1990)

pose and use of genetic engineering (such as gene mapping and transplants), to screening for genetic diseases, and the withholding of life-sustaining treatment. In this chapter we will address each of these issues as they relate to people with severe disabilities and their families. Our discussion begins with an overview of the principles of bioethics.

Bioethics

Focus 1:

Distinguish between the two philosophical positions of utilitarianism and deontological theories.

Each of us lives by a basic set of principles derived from a personal philosophy about who we are and how we fit into this world. Although we may not give these principles much conscious consideration, they are the foundation of a code of ethics that governs our actions. In recent years, ethicists have given considerable attention to two philosophical positions (ethical theories) that guide people in making decisions about what should or should not be done in any given circumstance: *utilitarianism* and *deontological theories.*

Utilitarianism is based on the premise that any action is "right" if it leads to the greatest good for the greatest number of people (Beauchamp & Walters, 1982). The utilitarian theory holds that the "end justifies the means." As such, the individual has ". . . only those rights granted by the larger society . . ." (Tymchuk, 1976, p. 45). Where utilitarianism is based on consequences that lead to the greater good, deontological theorists suggest that ". . . at least some acts are wrong and others right independent of their consequences" (Beauchamp & Childress, 1983). It is not the impact on society as a whole that is paramount, but the rights of an individual. Deontological theories hold that it is the individual ". . . with basic rights which cannot be abrogated nor curtailed by society and the individual's rights are superordinate to those of society" (Tymchuk, 1976, p. 45).

The application of either one of these theories in the extreme leads to difficult and complex dilemmas for both the individual and society. A literal interpretation of utilitarianism results in those with power remaining in power by limiting the rights of others. A literal interpretation of deontological theories, on the other hand, means that as we enhance the rights of some, we are infringing on the rights of others. Nowhere are the issues surrounding utilitarianism and deontological theories more evident than in the current national debate over abortion rights and the Supreme Court's decision in *Roe v. Wade.* As society attempts to legislate abortion rights (utilitarianism), people take up personal philosophical positions that range from "the greater good for society" to the individual rights of the woman and the fetus.

Similar issues are raised everyday in the newborn intensive care units of our nation's hospitals. When a child is born with serious and significant birth defects and requires life-sustaining support, should the parents and physicians have the right to choose life or death, or should the right of the infant to life always prevail? Whose rights carry more weight? When there are conflicts whose rights take precedence? Beauchamp and Childress (1983) suggest that any "answers to these questions, which may finally be unanswerable to everyone's satisfaction, can only come through systematic reflection on moral principles and rules" (p. 55). Three principles (Beauchamp & Walters, 1982) most often identified by ethicists as the driving forces in moral decision-making are:

1. Autonomy (self-rule, free of external control)
2. Beneficence (do no harm)
3. Justice (receiving what is deserved—fairness).

Differing perspectives on the application of these principles to a fetus or infant with severe disabilities creates societal dilemmas often referred to as "competing equities." When considering the issue of abortion, who is more autonomous the mother or the fetus? Who shall be considered first as the principle of "do no harm" is applied? What is fair?

In the following section, we examine bioethical issues as they apply to the prevention of severe disabilities. Developments in genetic engineering, organ transplantation, as well as genetic screening and counseling are addressed. The chapter concludes with a discussion of recent advances in medical care and treatment for the newborn with severe disabilities.

Prevention

The prevention of severe disabilities, particularly mental retardation, has historically been hailed by health care professionals, disability organizations, and the general public as a laudable goal. Over the years, efforts at preventing severe disabilities have taken on many forms. Isolation (quarantining people with severe disabilities) and mandatory sterilization procedures were predominant forms of prevention in the first half of the twentieth century. They were eventually replaced by less controversial forms of prevention, such as immunizations against disease, proper nutritional habits during pregnancy, and appropriate maternal prenatal care. Immunizations protect against the contraction of serious illnesses (such as rubella) that can result in mental retardation or blindness. Improper maternal nutritional habits during pregnancy may contribute significantly to fetal problems, such as low birthweight and prematurity. The failure of the mother to access appropriate prenatal care during pregnancy can have "significant health consequences, as many conditions that are amenable to timely medical treatment can develop serious complications if neglected" (President's Commission, 1983a, p. 111).

As medical science has continued to rapidly progress in its understanding of human genetics and accompanying diseases, prevention has now expanded even further into the areas of genetic engineering, organ transplantation, and biomedical screening. The importance of genetics research cannot be overstated. As the causes of these diseases are identified, more accurate diagnoses will be made and effective treatment procedures implemented.

Genetic Engineering

Focus 2:

What is the purpose of genetic engineering, and why are there concerns about its future use with human beings?

A leading human geneticist told this story recently. On a Friday morning he was called by a colleague, a neurologist, who said that a woman was in his office with her young son, who appeared to have a fatal inherited disease. In addition, she was pregnant—and the neurologist said he urgently needed advanced laboratory help to make a diagnosis. By Friday afternoon it was determined that the young boy did have the disease—but by Monday it was clear that, fortunately, the baby the mother was carrying did not. In the 21st century, such stories will probably be told many times, but with an added line: "By Tuesday we started effective therapy for the disease in the young boy." *(Choppin, 1991, p. 1)*

There are nearly 4,000 genetic diseases in human beings. Scientists believe that eventually most of these diseases can be prevented and treated (Howard Hughes Medical Institute, 1991). Where understanding the genetic structure of organisms was once thought to be forever out of reach, it is now possible that every one of the genes in the human body will be identified (mapped) sometime in the 21st century. Gene mapping, however, still has a long way to go since only about 4,500 of the possible 100,000 or so genes have been classified. The focus is on DNA, the substance that contains all genetic instructions. By identifying the genes we inherit from our parents, scientists are making significant progress against fatal genetic diseases. In fact, major strides have been made against sickle-cell anemia, hemophilia, Huntington's Disease, Tay-Sacs Disease, and cystic fibrosis (CF).

Genetic engineering is concerned with the conquest of disease. The prevention and treatment of genetic diseases first requires the identification of the faulty gene that causes the disease (as in cystic fibrosis). The next phase is to identify the protein that the gene normally produces. Finally, there is an attempt to fix or replace the defective protein or gene (Howard Hughes Medical Institute, 1991). A technique to fix or replace genes is known as *gene therapy* (cell manipulation). "Using recombinant DNA and other techniques of molecular biology . . . genetic material from one organism can be inserted into an organism of a different species" (President's Commission, 1983b, p. 40). Gene therapy has met with limited success over the past two decades. While some geneticists dismiss gene therapy as "pie in the sky," others suggest not only will it happen, but there will be major breakthroughs in the near future. While attempts at gene therapy failed in 1970 and 1980, doctors at the National Institutes of Health tried again with some success in 1990. They took the white blood cells of a four-year-old girl who had a grave immune deficiency, added the gene for the missing enzyme, and transplanted the altered cells back into her body (Schmeck, 1991).

Bioethical Issues

Genetic research holds considerable promise for altering human suffering in the future. As suggested by Pine (1991), "the miraculous substance that contains all our genetic instruction—DNA—is rapidly becoming a key to modern medicine." However, genetic research and engineering are not without detractors. In 1983, a Presidential Commission was organized to study the ethical problems in biomedical and behavioral research. In a report entitled *Splicing Life* (President's Commission, 1983c), the Commission found that the general public had "exaggerated" fears about genetic engineering research remaking human beings into Frankenstein's monster. They did, however, acknowledge that such techniques challenge ". . . some deeply held feelings about the meaning of being human and of family lineage" (President's Commission, 1983b, p. 41). The Commission stressed that the future of genetic engineering must be one of ameliorating genetic deficiencies, not enhancing or perfecting human beings.

NEWSWORTHY 4-1   Reading the Blueprint: The Human Genome Project
Reading the Human Blueprint

"All human disease is genetic in origin," Nobel laureate Paul Berg of Stanford University told a cancer symposium a few years ago. Berg was exaggerating, but only slightly. It has become increasingly evident that virtually all human afflictions, from cancer to psychological disorders and susceptibility to infection, are rooted in our genes. "What we need to do now is find those genes," says James Watson, who shared a Nobel prize for deciphering the structure of DNA and who now directs the national Center for Human Genome Research at the National Institutes of Health.

The necessary guide will be a map fixing each of the estimated 50,000 to 100,000 human genes to its correct location on the chromosomes. "Like the system of interstate highways spanning our country, the map of the human genome will be completed stretch by stretch," Watson says. He expects that this map, the goal of the federally funded Human Genome Project, will provide the key to understanding the nearly 4,000 known genetic disorders and the countless diseases whose origin may be due in part to genetic malfunctions, as well as the astonishing variety of normal human traits.

Such a map has been on the wish lists of molecular explorers for years. Without it, nailing the culprits responsible for genetic diseases requires not only hard work, ingenuity, and determination, but more than a little luck. Although researchers were aided by luck when they found the general location of the gene for Huntington's disease (HD) on chromosome 4 in 1983, for instance, since that time they have spent eight years painstakingly slogging through the target area at the tip of the chromosome and still have no gene in sight.

Yet single-gene diseases such as HD are relatively easy targets. Disorders that seem to be caused by the interplay of several genes—hypertension, atherosclerosis, and most forms of cancer and mental illness—are much more difficult to track down. Having a map of the entire human genome will make it possible to identify every gene that contributes to them.

A gene map can also lead researchers to new frontiers in drug development. Once all the genes are identified and their bases are sequenced, it will be possible to produce virtually any human protein—valuable natural pharmaceuticals, such as tissue plasminogen activator, interferon, and erythropoietin—as well as new molecules designed specifically to block disease-producing proteins.

The NIH gene-mapping project officially began in October 1990. But the map of the human genome has been in the making for a good part of the century. It started in 1911, when the gene responsible for red-green color blindness was assigned to the X chromosome following the observation that this disorder was passed on to sons by mothers who saw colors normally (see p. 23). Some other disorders that affect only males were likewise mapped to the X chromosome on the theory that females, who have two X chromosomes, were protected from these disorders by a normal copy of the gene on their second X chromosome—unlike males, who have one X and one Y chromosome.

The other 22 pairs of chromosomes remained virtually uncharted until the late 1960s. Then biologists fused human and mouse cells to create uneasy hybrid cells that cast off human chromosomes until only one or a few remained. Any recognizable human proteins in these hybrid cells thus had to be produced by genes located on the remaining human chromosomes. This strategy allowed scientists to assign about 100 genes to specific chromosomes.

Map-making really took off in the early 1970s, when geneticists discovered characteristic light and dark stripes or banks across each chromosome after it was stained with a chemical. These bands, when fluoresced under ultraviolet light, provided the chromosomal equivalent of latitudes. They made it easier to identify individual human chromosomes in hybrid cells and served as rough landmarks on the chromosomes, leading to the assignment of some 1,000 genes to specific chromosomes.

NEWSWORTHY 4-1 *Continued*

Around the same time, recombinant DNA technology began to revolutionize biology by allowing researchers to snip out pieces of DNA and splice them to bacteria, where they could be grown, or cloned, in large quantities. This led to two new mapping strategies, In one, *in situ* hybridization, scientists stop the division of human cells in such a way that each chromosome is clearly visible under a light microscope. Then they use probes to find the location of any DNA fragment on these chromosomes. Originally these probes were radioactively labeled, but chemically-tagged probes that can be made to fluoresce have been found to yield far more accurate and rapid results.

The other strategy is to use DNA variations as markers on the human genome, as proposed by Botstein, White, Skolnick, and Davis in 1980. This has resulted in a flood of new markers and an explosion in the knowledge of genes' chromosomal whereabouts. The number of genes mapped grew from 579 in 1981 to 1,879 in 1991. Gene mappers, who used to meet to coordinate their findings every year or so, now update the map every day via electronic databases.

Meanwhile, scientists learned to sequence the genes they isolated. This became possible in the mid-1970s when Frederick Sanger at Cambridge University and Walter Gilbert and Allan Maxam at Harvard University developed efficient new methods for determining the order of bases in a strand of DNA. Automated high-speed sequencing by machine followed in the 1980s. Now, once a new gene has been identified, it is immediately sequenced to understand the nature of the protein it codes for and to identify mutations that are related to disease.

Sequencing the entire genome, however, means sequencing at least 3 billion base pairs of DNA-one chromosome of each type, or half the total number of chromosomes in a human cell. This remains a daunting project.

Generally the most interesting or accessible genes have been located first, creating a disparity among chromosomal maps. While the map of the X chromosome appears to be as densely populated as the New York coast, for instance, chromosome 18 looks as lonesome as central South Dakota.

The Human Genome Project should even out the map by sending explorers into chromosomal *terra incognitae.* "The project really isn't doing anything new. What it's doing is creating order and accountability," says geneticist Eric Lander of the Whitehead Institute.

This orderly process is expected to produce a genetic linkage map in which the positions of genes for specific traits and diseases are superimposed on a grid of evenly spaced markers along the chromosomes. The project's five-year goal is to cover the entire genome with 1,500 genetic markers placed at equal intervals. Scientists will be able to determine any gene's location relative to these markers.

In addition, the project will create a physical map that shows actual distances along the chromosomes in terms of base pairs. The physical map probably will be constructed of long overlapping stretches of DNA cloned in yeast and known as yeast artificial chromosomes (YACs). Developed in 1987 by Maynard Olson, now a Howard Hughes Medical Institute (HHMI) investigator at Washington University in St. Louis, YACs make it possible to close and store very large DNA segments—much larger than those that can be cloned in bacteria. The technique has reduced the number of DNA pieces that need to be placed in the right order from 100,000 to 10,000. Recently, Olson assembled a YAC library of the entire genome and distributed it for the use of gene mappers.

At least two approaches have been developed to unite the genetic linkage map and the physical map so that a researcher can easily move back and forth between the two. One is to dot both maps with new kinds of markers known as sequence-tagged sites, or STSs—long sequences of DNA that generally occur only once in the whole human genome and can be used as common reference points. The other approach is to plot the

Continued

NEWSWORTHY 4-1   *Continued*

position of existing genetic markers onto the physical map by means of *in situ* hybridization.

Meanwhile, new strategies promise to speed up sequencing significantly. Some researchers have reported that it may not be necessary to sequence every base but to sequence certain pivotal regions of DNA and fill in the blanks later. Moreover, automated sequencing and computer software designed specifically for genome analysis are already reducing sequencing time.

As the pace of mapping and sequencing quickens, so does the pace of data collection. The Genome Data Base, developed by The Johns Hopkins University in collaboration with HHMI, integrates various kinds of mapping and sequencing data, as well as the constantly evolving genetic linkage map. The Paris-based Centre d'Étude du Polymorphisme Humain collates data from laboratories around the world to develop a series of consensus maps for each chromosome. Another international body, the Human Genome Organisation, is starting to coordinate gene-mapping efforts in 42 nations.

The Genome Project has often been criticized as the intrusion of "big science" on the traditionally "small science" of biology. However, "everyone's beginning to realize this isn't at all like putting up a space station or erecting a supercolliding superconductor," says Glen Evans of the Salk Institute in La Jolla, California. "We're not going to undertake large-scale sequencing until new technology makes it cheap to do," explains James Watson.

If a map of the genome and sets of overlapping clones had been available when researchers set out to find the cystic fibrosis gene, their task would have taken only a fraction of the time and cost, points out Thomas Caskey, of the HHMI unit at the Baylor College of Medicine. "The investigators wouldn't have had to clone region after region looking for the gene," he says. "They could have just reached into the freezer and pulled out two markers flanking it. The same would be true for many other diseases. And remember, once we make this map, we will never have to do it again."

Source: Merz, B. (1991). Reading the human blueprint. *Blazing a genetic trail: A report from the Howard Hughes Medical Institute*. Bethesda, MD: Howard Hughes Medical Institute.

Organ Transplantation

Focus 3:

Identify two problems associated with the advancement of organ transplantation.

Advances in medical technology, such as improved surgical techniques and medications that reduce rejection, have resulted in an ever-increasing rate of success for pediatric organ transplants. Patients with congenital heart and lung problems, as well as kidney and liver disease, have much greater chances of survival and an enhanced quality of life as a result of organ transplantations (Cohen, 1990). This advancing technology does, however, have its problems—specifically, a shortage of available organs, and the necessity to remove organs from a donor prior to the cessation of heart and breathing functions.

The lack of available organs for transplantation results from several factors. For infants and young children, the mortality rate is low and too few die from accidents to meet the need for nearly 500 hearts, and between 500 and 1,000 infant livers required each year for transplantation. Somewhere between 30 percent and 60 percent of all infants who need a transplant die each year because there are not enough matched organs available (Blakeslee, 1987). Other factors that contribute to a shortage of available organs for all possible recipients include no available matched donor, and the failure of the public to designate themselves as donors. While public support for organ donation remains strong and there is a Uniform Anatomical Gift Act in all 50 states, few people actually sign donor cards. Additionally, family members find it extremely difficult to donate organs after the death of a loved one (Childress, 1986).

Bioethical Issues

The second problem associated with transplantation—the removal of organs from a donor prior to the cessation of heart and breathing functions—is a bioethical issue. Most organs used in transplantation must be removed prior to the cessation of these circulatory actions. As such, normal circulation must be maintained, often by mechanical means, to preserve the organs until they are removed from the body and preserved for transplantation. Since medical life support techniques can maintain breathing and heart actions even when the brain is no longer functioning, it is possible to "harvest" organs following "brain death." A definition of brain death recommended by the President's Commission (1983d), and now adopted in the majority of states in the U.S., indicates that:

> *An individual who has sustained either (1) irreversible cessation of circulatory and respiratory functions, or (2) irreversible cessation of all functions of the entire brain, including the brain stem, is dead. A determination of death must be made in accordance with accepted medical standards. (p. 2)*

While not all states have adopted the above definition, current law in every state mandates that organ donors must be brain dead (Cohen, 1990). However, the actual determination of brain death is a difficult legal and moral issue, particularly as applied to infants with severe disabilities. One condition that is particularly problematic is anencephaly. Anencephaly is a congenital disorder in which the cerebral cortices (centers of higher cognitive operations) are missing. The condition, which affects about 3,000 babies each year, is irreversible and the majority of infants with this condition die in the first few days of birth. The baby with anencephaly usually dies slowly, and their organs atrophy rendering them unsuitable for organ transplantation once death occurs. The difficulty is that because the organs atrophy as the baby is dying, physicians may attempt to "harvest" them prior to brain death.

There are numerous ethical complexities associated with anencephaly and other similar conditions resulting in severe disabilities. Libby (1990) points out that when severe disabilities are diagnosed *in utero*, ". . . parents are faced with an agonizing dilemma. If the pregnancy is carried to term, their child will be stillborn or face almost certain death within a few days or months of birth" (p. 106). Libby suggests that the alternatives facing parents are either selective abortion following the *in utero* diagnosis, or carrying the fetus to term and donating the organs once the child is born. This dilemma has resulted in professional and parent groups speaking out in behalf of infants born with severe neurologic disabilities. Resolutions on organ transplantation have been adopted by both the Association for Persons with Severe Handicaps (Meyer, Peck, & Brown, 1991a) and the American Association on Mental Retardation (BOD passes, 1988). Both resolutions emphasize that organ donation should only occur when the donor is "brain-dead" and where proper consent has been obtained from the parents. Coulter (1991) argues that removing organs from an infant who is not brain dead constitutes active euthanasia. Coulter further acknowledges the ethical dilemma of protecting the rights of the baby with anencephaly while recognizing the benefits to infants that are the organ recipients:

> *Those who seek to permit this active euthanasia must recognize the significant ethical, legal, and historical risks inherent in such a policy. On the other hand, those whose concern for safeguarding the rights of persons with severe disabilities leads them to oppose active euthanasia must acknowledge the suffering of infants who might benefit from organ transplantation as well as their families. Perhaps some way can be found to provide organs without the necessity of active euthanasia.* (p. 74)

Genetic Screening

> **Focus 4:**
>
> Identify the three major types of genetic screening.

> *The prospect of being able to diagnose every known human genetic disease from as early as six to eight weeks gestation remains a futuristic, but tangible goal. (Manning, 1989)*

Genetic screening is a search for certain genes that are predisposed to disease, already diseased, or may lead to disease in future generations of the same family. There are three major categories of genetic screening: prenatal, newborn, and carrier.

Prenatal assessment involves several techniques, among which the more common are amniocentesis, fetoscopy, and ultrasonography. The purpose of amniocentesis is to access cells in the fetus where there is an increased risk of chromosomal or inborn metabolic error. A small amount of fluid is drawn from the amniotic sac in the mother. Cells are then extracted from this fluid, grown in a culture for several weeks, and then analyzed for various abnormalities. Amniocentesis is most often done when there are risk factors associated with advancing maternal age, a history of chromosomal defects in previous pregnancies, a family history of Down syndrome or other chromosomal abnormality, or a history of multiple miscarriages. Amniocentesis is now a routine test with a low (.5 percent) risk for maternal or fetal complications (President's Commission, 1983e). The procedure, which is usually conducted between the 14th and 16th weeks of pregnancy, can be used to diagnose such conditions as Down syndrome, hydrocephalus, Tay-sachs disease, and anencephaly, to name but a few.

Fetoscopy also involves inserting a needle into the amniotic sac, but this time with a viewfinder (endoscope) to directly observe the fetus. A thin needle can also be inserted alongside the endoscope to draw blood samples. The procedure is usually conducted between the 15th and 20th weeks of pregnancy, and has a miscarriage rate of 3–5 percent (President's Commission, 1983e). Fetoscopy has been successful in the diagnosis of several genetic disorders, including spina bifida and trisomy 13 (Cohen, 1990).

Ultrasonography, which is now a routine technique in prenatal care, involves the transmission of high frequency, low-intensity sound waves through the abdomen of the pregnant woman. These soundwaves pass through tissue and are then reflected back into two-dimensional visual images on a screen. The procedure is generally considered to be safe for both the fetus and the mother. There are three types of ultrasound techniques. The first, which generates two-dimensional pictures, can estimate fetal age, weight, location of the placenta, and body parts. The second can show the movements of the fetus, including heartbeat, breathing, swallowing, and the activities of the arms and legs. The third type can actually measure fetal heart rate and sound (Cohen, 1990). Ultrasound has been effective in diagnosing many conditions, such as hydrocephaly, anencephaly, renal dysplasia, duodenal atresia, and mengomyelocele. Ultrasound is often used in conjunction with amniocentesis to provide a more accurate diagnosis relative to the location of the fetus, determination of multiple pregnancies, and to assist in fetal surgery *in utero*.

Newborn screening may involve testing for "inborn errors of metabolism," and chromosomal abnormalities. Inborn errors of metabolism result from a defective gene(s) that has ". . . abnormal or missing enzymes or other protein" (President's Commission, 1983e, p. 12). These metabolic conditions, which are usually inherited, include phenylketonuria, Tay-Sachs disease, and sickle-cell anemia. Most inborn errors are now treatable if caught early in the child's life by supplying the body with the missing substance or by altering the environment to remove whatever is harmful to the individual. Since inborn errors of metabolism are inherited from an autosomal recessive gene, there is a 25 percent risk that future pregnancies will result in a child exhibiting the same symptoms.

The second type of newborn screening, chromosomal testing, attempts to identify inborn genetic errors that result from abnormalities in the configurations of chromosomes in the body. Chromosomes are the structures in the human body which contain the genes, which in turn are comprised of molecules of Deoxyribonucleic acid (DNA). Genetic disorders can result when a gene(s) along the chromosomes mutate—become altered in some way. There are some 500 genetic disorders that are inherited conditions, including cystic fibrosis and tuberous sclerosis (Widerstrom, Mowder, & Sandall, 1991). Genetic disorders may also result from "genetic accidents," and are therefore not inherited conditions. The most common type of Down syndrome, Trisomy 21, accounts for 95 percent of all cases of the disease, and is not linked to genetic predisposition (Drew, Logan, & Hardman, 1992).

Carrier screening is aimed at identifying people of reproductive age who carry abnormal genetic information that could be passed on to their offspring, although they may not have a genetic disease themselves. The technique, which began in the 1970s to screen for Sickle-Cell Anemia and Tay-Sachs prior to conception, is simple to conduct, and quite accurate. As stated by the President's Commission, the hope for carrier screening was that ". . . some serious (and often incurable) diseases could be prevented by counseling those people found through screening to be at increased risk of having affected children" (1983e, p. 18). For example, it was found that 1 in 10 U.S. African Americans are carriers for sickle-cell anemia.

Carrier screening, like its newborn screening counterpart, has been expanded to include numerous other genetic conditions, including cystic fibrosis and phenylketonuria (PKU). The importance of carrier screening may be seen in the fact that prior to 1970 when the testing began, between 50 and 100 children were born with Tay-sachs disease. After 1980, the number of children born with Tay-sachs decreased to less than 15 per year (President's Commission, 1983e).

Bioethical Issues

As the use of genetic screening techniques becomes widespread, their continued use and expansion has become a matter of ethical debate. Cohen (1990) reviewed the literature on ethical issues associated with prenatal diagnosis, and found opposing viewpoints on the subject. Some ethicists contend that prenatal diagnosis must be restricted in its use or society will be less willing to ". . . accept and care for abnormal children" (Ramsey, 1973, p. 148). Hauerwas (1986) suggests that ". . . it has become common in our society to assume that certain children born with severe birth defects who also happen to be retarded should not be kept alive in order to spare them a lifetime of suffering" (p. 54).

Fletcher (1983) expressed concerns that advances in genetic screening could pressure certain groups of people who were either carriers of genetic disease, or had the disease identified in utero to be screened on a compulsory basis. The rationale would be that the cost of raising a child who is disabled far exceeds the costs of a selective abortion. Morison (1973) agrees with this utilitarian approach, suggesting that it is in society's best interest to maintain limits of both quantity and quality in human reproduction:

> Now, when a defective child may cost the society many thousands of dollars a year for a whole lifetime without returning the benefit, it would appear inevitable that society should do what it reasonably can to assure that those children who are born can lead normal and reasonably independent lives. (p. 208).

Genetic Counseling

Focus 5:

What are the responsibilities of a genetic counselor, and how do they ensure their neutrality in the decision-making process?

The next logical step following genetic screening is for the family members to comprehend the test results, and their implications for the future. It is the responsibility of a genetic counselor to provide the information necessary for the individual(s) involved in the screening to make an informed decision in such areas as: (1) having children when screening has identified one or both parents as a carrier of a genetic disease, and there is a possibility (sometimes a probability) of the anomaly being passed on to their offspring; and (2) continuing or selectively aborting a pregnancy when the screening indicates that a genetic anomaly has occurred in the fetus. The genetics counselor then provides specific information regarding the long-term medical prognosis, and the potential consequences of whatever action is taken by the parents.

The primary role of the counselor is "information-giving," although there are paradigms of genetic counseling that involve this professional serving as a "moral advisor," or "psychotherapist." In the past, some counselors were directive, attempting to help family members make the "right" reproductive decision—a decision that was in the best interests of society, as a whole (President's Commission, 1983e). Today, however, it is widely accepted that the counselor's role is one of neutrality. This professional must be non-directive, so that the family can make an autonomous and fully informed decision.

Genetic counselors come from varied backgrounds and training. Some are physicians trained in counseling techniques, others come from outside the medical profession bringing with them extensive backgrounds in human genetics. Beyond a background in genetics, however, these counselors must also be highly trained in communication skills, and be able to work as a member of a medical genetics team. Other team members may include physician geneticists, nurses, social workers, and laboratory technicians.

Bioethical Issues

While the neutral role of the counselor in genetic decision-making has been strongly emphasized, there is still concern that the counselor must guard against becoming actively engaged in directing the family's decision for them. This is especially true given society's general reliance on physicians as family advisors and authority figures. To ensure neutrality, genetics counselors must become acutely aware of what constitutes informed consent in a decision-making situation.

The American Association on Mental Retardation developed a consent handbook (Turnbull, 1977) with the expressed intent of identifying the three critical elements of informed consent: capacity, information, and voluntariness. The first element, *capacity*, involves three factors to be taken into consideration: the person's age (age of majority), mental and emotional competence, and the specific situation in which the decision is to be made. In regard to genetic counseling, the question is does the family member(s) have the ability to process the information given, particularly in light of a situation that may be emotionally charged and extremely stressful?

Information must be presented in such a way as to ensure that within reason the possible situations and consequences have been taken into account—provide a balanced perspective on the issue at hand. As stated by Turnbull, ". . . the focus is on 'what' information is given and 'how' it is given since it must be effectively communicated (given and received) to be acted upon" (p. 8). It is also important that the family is encouraged by the counselor to seek out other opinions on the information provided to ensure as much knowledge about the issue as possible.

Voluntariness is defined as placing individuals in a situation where they are able to ". . . exercise free power of choice without the intervention of any element of force fraud, deceit, duress, overreaching or other ulterior form of constraint or coercion" (Turnbull, 1977, p. 10). This element of consent reinforces the counselor's position as an informant, and not a moral advisor. While the family's views may not be consonant with that of the counselor, this should not become a dilemma for the professional. As suggested by Drew, Logan, and Hardman (1992), this may be particularly difficult for the counselor who has his or her own personal beliefs and feelings about what should be done.

Abortion

Focus 6:

What is selective abortion, and what is its relationship to genetic screening?

The Court for the most part sustains this position: During the period prior to the time the fetus becomes viable, the Constitution of the United States values the convenience, whim, or caprice of the putative mother more than the life or potential of the fetus; the Constitution, therefore, guarantees the right to an abortion as against any state law or policy seeking to protect the fetus from an abortion not prompted by more compelling reasons of the mother. (Roe v Wade, 1973)

Selective abortion is the process by which a woman may make the decision to terminate a pregnancy. In the past several years, laws that have attempted to limit a woman's right to abortion have been significantly modified or struck down by the courts. In general, the rights of the mother to an abortion outweigh the rights of the fetus (Cohen, 1990; Beauchamp & Walters, 1982). In recent times, the most significant decision regarding abortion rights was made by the U.S. Supreme Court in *Roe v. Wade.* The Court upheld a mother's right to abortion until the time when the fetus becomes viable. *Viability* is defined by the Court as the point when the fetus is capable of meaningful life outside the uterus.

The reasons why a woman would choose selective abortion are numerous, and may include health risks to the mother or unborn child (e.g., heart complications), financial burden, emotional trauma, or the identification of metabolic or chromosomal disorders (e.g., Down syndrome) during genetic screening.

Bioethical Issues
The issues surrounding a woman's right to an *abortion* have arguably created the most highly visible and volatile debate in the United States today. No other single issue polarizes people like the unborn child's right to life versus the woman's right of choice. The issue becomes even more complex when viewed in the context of rapidly advancing medical technology, and the identification of the unborn fetus with disabilities. The progress made in genetic screening, including the number of chromosomal and metabolic disorders that can now be identified in utero, have placed the parents and the

physician in the most difficult of positions: deciding whether to abort a fetus. Opponents of selective abortion argue that while a woman has received considerable legal protection under the law, the fetus has been basically left unprotected. They argue that there is no justifiable reason for abortion. It does not matter whether the unborn child is damaged or not; the child has a right to life.

Those who favor selective abortion not only argue that the woman's rights may not be abrogated or curtailed, but that the quality of life for the child born with a severe disability may be so diminished that, if given the choice, they would choose not to live under such circumstances (the suffering child). Silver (1981) suggests the family may also benefit from a selective abortion as well. Some families are just not able to cope with a child who is disabled due to serious physical, emotional, and financial stress (Duff & Campbell, 1973). These arguments are countered by opponents to abortion who point out that no one has the right to decide for someone else whether a life will "be happy" or "a quality experience." In the case of children born with disabilities, major strides have been made to enhance the quality of life for these individuals in many areas, including education, medical care, technology, and social inclusion.

NEWSWORTHY 4-2   Attitudes Toward Abortion

In January of 1993 (one day after the 20th anniversary of the *Roe v. Wade* decision), some 75,000 anti-abortion protesters marched on Washington, D.C. The *Washington Post* (Warden, 1993) interviewed 742 randomly selected demonstrators on their attitudes toward abortion, and then compared the data with (1) a random sample of 881 abortion-rights demonstrators who marched on Washington in April of 1992, and (2) a national random sample of 1,510 adults.

Question: Should Abortion Be Legal under Each of the Following Circumstances: (shown: Percentage who said "yes."):

Question	Anti-abortion Marchers	Abortion-rights Marchers	National Sample
If the woman's life is in danger	35%	99%	91%
If the pregnancy is the result of rape or incest	9%	100%	86%
If the family cannot afford to have the child	1%	97%	49%
If the parents don't want another child	1%	95%	45%
If there is a chance that the child will be born deformed	*2%*	*97%*	*73%*

Source: Warden, S. (January 23, 1993). Anatomy of a march. *Washington Post*, A8.

Withholding Medical Treatment

Focus 7:

Distinguish between *active euthanasia* and the withholding of medical treatment (*passive euthanasia*).

> *The arrival of a wanted child, who is some way disabled, elicits a multitude of feelings and a painful paradox for the parents. The pregnancy is a symbol of growth and positive familial future; the arrival of the handicapped newborn often erroneously signals "failure," the demise of family "normalcy" and perceived long term suffering and hardship for family members. It is for this reason that some physicians hold that "forcing some infants to live with their crippling" handicaps is more cruel than letting them die. (Rue, 1985, p. 202).*

As is true with abortion, the issues surrounding withholding medical treatment, sometimes referred to as *passive euthanasia*, are extremely controversial whether the focus is on infants with disabilities, people with a terminal illness, or those who are in the latter years of their lives. Legal experts and ethicists have attempted over the years to distinguish between two types of euthanasia: active and passive. *Active euthanasia* is taking a direct action (voluntary or involuntary) designed to end the individual's life. Individuals may voluntarily carry out the act themselves (take an overdose), or have someone else do it for them. It is also possible for active euthanasia to be involuntary where the act is done on their behalf, but not with their knowledge or permission (mercy killing). Passive euthanasia is more often described as allowing the individual to die (Fletcher, 1983). Arguments have been made that there is a crucial difference between these two types of euthanasia. For example, active euthanasia may involve a doctor taking a direct action (giving a lethal injection) to bring about a patient's death; whereas in passive euthanasia, the doctor does nothing, and the patient dies. Rachels (1982), however, argues that it is misleading to say the doctor does nothing. The doctor lets the patient die—life-sustaining treatment is withheld.

Bioethical Issues
For individuals born with disabilities, particularly those with more severe conditions, issues involving active euthanasia and the withholding of medical treatment are enormously important to understand. The frequency with which infants with disabilities were being allowed to die in newborn nurseries first came to light in the literature in the early 1970s (Duff & Campbell, 1973). In several instances, it was found that treatment, considered routine for an infant who was not disabled, was being withheld on the basis that a child had a disability. For example, in one situation, an infant with Down syndrome was denied treatment for an intestinal obstruction even though it was clear the child would die without the treatment (See Point and Counterpoint 4-1). The obstruction, though fully correctable in a virtually risk-free operation, was not performed *because* the child had Down syndrome. It would have been routinely performed on a child who was not disabled. It was clear that a separate standard was applied to infants

with disabilities, that was not being applied to those who were not disabled. In the past twenty years, concerns regarding this separate standard have resulted in greater protections for infants with disabilities, but have not resolved some critical questions. As framed by Neal (1990), these questions are:

> *Does every living newborn have the right to the treatment that is most likely to preserve life, or is it permissible to sometimes let such an infant die, or even take active steps to end the life of the infant?*

> *Who has the responsibility, or the right, to make decisions on these matters, either for the individual infant or for such infants in general?*

> *How should the scarce and expensive resources required for neonatal intensive care (NIC) be allocated, both at the individual and general level? (p. 92)*

These questions are not easy to answer. The questions of "what is in the best interest" of the infant, and "who shall decide" immediately suggest that some type of criteria must be applied in the decision-making process. It can be argued that sustaining life is the physician's ultimate responsibility and most important role. It is not up to the physician to make moral decisions about what constitutes a quality life. However, the dilemma for the physicians is what happens when the commitment to sustain life conflicts with the duty to relieve suffering?

In the past several years, hospitals have established infant care review committees to assist physicians and family members in making the difficult decisions of treatment or nontreatment in the newborn nursery. However, these committees, which were established in law by the U.S. Congress in the Child Abuse Prevention and Treatment Act of 1984, have no authority in the decision-making process. They may only make recommendations to physicians concerning appropriate procedures in the treatment of seriously ill newborns. Coulter (1991) indicates that many of these committees have now become inactive, and that decisions regarding medical treatment are generally left to physicians and parents.

Weir (1984) suggested that four criteria be used to determine who is in the best position to either assist family members and physicians, or to serve as a proxy in making difficult and complex treatment decisions. First, anyone who decides whether treatment will be withheld from a seriously ill newborn should have: (a) all the medical facts in the case; (b) understand the dynamics of the family unit into which the baby has been born, and (c) be knowledgeable regarding possible alternatives for placement other than in the biological family (e.g., adoptive parents). The individual(s) must meet the fundamental moral requirement of impartiality. "To maximize the possibility of being objective, the persons making the . . . decision should be disinterested in the particular case and issue and dispassionate in weighing available alternatives" (p. 256). These possible proxies must also be emotionally stable and consistent from case to case. "In terms of the principle of justice, morally similar cases should be handled in similar ways" (Weir, p. 257).

Several organizations concerned with disability (i.e., the Association on Mental Retardation, the ARC—A National Organization on Mental Retardation, the Associa-

**POINT OF INTEREST 4-1   The Association for Persons with Severe Handicaps (TASH)
Resolution on Infant Care**

TASH opposes the withholding of medical treatment and/or sustenance to infants when the decision is based upon the diagnosis of, or prognosis for, retardation or any other disability. TASH
affirms the right to equal medical treatment for all infants in accordance with the dignity and
worth of these individuals, as protected by federal and state laws and regulations. TASH
acknowledges the responsibilities of society and government to share with parents and other
family members the support necessary for infants with disabilities. Finally, TASH acknowledges
the obligation of society to provide for life-long medical, financial, and educational support to
persons with disabilities extending to them opportunities offered to all members of society.
    The rationale for this resolution is as follows:

• The right to life and liberty is guaranteed by our Constitution, Bill of Rights, and federal
  and state laws and regulations.
• The life and liberty of persons with disabilities are threatened by the prejudice which results
  from the ignorance generated by segregation and separation.
• This prejudice can only be overcome when the next generation of children born without disabilities grow up, play with, go to school with, and live and work with their peers with disabilities.
• TASH is extremely concerned with the practice of withholding medical treatment and/or sustenance from infants based upon the diagnosis of, or prognosis for, disability.

Originally Adopted April 1983; Amended April 1989
Source: Meyer, L. H., Peck, C. A., & Brown, L. (1991). Resolution On Infant Care (Document VI.1). In L. H.
Meyer, C. A. Peck, & L. Brown (1991), *Critical Issues in the Lives of People with Severe Disabilities* (pp. 547).
Baltimore: Paul H. Brookes.

tion for Persons with Severe Handicaps) have taken positions opposing withholding medical treatment when any decision is based on the persons having a disability (See Point
of Interest 4-1). The crux of these positions is that all individuals are entitled to the right
to life under the Constitution of the United States, and that it is the obligation of society
to protect people from the ignorance and prejudices that may be associated with disability.

Advances in Newborn Intensive Care

Focus 8:

Identify recent advances in the treatment of high-risk infants in newborn intensive care units.

*Bright lights shine day and night; there is a din caused by monitors and high
technology machines. Incubators, intravenous tubes, and monitoring equipment abound . . . The babies, some of whom look no different from a fetus, lay*

in isolettes, bassinets, cribs, or on slanted hotbeds warmed by radiant lamps.
The smallest babies have arms that are not any bigger than their mother's
finger; their heels are as tiny as a pencil eraser. (Cohen, 1990, p. 75)

Advances in medical treatment for infants born prematurely, as well as those with low birthweight and birth anomalies, have resulted in the development of highly specialized hospital settings to comprehensively treat these newborns. Begun in the early 1960s, these settings are known variously as neonatal intensive care units (NICUs), high-risk neonatal centers, special-care nurseries, and perinatal centers. Since their inception, these units have had considerable success in reducing infant mortality, and improving the long-term prognosis for infants born with birth anomalies. Nearly 60 percent of all infants admitted to newborn intensive care units will develop normally. However, estimates are that one in four infants admitted to newborn intensive care units will not survive, and that about 16 percent will leave the hospital with moderate and severe disabilities (U.S. Congress, 1987).

Hospitals with newborn units are generally organized into three levels of care. Level I hospitals provide treatment for normally developing newborns. In level II hospitals, a newborn intensive care unit is available with a limited range of services. The full range of services, including a staff of neonatologists, and a neonatal transport system, is available in the level III hospital. Infants admitted to level III units have low birthweights, usually under 2,500 grams although some may be as low as 800 grams (under 2 pounds). Many of the infants weighing less than 800 grams will have significant medical problems, including respiratory distress syndrome (underdeveloped lungs), infections, asphyxia (lack of oxygen), hypothermia, heart problems, jaundice, and congenital malformations. The mortality rate for these infants may be as high as 65 percent (Stevenson, Peterson, Yates, Benitz, & Gale, 1988).

Recent advances in neonatal medicine have significantly reduced the incidence of the leading cause of death in preterm infants—respiratory distress syndrome. Preterm infants may be born with an inadequate supply of a natural substance in the lungs—surfactin. The preterm infant with a lack of surfactin is highly susceptible to disease that often results in death. Surfactant-replacement therapy is a process whereby a surfactant is instilled through the trachea to restore the depleted substance in the infant's lungs. This therapy has reduced the number of preterm infant deaths from 10,000 per year in the 1970s to about 5,000 per year in the 1980s (Avery & Merritt, 1991).

There are many other advances in the medical care available in newborn intensive care units beyond the use of surfactin. Oxygen therapy involves both mechanical ventilation to breathe for a baby unable to take in air spontaneously, and a plastic hood with oxygen that helps support an infant's breathing. Continuous positive airway pressure (CPAP) prevents the neonate's lungs from totally deflating by maintaining a gas pressure that is greater than atmospheric pressure. Ventricular shunts may be implanted in the infant's head to remove excessive cerebrospinal fluid in the brain and reduce head size. Neonatal surgery can correct many anomalies, such as esophageal atresia, perforations in the gastrointestinal tract, abdominal wall defects, and congenital heart disease.

While there have been concerns about such factors as the costs associated with intensive care, and some of the side effects resulting from the physical environment

****

POINT AND COUNTERPOINT 4-1   **The Parents' Right to Decide?**

The Family Setting:
Mother, 34 years old, hospital nurse.
Father, 35 years old, lawyer.
Two normal children in the family.

In late fall of 1963, Mr. and Mrs. ——— gave birth to a premature baby boy. Soon after birth, the child was diagnosed as a "mongoloid" (Down syndrome), with the added complication of an intestinal blockage (duodenal atresia). The latter could be corrected with an operation of quite nominal risk. Without the operation the child could not be fed and would die.

At the time of birth Mrs. ——— overheard the doctor express his belief that the child was a mongol. She immediately indicated she did not want the child. The next day, in consultation with a physician, she maintained this position, refusing to give permission for the corrective operation on the intestinal block. Her husband supported her in this position, saying that his wife knew more about these things (i.e., mongoloid children) than he. The reason the mother gave for her position—"It would be unfair to the other children of the household to raise them with a mongoloid."

The physician explained to the parents that the degree of mental retardation cannot be predicted at birth—running from very low mentality to borderline subnormal. As he said: "Mongolism, it should be stressed, is one of the milder forms of mental retardation. That is, mongols' I.Q.s are generally in the 50–80 range, and sometimes a little higher [this estimate varies from the information on p. 45]. That is, they're almost always trainable. They can hold simple jobs. And they're famous for being happy children. They're perennially happy and usually a great joy." Without other complications, they can anticipate a long life.

Given the parents' decision, the hospital staff did not seek a court order to override the decision. The child was put in a side room and, over an 11-day period, allowed to starve to death.

Following this episode, the parents undertook genetic counseling (chromosome studies) with regard to future possible pregnancies.[1]

Point:

The right to decide whether this baby has the operation to remove the intestinal blockage must ultimately rest with the parents. Their reasons for this decision should not be questioned, since the ultimate responsibility for raising this child, or deciding to let him die will rest with them. Only they can weigh all the factors that will affect their family, including impact on the other children, as well as emotional and financial burdens. No one should attempt to step into the shoes of these parents in what may be the most difficult decision of their lives.

Counterpoint:

It is the responsibility of the physician to override the parents' decision in this case. The rights of the baby must not be weighed against the "greater good" for the family or society. This child is going to be denied an operation that, were he not disabled, would have been done on a routine basis. Allowing this infant to starve to death because he has a disability can only be described as child abuse, if not murder.

[1]Source: Weir, R. (1984). *Selective nontreatment of handicapped newborns.* New York: Oxford University Press, p. 50–51.

****

of the unit (for example, strong lights and high noise levels resulting in some infants having visual and hearing impairments), there can be no doubt as to the growing impact of these units on the lives of high-risk infants. Many infants who virtually had no chance of survival only a few years ago now go on to lead normal healthy lives. Follow-up studies suggest that "major handicapping conditions are being prevented in these at-risk infants through improved care in neonatal intensive care units" (Widerstrom, Mowder, & Sandall, 1991, p. 7). Widerstrom et al. also suggest, however, that there is an increase in the number of neurodevelopmental and neurobehavioral delays that become evident during the school years as academic and behavioral problems.

Conclusion

This chapter has examined the complex biomedical issues associated with the prevention and treatment of severe disabilities. These issues include genetic engineering, organ transplantation, genetic screening and counseling, abortion, and withholding medical treatment. Bioethical concerns have been addressed in the context of both utilitarian and deontological philosophical positions. While the prevention of severe disabilities has historically been considered a laudable goal for society, advances in medical science are raising difficult questions about how far society will go. Will genetic engineering continue to focus exclusively on ameliorating genetic deficiencies, or eventually be used to perfect human beings? What will be the impact on people with severe disabilities as the need for organs for transplantation continues to increase? Will geneticists eventually be able to screen for every known human genetic disease, and, if so, will there be more demand for selective abortions? As more and more infants are kept alive through the advances in medical treatment in newborn intensive care units, how will the difficult decisions of resource allocation and selective treatment be made?

Focus Review

Focus 1: Distinguish between the two philosophical positions of utilitarianism and deontological theories.

- Utilitarianism suggests that ethical decisions be based on the greatest good for the greatest number of people—the end justifies the means. An individual has only those rights granted by the larger society.
- Deontological theorists indicate that it is not the impact of society as a whole that is most important, but the rights of an individual. It is the individual with basic rights which cannot be abrogated nor curtailed by society.

Focus 2: What is the purpose of genetic engineering, and why are there concerns about its future use with human beings?

- Genetic engineering is concerned with the conquest of the more than 4,000 genetic diseases in human beings. The prevention and treatment of these diseases requires the identification of the faulty gene that causes the disease.
- There are some fears that genetic engineering will result in the remaking of human beings, as well as the elimination of genetic disease.

Focus 3: Identify two problems associated with the advancement of organ transplantation.

- There is a lack of organs available for transplantation.
- Most organs used in transplantation must be removed prior to the cessation of heart and breathing functions. Since medical life support techniques can maintain breathing and heart actions even when the brain is no longer functioning, the question is when is what constitutes "brain death."

Focus 4: Identify the three major types of genetic screening.

- Prenatal assessment involves the use of amniocentesis, fetoscopy, and ultrasonography. In amniocentesis, a needle is used to withdraw a small amount of fluid from the amniotic sac to access cells in the fetus where there is an increased risk of chromosomal or inborn metabolic error. Fetoscopy also involves inserting a needle into the amniotic sac, but this time with a viewfinder (endoscope) to directly observe the fetus. Ultrasonography, which is now a routine technique in prenatal care, involves the transmission of high frequency, low-intensity sound waves through the abdomen of the pregnant woman. These soundwaves pass through tissue and are then reflected back into two-dimensional visual images on a screen.
- Newborn screening involves testing immediately after birth for "inborn errors of metabolism," and chromosomal abnormalities.
- Carrier screening attempts to identify people of reproductive age who carry abnormal genetic information that could be passed on to their offspring, although they may not have a genetic disease themselves.

Focus 5: What are the responsibilities of a genetic counselor, and how do they ensure their neutrality in the decision-making process?

- A genetic counselor has the responsibility to provide the information necessary for the person(s) involved in the screening to make an informed decision.
- Genetics counselors maintain neutrality by applying the principles of informed consent: capacity, information, and voluntariness.

Focus 6: What is selective abortion, and what is its relationship to genetic screening?

- Selective abortion is the process by which a woman may make the decision to terminate a pregnancy.

- Advances in genetic screening now result in a number of chromosomal and metabolic disorders being identified in utero. This has placed the parents and the physician in the difficult and complex position of deciding whether or not to abort a fetus based on the information from the genetic tests.

Focus 7: Distinguish between active euthanasia and the withholding of medical treatment (passive euthanasia).

- Active euthanasia is taking a direct action (voluntary or involuntary) designed to end the individual's life. Individuals may voluntarily carry out the act themselves, or have someone else do it for them. Active euthanasia may also be involuntary where the act is done on their behalf, but not with their knowledge or permission (mercy killing).
- Withholding medical treatment (passive euthanasia) is most often described as allowing the individual to die by taking no direct action (providing a treatment).

Focus 8: Identify recent advances in the treatment of high-risk infants in newborn intensive care units.

- Surfactant-replacement therapy can now restore the depleted substance in the lungs of infants born with respiratory distress syndrome. This therapy has significantly reduced the number of preterm infant deaths.
- Other advances include oxygen therapy (mechanical ventilation and oxygen hoods), continuous positive airway pressure (CPAP) (prevents lung deflation), ventricular shunts (reduces pressure on the brain), and neonatal surgery (corrects many birth anomalies).

References

Avery, M. E., & Merritt, T. A. (1991). Surfactant-replacement therapy. *The New England Journal of Medicine, 324*(13), 910–911.

Beauchamp, T. L., & Childress, J. E. (1983). *Principles of biomedical ethics.* Oxford, England: Oxford University Press.

Beauchamp, T. L., & Walters, L. (1982). *Contemporary issues in bioethics.* Belmont, CA: Wadsworth Publishing.

Blakeslee, S. (1987, October 19). Baby born without brain kept alive to give heart. *The New York Times,* 1, B9.

BOD passes resolutions on AIDS and transplants. (1988, July). *News & Notes—Quarterly Newsletter of the American Association on Mental Retardation,* 4.

Choppin, P. W. (1991). Foreword. In *Blazing a genetic trail: A report from the Howard Hughes Medical Institute* (p. 1). Bethesda, MD: Howard Hughes Medical Institute.

Cohen, L. G. (1990). *Before their time: Fetuses and infants at-risk.* AAMR Monographs (Michael J. Begab, Series Ed.). Washington, D.C.: American Association on Mental Retardation.

Coulter, D. L. (1991). Medical treatment. In L. H. Meyer, C. A. Peck, & L. Brown (Eds.), *Critical issues in the lives of people with severe disabilities* (pp. 553–558). Baltimore: Paul H. Brookes.

Crutcher, D. M. (1990). Quality of life versus quality of life judgments: A parent's perspective. In R. L. Schalock (Eds.), *Quality of life: Perspec-*

tives and issues (pp. 17–22). Washington, D.C.: American Association on Mental Retardation.

Drew, C. J., Logan, D. R., & Hardman, M. L. (1992). *Mental retardation: A life cycle approach* (5th ed.). New York: Macmillan Publishing Co.

Duff, R., & Campbell, G. (1973). Moral and ethical dilemmas in the special care nursery. *New England Journal of Medicine, 289,* 890–894.

Dunlop, M. (1983, June). When to preserve life? *World Press Review,* 56–57.

Fletcher, J. C. (1983). Ethics and trends in applied human genetics. *Birth defects, 19,* 143–158.

Gerry, M. H. (1985). The civil rights of handicapped infants: An Oklahoma experiment. *Issues in Law and Medicine, 1*(1), 15–44.

Hauerwas, S. (1986). Suffering the retarded. Should we prevent retardation? In P. R. Dokecki, & R. M. Zaner (Eds.), *Ethics of dealing with persons with severe handicaps* (pp. 53–70). Baltimore: Paul H. Brookes.

Howard Hughes Medical Institute (1991). *Blazing a genetic trail: A report from the Howard Hughes Medical Institute.* Bethesda, MD: Author.

Lyon, J. (1985). *Playing God in the nursery.* New York: W. W. Norton Co.

Manning, F. A. (1989). Reflections on future directions of perinatal medicine. *Seminars in Perinatology, 13*(4), 342–351.

Merz, B. (1991). Reading the human blueprint. *Blazing a genetic trail: A report from the Howard Hughes Medical Institute.* Bethesda, MD: Howard Hughes Medical Institute.

Meyer, L. H., Peck, C. A., & Brown, L. (1991a). Organ transplant unit (Document VI.3). In L. H. Meyer, C. A. Peck, & L. Brown (Eds.), *Critical issues in the lives of people with severe disabilities* (p. 549). Baltimore: Paul H. Brookes.

Meyer, L. H., Peck, C. A., & Brown, L. (1991b). Resolution on infant care (Document VI.1). In L. H. Meyer, C. A. Peck, & L. Brown (1991), *Critical issues in the lives of people with severe disabilities* (p. 547). Baltimore: Paul H. Brookes.

Morison, R. S. (1973). Implications of prenatal diagnosis for the quality of, and right to human life: Society as a standard. In B. Hilton, D. Callahan, M. Harris, P. Condliffe, & B. Berkley (Eds.), *Ethical issues in human genetics* (pp. 201–211). New York: Plenum.

National Association of State Directors of Special Education. (1991). *Reference notes for speechmaking or understanding the forces at work which are driving social policy.* Washington, D.C.: Author

Neal, B. W. (1990). Ethical aspects in the care of very low birth weight infants. *Pediatrician, 17,* 92–99.

Pine, M. (1991). Introduction. In *Blazing a genetic trail: A report from the Howard Hughes Medical Institute* (pp. 4–5). Bethesda, MD: Author.

President's Commission for the Study of Ethical Problems in Medicine and Biomedical and Behavioral Research (1983a). *Securing access to health care.* Washington, D.C.: Author.

President's Commission for the Study of Ethical Problems in Medicine and Biomedical and Behavioral Research (1983b). *Summing up: Final report on studies of the ethical and legal problems in medicine and biomedical and behavioral research.* Washington, D.C.: Author.

President's Commission for the Study of Ethical Problems in Medicine and Biomedical and Behavioral Research (1983c). *Splicing life.* Washington, D.C.: Author.

President's Commission for the Study of Ethical Problems in Medicine and Biomedical and Behavioral Research (1983d). *Defining death.* Washington, D.C.: Author.

President's Commission for the Study of Ethical Problems in Medicine and Biomedical and Behavioral Research (1983e). *Screening and counseling for genetic conditions.* Washington, D.C.: Author.

Rachels, J. (1982). Active and passive euthanasia. In T. Beauchamp, & L. Walters (Eds.), *Contemporary issues in bioethics* (pp. 313–316). Belmont, CA: Wadsworth.

Ramsey, P. (1973). Screening: An ethicist's view. In B. Hilton, D. Callahan, M. Harris, P. Condliffe, & B. Berkley (Eds.), *Ethical issues in human genetics* (pp. 147–161). New York: Plenum.

Roe v. Wade. 410 U.S. 113 (1973).

Rue, V. M. (1985). Death by design of handicapped newborns: The family's role and response. *Issues in law and medicine, 1*(3), 201–225.

Schmeck, H. M. (1991). The future of genetic research. In *Blazing a genetic trail: A report from the Howard Hughes Medical Institute* (pp. 50–55), Bethesda, MD: Author.

Silver, T. (1981). Amniocentesis and selective abortion. *Pediatric annals, 10,* 397–400.

Stevenson, D. K., Petersen, K. R., Yates, B. L., Benitz, W. E., & Gale, R. (1988). Outcomes of neonates with birth weights of less than 801 grams. *Journal of Perinatology, 8*(2), 82–87.

Turnbull, H. R., III. (1977). *Consent handbook.* Washington, D.C.: American Association on Mental Retardation.

Tymchuk, A. J. (1976). A perspective on ethics in mental retardation. *Mental retardation, 14*(6), 44–47.

U.S. Congress, Office of Technology Assessment (1987). *Neonatal intensive care for low birthweight infants: Costs and effectiveness* (High Technology Case Study 38). Washington, D.C.: Author.

Weir, R. (1984). *Selective nontreatment of handicapped newborns.* New York: Oxford University Press

Widerstrom, A. H., Mowder, B. A., & Sandall, S. R. (1991). *At-risk and handicapped newborns and infants.* Englewood Cliffs, NJ: Prentice Hall.

C h a p t e r **5**

Early Intervention Programs for Infants and Toddlers with Disabilities and Their Families

The time between the birth of a baby and that child's third birthday is an exciting and challenging time for any family. Both the child and the family undergo rapid developmental changes. The typically developing child begins this period as a newborn who is totally dependent on others for nutritional and self-care needs, is unable to hold up his or her head without support, and who communicates with others through (a) subtle changes in body tone and movement, (b) the use of eye contact and facial expressions, and (c) frequent and not so subtle cries. Three years later this tiny baby has become an active preschooler who is able to speak in short sentences, using hundreds of different words, who runs and jumps with ease, eats meals with their family, is toilet trained, and is rapidly learning about shapes, colors, letters, and numbers (Allen & Marotz, 1989).

Family members also undergo rapid developmental change during this time with the young child. If it is the first child in the family, parent(s) will experience one of the major adjustments of adult life (Turnbull, Summers, & Brotherson, 1986). Becoming a parent produces an overnight change from being a largely autonomous individual who has significant freedom in structuring their own routines and activities to assuming a 24-hour a day responsibility for another human being. To make this change even more overwhelming, becoming a parent is a responsibility that in all likelihood will last for at least eighteen years, with a lifelong continuation of the strong emotional attachment. If the parent(s) of a newborn have already had a child, the lifestyle and personal growth changes may be somewhat less dramatic. However, a return to the intensive caretaking and nurturing needs of infants and toddlers, and the adjustment to a new set of relationships within the family are always a major event.

The rapid developmental growth of the child and family members precipitated by the birth of an infant creates a challenging set of adjustments for any family, ones that

WINDOW 5-1   Edward's Story*

The neonatologist now attending in the nursery is the same one who seven years ago told my husband Alfred and me that our newborn son was going to die.

"Don't even hope," he said, pointing to the lengthy problem sheet taped to Edward's warming table, "any *one* of the problems could be fatal, but all of them together. . . ."

I was heartbroken by the end of my pregnancy—the seven happiest months of my life. I knew that our baby's chances of living and being normal were almost nonexistent. I was terrified that our son would die and even more terrified that he might somehow live. . . .

Alfred never shared my ambivalence about Edward's survival. He wanted Edward to live no matter what. He cheered him on the way he cheered for his favorite underdog hockey and football teams. So did the nursery staff, who marveled at "Big Ed" Harrison's incredible will to live. As I cradled Edward in my hands for the first time and looked into his newly opened eyes, I was overwhelmed by maternal feelings. But at home, my rational side took over. Edward's death, I felt, was in everyone's best interest and I tried to resign myself to it. I wondered whether Alfred, with his optimistic attitude, was a better, braver person, or whether I was simply more realistic.

A week after Edward's birth, the neonatologists called us in for a conference. Edward had suffered a massive brain hemorrhage. His brain waves were "grossly abnormal." The time had come to stop the respirator and let Edward die. "Quite frankly," said one of the doctors, "we don't think he has enough brain left even to breathe on his own. . . ."

. . . That evening we were with Edward when the respiratory therapist came and turned the dials. To everyone's amazement, Edward kept on breathing. He was still breathing on his own when we left the nursery at midnight. Edward was going to live.

. . . Our child could breathe, but what else could he do? No one would venture a guess. It distressed me to realize that behind the impressive nursery hardware were fallible human beings who were as puzzled by our baby as I was.

. . . Edward's problem list soon doubled. He was, as one the nurses graphically phrased it, "a real train-wreck of a kid." Edward had frequent seizures, he developed hydrocephalus as a result of his brain hemorrhage, and he was taken to shunt surgery weighing 2 1/2 pounds. Then his shunt became infected and the infection went into his brain. Again, he nearly died. We were sent from the nursery as doctors pounded on his chest to restart his heart. "This is the worst thing that could possibly happen," said the neurosurgeon. "Have you ever seen a baby this sick turn out to be normal?" I asked. "Very few," he replied, "and normal is a damned big category." (I am grateful to this man, and to the other doctors who told us the truth, even when the truth was painful.)

. . . As we took Edward home from the hospital, we were given contradictory instructions to "treat him like a normal baby but bring him in if he becomes irritable or lethargic or if he starts to vomit (signs of increasing hydrocephalus).

. . . I remember that first year as one long doctor's appointment—exhausting, anxious hours in waiting rooms and ERs, at radiology, in hospital wards, therapists offices, and the follow-up clinic. We spent our nights awake, coaxing our reluctant baby to eat, watching him for danger signs, checking to see if he was breathing.

We rebounded from crisis to crisis. . . . At the first eye appointment, the opthalmologist told us Edward had no functional vision. At the second follow-up clinic, his cerebral palsy was diagnosed. At each subsequent checkup a new developmental delay was discovered. He would almost certainly be retarded. . . .

Our lives were totally centered around Edward, I was afraid to leave him with a babysitter (the first time we did, to go out to dinner, I came home and promptly threw up). I was frightened that if I let down my guard and enjoyed myself, something dreadful would happen. There were many days and nights when I was too depressed, exhausted, or sick to function, and

(*continued*)

WINDOW 5-1   *Continued*

Alfred took over. His optimism, which had puzzled and irritated me in the beginning, was now my greatest source of strength. He was, and is, a wonderful father to Edward. . . .

We found babysitters who loved Edward and worked well with him. They became virtually a part of our family. I forced myself into activities that got me out of the house, and slowly I began to lose my fear of leaving my baby.

I became involved with a group for parents whose children required intensive care at birth. I found I had much more in common with these mothers and fathers than with my friends, whose main parental concerns were teething, diaper rash, and enrolling their toddlers in the right college preparatory nursery school. . . .

I had always been suspicious of the glowing accounts parents write about life with their special children, but life with Edward (once the horrible first year was over) was not the grim martyrdom I had expected. Despite his developmental problems, our son was a healthy, happy child. His loving, exuberant nature was a delight. We worked very hard with him, and he rewarded us with slow but steady progress. We were amazed at his perseverance and will to succeed. . . .

Still, Edward's development was highly uneven. While he could read, he could not identify the simplest picture unless he had memorized it. He rarely used words in a meaningful way. He had problems eating: he chewed poorly, gagged easily. With dim vision, no depth perception, and spasticity in his legs, he had difficulty navigating and walking. He reacted to unfamiliar or overstimulating surroundings by throwing tantrums.

Little by little, we introduced him to the outside world through trips to the supermarket, the drugstore, the zoo, and the park. . . . Dealing with the reactions of others is a problem for many parents of handicapped children. We found a straightforward, honest approach worked best. When children at the park would ask me why Edward walked "funny," talked "funny," or wore glasses, I'd tell them that he'd been very sick as a

baby and things that were easy for them to do were hard for Edward. Usually the children then became quite interested in him and tried to include him in their games, taking him under their wings. Adults were also curious. When I told Edward's story, they too became interested and helpful. . . .

When we first consulted developmental specialists we hoped for answers about Edward's condition and suggestions for helping him. What we got, instead, was confusion. Yes, Edward was ready for toilet training. No, he wasn't. Yes, heel cord surgery would help him walk better. No, it was the worst thing we could do. We soon learned that there was no right answer to any question about Edward's care and upbringing. We began to rely more and more on our own judgment. We continued to seek professional insight, but we tried to find doctors and therapists with whom we felt compatible, people whose advice made sense to us. . . .

And what is Edward like today? At age 7 he is a peculiar mix of abilities and disabilities. He reads at a first-grade level, but his speech is that of a two-year-old. He walks stiffly, but he can run, jump, stand on his head, climb and go down the highest slide at the playground. He writes his name and many other words on the board at school, but he can't unscrew a lid, turn on a faucet, or button a button. After years of heroic effort, he is almost toilet trained. He still indulges in occasional tantrums, but he is easier to take out in public. He is beginning to interact socially with other children and is developing a healthy sibling rivalry with his little sister, Amy (born April 10, 1980, two weeks *after* her due date).

I no longer have any ambivalence about Edward's survival. I'm very glad he lived. I *do* feel lucky, extremely lucky. I feel lucky that with all the brain damage our son sustained, he still turned out to be a fun-loving, affectionate, "bright" child. Alfred and I are lucky that our marriage has survived, that we have found the physical, emotional, and financial resources to cope. Not everyone is so lucky.

WINDOW 5-1 *Continued*

But even with everything Ed has going for him, I'm still worried about his future. A doctor recently told us Edward would never live independently.

I can only hope, unrealistically perhaps, that the doctor is wrong about Edward, that some day our son will manage on his own. Or, perhaps, some day our society, which puts such enormous resources into the saving of high-risk babies, will develop a similar commitment for providing the handicapped survivors with a decent life.

Source: Harrison, H., & Kositsky, A. (1983). *The premature baby book: A parent's guide to coping and caring in the first years* (p.p. 219-223). New York: St. Martin's Press.

are unique to nurturing a child of this age (Olson et al., 1983). Some formerly satisfying relationships and activities often must take a lesser role in family members lives in order to meet these new demands. The happiness and well-being of various family members is often intertwined at this time to a degree that may not be repeated at later stages of family life. For families that successfully meet most of the challenges of these early years, the rapid growth and increased responsiveness and competence of the typically developing child often seem like more than adequate rewards for the expended energy and numerous adjustments.

For adults who are asked to meet too many challenges with too few resources and supports, the results can be much less satisfactory for all concerned (Hanson & Lynch, 1992; LeLaurin, 1992). Sometimes overwhelming problems on the part of the parent(s) (e.g. substance abuse, mental health problems, poverty, dysfunctional relationships) may prevent or interfere with a parent's ability to effectively nurture and care for a young child (Hanson & Lynch, 1992; Musick, 1990). When this occurs it has negative impacts not only on the child's health, emotional well-being, and learning, but also on the way the parent(s) feel about themselves as individuals and as parents. There are very few adults who will not experience considerable unhappiness and lowered self-esteem if they are unable to adequately meet their child's needs.

Infants and toddlers with developmental delays or severe disabilities present some unique challenges and adjustments for parents and other caregivers and family members. The parent has many emotional adjustments in accepting the child's disability and learning to interact with a group of professionals who wish to help them in meeting the child's special needs (Blacher, 1984; Turnbull, Turnbull, Summers, Brotherson, & Benson, 1986). The child's health, behavioral, or other caregiving needs may be very intensive and their rate of growth and development will be much slower or different than that which occurs for typical children (Kohrman, 1990; Lehr, 1989). Even under the best of circumstances, the combined impact of increased caregiving demands and less rapid or "satisfactory" progress on the part of the child can seriously effect a parent(s) ability to meet the always significant challenges of early parenthood.

When considering the many additional challenges and adjustments faced by the families of a young child with severe disabilities, it is sometimes too easy to lose sight of the fact that these are first of all families with many of the same joys, dreams, problems, and issues as any other family. Similarly, an infant or toddler with severe disabilities is first of all a young child with many of the same sources of enjoyment, frustration, and need as any other child their age. As with any young child, their closest and most important ties are to their family, and their relationship with their family is much more influential than their relationship with service providers. It is for this reason that early intervention programs have been developed to support not only the health and developmental progress of the infant or toddler with disabilities, but the family that is so important to them as well. Sometimes the services will assist families in more quickly or more fully reestablishing a satisfying family relationship or in supporting the child in reaching their optimal potential. Sometimes the services may be critical to preserving the family unit, or to the child being able to live at home as a part of their family. Regardless of the specific goal or type of services provided as a part of early intervention programs, these services not only need to be based on the unique and constantly evolving strengths, needs, and preferences of the infant or toddler with disabilities, but the inevitably related, unique, and constantly changing strengths, needs, and preferences of that child's family as well.

This chapter will provide an overview of the types of services that have been available to infants and toddlers with disabilities and their families in the past, describe recent federal legislation related to early intervention, and discuss the characteristics of family-centered early intervention for infants and toddlers and their families.

Focus 1:

What types of services were made available in the past to infants and toddlers with disabilities and their families?

History of Early Intervention Services

The current availability of a variety of health, social service, educational, and family support services designed to meet the needs of infants and toddlers with disabilities and their families is a very recent development. The number of children with severe disabilities who survive early infancy is increasing due to the many advances in treating premature infants as well as those with life-threatening illnesses or birth defects (Lehr, 1989). Fifty years ago families had very limited service choices available to them if they had a baby with a recognizable condition or syndrome that might result in severe disabilities. This section will describe the changes in typical early intervention services from those formerly provided to institutionalized infants and toddlers, to current family-centered and family-directed early intervention models.

Institutionalization

As recently as the 1950s virtually all families were advised to place a family member with severe disabilities in a state institution at birth or at the time the extent of the disabilities was recognized. If the diagnosis of a physical condition associated with disability (e.g. Down Syndrome) was made at the time the child was born, the parents were frequently advised to decide to institutionalize the child before they had a chance to build a relationship or grow attached to the child through holding them in the hospital and taking them home to be a part of the family (Harbin, 1993). In some instances families were encouraged to act as though the child had died, sparing any other children knowledge of their child with disabilities, not visiting the child with disabilities in the institution, and basically getting on with what professionals perceived to be more productive and positive aspects of their lives.

Sometimes the presence of a severe disability would not be recognized until persistent patterns of seriously delayed development could be observed in the young child. For children with severe disabilities, this identification would usually occur during the infant or toddler years. Commonly, professional advice at the time would again center on institutionalization based on the rationale of what would be most beneficial for other family members. The role of staff in the institution was to replace or substitute for the parents as caregivers (Harbin, 1993), making sure that the child's physical needs were attended to, and that there was a safe, protective environment to shelter the child from harm.

Not all families followed professional recommendations to institutionalize their child. In the face of the identification of the disability, the advice to institutionalize the child, and an almost complete lack of services in the community for either the child or their family, some families still chose to take the child home to raise in the best way they knew how (Featherstone, 1980). In some instances, the decision concerning institutionalization was postponed to a later time. In other families, there was a definite intent to have the child with severe disabilities live within their family throughout their life.

Child-Centered Early Intervention

In the late 1950s and early 1960s professionals working with young children and their families began to pay closer attention to earlier research on the impact of a stimulating environment on the learning of young children, including those with disabilities. When a child with severe disabilities was born or identified parents began to be encouraged to take their child home and love them, and to access available services that would assist them in stimulating their child's development and in helping them deal with the emotional impact of having a child with disabilities (Harbin, 1993). During this same decade, powerful parent advocacy organizations were formed, such as the Association for Retarded Citizens. Parent groups and a variety of public and private agencies offered an increasing number of programs and services including infant stimulation programs, occupational, physical, and speech therapy services, family counseling, and respite care (Gentry & Olsen, 1985). Professionals concentrated their efforts on working directly with the child. Parents were encouraged to observe and carry over therapy or stimulation activities with the child at home (Harbin, 1993).

By the 1970s both the learning potential of children with severe disabilities and the importance of parent involvement in facilitating the child's learning were more widely recognized by service providers from a variety of professions. Federal legislation such as P. L. 94-142 and model demonstration projects federally funded through the Handicapped Childrens Early Education Program (HCEEP) were also requiring more extensive parental involvement and decision-making. Professionals began to view parents as important teachers of their young children with disabilities. Parent training programs, designed to have professionals teach parents to teach their own child were among the most widely utilized intervention strategies (Baker, Brightman, Blacher, Heifetz, Hinshaw, & Murphy, 1989; Baldwin, Fredericks, & Brodsky, 1973; Lillie, Trohanis, & Goin, 1976).

During the 1970s a number of curriculum materials were produced by federally funded model demonstration projects that were designed to assist parents in fulfilling this teaching role. Several of these curriculum or training guides and other publications written at the same time were specifically designed for use with parents of infants and toddlers, including those with moderate to severe disabilities. Many of these curricula and teaching tools, or their later editions, are still in widespread use in early intervention programs today. These curricula include the *Portage Guide to Early Education* (Bluma, Shearer, Frohman, & Hilliard, 1976), *Teaching the Infant with Down Syndrome* (Hanson, 1987), *Hawaii Early Learning Profile (HELP): Activity Guide* (Furuno, O'Reilly, Hosaka, Inatsuka, Allman, & Zeisloft, 1985), *The Carolina Curriculum for Infants and Toddlers with Special Needs*, 2nd ed. (Johnson-Martin, Jens, Attermeier, & Hacker, 1991), and *Handling the Young Cerebral Palsied Child at Home* (Finnie, 1975).

In spite of the many advances in providing programs during the 1970s and early 1980s, early intervention services continued to be fragmented or simply unavailable for many infants and toddlers with severe disabilities and their families (McDonnell & Hardman, 1988). This is not surprising considering that federal legislation did not require states to provide any special services to meet the needs of infants and toddlers with disabilities (Gentry & Olson, 1985). However, during the 1980s and early 1990s changing perceptions and policies about the relationship between professionals and families of individuals with disabilities combined with the 1986 passage of P. L. 99-457 to bring about major changes in the structure of early intervention programs and services.

Family-Focused to Family-Centered Early Intervention

Many parent training programs have reported success in teaching parents to use a variety of prescribed intervention strategies, and positive child outcomes have been reported for programs where parents had primary responsibility for direct intervention (Bailey & Simeonsson, 1988; Benson & Turnbull, 1986; Guralnick & Bricker, 1987; Hanson & Schwarz, 1978; Shearer & Shearer, 1976). In spite of these positive outcomes, families and interventionists began to express reservations about using parent training as the dominant early intervention model. For one thing, less positive parent training outcomes were reported for many families, particularly those in which parent(s)' socioeconomic status or educational level were low or the families were experiencing financial, marital, or health crises (Bailey & Simeonsson, 1988; Benson & Turnbull, 1986; Bromwich, 1978). Additional concerns related to the many families who (a) dropped out of the programs (Stile, Cole, & Garner, 1979), (b) did not use the intervention techniques effectively with their young children (Bailey & Simeonsson, 1988; Bromwich, 1978), and/or (c) had parent(s) who simply preferred to be a parent, not their child's teacher (Benson & Turnbull, 1986; McDonnell & Hardman, 1988). Even for families that had been very successful in learning to use the prescribed intervention techniques there was little evidence to suggest that families chose to continue in a "formal" teaching role for any length of time (Bailey & Simeonsson, 1988; Benson & Turnbull, 1986; McDonnell & Hardman, 1988), although many of the techniques may have been maintained or generalized to facilitate the child's development and learning in a more natural or incidental way within daily family routines (Baker et al, 1980; Benson & Turnbull, 1986). In summary, teaching parents to carry out intervention with their infants and toddlers had many positive outcomes within some families. However, because of the many families who did not select to adopt a "teaching" role, or who were unsuccessful in being effective in this role, training parents to be a primary interventionist or teacher for their child has evolved into being one of many options rather than the primary focus for early intervention programs.

Family advocacy, family systems theory (see Chapter 3), and research on families also changed perceptions about how early intervention programs should be structured. While the needs of the child with disabilities continued to be an important intervention focus, service providers began to realize how inseparable these needs were from those faced by other family members or the family unit as a whole. Families and interventionists also became increasingly concerned about the deficit focus of both child- and family-focused intervention (Dunst, Trivette, & Deal, 1988; Summers, Behr, & Turnbull, 1989; Turnbull & Turnbull, 1986). It almost seemed as if the purpose of early intervention could be condensed to answering one question "What is lacking/needed/wrong with this child and/or family and how do *we* get *them* to fix it?" To move away from a deficit focus, interventionists began to place more emphasis on acknowledging the strengths and individuality of families and on using the families, rather than professionals perceptions and insights as a basis for determining program goals and needed supports and services. The emphasis on "enabling and empowering" families became a new, and well-articulated model for early intervention services, family-centered early intervention (c.f. Dunst, Trivette, & Deal, 1988; McGonigel, Kaufmann, & Johnson, 1991).

One way of identifying major paradigm shifts in service programs is to identify the forces that most significantly drive service delivery. Figure 5-1 describes four major paradigms that could be used by early intervention programs. At the time P. L. 99-457 was passed in 1986 many early intervention programs were making a transition from being child-centered to family-focused. Changes in P. L. 99-457 in the 1991 Reauthorization of the Individuals with Disabilities Education Act (P. L. 102-119) mirrored the more recent shift from family-focused to family-centered services. Major federal legislation impacting the provision of early intervention services are described in the next section of this chapter.

System-Centered: The needs of, or benefits to, the service system drive the delivery of services.

Child-Centered: The strengths and needs of the child drive the delivery of services.

Family-Focused: The strengths and needs of the family, as determined by providers, drive the delivery of services.

Family-Centered: The priorities and choices of the family drive the delivery of services.

FIGURE 5-1   The Driving Forces of Service Delivery

Source: Adapted from Recognizing Family-Centered Services, Larry Edelman, Project Copernicus, 1992. Presented by M. McGonigel & L. Frederick during Summer Institute II for Professionals Working with Young Children with Special Needs and Their Families, August 3–4, 1992, Salt Lake City, Utah.

Federal Legislation and Early Intervention

While the 1975 passage of the Education of the Handicapped Act (EHA) (P. L. 94-142) had created incentive grants to encourage states to provide preschool special education programs, similar comprehensive federal incentives to provide services to infants and toddlers with disabilities did not occur until more than a decade later with the 1986 passage of an amended EHA, P. L. 99-457. As discussed in Chapter 3, P. L. 99-457 is the most significant federal legislation to date in terms of its impact on early intervention services for infants and toddlers with developmental delays or disabilities and their families. The 1986 passage of P. L. 99-457 not only extended the Part B full service mandate to preschoolers with disabilities (Section 619), it also established a new program for infants, toddlers, and their families, The Infant and Toddlers with Disabilities Program (Part H). States were not required to participate in Part H but they were eligible for federal funds if they chose to do so and agreed to meet federal implementation requirements after an initial five-year planning period.

As you will recall, in 1990, the title of EHA was changed to the Individuals with Disabilities Act (P. L. 101-476). Amendments to IDEA were passed in 1991 (P. L. 102-119), including several affecting the Infant and Toddler program. While the legislative changes reflected in P. L. 99-457, 101-476, and 102-119 represent a major policy shift in favor of more active federal involvement in early childhood special education and early intervention they fall short of mandating the availability of early intervention services for eligible infants, toddlers, and their families, an end desired by most of the involved families, advocates, and professionals.

> **Focus 2:**
>
> How are early intervention services currently defined in Part H of the 1991 Reauthorization of IDEA (P. L. 102-119)?

Early Intervention as Defined by P. L. 102-119, Part H

Several major components of Part H differentiate it from the Part B (preschool and school age) requirements. These components include:

1. *Eligibility.* Participating states are required to provide services to infants and toddlers who are developmentally delayed or who have a diagnosed physical or mental conditions with a high probability of resulting in developmental delay (e.g. cerebral palsy, Down Syndrome). States determine their own definition for developmental delay, and may choose to also define and provide services to a third group of infants and toddlers, those who are at-risk for future developmental delays. Regardless of how a state chooses to define developmental delay, establishing eligibility for Part H early intervention programs is noncategorical in nature. Parents will know whether or not their child is currently developmentally delayed, but states do not determine that a child has "severe disabilities" or "behavior disorders" or "profound mental retardation" in order to make the child and family eligible for early intervention services.

2. *Individual Family Service Plan (IFSP).* An IFSP is a required written document developed for every eligible child and their family. The IFSP is very important because it reflects the goals, plan of action, services, and evaluation strategies that parent(s) and multidisciplinary early intervention team members agree upon as defining the individualized early intervention most important for that child and family. Figure 5-2 lists required IFSP components.

3. *Service Coordination.* Service coordination was called case management in the original Infants and Toddlers with Disabilities Program (P. L. 99-457, 1987). Not too surprisingly many families were not enthusiastic about the idea of being a "case" that someone would "manage" (Dunst, 1991). Consequently, in the 1991 Amendments the language was changed from "case management" to "service coordinator." The identification of a service coordinator is a required part of the IFSP. The rules and regulations for Part H (Federal Register, Nov. 18, 1987) define service coordination as the "services provided to families of infants and toddlers with disabilities to assist them in gaining access to early intervention services identified in the individualized family service plan." According to the federal rules and regulations developed for the 1991 Amendments, specific service coordination activities include:

1. Coordinating the performance of evaluations and assessments;
2. Facilitating and participating in the development, review, and evaluation of individualized family service plans;
3. Assisting families in identifying available service providers;

1. Child's present level of development:
   a. Physical (including vision, hearing, & health)
   b. Cognitive
   c. Communication
   d. Social or emotional
   e. Adaptive

2. Family-directed assessment of the resources, priorities, and concerns of the family

3. Major outcomes or goals for the child and family, including criteria, procedures, and timelines

4. Early intervention services necessary to meet the unique needs of the child and family and to achieve identified outcomes

5. Dates and duration of services

6. Service coordinator

7. Plan for supporting transition at age three

8. Statement of natural environments in which early intervention services shall appropriately be provided

9. Informed, written consent from parents before services in IFSP are provided

---

FIGURE 5-2   Components of the Individualized Family Service Plan

4. Coordinating and monitoring the delivery of available services;
5. Informing families of the availability of advocacy services;
6. Coordinating with medical and health providers; and
7. Facilitating the development of a transition plan to preschool services, if appropriate (Federal Register, May 1, 1992, p. 303.22).

Service coordinators must be qualified to carry out these responsibilities. Often service coordinators are early interventionists from a variety of professions, or parents or paraprofessionals who have been specially trained for a service coordination role.

4. *Broadened Range of Services.* Early intervention services that may be provided under Part H include a broader range of services than the special education and related services which might be included on an IEP for a preschooler with disabilities. Early intervention services are identified and provided on an individual child and family basis, in order to achieve desired outcomes specified in the IFSP. The menu of early intervention services include:

a. Assistive technology
b. Audiology

   c. Communication (e.g. speech or language therapy)
   d. Family education and counseling
   e. Health care services, to enable the child to benefit from other early intervention services
   f. Nursing
   g. Nutrition
   h. Occupational therapy
   i. Physical therapy
   j. Psychological services
   k. Social work
   l. Special instruction
   m. Transportation needed to enable the child and family to receive early intervention services
   n. Vision services

Very few early intervention programs have a large and diverse enough staff to be able to provide this wide an array of services on their own. Interagency coordination is often needed to successfully implement the IFSPs. This is one of the reasons for the service coordination requirement in Part H of IDEA.

   6. *Interagency Coordinating Council.* Each state choosing to participate in the Part H Infant and Toddler program was required to select a lead agency and form an interagency coordinating council (ICC). The lead agency is responsible for Part H planning, with the advice and assistance of the state ICC. Different states selected different agencies to fill the lead agency role, including Education, Health, Mental Health, and Social Services. Federal regulations required membership on state-level interagency coordinating councils to include parents of infants and toddlers with developmental delays or disabilities, service providers, agency representatives, and representatives from higher education.

Family-Centered Early Intervention

Family-centered early intervention embraces a positive and holistic view of families, including families with an infant or toddler with severe disabilities or delays. The philosophy and practice of family-centered early intervention is consistent with federal legislation, but in many ways goes much farther in the attempt to empower families. Parent advocacy and educational groups and professionals from a variety of disciplines have participated in developing the key concepts and practices related to family-centered early intervention. While often regarded as "best practice" for early intervention programs or services at this time, family-centered early intervention did not develop until the late 1980s and early 1990s. Professional and family support is strongest for the philosophical base for family-centered early intervention. Implementation of family-centered early intervention practices and efficacy research on family-centered early intervention are still in the very early stages of development.

A Philosophy of Enabling and Empowering Families

The philosophy of *enabling* and *empowering* families (Dunst et al., 1988) is central to family-centered early intervention as well as increasingly accepted as a basis for a variety of professional-family partnerships. McGonigel (1991) defined these terms in relation to early intervention in the following manner:

> Enabling *families means creating opportunities and means for families to apply their present abilities and competencies and to acquire new ones as necessary to meet their needs and the needs of their children (Dunst, Trivette, & Deal, 1988).* Empowerment *is both a process and an outcome that takes different forms in different families (Rappaport, 1984).* Empowering families in *early intervention does not mean giving or bestowing power on families—the power is theirs by right. Rather, it means interacting with families in such a way that they maintain or acquire a sense of control over their family life and attribute positive changes that result from early intervention to their own strengths, abilities, and actions (Dunst, Trivette et al., 1988). (p. 8).*

A focus on enabling and empowering families creates a very different role for early interventionists than the previously common role of expert who focuses on child-centered intervention. Figure 5-3 summarizes the rationale and principles of family-centered early intervention as they relate to development of IFSP's. While these principles are not unique to families that have an infant or toddler with severe disabilities or developmental delays, their very responsiveness to individual child and family needs are likely to be beneficial to families who may be facing some very unique challenges that are not readily addressed by signing up for a prepackaged set of services or programs.

Focus 3:

What are the major goals of early intervention for infants and toddlers with severe disabilities and their families?

Goals of Early Intervention

As mentioned earlier, the empowerment of families is both an end goal and a means for reaching other goals of early intervention programs for infants and toddlers with disabilities and their families. Additional goals for early intervention programs and their importance for children with severe disabilities include:

1. *Mutually enjoyable family relationships that include the child with disabilities are established and maintained.* An important outcome for early intervention is the establishment of enjoyable and reciprocal family relationships that include the young child with disabilities (Bromwich, 1978; Hanson, 1987; Rose, Calhoun, & Ladage, 1989).

- Infants and toddlers are uniquely dependent on their families for their survival and nurturance. This dependence necessitates a family-centered approach to early intervention.

- States and programs should define "family" in a way that reflects the diversity of family patterns and structures.

- Each family has its own structure, roles, values, beliefs, and coping styles. Respect for and acceptance of this diversity is a cornerstone of family-centered early intervention.

- Early intervention systems and strategies must honor the racial, ethnic, cultural, and socioeconomic diversity of families.

- Respect for family autonomy, independence, and decision-making means that families must be able to choose the level and nature of early intervention's involvement in their lives.

- Family/professional collaboration and partnerships are the keys to family-centered early intervention and to successful implementation of the IFSP process.

- An enabling approach to working with families requires that professionals reexamine their traditional roles and practices and develop new practices when necessary—practices that promote mutual respect and partnerships.

- Early intervention services should be flexible, accessible, and responsive to family-identified needs.

- Early intervention services should be provided according to the normalization principle—that is, families should have access to services that are provided in as normal a fashion and environment as possible and that promote the integration of the child and family within the community.

- No one agency or discipline can meet the diverse and complex needs of infants and toddlers with special needs and their families. Therefore, a team approach to planning and implementing the IFSP is necessary.

FIGURE 5-3   Principles Underlying the IFSP Process

Source: McGonigel, M. J. (1991). Philosophy and conceptual framework. In McGonigel, M. J., Kaufmann, R. K., & Johnson, B. H. (Eds.), *Guidelines and recommended practices for the Individualized Family Service Plan* (2nd ed.) (pp. 9). Bethesda, MD: ACCH.

Infants with significant disabilities may have a number of atypical behaviors that can discourage the attempts of already stressed parents in establishing a satisfying relationship. For example, they may (a) sound different when they cry, cry more frequently, and be more difficult to soothe, (b) stiffen and pull away when being held, rather than molding to the caregivers body, (c) avert their gaze when caregivers attempt to establish eye contact, and (d) smile later, or less often or in response to different stimuli (Berger & Cunningham, 1981; Calhoun, Rose, & Pendergast, 1989; Cicchetti & Stroufe, 1978; Fraiberg, 1974). Early intervention can assist families in understanding these behaviors, and helping parents to learn to read their infants' cues and signals, and to adapt their own behavior to allow a more satisfying, reciprocal relationship to develop (Bromwich, 1978; Hanson & Lynch, 1989; Hedlund, 1989; Rose, Calhoun, & Ladage, 1989). As an infant develops, early intervention can also support family relationships by helping families cope with new challenges, such as teaching the infant to play, or to eat with the family, and to understand the importance of making time for other relationships within the family.

2. *The family unit as a whole is strengthened and individual family members have their critical needs met.* Central to the idea of family-centered early intervention is the recognition that the well being of various family members is interrelated, and that strengthening of the family unit as a whole, and the individual members within it will also benefit the child with severe disabilities. An example of support or intervention that may strengthen the family and benefit the infant or toddler is assisting a family in arranging quality daycare so that a parent who has been a full-time caregiver can return to work that they enjoy. Having a parent return to fulfilling work may have the added benefits of continuing medical insurance coverage, providing some caregiving respite for the parent, and increasing the family's income. With high-quality childcare the infant may also benefit from opportunities to interact with typically developing children, and to experience and learn to be a part of a new set of relationships, activities, and routines.

3. *The child's health is maintained or improved.* The physical health of a child has a profound impact on their learning and development, relationships with family and friends, and their overall quality of life. If a child is in constant pain or discomfort, suffers from frequent fatigue or exhaustion, or spends large amounts of time hospitalized, on life-support equipment, or receiving medical treatments, it may leave little room for the child to invest energy in new learning or for the child and family to just relax and have fun together. Many children with developmental delays or conditions that may result in severe disabilities have additional health problems. For example, about 12 percent of the children born with Down Syndrome also have clinically significant heart disease (Hanson, 1987). Also, premature infants or other individuals who have needed ventilator therapy may develop bronchopulmonary dysplasia (BDP), a chronic lung disorder which can result from scarring of the lungs. Children with BDP may require continued use of oxygen for long periods of time, may have a number of nutritional and feeding difficulties (McCamman & Rues, 1990), and are at higher risk for Sudden Infant Death Syndrome and serious respiratory infections. Up to 85 percent of infants with BDP develop pneumonia or bronchitis before their first birthday (Harrison & Kositsky, 1983). Rehospitalization will be required for many of them. For many infants and toddlers with severe disabilities good health can not be taken for granted. Achieving the best possible health outcomes is an important function of early intervention, one that will support the success of all other goals.

4. *Secondary disabilities are prevented.* Many young children with severe developmental delays have multiple disabilities and/or delayed development in a number of different performance areas. For example, a young child with severe cerebral palsy may have mild to moderate cognitive impairments, severe physical impairments, and be very delayed in the development of communication skills, due to the impact of the physical disabilities on the ability to control the muscles needed for speech, facial expressions, and gestures. Additionally, the limitations in the motor and communication areas will very likely lead to delays or deficits in adaptive and social interaction skills. The physical limitations alone may keep the child from being able to move, to explore and interact with the physical environment, and to develop the typical communication patterns and methods that foster satisfying personal relationships with family and friends. These difficulties, in turn, may hamper optimal cognitive development, and the development of the motivation to be an active learner and to optimize any potential for controlled, purposeful movement.

While none of these impairments or difficulties can be completely prevented, a failure to intervene early can result in permanent physical impairments, such as *contractures*, an irreversible shortening of muscles or tendons. With early and ongoing physical therapy many of the undesirable outcomes of untreated cerebral palsy can be prevented. Early intervention can also help caregivers to facilitate the developmental potential of the child, and to adapt or support the child's physical and social environment in ways that will allow them to have contingent and fulfilling interactions.

5. *The child's learning and development are enhanced.* Research has demonstrated that systematic and early intervention can improve the developmental, educational, and social outcomes for young children with disabilities (see Guralnick & Bennett, 1987 for a series of comprehensive reviews of existing research on early intervention). Because learning and performance builds on previous learning and performance, earlier attainment of various critical skills can open the opportunity for future learning and more proficient performance at many levels and in many contexts. The transactional model of child development (Sameroff & Chandler, 1975) describes how an interactive sequence of child-caregiver-environmental interactions continually modifies or impacts each contributor to the interactions, influencing future interactions and learning in either a facilitative or hindering fashion. The Down Syndrome Infant-Parent Program provides an example of how early intervention can influence developmental outcomes for children. This home-based early intervention program was a federal model demonstration project which operated in the mid-1970s at the University of Oregon (Hanson, 1987; Hanson & Schwarz, 1978). The project compared the age at which the projects' parent-taught infants with Down Syndrome, normal children, and children with Down Syndrome who were raised at home but did not participate in early intervention attained a number of key early developmental milestones. Point of Interest 5-1 displays some of the results of the study. While there is obviously considerable variation for all three groups of children, the children with Down Syndrome who were in early intervention attained the milestones at ages more like the normally developing children than the children with Down Syndrome who had not participated in early intervention. It is important to note that this program and the reported data are based on a small number of infants (n = 9–12) and are not necessarily representative of what would be achieved for a larger number of children and families. During a follow-up on the children at 8-

POINT OF INTEREST 5-1   Comparative Ages at Which Infants and Young Children Attained Developmental Milestones

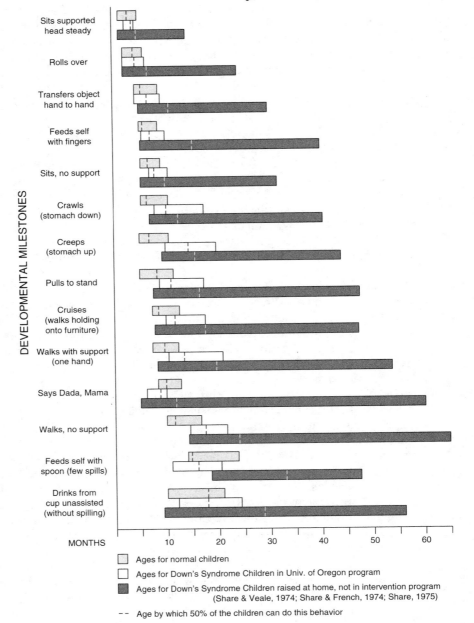

Source: Hanson, M. J. (1987). Progress of infants with down syndrome taught by their parents. In M. J. Hanson, *Teaching the Infant with Down Syndrome: A Guide for Parents and Professionals.* Austin: Pro-Ed.

10 years of age, the children who had participated in the early intervention project showed a large range of abilities, with individual children performing anywhere between the normal range on cognitive and academic measures, to being considered severely delayed. However, as Hanson (1987) notes, "The most striking finding in a follow-up observation is that these children are **all** accepted and complete members of their families and that their parents are **all** confident and caring parents." (p. 30).

6. *The independence and inclusion of the child and family are facilitated.* The infant and toddler years may seem early to be concerned about independence, particularly for a child with severe developmental delays or disabilities. However, it is in these years that parents and children not only develop an intimate relationship but also begin to reassert their individuality and independence (e.g. Brazelton, 1974; Rubin, Fisher, & Doering, 1980). If either the child with severe disabilities or their family is denied the opportunity to begin this process during the infant and toddler years, they miss an important chance to build a foundation for later independence and inclusion within the society at large.

Taking a baby or toddler along on parent ventures into the community is often a challenging and time-consuming enterprise at best. Parents of young children with severe disabilities may find this task to be even more difficult. They may have concerns about how they will feel and respond to comments or reactions from other people about their child's appearance, behavior, or specialized equipment (Calhoun, Rose, & Armstrong, 1989). They may also have concerns about physical and architectural barriers, or exposing their child to illnesses, cigarette smoke, or other potential health threats. Early intervention can play an important role in supporting families in overcoming these barriers to joint family participation in the community. It can also support childcare providers, family friends, or community members who can include the young infant or toddler with disabilities in activities that will allow them to interact on a frequent basis with typically developing children of similar ages. This provides the child with disabilities with a wider and more enjoyable base of experience, and an opportunity to learn to respond to the challenges of the world outside their own family and home.

Implementing Family-Centered Early Intervention

Families and early interventionists work in partnership to develop an IFSP that can guide early intervention during a period of the child's infant or toddler years. While IFSP's must be reevaluated at least every six months, they are designed to be a fluid document, reflecting the rapid and often unpredictable changes that occur with very young children and their families. Any part of the IFSP can be updated or altered when the family-early intervention team believe that such changes can better characterize current needs. Examples of changes that might be desirable before it is time to write a new IFSP are adding new outcome statements and changing the methods for meeting or evaluating outcomes if previous methods have been unsuccessful or are disliked. Four important components of IFSP development include: (1) conducting a family-directed assessment, (2) developing goals/outcome statements and identifying the needed supports and services to achieve the outcomes, (3) identifying the service coordinator and service coordination plan, and (4) planning for any forthcoming transitions.

Focus 4:

Describe family-directed assessment, Individualized Family Service Plans, service coordination, and transition planning, and discuss how they are used to achieve the goals of family-centered early intervention.

Family-Directed Assessment and Selecting Intervention Goals

Professionals from a variety of disciplines have been used to conducting test-based standardized or curriculum-based assessments in their area of expertise and summarizing and sharing the results and their recommendations with families and other team members. Numerous concerns have been raised about the meaningfulness of such test results for intervention planning, particularly when they are used to assess the performance of very young children, or individuals with severe disabilities, and are done in isolation of professionals with other types of expertise or the family who are so important to the child.

P. L. 99-457 introduced a new component to early intervention assessment, that of *family assessment*, in which with a family's permission, their strengths, and needs in relation to the child with disabilities would be assessed by professionals as a key to planning intervention. While acknowledging the importance of the family to the young child with disabilities, this approach had the potential to be intrusive to the family, creating a situation where a family might feel that they needed to complete an endless series of interviews and checklists in order to obtain early intervention services for their child. To counter these possible misuses of family assessment the 1991 reauthorization of IDEA changed the language to a "family-directed assessment."

Family-directed assessment can address issues related to both the child and family and is used for purposes of IFSP development, implementation, and evaluation. "A family's agenda—its priorities for how early intervention will be involved in family life—shapes the entire family-centered IFSP process" (McGonigel, 1991). One of the primary purposes of family-directed assessment is to identify family concerns, priorities, and resources. Figure 5-4 outlines principles that can assist professionals in working in partnership with families in this identification process.

Families also play an important role in directing and shaping assessment related to their child with developmental delays or disabilities. This can occur through sharing information about their child's current level of performance, including strengths and needs, by making suggestions on how to get optimal performance from their child, or by sharing information on the relevant people, places, and routines in the child's life, as well as their vision for the child's future. Family priorities for the child and the family may be very different from priorities generated by a group of professionals, who

- The inclusion of family information in the IFSP is voluntary on the part of families.

- The identification of family concerns, priorities, and resources is based on an individual family's determination of which aspects of family life are relevant to the child's development.

- A family need or concern exists only if the family perceives that the need or concern exits.

- Families have a broad array of formal and informal options to choose from in determining how they will identify their concerns, priorities, and resources.

- Families have multiple and continuing opportunities to identify their concerns, priorities, and resources.

- Family confidences are respected, and family-shared information is not discussed casually among staff.

- The process of identifying family concerns, priorities, and resources leads to the development of IFSP outcomes, strategies, and activities that help families achieve the things they want from early intervention for their children and themselves.

FIGURE 5-4   Principles for Identifying Family Concerns, Priorities, and Resources

Source: Kaufmann, R. K., & McGonigel, M. J. (1991). Identifying family concerns, priorities and resoures. In McGonigel, M. J., Kaufmann, R. K., & Johnson, H. H. (Eds.), *Guidelines and recommended practices for the Individualized Family Service Plan.* (2nd ed.) Bethesda, MD: ACCH.

tend to focus on achieving physical health for the child and maximizing developmental progress. Figure 5-5 includes some typical family priorities. While the individual expression of the achievements may be very different in form from person to person, there are very few parents who not want the majority of these outcomes for their children and family. Clearly some of these priorities (e.g. skills to drive car, employment) are very long range for infants or toddlers with disabilities. However, many of them (e.g. ability to walk and communicate, understanding that he/she is loved, personal happiness, feelings of accomplishment, skills to feed and dress themself, being comfortable enough to sleep through the night) are very much the focus of early intervention. All of the priorities listed in the section of Figure 5-5 that address what parents want for their family are outcomes that can be important to address as early as when an infant with severe disabilities is coming home from the hospital.

The overriding intent of family-directed assessment is to gather and share information that will assist families and early interventionists in developing an effective and supportive Individualized Family Service Plan. A multidisciplinary team of skilled professionals is unable to effectively design either an assessment plan or IFSP without the active participation of the family on some level. As Hunt and colleagues (1990) indicated to family

For our child we want

- Independence
- Personal happiness
- Feelings of accomplishment
- Respect
- Ability to walk
- Ability to communicate
- Good friends
- Understanding that he/she is loved
- Employment
- Skills to feed him/herself
- Skills to dress him/herself
- Comfortable enough to sleep through the night
- Skills to drive car
- The experience of having a loving relationship with a member of the opposite sex
- To know and love God

For our family we want

- Social outings (especially restaurants)
- Sleep-filled nights
- Enjoyment of an evening out (as a couple)
- Normal sibling relationships
- Relatives and friends to understand the nature of our child's disabilities
- Help with planning some adaptations to our home

FIGURE 5-5   Typical Family Priorities

Source: Hunt, M., Cornelius, P., Leventhal, P., et al., (1990). *Into our lives*. Akron, OH: Children's Hospital Medical Center.

members, "Your identification of resources, strengths, and concerns becomes the foundation of your individual plan—and no one knows these better than you do." (p. 3).

Important priorities for the child or family that have been identified through family-directed early intervention are developed into goal or outcome statements on the IFSP. A goal or outcome statement may focus on a desired end for either the child with disabilities or some other member of their family. The emphasis in the wording of the goal or outcome statement is one that reflects the family's way of expressing the goal and is free of professional terminology and jargon. The resources and supports for achieving the goal or outcome statement are included, as are the criteria by which attainment of the goal will be judged. An example of an IFSP for a young child with severe disabilities and their family is included in Figure 5-6.

Focus 5:

Describe the role of natural supports, natural contexts, and interagency coordination and collaboration in family-centered early intervention.

Western Carolina Center
Family, Infant and Preschool Program
Individualized Family Support Plan

Background Information:	Family Member's Name:	Relationship to Child:
Child's Name: Tammy Natasha	Sandy	Mom
Family's Name: Shook	Woody	Dad
No OPD 0 2: 0000	Amy	Sister
Date of Birth: 8 19 88 Age: 12 mos		
County: Cook		

Family Support Plan Team

Name	Title	Agency	Date
Sandy Shook	Parent		10-12-89
Woody Shook	Parent		10-12-89
Patricia N. Bill RN	Case coordinator	Family, Infant and Preschool Program	10-12-89
Jim Given, MD	Pediatrician	Family, Infant and Preschool Program	10-12-89
Mary Lou O'Keefe	Physical therapist	Family, Infant and Preschool Program	10-12-89
Pam C. Brule exc-SLP	Speech language therapist	Family, Infant and Preschool Program	10-12-89
Laurel Hensley	Social worker	Family, Infant and Preschool Program	10-12-89
Donald Whisit	Staff psychologist	Family, Infant and Preschool Program	10-12-89
Lynda Patch	Teacher	Family, Infant and Preschool Program	10-12-89
Marilyn Yakinovich	Family resource specialist	Family, Infant and Preschool Program	10-12-89

Team Review Dates

0 Months	3 Months	6 Months	9 Months

Griffiths Scale of Mental Development   Child's Functioning Level

Domain	CA	Age Level/Range	Domain	CA	Age Level/Range	Domain	CA	Age Level/Range
Locomotor	12 mos	2.7 mos	Eye/Hand	12 mos	2.3 mos	Gen. quot.		24.5
Personal/Social	12 mos	2.3 mos	Performance	12 mos	2.7 mos	Mental age	12 mos	2.9 mos
Hear/Speech	12 mos	4.6 mos						

Child's Strengths	Family's Strengths
Vocalizes and makes sound imitations Sleeps through the night Enjoys being held More alert to surroundings	Love one another Have good coping skills for dealing with stress Commitment to getting treatments for Tammy Take preventive measures with the children Advocate for children's needs

Formal Resources and Support Services	Dates Started	Ended	Informal Resources and Support Services	Dates Started	Ended
Cook Co. DSS	8-88		Maternal grandparents		
Cook Co. Mental Health	2-90		Pastor		
Cook Co. Cluster	7-89		Contribution fund from church		
FIPP Home-based serv.	6-89		Friends Gail		
Social Security	7-89		Tim		
Cook Co. Health Dept.	8-88		Cousins Michele & Albert		
Private pediatricians	8-88				
Private PT	7-89				

FIGURE 5-6   Individualized Family Service Plan

(continued)

Source: Noonan, M. J., & McCormick, L. (1993). *Early intervention in natural environments: Methods and procedures.* Pacific Grove, CA: Brooks/Cole.

Child's Name: __Tammy__ OPDO: __2-0000__ Family's Name: __Shook__ FIPP Staff Member: __P. Bell__ IFSP#: __1__ Page#: __1__

Date / #	Need/Project Outcome Statement	Source of Support/Resource	Course of Action	Family's Evaluation Date	Rating
06-12-89 / 1	Parents will obtain information about FIPP in order to decide which resources are going to best meet their needs.	Parents–ability to process information and choose resources Case coord.–information on FIPP Social worker–information on FIPP	Case coord. & social worker will provide information about FIPP during home visit. Parents will review information, ask questions and decide if they wish to access FIPP resources. If FIPP resources are not chosen, other alternative resources will be explored.	07-12-89 08-08-89	4 7
06-22-89 / 2	Parents will obtain information on avaliable financial resources in order to meet expenses related to Tammy's care.	Parents–ability to gather information Case coord.–information Social security–information	Case coord. will share information about community financial resources during weekly home visit. Parents will contact social security and social services for eligibility information and gather family financial records.	07-12-89 08-07-89	3 6
07-12-89 / 3	Parents will obtain information on available physical therapists in order to obtain service for Tammy.	Parents–ability to process information & schedule appointment with PT Case coord.–information PT–consultation	Case coord. will share names of PTs in the area during weekly home visit. Parents will contact PTs to ask about availability and schedule a consultation with PT of choice.	07-19-89 08-07-89 08-28-89	4 6 7
07-19-89 / 4	Woody will obtain counseling in order to learn ways to control his anger.	Woody–ability to schedule appointment and utilize counseling Family members–support & encouragement Case coord.–information & support DSS caseworker–information & support	DSS caseworker & case coord. will provide information on Woody on available counseling services during weekly home visit. Woody will make an appointment & attend counseling sessions. Family will give support & encouragement.	08-07-89 09-20-89 10-23-89 on hold	2 4 5
08-01-89 / 5	Parents will participate in PT sessions in order to learn handling techniques for Tammy.	Parents–abilities to utilize PT suggestions & provide feedback on usefulness of techniques PT–evaluation of Tammy & information on handling techniques	Parents will schedule PT evaluation & share information about Tammy with PT. PT will evaluate Tammy's motor development & demonstrate handling techniques during weekly PT sessions held at local recreation department.	08-28-89 09-20-89 ongoing	4 7
08-21-89 / 6	Parents will identify their goals and priorities for Tammy in order to prepare for assessment and intervention planning day at FIPP.	Parents–ability to identify goals Case coord.–developmental screening of Tammy & provide information about assessment procedures	Case coord. will administer Griffiths during weekly home visit & discuss results with parents. Parents & case coord. will discuss family's goals & priorities for Tammy and decide on objectives for the assessment & IPD.	09-20-89 10-01-89	3 7

Family's Evaluations:
1 .... Situation changed, no longer a need
2 .... Situation unchanged, still a need, goal or project
3 .... Implementation begun; still a need, goal or project
4 .... Outcome partially attained or accomplished
5 .... Outcome accomplished or attained, but not to the family's satisfaction
6 .... Outcome mostly accomplished or attained to the family's satisfaction
7 .... Outcome completely accomplished or attained to the family's satisfaction

FIGURE 5-6 *Continued*

Child's Name: __Tammy__ OPDO: __2-0000__ Family's Name: __Shook__ FIPP Staff Member: __P. Bell__ IFSP#: __1__ Page#: __2__

Date / #	Need/Project Outcome Statement	Source of Support/Resource	Course of Action	Family's Evaluation Date	Rating
09-20-89 / 7	Parents will use firm, deep pressure during physical contact with Tammy in order to increase her tolerance for touch.	Parents–ability to use PT techniques PT–consultation on handling techniques Case coord.–support & feedback	Parents will schedule & participate in weekly PT sessions with Tammy. PT will demonstrate handling techniques. Case coord. will assist family in incorporating techniques into daily routines & give feedback on use of techniques.	09-27-89 10-05-89 ongoing	4 7
09-20-89 / 8	Parents will obtain as much information as possible about Tammy's medical history in order to have a better understanding of events that occurred during her hospitalization.	Parents–skill in generating questions Case coord.–medical information Family physician–information & consultation FIPP physician–consultation	Case coord. will obtain medical records and schedule meeting with FIPP physician. Parents will identify their questions and consult with physicians. Family physician & FIPP physician will interpret records & answer questions.	10-12-89 11-06-89 12-18-89	4 4 6
09-20-89 / 9	Tammy will consistently hold her head up in order to work toward sitting independently.	Parents–abilities to use techniques to promote head control PT–consultation on techniques to promote head control Case coord.–support & information	Parents will attend PT consultation weekly and use suggested techniques with Tammy. PT will evaluate Tammy's motor abilities and suggest techniques for promoting head control. Case coord. will provide support to family in using techniques during weekly home visits.	10-12-89 11-06-89 12-11-89 See goal #18	3 4 4
10-12-89 / 10	Parents will take Tammy for an eye examination in order to determine her visual abilities.	Parents–abilities to schedule exam & understand results Private physician–information Eye doctor–evaluation & information Case coord.–support & information	Parents will obtain names of eye doctors from private physician and schedule eye evaluation. Parents will take Tammy for eye exam & consult with doctor. Case coord. will provide support & information related to eye evaluation during weekly home visits.	10-12-89 11-06-89	3 6
10-12-89 / 11	Tammy will use her hands to bring toys to her mouth in order to explore and become aware of her surroundings.	Case coord.–information Parents–abilities to use suggested techniques to promote hand use	Case coord. will demostrate techniques for promoting hand use during weekly home visits. Parents will use techniques in daily routines with Tammy.	10-12-89 11-06-89 12-11-89 See goal #19	3 3 3
10-12-89 / 12	Tammy will tolerate being in water in order to make bathtime more relaxing.	Parents–skills in using suggested techniques for bathtime Case coord.–bathchair, information on use of chair & feedback on use of techniques	Case coord. will provide a bathchair on loan & demonstrate use during weekly home visits. Parents will use chair & other techniques such as keeping Tammy wrapped in towel until placed in the tub, gently placing her in warm water, having the bathroom warm, using gentle but firm motions & holding Tammy firmly.	11-13-89 12-11-89 01-22-90	4 4 7

Family's Evaluations:
1 . . . . Situation changed, no longer a need
2 . . . . Situation unchanged, still a need, goal or project
3 . . . . Implementation begun; still a need, goal or project
4 . . . . Outcome partially attained or accomplished
5 . . . . Outcome accomplished or attained, but not to the family's satisfaction
6 . . . . Outcome mostly accomplished or attained to the family's satisfaction
7 . . . . Outcome completely accomplished or attained to the family's satisfaction

FIGURE 5-6 *Continued*

Child's Name: __Tammy__ OPDO: __2-0000__ Family's Name: __Shook__ FIPP Staff Member: __P. Bell__ IFSP#: __1__ Page#: __3__

Date / #	Need/Project Outcome Statement	Source of Support/Resource	Course of Action	Family's Evaluation Date	Rating
10-17-89 / 13	Parents will obtain information on respite options in order to make decisions on the best respite resources for their family.	Case coord.–information on formal respite programs–feedback & support Parents–ability to identify people they know for child care Grandmother–support & feedback	Case coord. will provide information on respite programs during weekly home visits. Parents will identify people they know (with Grandmother's help) who might provide respite. Parents will decide which options to pursue for respite.	10-30-89 11-06-89 12-11-89	3 6 7
10-17-89 / 14	Parents will gather information on preschool programs in their community in order to decide if attending preschool will further promote Tammy's development.	Case coord.–information on local preschools & feedback DSS–information on preschools Parents–ability to gather information & select services	Case coord. will provide information on available preschools & assist family in knowing what to look for in selecting a program, during weekly home visits. Will provide support to family as they consider programs. Parents will contact DSS for information on local programs and contact programs they choose to visit.	10-30-89 11-13-89 12-11-89 See goal #17	4 4 6
11-06-89 / 15	Parents will obtain a second neurological consultation in order to better understand the reasons for Tammy's delays.	Parents–ability to access community resources Physician–referral to neurologist Neurologist–evaluation of Tammy & interpretation of results Case coord.–emotional support & feedback	Parents will ask private physician for names of neurologists, schedule a neurological & ask their questions concerning Tammy's delays. Case coord. will assist the parents in listing their questions for the neurologist & provide emotional support during weekly home visits.	12-18-89 01-06-90 01-22-90	3 3 3
12-11-89 / 16	Woody will obtain information on local literacy programs in order to decide on enrolling in a program.	Woody–ability to get information & decide on enrolling Family–support & encouragement to Woody Case coord.–medical information Community college–information on enrollment	Case coord. will provide information on literacy programs during weekly home visits. Woody will contact community college for information. Other family members will provide encouragement to Woody in learning to read.	01-22-90 02-28-90 on hold	4 4
12-11-89 / 17	Parents will complete application papers for Family Place in order for Tammy to be enrolled in the preschool program.	Parents–ability to complete application & provide information on their goals for Tammy Family Place staff–information on application process Case coord.–support & feedback for family	Parents will make appointment & meet with Family Place staff to complete application process & share their goals for Tammy. Case coord. will provide support to family in completing application process. Family Place staff will meet with Tammy's parents & keep them informed on enrollment process.	01-16-90 01-22-90 on hold	3 6
12-11-89 / 18	Tammy will consistently hold her head up for 30 seconds during playtime in order to develop skills for sitting independently.	Case coord.–support & information Parents–ability to use suggested techniques to promote head control PT–techniques for head control	Parents will take Tammy to weekly PT sessions & use suggested techniques with Tammy during playtimes. PT will demonstrate techniques during weekly sessions. Case coord. will provide feedback on use of techniques during weekly home visits.	01-22-90 02-28-90	3 4

Family's Evaluations:
1 . . . . Situation changed, no longer a need
2 . . . . Situation unchanged, still a need, goal or project
3 . . . . Implementation begun; still a need, goal or project
4 . . . . Outcome partially attained or accomplished
5 . . . . Outcome accomplished or attained, but not to the family's satisfaction
6 . . . . Outcome mostly accomplished or attained to the family's satisfaction
7 . . . . Outcome completely accomplished or attained to the family's satisfaction

FIGURE 5-6 *Continued*

Child's Name: __Tammy__ OPDO: __2-0000__ Family's Name: __Shook__ FIPP Staff Member: __P. Bell__ IFSP#: _1_ Page#: _4_

Date / #	Need/Project Outcome Statement	Source of Support/Resource	Course of Action	Family's Evaluation Date	Rating
12-11-89 / 19	Tammy will use her hands to bring her 6 oz. bottle with handles to her mouth in order to become more aware of hand use.	Case coord.–information Parents–ability to teach Tammy to hold her bottle	Case coord. will demonstrate ways to encourage Tammy to hold bottle during weekly home visits. Parents will talk to Tammy about what they are doing as they place the bottle in her hands and use prompts to encourage her to hold it.	01-22-90 02-28-90	3 6
12-11-89 / 20	Parents will explore financial resources in order for Amy to be able to attend Family Place.	Case coord.–information on resources DSS & Family Place–information on financial resources Parents–ability to access community resources	Case coord. will provide information on possible financial resources during weekly home visits. Parents will contact DSS & Family Place to inquire about other possible financial resources for funding daycare for Amy and pursue options they think are appropriate.	01-16-90 01-22-90 02-28-90	3 4 7
01-16-90 / 21	Parents will consult with physician in order to determine if Tammy may receive immunizations.	Case coord.–information on immunizations Parents–ability to access & share information with physician Physician–information & recommendations on immunization	Case coord. will share information about importance of immunizations with parents during weekly home visits. Parents will consult with private physician about immunizations for Tammy & their plans to enroll her in daycare. If immunizations are not advised, parents will obtain statement from physician for Family Place.	01-22-90 02-28-90	3 3
01-22-90 / 22	Parents will gather information on housing options in Cook County in order to consider the possibilities of buying a house.	Case coord.–information & emotional support DSS, Housing Authority, & FHA–information on housing options Parents–ability to gather information & consider options	Case coord. will provide information on local housing agencies & provide emotional support during weekly home visits. Parents will contact local DSS, Housing Authority & FHA to gather information on options & provide information on their financial status.	02-28-90	4
01-22-90 / 23	Tammy will eat 2 or 3 mashed table foods in order to adjust to more texture in her food.	Case coord.–demonstration of ways to add texture to food & feeding techniques Parents & grandparents–abilities to teach Tammy to eat table foods	Case coord. will provide information on adding texture & suggestions on foods to try (bananas, cooked carrots, scrambled eggs, etc.) during weekly home visits. Parents & grandparents will give Tammy 1 or 2 bites of mashed foods as she will tolerate.	02-28-90	5
01-22-90 / 24	Parents will obtain a third neurological consultation in order to get another opinion on the reasons for Tammy's delays.	Parents–abilities to access community health resources Case coord.–emotional support & feedback Neurologist–evaluation of Tammy & interpretation of results	Parents will select a neurologist from previously recommended list, make appointment & ask questions at neurological. Case coord. will assist family in reviewing their question list & provide emotional support during weekly home visits.	02-28-90	3

Family's Evaluations:
1 .... Situation changed, no longer a need
2 .... Situation unchanged, still a need, goal or project
3 .... Implementation begun; still a need, goal or project
4 .... Outcome partially attained or accomplished
5 .... Outcome accomplished or attained, but not to the family's satisfaction
6 .... Outcome mostly accomplished or attained to the family's satisfaction
7 .... Outcome completely accomplished or attained to the family's satisfaction

FIGURE 5-6 *Continued*

IFSP Goal # / Date Started	Objectives	Routines						Date Attained
		Mealtimes	Dressing & Diapering	Bathtime	Independent Playtime	Playtime with Others		
#9 / 09-20-89	Tammy will consistently hold her head up in order to work toward independent sitting.	X	X	X				See #18
#11 / 10-12-89	Tammy will use her hands to bring toys to her mouth in order to explore and become more aware of her surroundings.				X	X		See #19
#12 / 10-12-89	Tammy will tolerate being in water in order to make bathtime more relaxing. (Use bathchair for support and put Tammy in the water slowly.)			X				1-22-90
#18 / 12-11-89	Tammy will consistently hold her head up for 30 seconds during playtime in order to work toward independent sitting.					X		2-28-90
#19 / 12-11-89	Tammy will use her hands to bring her 6 oz. bottle with handles to her mouth in order to become more aware of her hand use.	X						3-28-90
#23 / 01-22-90	Tammy will eat 2 or 3 mashed table foods in order to adjust to more texture in her food (start with one or 2 bites of the food).	X						2-28-90

Child's Name: Tammy   OPD 0: 0000   Matrix#: 1

FIGURE 5-6 *Continued*

Natural Supports and Natural Contexts

Natural supports and natural contexts are critical to family-centered early intervention. The concept of natural supports was introduced in Chapters 2 and 3. At the early intervention age level, natural supports are identified as part of the family-centered assessment process, and are often called "informal supports" because they are based on a family's network of friends and the services and settings available to all community members. These natural or informal supports or resources are identified as strengths on the IFSP, and are linked to individual goal or outcome statements as a primary and preferred means of achieving the outcome. While professional services and supports are valued, and often incorporated, strengthening the use of natural supports is one of the primary mechanisms for empowering families.

WINDOW 5-2   Sharon: Almost Three

Sharon is just three months away from her third birthday. Sharon has Down Syndrome and a mild hearing impairment. She lives with her mother and her ten-year-old brother. Her parents are divorced but she usually sees her father several times a week. Her father has remarried and Sharon has a four-year-old stepsister. She and her brother stay with her father, stepmother, and stepsister every other weekend and she goes to their home for late afternoon play and dinner at least one weekday evening every week. Sharon's mother works as an administrative assistant at the local community college and Sharon needs full-time childcare. Sharon attends a daycare center while her mother works. There are ten other children in her toddler group and their are two caregivers assigned to the group at any one time.

Sharon has been walking for over a year. She likes to play outdoors with the other children in her daycare center, and is particularly fond of playing in the sandbox, climbing on the toddler size jungle gym and going down the small slide. She can feed herself well and likes most foods, especially macaroni and cheese, ice cream, and chocolate chip cookies. Sharon can put on and take off her coat and hat by herself, but usually needs help with other clothing. Sharon is not toilet trained, and has not showed much interest, even though some of the other children in her daycare class are using potty chairs and wearing training pants or underpants. Sharon enjoys baths and likes to have her hair fixed pretty, although she has a hard time sitting still if her mother wants to do anything more than put a bow in it. Sharon knows about fifty different words and says them clearly enough that people who know her can usually understand what she is saying. She usually uses one word at a time, and will try to repeat things she has heard other people say that she is interested in. Sharon loves to play with her parents and older brother, and will try to copy everything her stepsister does, although they are inclined to fight over toys or her stepsister trying to tell Sharon what to do. Sharon likes to play around the other children in her daycare class and

enjoys most of the same activities they do. Sometimes she gets frustrated because she can't talk as well, or use her hands as skillfully as many of the other children. This can make it hard to play some of their games, or to do the art activities that their teachers ask them to do for holidays or other special occasions. Sharon goes to Sunday school, shopping, and out to restaurants with both her mom and dad's families. She also likes to go to the park or to her cousins house to play.

Sharon's mother and father have both been pleased with the early interventionists they have worked with since Sharon was two weeks old. The early intervention program staff have included both of Sharon's parents and their families and have also been available to provide training or support to teachers at the daycare center that Sharon attends. While her parent's really want to help Sharon learn as much as much as she can, they also feel that while Sharon is a very important part of the family that not everything can revolve around doing teaching or intervention with her. The interventionists have helped them see how to include "teaching" within the other things Sharon does on a regular basis, and in particular in the things she really enjoys, like play and meal times.

Sharon's family is concerned as they approach the transition to preschool special education programs. They are a little worried that the school district will want Sharon to attend a class that has been specially designed for preschoolers with developmental delays or disabilities rather than a regular preschool classroom. The fact that Sharon is not talking much and is not toilet trained is also raising some new issues at her daycare center. The staff there feel that she is not "ready" to be moved into the three-year-old class until she is toilet trained. They feel that in this, as in many other areas, she is more like the two-year-olds and would benefit from an extra year in that class. Sharon's family and early intervention team plan to begin working on the transition to preschool and the three-year-old class within the next two weeks. They want to have time to plan and sup-

(continued)

WINDOW 5-2 *Continued*

port the daycare and preschool staff, but still be assured that Sharon can receive the specialized services she needs, while participating in preschool and childcare programs with typical children of her own chronological age. Her family feels that the extent to which Sharon has been actively included in family, childcare, and community activities up to this point in her life will help her make whatever adjustments will be necessary to continue to be included in school and community life as she gets older.

A reliance on *natural contexts* is not only consistent with best practice family-centered early intervention, it is tied to the implementation of the least restrictive environment within the federal regulations for the Part H Infant and Toddler Programs. *Natural contexts* refer to the settings and routines that typically developing children participate in in family, daycare, and community contexts. P. L. 101-119 requires that "to the maximum extent appropriate, [services] are provided in natural environments, including the home and community settings . . . in which children without disabilities participate."

The IFSP itself must include "a statement of the natural environments in which early intervention services shall appropriately be provided." Figure 5-6, p. 121, included a goals by routines matrix, which identified which child-focused goals could be incorporated within which daily routine. This is one way of looking at how intervention can be included in natural contexts and specified in the IFSP.

Transition Planning

Transitions are often a very stressful time for individuals with disabilities and their families (Turnbull, et al., 1986). Recognizing the need for support of families and children during transitions, Part H requires a transition plan to be developed as children receiving early intervention services approach their third birthday, or move between early intervention programs. The goals of transition include uninterrupted provision of necessary services, and supporting children, families, and service providers. Many children in early intervention will transition to preschool special education programs around the time they turn three. Preschool special education programs are often administered by different agencies than early intervention programs, are classroom-based, and have different eligibility criteria. Many children beginning to attend preschool at age three will be expected to ride a school bus with other preschoolers, and the family-centered nature of early intervention is often replaced by more typical parent-teacher-child relationships. These differences between early intervention and preschool programs can create many adjustments for the parent and child. These adjustments and stresses may be more intense when the child entering preschool has severe disabilities. Many families will want the preschooler included in a high-quality early childhood program in which most of the children are typically developing, while still having their child's individual educational, health, and related service needs met by specially trained personnel. The extent to which both inclusion and intensive educational support needs are met in the same classroom is very variable at this time in preschool programs around the country. Transition plans may also be developed as children move from a hospital to home setting, between communities, or when children and families make other shifts during the infant or toddler years. Part H requires IFSP's to include "steps to be taken to support the transition." These steps will usually include educating parents about available preschool options and the changes and expectations that occur when their child begins preschool, visiting preschool programs and teaming with preschool staff to develop the final IFSP and the first preschool IEP, and sharing information or providing support that will enhance the effectiveness of the transition in meeting child, family, and interventionist's needs.

Service Coordination

Early intervention as defined by Part H has been described as a linking mechanism rather than as a separate program. The reason for this rests in the fact that one of the primary purposes of early intervention is to identify and coordinate formal and informal resources to meet needs and priorities identified by the family. Rather than funding a new program to meet all of the needs, the program develops, links, and supplements existing resources. The degree of reliance on informal or natural supports and interagency cooperation has many advantages but can also create a significant challenge in attempting to keep all of the resources and services coordinated and functioning effectively to meet the child and family's needs. Recognizing this challenge, Part H requires the identification of a service coordinator who will fill a service coordination role. The service coordinator is identified as a part of IFSP development and is recorded on the document itself. The IFSP should also show the services and informal supports that will be utilized for IFSP implementation.

Changing Needs: Birth to Three

The most critical feature of family-centered early intervention is that it meets the individual and changing needs of infants or toddlers with disabilities and their families. While the individual nature of early intervention limits the usefulness of generalizations across children and families, there are some similarities that often occur. One of these similarities is the changing focus and form of early intervention as the child with developmental delays or disabilities matures through early infancy, being an older baby or young toddler, and being an almost three-year-old, ready to move on to preschool experiences. The priorities and roles of families and interventionists change along with the developing child. Figure 5-7 summarizes some of the common concerns, goals, and priorities for the child and family at two months after birth, one and half years, and two and a half years. Common intervention strategies or interventionist roles are also summarized as a part of the figure.

Child's Age:	Two Months	One and a Half Years	Two and a Half Years
Major Concerns	• Understanding and accepting child's developmental delay or disability • Explaining disability to family and friends • Resolving or planning for ongoing health care needs of child • Establishing workable family routines that meet the child's needs • Establishing a satisfying, reciprocal relationship with infant	• Helping child maximize developmental progress • Being able to communicate with child, and have child communicate with others • Having some relief from constant caregiving demands • Having time to play and have fun with child, other family members, and friends • Overcoming any barriers to community participation for child or family	• Discipline related issues • Explaining child's disability and special needs to school and community members • Child's readiness for classroom program and peer relationships • Obtaining desired preschool program placement and special services • Changing nature of services from family-centered to child-centered
Goals for Child	• Regulation of feeding, sleeping, and elimination patterns • Responding to caregiver and self comforting and consoling • Interacting with caregiver(s) through making eye contact, vocalizing, smiling, and responsive body movements • Showing interest in sounds, objects, people, and activities in the environment	• Communicating through gestures and single words • Walking • Feeding self at meals • Enjoying playing with simple toys • Playing simple games with caregivers, and imitating caregiver actions	• Following routines and directions • Understanding and using simple phrases and sentences to communicate • Playing alone for brief periods of time • Showing interest and enjoyment in other children and ability to play with them for a brief time • Toilet training
Common Roles for Interventionist	• Supporting parent(s) in developing a positive, enjoyable relationship with child • Helping parent(s) link with services and agencies that can support meeting their own or the child's needs • Supporting parents in finding out about, trying out, and choosing caregiving strategies and routines that work for their family • Support to families in linking with other parents of children with disabilities or other sources of understanding and emotional support	• Providing caregivers with ideas on how to facilitate the child's development across a variety of developmental areas and within natural play and caregiving routines • Working with family members to integrate and coordinate input from a variety of service providers with other family priorities and demands	• Providing support for family in assuming more of service coordination role • Collaborating with early intervention team, preschool team, and family in planning for transition to preschool • Facilitating intervention on goals that will help child as preschooler
Common Intervention Strategies	• Listening very carefully to parents concerns, priorities, and requests for assistance • Helping families to be aware of available options and to feel comfortable with the choices and decisions they make • Focusing on short term, high priority concerns, and refocusing intervention as often as needed to respond to rapidly changing infant and family needs	• Working with family members on developing and trying intervention strategies that are designed to teach the child skills that have been identified as a priority goal by parents as a part of IFSP • Working with family members on integrating intervention strategies across different developmental goals, as they would naturally occur within play or caregiving routines • Supporting families in identifying supports or services that will allow the child's needs to be met while other family members have time to pursue other needs or goals	• Developing transition plan with family and preschool team • Involving child in frequent activities with typical peers of similar ages • Identifying ways to increase child's independence • Using modeling and expansion of child's communication to increase the flexibility and effectiveness of the child's communication with others

FIGURE 5-7 Common Concerns and Changing Needs in Early Intervention

Conclusion

Future Directions in Early Intervention

In the last forty years, the quality and availability of services for infants and toddlers with severe disabilities and their families has improved dramatically. Research studies which have examined the effectiveness of early intervention for these infants and toddlers have often focused on developmental outcomes for the child or a reduction of later intervention costs. While there are a number of other meaningful outcomes to be examined, past research has been supportive of the effectiveness of early intervention for children with autism or cognitive delays (Guralnick & Bricker, 1987; Simeonsson et al., 1987). For example, the combination of not institutionalizing infants with Down Syndrome and the availability of early intervention for many of these children has been sufficiently successful that Down Syndrome is now viewed as a condition most likely to result in mild-moderate delays or impairments, rather than severe-profound impairments as was the prognosis a generation ago. In an extensive review of existing research, Guralnick & Bricker (1987) concluded that "There is . . . . reason to project confidence that the decline in measured intelligence with increasing chronological age common to children with Down Syndrome can be prevented and to some extent reversed" (p. 166). A select group of early intervention programs for children with autism have attained similar results when the intervention has (a) begun at an early age, (b) included structured, behavioral treatment, (c) been intensive in nature (multiple hours per day, year round, home and center), (d) involved parents in carrying out intervention, and (e) systematically focused on the generalization of learned skills (Simeonsson, et al., 1987). In fact, some of the children in programs that met these criteria seemed to show near "recovery" by the time the children were ready to enter school.

The intensity of the intervention, the degree of family involvement in intervention, and the comprehensiveness of the provided services have been several of the key variables associated with positive outcomes in the more child-centered early intervention on which most currently referenced research is based. Intensity, comprehensiveness, and family involvement are conceptualized differently in family-centered early intervention. While the policy, family, and professional support are strong for family-centered early intervention, we are not yet certain whether it will yield similar child outcomes or what the potential benefits will be. We are also still uncertain as to what kinds of programmatic variables make family-centered early intervention most likely to be a success. Guidelines provided to interventionists at this point are largely based on values or philosophical positions and are not empirically validated for large numbers of children and families. Future directions for early intervention will include developing this understanding of the parameters of how to make family-centered early intervention work.

Several of the variables associated with successful early intervention outcomes in the past (i.e. intensity of services, comprehensiveness of services) may require an expanded funding base for either early intervention or for the community programs (e.g. childcare, preventive health care) to which early intervention can link. While the concept of linking existing services and building on informal or natural supports has many strengths, in a number of communities, needed services or supports are still not

****

POINT AND COUNTERPOINT 5-1   Family-Centered Care:
                                 Is It Always in the Child's Best Interests?

Kylie is a nine-month-old baby with cerebral palsy and a controlled seizure disorder. She was born two and a half months prematurely and had anoxia (oxygen deprivation) at birth, as well as seizures and symptoms associated with cocaine withdrawal. Kylie has very limited voluntary control or movement of her arms and legs and is unable to hold up her head independently. The rigidity of her body makes her difficult to carry or hold. She is alert and responsive to interactions but tends to be irritable and hard to soothe. Kylie has serious feeding difficulties and dislikes being fed.

Marcy is Kylie's mother. Marcy was fifteen when Kylie was born and is now sixteen years old. She is no longer dating Kylie's father and he has no contact with the baby. Marcy became addicted to cocaine when she was fourteen. She has been treated at substance abuse centers on several occasions but has been unable to stay "clean" for more than a few weeks at a time. Marcy tried living with her mother after Kylie was born but couldn't take her mother's interference in her life, particularly her constant criticism of the men Marcy was seeing and of her suspected return to cocaine usage. Marcy is currently estranged from her mother and receiving public assistance. She has a steady boyfriend who usually stays with her, a man named Michael who is ten years older than herself, and who is also a user. Michael doesn't pay much attention to Kylie one way or another, although he does find her crying very irritating and asks Marcy to put her in her crib in the other room if Marcy is unable to quickly quiet her.

Kylie is being seen by a pediatrician, occupational therapist, and physical therapist at a public health agency which provides early intervention services to children with developmental delays. The physical therapist is her service coordinator and she makes home visits twice a week. Kylie's pediatrician is very concerned about her minimal weight gain, or failure to thrive, and seriously doubts that Marcy is following through on the admittedly very time-consuming procedures that he and the occupational therapist are recommending to improve her nutritional and health status. Her physical therapist is also very concerned about lack of follow through on the range of motion exercises she asks Marcy to do with Kylie twice a day. If these exercises are not carried out on a regular basis muscle contractures will permanently limit Kylie's movement.

The early intervention team who work with Kylie and Marcy are uncertain how to proceed. They have very genuine concerns about Kylie's welfare, and suspect that she is left to lie around much of the time, without the attention to her special needs that will assure her health and development. On the other hand, Marcy does bring her to the clinic, is home when the therapist comes for home visits, gives Kylie the medication needed to control her seizures, and talks about her love and concern for Kylie. There are no signs that Michael or Marcy have ever abused Kylie. The team feels that if Kylie were a typically developing child who did not require so much extra time and attention that her physical needs could be adequately met within her current home environment.

Point:

While Marcy may have good intentions she is currently unable to meet Kylie's basic health and developmental needs on her own. Marcy obviously loves Kylie but if Kylie continues in her care at this time she may suffer damage that will permanently limit her development and well being, e.g., through the development of muscle contractures or through an extended period of malnutrition. Kylie must receive the care she needs now. The early intervention team should contact child protective services and push for the addition of home care services or the temporary removal of Kylie from her home. They have tried to reach Marcy about the importance of the

POINT AND COUNTERPOINT 5-1   *Continued*

feeding and therapy procedures. She is too young and has too many problems of her own to respond as needed at this time. If Marcy is unable to get her life turned around within a reasonable period of time child protective services should seek to terminate her parental rights. While Marcy has rights, Kylie should also have the right to grow up in a family which can not only love her but also take care of her.

Counterpoint:

The early intervention team should continue working with Marcy, using a family-centered approach to respond to the concerns, priorities, and needs she identifies. While Kylie's needs are not being adequately met in many ways it is important for her sake to keep the family intact and to support Marcy in doing her best with her child. If child protective services is contacted, Marcy may lose all trust in professionals and simply not take Kylie in for any type of treatment. Look what happened when her mother tried to "interfere"; Marcy cut her off both from herself and her granddaughter. However inadequate the current situation is it's better than having Marcy take off with Kylie, with both of them receiving no support at all.

****

available or cannot be readily developed on existing resource bases. Examples of needed services for which funding is currently tenuous or missing in many communities include supported daycare (extra staff or training available to meet the needs of children with disabilities), a cadre of respite care providers trained to handle technologically dependent children, and a lending/funding resource for programmable computer-assisted communication devices. To really take advantage of the potential of early intervention it may be necessary not only to pass federal legislation mandating the availability of early intervention services but to also increase funding to the agencies and services with which early intervention needs to link as well. As a society can we afford an intensive early intervention program for children with autism that results in regular class placement for many of its graduates, or in early intervention services that provide sufficient family and community health support to maintain a technologically dependent child at home? While there are no easy answers to questions such as this, as one examines the alternative costs to society for not intervening, another reasonable question is whether we can afford not to.

Meisels (1992) ties together many of the issues in building on the demonstrated successes and difficulties of previous early intervention models or paradigms as we seek to enhance the effectiveness of more family-centered early intervention.

> *As we review the efforts of the past, and as we anticipate the needs of the future, we can see distinct need for a better match between the child's and family's lived context and the context of early intervention, with particular attention paid to the manner in which services are delivered. It is essential that we shift the way that systems and structures are organized so that they work more effectively for families. No longer can we consider the child as isolated from his or her family. No longer should we attend to the needs of parents without*

also recognizing that they must know how to respond to the changing needs of their children. No longer is it appropriate to follow the dictates of a theoretical view of intervention without questioning its relevance to a particular child and family's social and community situation. Rather, we must foster highly individualized programs of intervention that consider the needs of children and families in tandem, and that seek to address these needs through theoretically-driven and empirically-substantiated models that are consistent with the family's world.

Instead of searching "out there" for the "best" intervention or assessment model overall, we must pay systematic attention to the child and family in context. As we learn to appreciate and intervene with their context, we will become more successful in enhancing development and strengthening families. (Meisels, 1992, p. 5-6).

Focus Review

Focus 1: What types of services were made available in the past to infants and toddlers with disabilities and their families ?

- Institutionalization was recommended to families of infants and toddlers with severe disabilities through the 1950s.
- Child-centered early intervention services became increasingly available between the late 1950s and the mid-1980s. These services were initially developed and operated by parent advocacy groups and private and public agencies and focused on enhancing the child's skill development and preventing secondary disabilities.
- Federally funded model development projects increased the quality, comprehensiveness, and availability of early intervention services.
- Parents played prominent roles in early intervention services, including as teachers for their child with disabilities.

Focus 2: How are early intervention services currently defined in Part H of the 1991 Reauthorization of IDEA (P.L. 102-119)?

- Eligibility is based on the determination of developmental delay or the existence of a diagnosed physical or mental condition with a high probability of resulting in developmental delay. States have the option of defining and providing services to children who are at risk of developmental delay.
- Individualized Family Service Plans (IFSPs) are developed for every eligible child and family. Required components of the IFSP include a statement of the child's present level of development, a family-directed assessment of the resources, priorities, and concerns of the family, major desired outcomes or goals for the child and family, and the identification of a service coordinator and the early intervention services necessary to meet the unique needs of the child and family.

- States participating in the Part H Early Intervention program must identify a lead agency and form an Interagency Coordinating Council.

Focus 3: What are the major goals of early intervention for infants and toddlers with severe disabilities and their families ?

- Mutually enjoyable family relationships that include the child with disabilities are established and maintained.
- The family unit as a whole is strengthened and individual family members have their critical needs met.
- The child's health is maintained or improved.
- Secondary disabilities are prevented.
- The child's learning and development are enhanced.
- The independence and inclusion of the child and family are facilitated.

Focus 4: Describe family-directed assessment, Individualized Family Service Plans, service coordination, and transition planning, and discuss how they are used to achieve the goals of family-centered early intervention.

- Family-directed assessment involves family members in directing and/or shaping the process of gathering and sharing information that will assist their family and early intervention team in developing and implementing an effective and supportive Individualized Family Service Plan (IFSP).
- Individualized Family Service Plans (IFSPs) are the required written documents used to define the goals, plan of action, services, and evaluation strategies that family members and multidisciplinary early intervention team members agree upon as defining the early intervention most important for an individual child and family.
- Service coordination services are designed to assist families of infants and toddlers with developmental delays in accessing and benefitting from a variety of services and supports identified within a child and family's IFSP. Regulations require the identification of a service coordinator on every IFSP.
- Transition planning is a required component of IFSPs as children receiving early intervention services approach their third birthday. IFSPs must include the "steps to be taken to support the transition" [to preschool special education].
- One of the goals of early intervention is to enable and empower families to meet the needs of family members, including those of the infant or toddler with developmental delays. Family-directed assessment uses methods that are meaningful to the family to gather and share information about child and family strengths, needs, supports, and priorities. This information is used to assist in the development of the IFSP which includes family priorities for goals, the natural contexts in which intervention will occur, and the supports and services which will best assist a family in achieving the identified goals or outcomes. Service coordination services are provided to help tie together the formal and informal supports and services that are used to implement an IFSP. Transition planning assists families in preparing for the next phase in their child' and their family's life.

Focus 5: Describe the role of natural supports, natural contexts, and interagency coordination and collaboration in family-centered early intervention.

- Natural or informal supports are identified as strengths on a child and family's IFSP, and are linked to individual goals or outcome statements as a primary or preferred means of achieving many outcomes.
- Natural contexts refer to the settings and routines that typically developing children of similar ages participate in within family, daycare, and community settings. Part H requires that "to the maximum extent appropriate, [services] are provided in natural environments, including the home and community settings . . . in which children without disabilities participate." These natural environments or contexts must be identified as a part of the IFSP.
- Interagency coordination and collaboration are required to make early intervention successful. One of the primary purposes of early intervention is to identify and coordinate formal and informal resources, services, and supports, in order to meet the needs and priorities identified by the family. The requirements to include service coordination and interagency coordinating councils (ICCs) as a part of early intervention reflect how critical this type of coordination and collaboration are to successful intervention.

References

Allen, K. E., & Marotz, L. (1989). *Developmental profiles: Birth to six*. Albany, NY: Delmar Publishers.

Bailey, D. B., & Simeonsson, R. J. (1988). Home-based early intervention. In S. L. Odom & M. B. Karnes (Eds.), *Early intervention for infants and children with handicaps: An empirical base* (pp. 199–215). Baltimore: Paul H. Brookes.

Baker, B. L., Brightman, A. J., Blacher, J. B., Heifetz, L. J., Hinshaw, S. P., & Murphy, D. M. (1989). *Steps to independence: A skills training guide for parents and teachers of children with special needs* (2nd ed.). Baltimore: Paul H. Brookes.

Baker, B. L., Heifetz, L. J., & Murphy, D. M. (1980). Behavioral training for parents of mentally retarded children: One-year follow-up. *American Journal of Mental Deficiency, 85*(1), 31–38.

Baldwin, V. L., Fredericks, H. D., & Brodsky, G. (1973). *Isn't it time he outgrew this? or a training program for parents of retarded children*. Springfield, IL: Charles C. Thomas.

Bennett, T., Lingerfelt, B. V., & Nelson, D. E. (1990). *Developing Individualized Family Support Plans: A training manual*. Cambridge, MA: Brookline Books.

Benson, H. A., & Turnbull, A. P. (1986). Approaching families from an individualized perspective. In R. H. Horner, L. H. Meyer, & H. D. Fredericks (Eds.), *Education of learners with severe handicaps: Exemplary service strategies* (pp. 127–157). Baltimore: Paul H. Brookes.

Berger, J., & Cunningham, C. C. (1981). The development of eye contact between mothers and normal versus Down's syndrome infants. *Developmental Psychology, 17*, 678–689.

Blacher, J. (Ed.). (1984). *Severely handicapped young children and their families: Research into review*. New York: Academic Press.

Bluma, S. M., Shearer, M. S., Frohman, A. H., & Hilliard, J. M. (1976). *Portage guide to early education*. Portage, WI: CESA 5.

Brazelton, T. B. (1974). *Toddlers and parents: A declaration of independence*. New York: Delta.

Bromwich, R. (1978). *Working with parents and infants: An interactional approach*. Austin, TX: Pro-Ed.

Calhoun, M. L., Rose, T. L., & Armstrong, C. (1989). Getting an early start on community participation. *Teaching Exceptional Children, 21*(4), 51–53.

Calhoun, M. L., Rose, T. L., & Prendergast, D. E. (1991). *Charlotte Circle intervention guide for parent-child interactions.* Tucson, AZ: Communication Skill Builders.

Cicchetti, D., & Stroufe, L. A. (1978). An organizational view of affect: Illustrations from the study of Down's syndrome infants. In M. Lewis & L. A. Rosenblum (Eds.), *The development of affect* (pp. 309–350). New York: Plenum Press.

Dunst, C. J. (1991). Implementation of the Individualized Family Service Plan. In M. J. McGonigel, R. K. Kaufmann, & B. H. Johnson (Eds.), *Guidelines and recommended practices for the Individualized Family Service Plan* (2nd ed.), (pp. 67–78). Bethesda, MD: Association for the Care of Children's Health.

Dunst, C. J., Trivette, C. M., & Deal, A. G. (1988). *Enabling and empowering families: Principles and guidelines for practice.* Cambridge, MA: Brookline.

Featherstone, H. (1980). *A difference in the family: Living with a disabled child.* New York: Penguin Books.

Finnie, N. R. (1975). *Handling the young cerebral palsied child at home.* New York: E. P. Dutton.

Fraiberg, S. (1974). Blind infants and their mothers: An examination of the sign system. In M. Lewis & L. A. Rosenblum (Eds.), *The origins of behavior: Vol. I The effect of the infant on its caregiver* (pp. 215–232). New York: Wiley.

Furuno, S., O'Reilly, K. A., Hosaka, C. M., Inatsuka, T. T., Allman, T. L., & Zeisloft, B. (1985). *Hawaii Early Learning Profile (HELP): Activity guide.* Palo Alto: VORT Corporation.

Gentry, D., & Olsen, J. (1985). Severely mentally retarded young children. In D. Bricker & J. Filler (Eds.), *Severe mental retardation: From theory to practice* (pp. 50–75). Reston, VA: The Division on Mental Retardation of the Council for Exceptional Children.

Guralnick, M. J., & Bennett, F. C. (1987). *The effectiveness of early intervention for at-risk and handicapped children.* Orlando, FL: Academic Press.

Guralnick, M. J., & Bricker, D. (1987). The effectiveness of early intervention for children with cognitive and general developmental delays. In M. J. Guralnick & F. C. Bennett (Eds.), *The effectiveness of early intervention for at-risk and handicapped children* (pp. 115–174). Orlando: Academic Press.

Hanson, M. J. (1987). *Teaching the infant with Down Syndrome: A guide for parents and professionals* (2nd ed.). Austin, TX: Pro-Ed.

Hanson, M. J., & Lynch, E. W. (1989). *Early intervention: Implementing child and family services for infants and toddlers who are at-risk or disabled.* Austin: Pro-Ed.

Hanson, M. J., & Lynch, E. W. (1992). Family diversity: Implications for policy and practice. *Topics in Early Childhood Special Education, 12*(3), 283–306.

Hanson, M. J., & Schwarz, R. H. (1978). Results of a longitudinal intervention program for Down's syndrome infants and their families. *Education and Training of the Mentally Retarded, 13,* 403–407.

Harbin, G. L. (1993). Family issues of children with disabilities: How research and theory have modified practice in intervention. In N. J. Anastasiow & S. Harel (Eds.), *At-risk infants: Interventions, families, and research* (pp. 101–114). Baltimore: Paul H. Brookes.

Harrison, H., & Kositsky, A. (1983). *The premature baby book: A parent's guide to coping and caring in the first years.* New York: St. Martin's Press.

Hedlund, R. (1989). Fostering positive interactions between parents and infants. *Teaching Exceptional Children, 21*(4), 45–48.

Hunt, M., Cornelius, P., Leventhal, P., Miller, P., Murray, T., & Stoner, G. (1990). *Into our lives.* Akron, OH: Children's Hospital Medical Center.

Johnson-Martin, N. M., Jens, K. G., Attermeier, S. M., & Hacker, B. J. (1991). *The Carolina Curriculum for Infants and Toddlers with Special Needs*, (2nd ed.). Baltimore, MD: Paul H. Brookes.

Kaufmann, R. K., & McGonigel, M. J. (1991). Identifying family concerns, priorities, and resources. In M. J. McGonigel, R. K. Kaufmann, & B. H. Johnson (Eds.), *Guidelines and recommended practices for the Individualized Family Service Plan* (2nd ed.), (pp. 47–56). Bethesda, MD: Association for the Care of Children's Health.

Kohrman, A. F. (1990). Bringing home a medically complex baby: Psychological issues for families, caretakers, and professionals. *Zero to Three, 11*(2), 36–41.

Lehr, D. H. (1989). Educational programming for young children with the most severe disabilities. In F. Brown & D. H. Lehr (Eds.), *Persons with profound disabilities: Issues and practices* (pp. 213–237). Baltimore: Paul H. Brookes.

LeLaurin, K. (1992). Infant and toddler models of service delivery: Are they detrimental for some children and families? *Topics in Early Childhood Special Education, 12*(1), 82–104.

Lillie, D. L., Trohanis, P. L., & Goin, K. W. (Eds.). (1976). *Teaching parents to teach.* New York: Walker and Company.

McCamman, S., & Rues, J. (1990). Nutrition monitoring and supplementation. In J. C. Graff, M. M. Ault, D. Guess, M. Taylor, & B. Thompson, *Health care for students with disabilities: An illustrated medical guide for the classroom* (pp. 79–118). Baltimore: Paul H. Brookes.

McDonnell, A., & Hardman, M. (1988). A synthesis of "best practice" guidelines for early childhood services. *Journal of the Division for Early Childhood, 12*(4), 328–341.

McGonigel, M. J. (1991). Philosophy and conceptual framework. In M. J. McGonigel, R. K. Kaufmann, & B. H. Johnson (Eds.), *Guidelines and recommended practices for the Individualized Family Service Plan* (2nd ed.), (pp. 7–14). Bethesda, MD: Association for the Care of Children's Health.

McGonigel, M., Kaufmann, R. K., & Johnson, B. H. (Eds.). (1991). *Guidelines and recommended practices for the Individualized Family Service Plan* (2nd ed.). Bethesda, MD: Association for the Care of Children's Health.

Meisels, S. J. (1992). Early intervention: A matter of context. *Zero to Three. 12*(3), 1–6.

Musick, J. S. (1990). Adolescents as mothers: The being and the doing. *Zero to Three, 11*(2), 21–28.

National Center for Family-Centered Care. (1990). *What is family-centered care?* Washington, DC: ACCH.

Noonan, M. J., & McCormick, L. (1993). *Early intervention in natural environments: Methods and procedures.* Pacific Grove, CA: Brooks/Cole Publishing Co.

Olson, D. H., Russell, H. I., Barnes, H., Larsen, A., Muxen, M., & Wilson, M. (1983). *Families: What makes them work.* Beverly Hills: Sage Publications.

Public Law 94-142 (1975).

Public Law 99-457 (1986).

Public Law 101-476 (1990).

Public Law 102-119. (1991).

Rappaport, J. (1984). Studies in empowerment: Introduction to the issues. In J. Rappaport, C. Swift, & R. Hess (Eds.), *Studies in empowerment: Steps toward understanding and action* (pp. 1–37). New York: Haworth Press.

Rose, T. L., Calhoun, M. L., & Ladage, L. (1989). Helping young children respond to caregivers. *Teaching Exceptional Children, 21*(4), 48–51.

Rubin, R. R., Fisher III, J. J., & Doering, S. G. (1980). *Ages one and two: Your toddler.* New York: Collier Books

Sameroff, A. J., & Chandler, M. J. (1975). Reproductive risk and the continuum of caretaking causality. In F. D. Horowitz, (Ed.), *Review of child development research* (Vol. 4, pp. 187–244). Chicago University: University of Chicago Press.

Shearer, D. E., & Shearer, M. S. (1976). The Portage Project: A model for early childhood intervention. In T. D. Tjossem (Ed.), *Intervention strategies for high risk infants and young children* (pp. 335–350). Baltimore: University Park Press.

Simeonsson, R. J., Olley, J. G., & Rosenthal, S. L. (1987). Early intervention for children with autism. In M. J. Guralnick & F. C. Bennett (Eds.), *The effectiveness of early intervention for at-risk and handicapped children* (pp. 275–296). Orlando, FL: Academic Press.

Stile, S., Cole, J., & Garner, A. (1979). Maximizing parental involvement in programs for exceptional children: Strategies for education and related service personnel. *Journal of the Division for Early Childhood, 1*, 68–82.

Summers, J. A., Behr, S. K., & Turnbull, A. P. (1989). Positive adaptation and coping strength of families who have children with disabilities. In

G. H. Singer & L. K. Irvin (Eds.), *Support for caregiving families: Enabling positive adaptation to disabilities* (pp. 27–40). Baltimore: Paul H. Brookes.

Turnbull, A. P., Summers, J. A., & Brotherson, M. J. (1986). Family life cycle: Theoretical and empirical implications and future directions for families with mentally retarded members. In J. J. Gallagher & P. M. Vietze (Eds.), *Families of handicapped persons: Research, programs, and policy issues* (pp. 45–65). Baltimore: Paul H. Brookes.

Turnbull, A. P., & Turnbull, H. R. (1986). Stepping back from early intervention: An ethical perspective. *Journal of the Division for Early Childhood, 10*(2), 106–117.

Turnbull, A. P., Turnbull, H. R., Summers, J. A., Brotherson, M. J., & Benson, H. A. (1986). *Families, professionals, and exceptionality: A special partnership*. Columbus, OH: Merrill Publishing.

Chapter **6**

Programs for Preschool Children

Three- through five-year olds are known for their active, energetic, enthusiastic, and noisy exploration of the world around them. While often shy or in need of adult assistance or reassurance, preschoolers enjoy enlarging their world to include regular classmates and playmates, and to building relationships with adults beyond their immediate family and caregivers (Allen & Marotz, 1989). As with younger children, this age is characterized by rapid physical and developmental growth. Preschoolers not only learn many new skills, they also become much more sophisticated in both applying skills and learning new ones. Preschoolers are absorbed with play and with becoming more independent in daily routines. Play and daily routines are the natural contexts for learning for children of this age (Rubin & Fisher, 1982). As they approach school age children become increasingly interested in the wider world, in the relationships between people and events, and in the mystery of books and reading (Caplan & Caplan, 1983). Most preschoolers are very social and want to be included in everything that their family, classmates, and friends do. While many preschool age children attend preschool or daycare programs, the number of hours of participation varies widely (Willer et al., 1991). A number of preschoolers continue to spend much of their time at home with family members. If families have developed close relationships while the child was an infant and toddler, the preschool years are often a very enjoyable time for both parents and children.

For the parents of a child with severe developmental delays or disabilities the preschool years may present new challenges. The gap between what their child and typically developing children of the same age can do is noticeably widening. Having their child attend a preschool special education program that includes normally developing age peers may accentuate this realization, particularly if the child has been at home or in a mixed-age family daycare program up to this point in time. There may also be the adjustment to meeting and conversing with the parents of typically developing children

---

WINDOW 6-1   Beginning Preschool

As my daughter's third birthday approached, I lived in dread, not wishing to leave the familiar, comfortable environment of her infant program. The infant program had become home away from home for me. It was supportive and intimate. I had made some lifelong friendships, as well as had established a comfortable routine in our lives. I saw making the transition to a preschool program in the school district as an extremely traumatic experience, second only to learning of Amy's diagnosis.

What were my fears? First, I was concerned that my husband and I, along with professionals, would be deciding the future of our child. How could we play God? Would our decisions be the right ones? Second, I feared loss of control, as I would be surrendering my child to strangers—first to the school district's intake assessment team and then to the preschool teacher. The feeling of being at the mercy of professionals was overwhelming. In addition, I had more information to absorb and a new system with which to become familiar. Finally, I feared the "label" that would be attached to my child and feared that this label would lower the world's expectations of her.

The first week Amy attended her new preschool was wonderful, as I was in the classroom with her everyday. Then came the reality of being in the classroom only one day a week. That change was most difficult, as I was going through separation anxiety. I was convinced that the staff was incompetent, and I had made the worst decision possible. However, the staff sensed my anxieties and were extremely patient and cooperative. We have now established a pattern of mutual support and partnership. I feel fortunate, as my daughter has done remarkably well in the preschool.

Patti Wood, parent

From: Hanline, M.F. & Knowlton, A. (1988). A collaborative model for providing support to parents during their child's transition from infant intervention to preschool special education public school programs. *Journal of the Division for Early Childhood, 12* (2), 116–125.

who are their child's classmates. The parents of other children they met in the early intervention program were probably also the parents of a child with developmental delays. The public school years begin to seem much closer, with all of the attendant concerns about whether the child will be accepted by other children, where will they attend school, and how productive and enjoyable will the whole school experience be for their child. For some families getting their child ready for school becomes a focus. Other families may struggle with the realization that their child will not be "ready" to blend in to a kindergarten classroom, no matter how hard they, the child, and their child's preschool teachers work. While clearly not the intent of federal legislation, most families realize that the decisions that they and school district teams make about their child's initial school placement may have substantial impact not only on the type of curricular goals that are emphasized for their child (e.g. academic or adaptive) but also on the amount of time their child will be educated with peers without disabilities.

Even though the preschool years introduce a new set of concerns and stresses for families of young children with severe developmental delays, there is often diminished program support for other family members. While early intervention has become increasingly family-centered, preschool programs continue to be primarily child-focused and to be offered in center-based settings. However positive the parent-teacher-team relationship, the increased focus on the child may make parents feel less supported and as though the family issues and contexts are treated as less central or less well understood. This chapter will examine these issues which are unique to preschool programs, and also provide an overview of (a) the historical and legislative basis for preschool services, (b) the educational needs of preschool children, and (c) the characteristics and features of best practice preschool programs for young children with severe developmental delays and their families.

Focus 1:

What types of services were made available in the past to preschoolers with developmental disabilities and their families?

The History of Preschool Services

Types of Services and Service Delivery Models

The history of preschool programs for children with severe developmental delays is similar to that described for infants and toddlers and their families in Chapter 5. Until the last forty or fifty years, most individuals with severe disabilities, including preschool age children, were either living in institutions or at home with their families (Gentry & Olsen, 1985; Harbin, 1993). If children lived at home they were usually without the benefit of either specialized services or access to public education or community programs. During the late 1950s through the mid-1980s, there were growing opportunities for children with disabilities to attend preschool special education programs or to access other specialized services (Gentry & Olsen, 1985). However, these opportunities were not consistently available, and generally appear to have been less available to young children with severe disabilities and their families (Bailey & Bricker, 1984; Bricker & Kaminski, 1986). Many preschoolers with severe disabilities were not able to attend preschool programs that would provide appropriate special education and related services until after P. L. 99-457 was enacted in 1986.

Preschool special education programs have traditionally been organized as center-based, home-based, or combined home- and center-based programs (see Thurman & Widerstrom, 1990 for a thorough description and numerous examples of early childhood intervention models). Center-based preschool programs usually provide IEP-based special instruction and related services within a variety of preschool classroom activities and routines. Part of this intervention might be planned to ensure many practice opportunities, and part of it might include providing just one or two opportunities for a child to use a specific targeted skill throughout the entire class activity. Window 6-2 provides an example of how IEP goals might be infused within preschool activities and routines.

Preschool classes may be part-day or full-day and may meet every day or only a few times during a week. Examples of center-based model demonstration projects that have enrolled preschool children with severe disabilities include the Infant, Toddler, and Preschool Research and Intervention Program (Bricker & Bricker, 1973, 1976), The Down

WINDOW 6-2 Joshua's Day at Preschool

Joshua is a three-year-old child with severe and multiple disabilities. He lives with his Mother and Father, and will have a new brother or sister in a few months. His mother stays home with Joshua when he is not attending preschool. Joshua attends a community preschool program located in his local elementary school. Joshua's family and preschool team (which includes his parents, the community preschool teacher, a preschool special education consulting teacher, an instructional aide, a physical therapist, a speech and language pathologist, and an occupational therapist) have identified high priority goals on Joshua's IEP. These goals include:

1. maintaining head control, or keeping his head erect when properly positioned,
2. supported sitting, or maintaining his balance when supported at hips and trunk by an adult or adaptive chair,
3. purposefully reaching for objects or people when in a prone position,
4. using adaptive switches to activate toys and media,

5. playing functionally with three or more toys, i.e. playing with them in their usual or intended fashion; toys must be selected so that batting, pushing, or tapping motions are all that is needed for play,
6. responding to peer initiations through eye contact, facial expression, and/or vocalization,
7. using lip closure to pull food off a spoon when eating snacks and meals, and
8. using a purposeful reach to request desired objects, activities, and interactions with people.

The matrix below lists Joshua's preschool class schedule down the left side of the matrix. A short description of Joshua's IEP goals are listed across the top. Checks are used to indicate for which IEP goals intervention can most naturally be included in the context of each of the daily preschool activities. The abbreviations at the right hand side of the page show the physical therapist's recommendations for positioning Joshua during each activity.

Joshua's Preschool Day	GOALS head control	supported sitting	purposeful reach, prone	uses switch to activate	funct. use 3+ toys	responds to peers	pulls food off spoon	uses reach to request	Recommended Position
9:00—Arrival (coats off, diaper change, free play)	✓	✓				✓		✓	WC
9:15—Circle (Finger plays, weather, show and tell)	✓	✓				✓			SS
9:30—Manipulative Toy or Block Area	✓	✓	✓	✓	✓	✓		✓	SS PB
9:50—Science or Social Studies Activities (Preacademic skills and stories included)	✓				✓	✓		✓	WC
10:10—Outdoor Play (Gross motor activities)	✓				✓	✓		✓	PS or M

(continued)

WINDOW 6-2 *Continued*

Joshua's Preschool Day	GOALS head control	supported sitting	purposeful reach, prone	uses switch to activate	funct. use 3+ toys	responds to peers	pulls food off spoon	uses reach to request	Recommended Position
10:30—Imaginative Play (Diaper change included)	✓		✓	✓	✓	✓		✓	PB
11:00—Snack	✓					✓	✓	✓	WC
11:20—Art or Music	✓	(✓)		(✓)		✓		✓	WC or SS
11:50—Closing Circle	✓	✓				✓			SS d WC
12:05—Bus to Go Home									

Positioning Abbreviations

PS—Prone Stander
PB—Prone on Bolster
WC—Wheel Chair
SS—Adult Supported Sitting
M—Mat (range of motion)

Excerpt adapted from: McDonnell, A. (1990). *Selecting play and natural routines as contexts for goal-based interventions for infants, toddlers, and preschoolers with disabilities.* University of Utah, Department of Special Education, Salt Lake City.

Syndrome Program at the Experimental Education Unit at the University of Washington (Hayden & Dmitriev, 1975; Hayden & Haring, 1976), The Teaching Research Infant and Child Center Data-based Classroom for the Moderately and Severely Handicapped (Fredericks, et al, 1977), and The Social Integration Program (Rule et al., 1987) which served children enrolled in community daycare centers. Some advantages for center-based programs include the opportunity for the child with disabilities to interact with other children of the same age, the provision of some respite or daycare help for the child's family, the opportunity for specially trained professionals to work directly with the child and to team with each other on intervention issues, and the opportunity the child receives to become competent in the many skills needed to successfully learn and get along with others in a classroom environment before beginning kindergarten.

Home-based programs for preschoolers with disabilities have usually concentrated on teaching other family members to carry out intervention within the child's home, either in teaching sessions or within the context of daily family routines. Figure 6-1 provides an example of how intervention for Joshua's IEP goals could be infused into his family's typical activities and routines. Given an option, many families choose to have preschool age children spend most of their time at home with their family and home-based programs support these families if they choose to be the primary inter-

Recommended Position

Time / Activity									Recommended Position
7:00 – Wake-up cuddle, diaper change	✔	✔	✔						
7:20 – Breakfast, watch Mom clean up kitchen	✔					✔	✔		WC
8:00 – Get ready for school, play with Mom	✔	✔		✔	✔				
8:40 – Bus arrives									WC
12:15 – Diaper change, lunch	✔					✔	✔		WC
12:45 – Story or singing							(✔)		
1:00 – Nap									
3:30 – Diaper change, range of motion	✔	✔					(✔)		M
4:00 – Snack	✔					✔	✔		WC
4:30 – Play w/Mom (or have friend over)	✔	✔	✔	✔	✔	(✔)			SS, PB
5:00 – Play by self, watch Mom cook dinner	✔		✔	✔	✔				SS or PB
5:30 – Sit w/Dad while he watches the news	✔	✔			(✔)		(✔)		SS PB
6:00 – Diaper change, dinner	✔					✔	✔		WC
6:45 – Bath	✔	✔			✔		✔		
7:15 – Play with Mom or Dad, diaper change	✔					✔	✔		SS PB
7:45 – Story, singing							(✔)		
8:00 – Bedtime									

Positioning Abbreviations

PS - Prone Stander
PB - Prone on Bolster
WC - Wheel Chair
SS - Adult Supported Sitting
M - Mat (range of motion)

FIGURE 6-1   A Day at Home for Joshua Family/Child Routine

ventionist(s) for their child at this age. Home-based programs may also be more appropriate for children with very fragile or failing health, when exposure to infectious diseases carried by other children could be a threat. Prior to federally mandated preschool special education programs, homebased programs were also sometimes favored because they could be less expensive to operate, particularly in rural areas or for children with low-incidence disabling conditions (Bailey & Simeonsson, 1988). An example of a home-based model program which included some preschool age children with severe disabilities is the Portage Project, originally developed in rural Wisconsin (Shearer & Shearer, 1976). Not all home-based programs have concentrated on teaching family members to be interventionists for their child. Some programs have introduced intervenors into the home to provide support for the child and family (Thurman & Wiederstrom, 1990). While many people favor home-based over center-based programs for infants and toddlers, some preschool classroom experience is generally favored for three-, four-, and five-year olds, unless individual family preferences or other extenuating circumstances prevent this from being a desirable option.

Many preschool programs combine center and home-based components, for example having children attend classes three or four days a week and having staff do home visits or parent education groups an additional one or two days. Prior to the implementation of P. L. 99-457 preschool programs generally made commitments to the funding agency outlining the range and types of service delivery options they would provide. With the 1986 passage of P. L. 99-457, the IEP became the document that legally determined the amount and type of services the individual child would receive. Changing philosophies about family-centered early intervention and the importance of inclusive preschool and early childhood programs have expanded and modified the ways service delivery models are conceptualized.

Philosophical and Curricular Models

Several different philosophical and curricular models have defined the ways in which preschool special education programs have approached intervention for children and families. These models have included the developmental, behavioral, cognitive, and functional/ecological curricular approaches (Hanson & Lynch, 1989). Interventionists often blend these models to varying degrees at the program implementation level. Bailey & Wolery (1992) summarized the assumptions of three of these perspectives as they are related to children, the nature of learning and development, and assessment and intervention (see Figure 6-2). The ecological model has gained increasing favor in recent years (Bailey & Wolery, 1992), and is particularly valid and useful for children with severe and/or multiple delays or disabilities (Hanson & Lynch, 1989). The ecological model is holistic, blends many of the strengths of the other perspectives, and is applicable to children with widely varying abilities, interests, and family and cultural backgrounds.

In the past, children with severe and profound disabilities most likely attended preschool programs that used a developmental or functional curricular orientation as the basis for selecting intervention goals and emphasized the use of behavioral teaching strategies for intervention (for recent reviews of model evaluation reports and research studies see Guralnick & Bricker,1987, and Simeonsson, Olley, & Rosenthal,

Theoretical Perspective	Basic Assumptions About the Nature of Children	Basic Assumptions About Learning and Development	Assessment Implications	Intervention Implications
Developmental	Children are born with an intrinsic motivation to explore and master the environment. Skills emerge in a relatively predictable sequence.	Development is primarily a result of physical maturation. Competence is gained through self-initiated exploration and play.	Document the extent to which the child has attained specific developmental milestones.	Arrange the environment and provide materials that are highly interesting to children and are most likely to facilitate competence in developmentally appropriate skills.
Behavioral	Children are born with the capacity to learn. The skills that a child displays emerge as a result of experiences with the environment. Biological and physiological processes also are acknowledged as important.	Antecedents and consequences serve to shape behavior. Children learn behaviors through repeated reinforcing interactions with the environment.	Identify the functional skills needed by the child to increase the likelihood of success in current and future environments.	Provide experiences and support that promotes success: Identify and use effective reinforcers to ensure rapid and efficient learning.
Ecological	Children influence and are influenced by the environment. Children inevitably are a part of a family system. Likewise, families are embedded within larger neighborhood, community, and institutional systems.	Development results from the complex interactions or transactions between children and the environment over time. Development cannot be examined in isolation, but rather must be examined over time and in the context of systems within which children and families function.	Determine the child's skills, the characteristics of the caregiving environment, and the family's needs, resources, expectations, and aspirations.	Provide services that support families and children in ways that are congruent with their ecology and are consistent with expressed family goals.

FIGURE 6-2 Three theoretical perspectives and their implications

From: Bailey, Jr., D. B., & Wolary, M. (1992). *Teaching infants and preschoolers with disabilities.* (2nd ed.) New York: MacMillan Publishing.

1987). As with model programs for infants and toddlers with disabilities and their families, many of these projects were originally funded through the federal government's Handicapped Children's Early Education Program (HCEEP). The HCEEP projects have been highly successful in many regards, with nearly 80 percent of the almost 600 funded demonstration projects continuing after federal funding ended (Bailey & Wolery, 1992). As a group, these programs and similar projects were successful in demonstrating that educational gains can be made by young children with severe and profound developmental disabilities if they have access to effective instruction or intervention, although they are likely to be proportionally smaller than the gains demonstrated by children with more mild to moderate developmental delays (Bailey & Bricker, 1984; Dunst, 1986; Guralnick, 1991; Guralnick & Bricker, 1987).

Models of Integration

The Infant, Toddler, and Pre-School Research and Intervention Program (Bricker & Bricker, 1973) was among the first programs to systematically integrate preschool children with disabilities with their typical peers. In the broadest sense, any program that actively mixes children with and without disabilities can be considered integrated (Odom & McEvoy, 1988). A variety of different approaches have been utilized to achieve integration, including *reverse mainstream, integrated*, and *fully mainstreamed or inclusive* preschool programs. These terms have been used in a variety of ways and to describe a wide range of organizational and teaching practices (Odom & McEvoy, 1988). For the purposes of this chapter, a common definition of each is included. Reverse mainstream preschool programs have usually been designed to meet the needs of children with disabilities and have "recruited" typically developing children to attend and serve as role models, peer interventionists, and/or playmates for the children with disabilities (Striefel, Killoran, & Quintero, 1991). In reverse mainstream preschool programs, the group of children is usually quite heterogenous, and often more than 50 percent of the enrolled children have developmental delays (Odom & McEvoy, 1988). The definition of integrated preschools, as distinct from reverse mainstream or inclusive programs, is probably the most ambiguous. Integrated preschools can be used to refer to a variety of arrangements which have resulted in part-time integration into a regular preschool class and part-time participation in special class or pull-out services. An example of an integrated preschool program would be one where children with moderate to severe developmental delays attend a special education preschool class adjacent to a Head Start classroom. The children with severe disabilities join the Head Start class for opening and closing circle, outdoor play, snack, music, and art, but also receive special instruction and individual therapy in the special preschool program. Fully mainstreamed or inclusive preschool programs are those that were designed to meet the needs of either typically developing children or *all* children, including those with developmental delays. These programs strive to meet the needs of the child with developmental delays within the "regular" or generic early childhood program, although this may involve the provision of substantial adaptation, individualized intervention, and/or support. In an inclusive preschool program the child with developmental delays would not usually spend parts of the classroom experience segregated from typically developing children. Children with developmental delays are substantially "outnumbered" in fully mainstreamed or inclusive preschool programs by typically developing children. The number of children with developmental delays in inclusive preschool programs would be expected to represent natural proportions, or the incidence of developmental delays in society as a whole.

Traditionally, children were believed to receive more intensive and specialized intervention in reverse mainstream or integrated programs, than would occur in fully mainstreamed programs (Striefel et al., 1991). However, as Taylor (1988) has pointed out, a location-based interpretation of intensity is conceptually flawed. It is perfectly possible to offer the same variety and intensity of services in an inclusive class as in a completely separate special class setting, although the manner in which such services are delivered may vary. Conversely, grouping children with severe and profound disabilities in a separate classroom does not assure a high quality or intensity of specialized instruction and therapy services; it only assures that children are isolated from the positive outcomes of being jointly educated with their typically developing peers.

Children with multiple or severe and profound disabilities have usually been the least likely to be included in integrated or inclusive preschool programs (Demchak & Drinkwater, 1992; Gentry & Olsen, 1985; Hanline, 1993). While it has not been customary to include children with the most intensive needs in generic early childhood programs, the foundation for this tradition is not rooted in unfavorable research results or in an individual assessment of children's educational or support needs (Demchak & Drinkwater, 1992; Strain, 1990). In listing several summary statements of what research tells us about preschool integration Strain (1990) comments that:

> *The sixth thing that we know is particularly troubling to those with administrative authority. There is no evidence that children with certain handicapping conditions or levels of disabilities make more or less good candidates for integration. Now obviously children with severe disabilities require more accommodations to maximize their growth and development. Here we have the root of the conventional wisdom that children with mild handicaps are better candidates for integration. What is true is that they may, only may, require less change in the structure and function of current service delivery to meet their learning needs. (Strain, 1990, p. 293).*

Issues related to educating preschool children with severe disabilities in inclusive settings will be discussed in a later section of this chapter.

The Influence of Federal Legislation on Preschool Programs

During the last twenty-five years, federal legislation has had a substantial impact on the availability and quality of preschool services for young children with disabilities (for a recent comprehensive review see Hebbler, Smith, & Black, 1991). As discussed in Chapter 3, P. L. 99-457, Section 619 has had the greatest impact on preschool special education services, by extending the mandate to provide appropriate special education and related services to all eligible three- to five-year olds. The earlier Education of the

Handicapped Act (P. L. 94-142) paved the way for this new mandate by having established Preschool Incentive Grants for the purpose of encouraging states to establish preschool programs for children with disabilities. As with programs for infants and toddlers and their families an early positive influence was P. L. 90-538, the Handicapped Children's Early Education Assistance Act. This Act established the Handicapped Children's Early Education Program (HCEEP) which stimulated the development of model programs, curricula, and assessments, as well as evaluation and research and the continuation and expansion of model programs to additional young children with disabilities and their families. The reader is encouraged to review information in Chapter 3 on Preschool Incentive Grants and the P. L. 99-457 requirements for preschool special education services. This chapter will briefly discuss Head Start legislation, which has also had a significant impact on preschool programs for children with disabilities.

Head Start Legislation and Regulations

"The major significance of the original Head Start legislation was not the substance of the law but what it represented. It was the first indication of legislative concern for early education for children with special needs and the beginning of a national expansion and consolidation of early intervention efforts" (Noonan & McCormick, 1993, p. 8). No specific mention of children with disabilities was made in the original 1966 Head Start legislation. However, following the 1972 passage of P. L. 92-424 (the Economic Opportunity amendments) Head Start programs were required to ensure that at least 10 percent of the enrollment opportunities were reserved for children with disabilities. Comparatively few children with severe disabilities were enrolled in Head Start as the result of this act. Most of the openings were used to enroll children with mild to moderate disabilities. Nevertheless, the role of Head Start in providing integration opportunities for young children with developmental delays or disabilities has been an important one, and one that is likely to become even more critical in the future.

In January of 1993, the new Head Start Disability Regulations were released. The regulations require Head Start Programs to (a) develop a disabilities service plan to meet the special needs of children with disabilities and their families, (b) designate a coordinator of services for children with disabilities, and (c) arrange or provide necessary special education and related services for eligible children with disabilities, unless these services are already being provided by another agency. Interagency cooperation is specifically encouraged as a part of the regulations, and Head Start programs are reminded of relevant state and federal regulations or standards governing services provided to three- through five-year olds with disabilities and their families. Two components of the regulations are particularly likely to make enrollment in Head Start Programs more available to children with severe or profound disabilities, when an IEP team has determined that this is the most appropriate placement for the child.

Among other things, the regulation . . . :

- States that a grantee *"must not deny placement on the basis of a disability or its severity to any child when:*

   1. The parents wish to enroll the child,

2. *The child meets the Head Start age and income eligibility criteria,*
3. *Head Start is an appropriate placement according to the child's IEP, and*
4. *The program has space to enroll more children, even though the program has made 10 percent of its enrollment opportunities available to children with disabilities."*

- *Indicates enrollment cannot be denied because of staff attitudes, and/or apprehension, inaccessibility of facilities, need to access additional resources to serve a specific child, unfamiliarity with a disabling condition or special equipment, such as a prosthesis, or need for personalized special services, such as feeding or suctioning, and assistance with toileting, including catheterization, diapering, and toilet training. (Walsh, 1993, p. 3).*

Current Status of Preschool Programs

During the last few years preschool personnel in many school districts and states have concentrated on beginning or expanding programs in order to implement the recent federal mandate for preschool special education services. Some of the challenges facing school districts and state offices of education during this time include: (a) providing for increasing numbers of children; (b) hiring qualified preschool special education teachers and related service providers; (c) considering how to offer preschoolers opportunities to be educated in the LRE when many districts educate only a limited number of nondisabled preschoolers, if any; (d) locating classroom space and funds for personnel, transportation, and other costs, which are only partially funded through new federal funds; (e) developing procedures for transitioning children into preschool from early intervention and for transitioning children into school programs as they reach kindergarten or school age; (f) establishing child find and eligibility procedures, which differ from those previously used for special education; and (g) examining due process procedures used with preschoolers and their families to assure that they meet all of the requirements of IDEA. Given these many challenges, it is not surprising that in many parts of the country extensive efforts have been directed to getting universal preschool programs for children with developmental delays in place and to assuring that they are in compliance with the requirements of IDEA. The next decade should be an exciting time for preschool programs. Now that programs are established there will be an opportunity to devote more time and resources to focusing on providing an enjoyable and effective experience for children and their families. The next section of this chapter will examine the educational needs of preschool children and the goals of preschool services, as well as the characteristics of best practice programs for preschoolers with developmental delays and their families.

Issues Related to the Educational Needs of Preschoolers with Severe Disabilities

Preschool children with severe developmental delays or disabilities have many of the same educational needs as typically developing children of the same age. These educational needs include developmentally appropriate learning experiences, inclusion in learning and social environments that value and respect individuality and diversity, and comprehensive and individually appropriate educational intervention.

Focus 2:

What is developmentally appropriate practice and how does it apply to preschool children with severe disabilities?

Developmentally Appropriate Learning Experiences

Like other preschoolers, children with severe developmental delays or disabilities need to have access to high quality, developmentally appropriate learning experiences. In order to assist early childhood educators in planning and providing these learning experiences, the National Association for the Education of Young Children (NAEYC) developed a paper (Bredekamp, 1986) defining and describing *developmentally appropriate practice (DAP)*, which has since been revised and used as the basis for a position paper and guidelines and recommendations for assessment, curriculum, training, and accreditation efforts [e.g. Bredekamp, 1987; Bredekamp, S., & Rosegrant, T. (1992); National Association for the Education of Young Children (NAEYC) and the National Association of Early Childhood Specialists in State Departments of Education (NAECS/SDE), 1991]. NAEYC is the largest national organization for early childhood professionals and other interested individuals dedicated to the education of children between the ages of birth and eight years. Through its policy, advocacy, and informational activities NAEYC has had a substantial influence on the way childcare and educational services for young children are conceptualized and implemented in the United States. Within the NAEYC position paper, developmentally appropriate practice guidelines are used to define appropriate learning environments and experiences for young children as distinct from those provided to children in the upper elementary grades, and intermediate and secondary school. These distinctions include (a) a need for learning activities that are initiated and directed by the child and supported by the teacher, and (b) an emphasis on learning through play, exploration, social interaction, and inquiry, rather than directive teaching to specific goals (Bredekamp, 1987; Carta et al., 1991; NAEYC & NAECS/SDE, 1991; Wolery, Holcombe, Venn, & Werts, 1992).

Developmentally appropriate practice has sometimes been interpreted to stipulate the use of learning environments, expectations, and practices that are based strictly on the child's achievement of "normal" developmental milestones; i.e., if you act like a two-year old, your learning environment should be structured in ways that are congruent to those that would facilitate learning for a two-year-old. This interpretation of developmentally appropriate practice conflicts with recommendations for age appropriate practice in special education (McDonnell & Hardman, 1988) and would be especially restrictive when applied to children with severe disabilities whose developmental skill level, by definition, is significantly delayed from their typically developing chronological age peers. *Age appropriateness* deliberately emphasizes an individual's chronological age over their "mental age" or developmental level. This perspective values the idea that a four-year old is first of all a four-year old, regardless of the presence or absence of disabilities, and should be treated as such, including being involved with the same kinds of instructional opportunities, materials, patterns of interaction, and social and instructional groupings as are typically developing peers of the same chronological age (Fink, 1982; McDonnell & Hardman, 1988).

While age appropriateness and an interpretation of developmentally appropriate practice that ties such practice exclusively to normal development may be in conflict, there are many ways to create learning experiences for young children that are *both* developmentally appropriate and age appropriate. For example, Mark is a five-year-old child with limited gross and fine motor movement and control. His cognitive development is similar to a typically developing eleven-month old. Mark is learning to use adaptive switches to activate toys and a radio or tape player. Mark enjoys listening to music and toys that make noise and move simultaneously. Mark would enjoy the lullabies and battery-operated lamb and giraffe toys that might usually be purchased for an eleven-month old. However, he also enjoys Raffi songs and songs from the Disney movies, as well as automated race tracks and battery-operated dinosaurs and robots. The latter selection of music and toys would also interest other children his age, and could provide some familiar and pleasurable experiences for Mark to enjoy in classroom and play settings with typical peers.

The applicability of DAP to young children with disabilities has sparked a lively debate in early childhood special education and early childhood education journals and professional forums (e.g. Carta et al., 1991; Johnson & Johnson, 1982; Kostelnik, 1992; Mallory, 1992; NAEYC & NAECS/SDE, 1991; Wolery, Strain, & Bailey, 1992; Wolery et al., 1993). One of the primary concerns expressed by many special educators is that while empirical research supports the effectiveness of intensive, focused and/or directive intervention for young children with disabilities, at this point in time there is no established body of research to support the effectiveness of DAP for young children with disabilities or developmental delays. In a research review on DAP and the efficacy of early intervention with children with disabilities, Carta et al. (1991) comment, "In summary, these studies have not provided convincing evidence that teacher-directed instruction is harmful, nor have they substantiated that adherence to developmentally appropriate practice (e.g, child-directed and nonacademic in focus) leads to better outcomes for average children, or more importantly, *for children who are at risk or who have disabilities*" (p. 10). Additionally, "The studies cited above, as well as many others, provide empirical support for the effectiveness of structured interventions for young children with special needs, and demonstrate that failure to intervene places children at relatively greater risk for developmental decline and restricted educational opportunities (Guralnick & Bennet, 1987)." (p. 11–12). Taken together these are serious issues for families and professionals who are concerned about individuals with disabilities and the important impact that effective early intervention can have on their lives.

While there are many commonalities between quality indicators or recommended practices in developmentally appropriate early childhood education and early childhood special education, at this time there are also significant differences or points of divergence (Carta et al., 1991; Wolery et al., 1992, 1993). Both DAP and best practice

POINT OF INTEREST 6-1

Read the following examples of recommended goals for children from the most influential professional organization for educators of young children.

A sample* set of goals from "Guidelines for Appropriate Curriculum Content and Assessment in Programs Serving Children Ages 3 Through 8"

Responsible adults want children to:

Develop a positive self-concept and attitude toward learning, self-control, and a sense of belonging

Develop curiosity about the world, confidence as a learner, creativity and imagination, and personal initiative

Develop relationships of mutual trust and respect with adults and peers, understand perspectives of other people, and negotiate and apply rules of group living

Understand and respect social and cultural diversity

Know about the community and social roles

Use language to communicate effectively and to facilitate thinking and learning

Become literate individuals who gain satisfaction as well as information from reading and writing

Represent ideas and feelings through pretend play, drama, dance and movement, music, art and construction

Think critically, reason, and solve problems

Construct understanding of relationships among objects, people, and events such as classifying, ordering, number, space, and time

Construct knowledge of the physical world, manipulate objects for desired effects, and understand cause and effect relationships

Acquire knowledge of and appreciation for the fine arts, humanities, and sciences

Become competent in management of their bodies and acquire basic physical skills, both gross motor and fine motor

Gain knowledge about the care of their bodies and maintain a desirable level of health and fitness

*For illustrative purposes only—not an official position.

Source: A position statement of the National Association for the Education of Young Children (NAEYC) and the National Association of Early Childhood Specialists in State Departments of Education (NAECS/SDE). Adopted November, 1990.

Consider this:

1. How many of these goals seem realistic and/or functional for a preschool age child with severe or profound disabilities?
2. In what ways would the inclusion of one or more children with severe or profound disabilities in a preschool educational program assist typically developing children in meeting these goals?
3. What might be some of the potential advantages and disadvantages for a preschool age child with severe or profound disabilities in attending an inclusive preschool program with broad and high expectations for all children? What could teachers and parents do to help the child benefit from the advantages and to minimize any potential disadvantages?

recommendations in early childhood special education are evolving (NAEYC & NAECS/SDE, 1991; Wolery et al., 1993), and are being heavily influenced by one another through an unprecedented amount of professional dialogue and collaboration, such as that between NAEYC and DEC. Perhaps the most accurate summary of many early childhood special educators viewpoints at this time is provided by Carta et al. (1991) and Wolery et al. (1992); i.e., that DAP is "appropriate but not sufficient" for children with disabilities. Appropriate but not sufficient means that enrollment in a high-quality preschool which implements DAP is an appropriate and desirable beginning for children with special needs, but that the educational experience can only be fully appropriate or sufficient if it also includes implementation of the types of intervention practices that have been repeatedly demonstrated to be effective with children with disabilities or developmental delays.

Inclusive Learning Environments

A second educational need that preschoolers with severe developmental delays share with normally developing peers is the opportunity to learn and develop friendships in inclusive educational, home, and community settings. The underlying rationale for inclusion was presented in Chapter two, and applies to preschool-age children. Many people feel that preschool is a very important time to implement inclusive programs, because it is the time that many children first learn to participate in classroom activities and to interact with a number of similar age peers. If children always attend programs that include children with developmental delays or disabilities, then there is essentially no need to "change attitudes" or "teach acceptance" or get children "ready" to be mainstreamed because inclusion will simply seem natural to the children. While there are methodological flaws in many research studies, and variability in research results, ". . . several recent reviews of the research on [preschool] mainstreaming all have concluded that mainstreaming can be implemented successfully and almost always results in positive outcomes. . . ." (Bailey & Wolery, 1992, p. 50). Not only do the vast majority of studies indicate that the developmental outcomes of integrated and fully mainstreamed programs are at least as positive as those for special segregated early childhood programs, they appear to be superior in some important respects. For example, a number of studies have found integrated or mainstreamed programs to be more successful in facilitating the frequency and competence of social, communicative, and play behavior on the part of children with developmental delays (e.g., Cooke, Ruskus, Apolloni, & Peck, 1981; Esposito & Koorland, 1989; Guralnick & Groom, 1987; Jenkins, Odom, & Speltz, 1989). It is important to note that no studies have documented negative outcomes for either developmentally delayed or typically developing children who have been enrolled in integrated or mainstream preschool programs (Bailey & McWilliam, 1990). In fact, a number of studies have documented positive developmental and attitudinal outcomes for preschoolers without disabilities (Guralnick, 1990; Hanline, 1993; McLean & Hanline, 1990; Odom & McEvoy, 1988). For recent reviews of the outcomes of integrated and/or inclusive preschool programs see Bailey & McWilliam (1990) and Odom & McEvoy (1988).

WINDOW 6-3   April's Preschool

April is a four-year-old child with autism who attends A Place for Children, a "regular" preschool/childcare program associated with the child development training program at the local community college. She lives with her mother and eight-year-old brother. Her parents are divorced and April's father lives out of state. She and her brother visit him for a month every summer. Her mother is employed full-time and April is enrolled in the full-day program at her preschool. Three other children with developmental delays are enrolled in other classrooms at April's preschool program and her school district pays for a teaching assistant to be on-site at the facility five hours a day to support the children, including carrying out individualized instruction within the various preschool activities. The teaching assistant is in April's class more than the other children's. April is the only one of the four children with severe developmental delays. The teaching assistant is supervised by an itinerant special education preschool teacher. A communication disorder specialist is also a part of April's preschool IEP team, as are the teacher and assistant teacher of the preschool program and April's parents.

April has moderate developmental delays in gross and fine motor skills, and severe developmental delays in cognitive, social, communication, and self-help skills. April is very physically active and has high rates of stereotypic behaviors such as hand flapping, jumping in place, and grimacing. She is interested in other children, and is affectionate with familiar adults and her older brother. April uses a few word approximations appropriately, and on occasion will spontaneously imitate the actions of other children and adults. She is not toilet trained and dislikes washing and grooming activities. April eats well and is able to dress and undress herself with some assistance. April likes to play with Legos and puzzles and hugs dolls and stuffed animals. She loves to swing and climb on playground equipment. April does not play games or engage in imaginative play at this time, although she seems to enjoy watching other children involved in these play activities. April will usually follow simple directions from a familiar adult if they first use her name.

April's preschool class has 20 children, and is staffed by one teacher, one assistant teacher, and one to three students in training, in addition to the part-time help from the special education teaching assistant. April is included in the ongoing preschool activities throughout the day. Except for snack and outdoor play times there are usually two or three activities going on simultaneously in the preschool class. Children are allowed to choose which activity they will join and most activities are planned to facilitate many opportunities for child initiation and interaction with each other and with the activity materials. If left to her own devices, April has a tendency to wander between activities at a very frequent rate, sometimes observing briefly before moving on, but often seeming to be very restless, and more interested in humming, hand flapping, and jumping in place than the very creative high-interest activities which are characteristic of the program she attends. The adults in April's preschool have learned to encourage April to make a choice and to then ask her to sit down near the center of the action. If she begins to engage in stereotypic activities they quickly redirect her to an activity that is more socially appropriate and more likely to be a learning experience for her. They work with the preschool special education teacher, the teaching assistant, and the communication disorders specialist to make sure that many teaching and practice opportunities on the skills on April's IEP are included throughout April's day. Because April is primarily working on communication, cognitive, and social goals it is easy for the early childhood educators to see how to include these within preschool activities; they are used to facilitating learning in these areas for other children throughout a variety of activities, although the other children are at a more sophisticated developmental level.

The other children in April's class have mixed reactions to her, just as they do to each other. Many of them have noticed that April often

WINDOW 6-3 *Continued*

behaves differently than other children in the class and have expressed curiosity about this. Some of the children ignore April, some are sometimes irritated by her humming or jumping, and others have shown interest in playing with April or in helping her learn to do things that they can do. The teachers have encouraged other children who have shown an interest in being April's friend or helping her learn things, but are always careful to insist that she be treated as another four-year old who is a part of their class. Some of the strategies her teachers have found most successful in helping the children relate to April are helping to interpret what she is saying, showing them how to help April play or communicate, and making suggestions on how they can include April in their play and learning activities. The

teachers have been pleased to see that a number of the children have become very good at understanding and helping April and that several children consider her to be a good friend.

During the last month that April has been in preschool she has been invited to play at another child's house and has also been invited to a birthday party. April's mom can see that April looks forward to preschool and seeing the other children, even though she isn't able to tell her mother much about what goes on during the day. April's teacher has started taking at least one instant photograph of April every day and writing a brief note on the back to tell what April is doing and who she is with. This has helped April and her mother be able to talk about her classmates and what happened in preschool that day.

Focus 3:

What policy statements have been made about preschoolers with developmental delays and inclusion? How well do these statements correspond to federal regulations related to educating preschoolers with disabilities in the least restrictive environment?

An example of the strong philosophical support for inclusive early childhood programs is provided by the Position Statement on Inclusion recently adopted and published by DEC (see Figure 6-3). This statement in no way makes an exception to the recommendation for full inclusion for children with severe or profound disabilities.

The reality of opportunities for inclusion for young children with severe and profound disabilities continues to be quite different; they are often excluded. One of the reasons for this gap between philosophical position and day-to-day reality is that inclusion in generic or mainstream early childhood programs is not required by federal regulations governing the education of preschoolers with disabilities in the Least Restrictive Environment. While children are to be educated "to the maximum extent possible" with children without disabilities, as with other special education programs intensive needs are often used to justify a special, segregated program placement. An additional challenge is faced by school districts in attempting to offer inclusive programs for preschoolers with developmental delays. Most school districts administer or have access to only a few preschool classes or programs for normally developing three-, four-, and five-year olds. Districts will need to expand their overall efforts to educate preschoolers or develop contractual arrangements with private preschool and child-

Inclusion, as a value, supports the right of all children, regardless of their diverse abilities, to participate actively in natural settings within their communities. A natural setting is one in which the child would spend time had he or she not had a disability. Such settings include but are not limited to home and family, play groups, child care, nursery schools, Head Start programs, kindergartens, and neighborhood school classrooms.

DEC believes in and supports full and successful access to health, social service, education, and other supports and services for young children and their families that promote full participation in community life. DEC values the diversity of families and supports a family guided process for determining services that are based on the needs and preferences of individual families and children.

To implement inclusive practices DEC supports: (a) the continued development, evaluation, and dissemination of full inclusion supports, services, and systems; (b) the development of preservice and inservice training programs that prepare families, administrators, and service providers to develop and work within inclusive settings; (c) collaboration among all key stakeholders to implement flexible fiscal and administrative procedures in support of inclusion; (d) research that contributes to our knowledge of state of the art services; and (e) the restructuring and unification of social, education, health, and intervention supports and services to make them more responsive to the needs of all children and families.

FIGURE 6-3   Position Statement on Inclusion

Source: Division for Early Childhood of The Council for Exceptional Children (Adopted: April, 1993)

care providers if they are to be able to educate preschool children in inclusive programs with natural proportions of children with and without developmental delays. At this time, federal regulations allow and in some ways encourage such arrangements but there are definite financial disincentives for districts in pursuing either of these options.

Comprehensive and Individually Appropriate Interventions

A third educational need for preschoolers with severe developmental delays is for comprehensive and individually appropriate intervention. While all children might in fact benefit from access to intensive and individualized intervention, most children will successfully learn and develop from a broad range of planned and unplanned learning activities, even if that learning and development is not at an optimal level. Because they experience so many more difficulties in both learning and applying new skills in a variety of meaningful contexts, it is critically important to facilitate the development of children with severe disabilities during the preschool years. Effectively facilitating this development requires the use of intervention strategies that have been demonstrated to be effective with learners with significant impairments. It also requires the frequent rather than sporadic or occasional use of these strategies. For example, for a preschool-age child with severe developmental delays, a teacher might try to plan for ten to twenty practice trials/day for each specific learning objective or IEP goal. (For goals like handwashing this would obviously be less often!). Some of the components of effective intervention for preschoolers with severe developmental delays include (a) the use of ecologically or environmentally based assessment, (b) family and team selection of priority IEP goals, (c) careful specification of intervention steps and strategies for meeting these IEP goals, (d) teaching within the context of natural caregiving, preschool, play, and family routines and activities, (e) using strategies which are not only effective in teaching new skills or behaviors, but that will help the child generalize and maintain use of those skills, and (f) monitoring the effectiveness of intervention strategies by assessing the child's performance in natural settings, how family members and peers perceive the child's progress, and the changes which have occurred in the child or family's life as a result of intervention. Several of these components will be described in this chapter. Complete descriptions of effective naturalistic intervention strategies for young children with severe developmental delays can be found in Bailey & Wolery (1992) and Noonan & McCormick (1993).

Focus 4:

Describe the major goals of preschool programs for children with disabilities.

Goals for Preschool Services

The goals for preschool services include many similarities to the early intervention goals discussed in Chapter 5. Four goals which are often stressed by families and educational programs during the preschool years include:

1. *Maximizing the child's development in a variety of important developmental areas.* The goal of maximizing development includes meeting specific high priority goals identified as a part of the child's IEP as well as creating learning environments that will facilitate learning and growth in many other important skills and activities. For most preschool children some of the important areas in which to facilitate development include social, communication, motor, cognitive, preacademic, self-care, play, and personal management. The learning and development that takes place in the preschool years creates a critical foundation for the school years. For preschoolers with severe developmental delays, part of maximizing development is the identification of effective alternatives for the behaviors or functions of behavior that child is unable to perform in the usual way. Some examples of alternatives or functional equivalents (Noonan & McCormick, 1993) that might be used by preschool children include (a) indicating words or ideas by pointing to a photo on a communication board, rather than talking, (b) pushing a switch to activate toys, rather than grasping and moving the usual on/off switches, (c) nodding yes/no rather than speaking, (d) or using a wheelchair to get places instead of walking.

2. *Developing the child's social interaction and classroom participation skills.* Many children have limited experiences with peers prior to entering preschool, and any experiences they have had have often been limited to a few familiar siblings, cousins, and neighbors, and/or other children attending the same family daycare or infant/toddler childcare program. Even if a child has regularly attended a center-based daycare program, they will face substantial adjustments to larger preschool classes which usually contain more structured activities and higher performance expectations than are found in toddler classes. One of the most important developmental tasks for preschool-age children is learning to establish successful relationships with peers, including learning to play together, share, stick up for yourself, communicate thoughts and feelings, and make and keep friends. These skills are not only important to being successful in school, but also form the basis of the child and adult friendships that are such an important contributor to an individual's enjoyment and quality of life. In addition to developing social skills and relationships with peers, preschool-age children need to learn to follow adult directions and classroom rules and routines, to ask for assistance appropriately, and to complete activities and tasks as requested by teachers without constant adult supervision or attention. The acquisition of such task-related skills may be even more important to kindergarten teachers than the child's play or social competence with peers (Walter & Vincent, 1982), and has resulted in their inclusion in the development of "survival skills" curricula for preschoolers with developmental delays (McCormick & Kawate, 1982; Rule, Fiechtl, & Innocenti, 1990; Vincent et al., 1980).

3. *Preparing the child for inclusive school placements and providing support for the transition to kindergarten or elementary school.* Maximizing the child's skill development, learning and practicing social skills with typical peers, and successfully adjusting to classroom patterns and expectations are important ways to prepare children for inclusive school placements. Additionally, it is important for the preschool team and the child's family to work collaboratively with the elementary school staff who will be responsible for educating the child when they enter kindergarten or first grade. Together the family, preschool team, and elementary team can plan for the preschool-kindergarten transition and assure that the child, their family, and the school staff have received the preparation and support necessary to make the transition as smooth and successful as possible for all concerned.

4. *Increasing community participation through support to family members and other caregivers.* One of the goals of preschool services primarily takes place outside of preschool classrooms. As the child with developmental delays gets older, families are often very anxious to return to employment, social, and recreational activities that they had participated in before the child was born. As the child with developmental delays becomes older, it is also important for the child to extend their experiences and social networks beyond the immediate family and preschool. While some families may wish to wait and many families will have begun the process during the infant/toddler years, preschool is a good time to support families in identifying and extending alternative caregivers so that family members have more flexibility to pursue their own interests. Similarly, these years are a very good time to identify community or neighborhood activities or relationships that their preschooler might enjoy. Examples of such activities might include swim or dance lessons, playing with neighborhood friends, joining a neighborhood soccer team, community outings with grandma, attending community childcare or preschool programs, or eating in restaurants once a week as a family. Similar to the role of early interventionists, preschool team members can be an important source of information and ideas on what is available in the community and who to call to make arrangements. They can also help families work with community program staff in identifying ways to include the child.

Recommended Practices for Preschool Programs

The identification of best practices for preschool programs serving children with disabilities has been an important area for professional and advocacy attention, as indicated by the books, articles, and chapter sections devoted to this task (e.g., DeStefano, Howe, Horn, & Smith, 1991; Hanson & Lynch, 1989; McDonnell & Hardman, 1988),

Integrated

Supported placement in generic early childhood service sites
Systematic contact with nonhandicapped peers
Planned integration at all levels

Adaptable

Flexible procedures within noncategorical models
Support of different family structures
Emphasis on function rather than form of response
Programmming changes based on individual, formative evaluation

Comprehensive

Comprehensive assessment, planning, programming, service coordination, and evaluation
Models theoretically and procedurally well-defined
Transdisciplinary approach to the delivery of related services
Direct instruction of generalized responding

Peer and Family Referenced

Curriculum that is referenced to individual child, family, peers, and community
Parents are full partners in educational planning and decision-making
Systematic communication between family and service providers
Planned enhancement of child's skill development within daily family routine

Normalized

Support for parenting role
Age appropriate skills and instructional strategies
Concurrent training across skill areas
Distributed practice across settings
Establishment of self-initiated responding
Avoidance of artificial reinforcement and aversive control techniques

Outcome-Based

Variety of outcome measures
Preparation for future integrated settings
Curricular emphasis on skills with present and future utility
Transition planning

FIGURE 6-4   A Synthesis of "Best Practice" Guidelines for Early Childhood Services

Source: McDonnell, A. & Hardman, M. (1988). A synthesis of "best practice" guidelines for early childhood services. *Journal of the Division for Early Childhood, 12* (4), 328–341.

and the formation of a Best Practice task force by the Division for Early Childhood of the Council for Exceptional Children (DEC). Recommended or best practices for preschool programs have been organized in a variety of different ways and continue to evolve at a rapid pace. Figure 6-4 lists some overall characteristics of best practice early childhood programs, and includes descriptors of specific recommended practices under each characteristic. While family-centered early intervention may be the defining characteristic of best practice early intervention the application of family-centered philosophy and practice to preschool services is somewhat less defined at this time. It will be interesting to see how preschool programs adapt the philosophy and practices of family-centered intervention so that it can be combined with providing effective intervention within inclusive, developmentally appropriate early childhood programs.

Developing and Implementing IEPs for Preschoolers

The Individualized Education Plan (IEP) is intended to guide the collaborative planning and implementation of special education and related services for preschoolers with developmental delays, including those with severe disabilities. IEPs for preschoolers have the same required components as IEPs written for much older students. However, because of the uniqueness of the preschool years, these IEP components are often developed and implemented quite differently than they would be for an older child.

Team Membership and Collaboration

IFSP development for infants and toddlers is generally conceptualized as family-centered or family-driven, with the child's family and the selected service coordinator having the strongest or most prominent influence on team decisions or actions. Early intervention service coordinators are often not special educators, nor are special educators required members of early intervention teams. In contrast, regulations regarding the make-up of IEP teams for preschoolers with developmental delays are essentially the same as those for school-age children. A preschool special education teacher usually serves in the service coordinator role, although a formal identification of a service coordinator is not required as it is for early intervention services. Parents are very important team members, although they do not usually have as prominent a role in team decisions and actions as is true in early intervention programs. In addition to a preschool special education teacher and family members, a mainstream early educator or preschool teacher, a school district administrator or their designated representative, and relevant related service providers, such as a speech and language pathologist, occupational therapist, or physical therapist, are all key members of preschool IEP teams. Because children transition into preschool at around age three, and move into school services at around age five, IEP development teams also commonly include one or more team members from a transition program. Many preschoolers are involved in childcare or community recreation programs, or spend significant amounts of time with neighborhood friends or extended family members. These other caregivers can be an invaluable part of a preschool team. For some children, additional collaboration with community health care or social service providers may also be important.

Collaborative teaming between family members and caregivers, early educators, early childhood special educators and related servers, transition program professionals, and other community members or agencies presents some obvious challenges. It is virtually impossible to collect all of these team members for regular meetings or planning sessions, and too many individuals would be involved to give everyone a chance to communicate effectively anyway. Transdisciplinary teaming can provide the flexibility in team roles and communication strategies to be able to ensure opportunities for information sharing, brainstorming, collaborative problem solving, and team implementation and evaluation of the IEP without requiring *all* team members to be physically present for each interaction. Family and other team members can all select the types of decisions or actions in which they would most like to be direct participants, and those for which they would primarily like to be informed about how things are going on a less frequent or direct basis.

Ecologically-Based Curriculum and IEP Development for Preschool Children

As mentioned earlier in the chapter, ecologically-based, naturalistic, or functional curricular models are usually favored for preschoolers, particularly for those with severe developmental delays (Hanson & Lynch, 1989; McDonnell & Hardman, 1988; Noonan & McCormick, 1993; Vincent et al., 1980). (For the purposes of this chapter, ecologically-based, environmentally-based, functional, and naturalistic curricula will be used interchangeably.) The use of ecologically-based curriculum influences the IEP development process, including the way assessment activities are conducted, the types of goals that are selected, and the way that intervention is implemented and evaluated. The ecologically-based curriculum approach emphasizes the importance of teaching skills that will increase participation in the natural contexts in which the child is currently involved, and in those in which they are likely to participate in the future (Vincent et al., 1980; McDonnell & Hardman, 1988; Noonan & McCormick, 1993). Natural contexts and the child and family preferences are important considerations in the planning and implementation of all phases of the intervention process. The rationale for teaching young children within natural play and caregiving routines is summarized in Figure 6-5.

Ecologically-based assessments are used more extensively than formalized testing in ecologically-based curriculum models. Observing the child in natural contexts and talking with significant individuals who spend time with the child on a regular basis are important sources of information for selecting IEP and other intervention goals. Assessment strategies that simulate natural contexts may also be used in order to facilitate team observation and collaboration and to gather information about the child's performance across a number of different developmental areas within a condensed time period. An example of a detailed and well-designed assessment strategy that simulates natural contexts for the purpose of observing the child's performance is transdisciplinary play-based assessment (TPBA) (Linder, 1990).

1. Child learns where and when to use targeted skills as part of the learning process. Integration of skill performance is more likely.

2. Communication between team members is increased, as is the role of parents and caregivers in facilitating the child's learning.

3. It multiplies the learning opportunities available to the child.

4. Chidren enrolled in group care or early childhood programs have an opportunity to learn from competent peer models.

5. The purpose for learning is more obvious to the child, and the learning experiences tend to be more enjoyable. Motivation may be increased, and the reinforcement is more likely to be intrinsic. Maintenance of learning is more likely.

6. Learning in natural contexts increases the range of stimuli that the child will need to respond to, and the range of responses that will be required of them. Stimulus and response generalization are improved.

7. It provides a reality check as to whether the skill is really important for the child to learn. If it doesn't fit into the child's daily routines, why are we teaching it?

FIGURE 6-5   Rationale for Using Play and Natural Routines as Contexts for Intervention

From: McDonnell, A. (1990). Selecting play and natural routines as contexts for goal-based interventions for infants, toddlers, and preschoolers with disabilities. University of Utah, Department of Special Education, Salt Lake City, Utah.

TPBA involves arranging and facilitating a variety of play and other activities for a child. The adult play facilitator initially watches or responds to the child's spontaneous play or behavior, and later facilitates play more directly to try to elicit the child's highest level of performance. Another child is usually brought in for one segment of the play activities to give team members a chance to observe peer interactions and play. Parent(s) and other team members who are not serving as the play facilitator watch the facilitated play and activity. The play session is often videotaped as well. The joint observation and tape allow team and family members to comment on how typical the child's performance is for that child and to share insights about what they have observed. Results are summarized and used as the basis for selecting intervention goals and strategies.

An example of an environmentally-based curriculum for preschoolers is one which is part of a cross-age ecological curriculum produced by several grant projects in the School and Community Integration Program (SCIP) in the Department of Special Education at the University of Utah (J. McDonnell, et al., 1992). The SCIP curriculum framework and IEP development process is similar across the preschool, early elementary, upper elementary, intermediate school, secondary school, and early adult (19–21) age levels. The curricular framework at each age level is organized around naturally occurring routines in which typically developing individuals of that age would

Programs for Preschool Children

often participate on a daily or weekly basis (see Figure 6-6 for a sample page from the preschool curricular framework). Contexts are used as an organizer and include the time of day (e.g. morning, evening) and the location of the routines (e.g. home, preschool/daycare, community). Within each context, common routines are listed, as are activities that might occur as a part of that routine. Broad skill areas which include specific skills that an individual would need to perform to complete activities or routines are also included within the curricular framework.

Curriculum catalogs have been developed at each level to assist family members and transdisciplinary teams in identifying priority IEP goals (see Figure 6-7 for sample pages from the Preschool Curriculum Catalog). The Preschool Activities Curriculum Catalog organizes preschool activities within leisure/play, personal management, and social relationships domains. For each domain, activities are organized by the location

CONTEXT: EVENING: HOME

ROUTINES	ACTIVITIES	SKILLS
Has dinner	Helps prepare Gets self to table Eats meal Helps clean up Other: (See Activities Catalog)	Social/Communication Motor Mobility Self-Help Self-Management Cognitive/Pre-Academics Play
Free time	Plays with friends, siblings Plays with toys, games Other: (See Activities Catalog)	
Personal care	Toileting Bath Grooming Other: (See Activities Catalog)	
Prepares for bed	Dressing/Undressing Grooming Listen to stories Other: (See Activities Catalog)	
Ends Day	Goes to bed	

FIGURE 6-6   Sample Page from SCIP Curricular Framework for Preschoolers

Curricular Domain	I. LEISURE/PLAY		
ENVIRONMENTAL CONTEXT	HOME AND/OR HOME-BASED CHILDCARE	SCHOOL AND/OR CENTER-BASED CHILDCARE	COMMUNITY
Activities	Have friends over Participate in play group Interactive games (tag, ring around the rosy) INDOOR Record player Tape recorder Radio TV, VCR Home video, computer game Hand-held video game Books Board games Card games Musical instruments Drawing, painting, coloring Playdoh, clay PRESCHOOL AGE TOYS Dress ups Child size kitchen Tool bench Action figures Dolls Construction (legos, blocks) Puppets Battery operated toys Car, road sets Puzzles OUTDOOR Swing set, jungle gym Tricycles, big wheels Hopscotch Water play (pool, slide, sprinkler) Sand play Ball activities	Participate in whole school activities (assemblies, carnivals) Interactive games Library, story time INDOOR Record player Tape recorder Radio TV, VCR Video, computer games Card games Musical instruments Drawing, painting, coloring Playdoh, clay PRESCHOOL AGE TOYS Dress ups Child size kitchen Tool bench Action figures Dolls Construction (legos, blocks) Puppets Battery operated toys Car, road sets Puzzles OUTDOOR Swing set, jungle gym Tricycles, big wheels Hopscotch Sand play Ball activities	ORGANIZED ACTIVITIES Attending religious group activities Team sports Lessons (dance, swimming) INFORMAL ACTIVITIES Playing at friend's house Playing at park, playground Swimming Skating Going for walks Library Movies

FIGURE 6-7 **Sample Parent IEP Worksheet and Sample Pages from SCIP Activity and Skill Curriculum Catalogs for Preschoolers**

SKILL AREA	SOCIAL/ COMMUNICATION	MOTOR	MOBILITY
Skills/Skill Group	Attends to environment Expresses needs, desires, and refusals Responds to communication Initiates communcative Interactions Uses new word/ symbols and word/symbol combinations in communication Follows directions Behaves appropriately for setting Maintains social interactions Other	Range of motion Head control Righting, protective reactions Sitting, trunk control Standing Lifting/carrying Use of Hands Pushing, pulling Reaching Grasping, releasing Twisting, turning manipulations Coordinated use of two hands Other	Moves to people or activities within same room Moves to people or activities beyond immediate room Moves to people or activities, outdoors Opens/closes doors Goes up/down stairs Maneuvers curbs/ barriers Moves safely with supervision, in community setting Other

Parent IEP Preparation Worksheet for Activities

1. Choose 3–7 activities you feel are most important for your child to learn during the next school year. Activities are listed on the pink pages in the Curriculum Catalog. You may select activities within home, school, and/or community environments.

2. Write the activities in the space provided. Write the activity you think is most important on line 1, the next most important activity on line 2, etc.

3. If you have ideas about where your child can practice or use the activity, answer the other questions about the selected activities. An example has been included at the top of the chart.

Activity	When?	Where?	With Whom?	Other
Example: Tricycle, bike	After Preschool	In front of house At park with family In front of friend's house	Brother Kid across street	Training wheels
1.				
2.				
3.				
4.				
5.				
6.				

Please remember to bring these worksheets with you to your child's IEP meeting.

Date: _____

Time: _____

Place: _____

FIGURE 6-7 *Continued*

in which they occur, specifically within home or home-based childcare settings, school and/or center-based childcare settings, or the community. The Preschool Skills Curriculum Catalog organizes generic skills or skill groups within six skill areas; social/communication, motor, mobility, self-help, cognitive/preacademic, and play. Both the activities and skill groups are still very broad and need to be identified much more specifically before they can serve as a complete IEP goal or objective. Parent IEP Preparation worksheets are included within the Preschool Curriculum Catalog to assist parents in prioritizing goals and providing the rest of the IEP team with critical information about how the goals fit into the child's daily life.

The SCIP/Utah Statewide Preschool Inservice Network (U-SPIN) IEP development process (A. McDonnell, Berki, Hoagland, & S. Kiefer-O'Donnell, 1992) uses the curricular framework and curriculum catalogs as a key part of individual, ecologically-based curriculum development. The process begins with pre-assessment planning, during which individual-, peer-, and family-referenced routines are generated and analyzed to select high-priority routines for increased child participation or performance. The chosen routines, current assessment information, progress in past interventions, and team concerns and priorities serve as the basis for selecting additional assessment strategies and participants. Functional and ecologically-based assessment strategies are emphasized. After assessment activities have been completed the results are shared with all team members. Parents and other preschool team members then use the routine-based curricular framework and curriculum catalogs to select priority IEP goals. During the IEP meeting, parent and preschool team goals are listed and collaborative negotiation is used to (a) select the highest priority goals, (b) to examine the possibilities for integrating goals across curricular areas, and (c) to infuse goals into peer and family routines. Examples of IEP goals and objectives for a child with severe developmental delays that might result from the use of this IEP process are provided in Figure 6-8.

Focus 5:

How do interventionists implement ecologically-based curriculum for preschool children with developmental delays?

Implementing Intervention in Natural Routines and Activities

Much of the planning for implementing intervention in natural routines and activities has already occurred by the time the IEP is written if assessment activities, goal selection and development, and the infusion of goals in natural routines have been conducted in ways that are consistent with an ecologically-based curriculum model. However, it is still necessary for families and team members to collaborate on ways to assure that focused intervention on IEP goals can be integrated within these natural routines. One way to assure that quality planning and evaluation strategies have been developed is through the development of individual program or intervention plans for each IEP goal.

1. Jason will respond socially to others by establishing and maintaining eye contact when he is spoken to.

   A. Given a verbal cue (name and/or "look") and a physical prompt, Jason will respond by making eye contact within 5 seconds and maintaining it for at least 3 seconds, in at least 3 different preschool activities, for 3 consecutive days.

   B. Same as A but with verbal cue only.

   C. In a variety of activities in preschool, the community, or at home, when Jason is spoken to (by name), he will respond by making eye contact within 5 seconds and maintaining it for at least 3 seconds, at least 9/10 opportunities during a 1 week probe for 6 consecutive weeks.

2. Jason will spontaneously express his wants and needs by signing "eat" and "drink" to request items.

   A. When given the verbal cue, "Do you want (eat)/(drink)?", in presence of desired items, Jason will imitate a model of the sign with 90% accuracy for 3 days.

   B. When given a verbal cue that does not contain a model (e.g., "What do you want?"), Jason will use the appopriate sign to make a request when presented with one preferred and two non-preferred items with 90% accuracy for 3 days.

   C. During time when food is available (lunch, snack, etc.) and visible to Jason, he will independently use the appropriate sign to make a request at least twice per day for 6 consecutive weeks, during 1 x week probe.

   D. During times when food/drink is not immediately available, at home or in community settings, Jason will initiate signing his requests for food and drink according to his own needs at least 2 x/day for 6 consecutive weeks during 1 x week probe.

   (continued)

FIGURE 6-8   Examples of Jason's IEP Goals and Objectives

3. Jason will independently use 3 different adaptive switches to activate battery-operated recreational activities and will maintain appropriate involvement for at least 5 minutes.

A. When presented with switches that activate simple, battery-operated, toys (e.g. car, radio), Jason will independently activate one and maintain involvement for at least 10 seconds with the adult in his immediate presence, 90%+ of opportunities for 3 consecutive sessions.

B. Same as A but for 3 minutes.

C. Same as A but with adult anywhere in room, for 5 minutes.

D. Given free play (at preschool, daycare, home, or friend's house) and access to switches that activate simple, battery-operated toys, Jason will use the activity and maintain appropriate involvement with it for at least 5 minutes with no more than 1 verbal reminder from an adult or peer, at least 80% of activity periods for 4 weeks.

FIGURE 6-8   *Continued*

The development of specific intervention plans that pay careful attention to the use of response prompting and fading procedures, reinforcement strategies, and corrections is particularly important for children with severe developmental delays, due to their significant learning difficulties. An example of a simple plan that has been developed for a preschool IEP goal is included in Figure 6-9.

The collection and monitoring of instructional and performance data is also very important to assure that intervention is being carried out as intended, and that intervention changes are made promptly unless the child is making regular progress towards meeting the intervention goal. Data collection within natural routines is a challenge for most preschool teachers, and may be viewed as an unwarranted intrusion in home and community settings. This is one of the many reasons why it is important to include family members and other caregivers as part of the intervention team, so that they can make informed decisions about if and how they would like to participate in evaluation efforts.

While individual intervention plans may be developed for specific IEP goals intervention on different goals is usually integrated within the same activity period or natural context. For example, if Jason is about to eat snack with his preschool classmates, he will be expected to use his wheelchair to transition to the snack activity, to sign "eat" and "drink" to request snack items, to sign "more" if he wants seconds on something, and to make eye contact when someone is talking to him. This same type of integration of intervention across goals would ideally occur throughout the routines in Jason's day.

Date begun: _4/1/92_

Infant/Child: ___Sarah B.___

Date completed: _____

Objective: _Turn-taking_

Interventionist: _Casey Kealoha_

Conditons: _When an adult or child begins a game and pauses, or passes the material/toy to Sarah._

Response: _Sarah will take a turn by playing for a few moments, and pausing or passing the material/toy back to the adult or child._

Criterion: _Plays for 10-60 seconds; pauses or passes material/toy 3 of 4 times._

Intervention Context	Prompting/Facilitation Techniques	Consequences
Setting(s): • In the morning at the sitter's • After school with her brother • After dinner with Mom, Dad or Grandpa **Routine(s)/Activity(ies):** • Clapping games, rocking or "dancing" to music, playing with toys that shake **Skill Sequence(s):** 1. Vocalizes to request attention 2. Turn-taking 3. Request "more" Occasions for incidental Intervention: n/a	**Positioning and Handling; Special Equipment/Materials:** • Supported sitting in high chair, propped against couch or in corner of couch, or on someone's lap; a table top (lap tray or high chair tray) will help her to manipulate and shake toys. **Environmental Modifications:** n/a **Prompting/Facilitation:** • Start a turn-taking game and play for about 30 seconds. • Then implement time delay: Physically assist Sarah to take her turn 2 times. For all additional turns, wait 4 seconds. If Sarah takes her turn within the 4-second delay, reinforce. If Sarah does not take her turn with 4 seconds, implement correction 1.	**Reinforcement:** • Verbally praise Sarah, laugh and show lots of excitement as she takes her turn. • Immediately take a turn when Sarah stops (play for about 30 seconds). **Corrections:** 1. (If Sarah waits beyond the 4-second delay) Physically assist Sarah to take her turn. 2. (If Sarah starts doing something else) Start the turn-taking game again. If she doesn't attend and does something else again, stop the intervention and try again later.

FIGURE 6-9   Sample Intervention Plan for Preschool IEP Goal

From: Noonan, J. J. & McCormick, M. J. (1993). *Early intervention in natural environments*: *Methods and procedures.* Pacific Grove, CA: Brooks/Cole Publishing Co.

Transition Planning and Preschool IEPs

Preschool programs usually serve children in the limited age range between three and five years. Sometimes children with developmental delays will continue in a preschool program for the remainder of the school year in which they turn six. In these instances, or in districts which do not have kindergarten, children may transition directly between preschool special education services and first grade. Most children enter preschool around their third birthday, and begin kindergarten two years later. Consequently, preschool programs are continuously involved in assisting children and families in making transitions between programs. The inclusion of steps and services to support transition are required as a part of IFSPs and IEPs as children and families prepare to transition from early intervention to preschool programs, and again as the child enters kindergarten or first grade.

While transitions are a natural part of life, even planned and positive transitions are often difficult due to the many adjustments. Families of individuals with disabilities have identified major service transitions as one of the more stressful and repetitious events they experience. Window 6-1 provided one parent's reaction to the early intervention-preschool transition. While generally stressful, transitions are also often a time of opportunity and growth. The role of program personnel during the transitions at either end of the preschool years is primarily to provide support and to facilitate a smooth adjustment on the part of the child, family, and individuals in the new program(s) who will be involved with the child. Conn-Powers, Ross-Allen, & Holburn (1990) summarized the goals for a preschool-elementary transition as follows:

Goals of a Successful Transition

1. *To promote the speedy adjustment of the child and family to the new educational setting*
2. *To enhance the child's independent and successful participation in the new educational setting*
3. *To insure the uninterrupted provision of appropriate services in the least restrictive school setting*
4. *To support and empower the family as an equal partner in the transition process*
5. *To promote collaboration among all constituents in the transition process*
6. *To increase the satisfaction of all constituents with*
   a. *the outcomes of the transition process, and*
   b. *the transition process itself, including their participation,*
7. *To increase the likelihood that the child is placed and maintained in the regular kindergarten setting and elementary school mainstream. (p. 94).*

These goals also apply, with minor modifications, to the early intervention to preschool transition. Figure 6-10 provides examples of some of the common concerns and transition-related child goals associated with the two preschool program transitions.

A number of model demonstration projects, school districts, and other program planners or providers have identified recommended steps or processes for preschool

Transition:	Early Intervention to Preschool	Preschool to Elementary School (K or 1)
Common Concerns	• Child's readiness for classroom program, peer relationships, and bus transportation • Changing nature of services from family-centered to child-centered • Safety of child with active peers and in playground and bus settings • Obtaining desired preschool placement and special services • Whether child's individual health and caregiving needs will be met in group setting	• Child's readiness for more structured school programs and full-day program (when applicable) • Whether child will be disruptive, ignored, or rejected in "regular" elementary classes and by typical peers • Obtaining desired school placement and special services • Safety of child in less closely supervised school settings
Common Child Goals Related To Transition	• Follows directions, rules, and routines • Communicates with familiar adults and peers • Toilet training • Is socially appropriate with peers in a variety of play and preschool activities • Transitions between activities at appropriate time • Occupies self and sustains attention during caregiving, preschool group, and play activities	• Completes seat work independently • Pays attention and participates without disruption in large and small group activities and instruction • Locates and manages own belongings • Is socially appropriate with peers in a variety of classroom and school activities • Takes care of own toileting, eating, grooming, and dressing needs as required in school setting • Demonstrates early academic or "readiness" skills

FIGURE 6-10 Common Concerns and Intervention Goals Related to Preschool Transitions

program transitions (e.g., Bennett, Raab, & Nelson, 1991; Conn-Powers et al., 1990; Diamond, Speigel-McGill, & Hanrahan, 1988; Hains, Rosenkoetter, & Fowler, 1991; Hanline & Knowlton, 1988; Kilgo, Richard, & Noonan, 1989; McDonnell, Thorson, & Freston, 1991). Some of the steps or activities that are recommended by many of these programs include:

1. Collaborative teaming between the family, sending program, and receiving program staff in developing a written transition plan that identifies steps or actions to be taken, who will do them, and when
2. Staff and family visits to the receiving program to (a) identify the environmental performance demands, (b) determine important skills to teach the child, and/or (c) identify supports or adaptations to be made in the environment to support the child's success
3. Receiving program staff observations of the child in the current environment, and suggestions on what they believe would (a) be most helpful to teach the child, or (b) be important areas on which to provide training or support to receiving staff

4. Family education and support are made available in a variety of ways and throughout the transition process
5. Child visit(s) to the receiving program environment occur shortly before the transition takes place

It is important to note that transitions are not a one time meeting with follow-up phone calls. To be effective, transition planning and support must begin well before the program change and continue support and evaluation of the transition for a period after the change has occurred (Conn-Powers et al., 1990; McDonnell & Freston, 1990).

Conclusion

Future Directions for Preschool Programs

During the last decade the passage of P. L. 99-457 mandated the provision of preschool special education and related services to all eligible children with disabilities. As a result of this mandate there has been a substantial growth in the number of children receiving services, as well as in the comprehensiveness and quality of the services themselves. While legislation can assure some things, at this point in time the strongest push for a continued striving towards excellence may come from families, and leadership and interagency collaboration at the state and local levels (Hebbler et al., 1991). Some of the greatest challenges for preschool programs in the next decade will include removing or overcoming the barriers to full inclusion for all preschool children with developmental delays, developing a firmer understanding of how to make programs both developmentally appropriate and effective for learners with intensive needs, and developing a stronger sense of how preschool programs can maintain the strong family-professional partnerships developed in early intervention through a more family-centered approach. Effectively meeting these challenges will require a redefinition of the early childhood professions as well as a redefinition of professional relationships with families and other caregivers. The editors introduction to a chapter on reaching the potentials of children with special needs in a recent NAEYC publication talks about this redefinition of the professions, as well as the inclusion of all children.

> *Both political and pedagogical trends are causing the fields of early childhood education and early childhood special education to converge. From a political perspective national laws now ensure access to services for children with disabilities. Due to the recent passage of the landmark civil rights legislation, the Americans with Disabilities Act (ADA), all early childhood programs must be prepared to serve children with special needs. Full implementation of the ADA, coupled with the Individuals with Disabilities Education Act, means the full inclusion of children with disabilities will become a reality, thus bringing early childhood education and early childhood special education closer together than ever before. Work remains to be done to expand the knowledge*

****

POINT AND COUNTERPOINT 6-1   How Important Is Inclusion for a Preschool Child with Profound Disabilities?

Shannon is a four-year-old child with multiple and profound disabilities. She is the third child in a warm and loving family. Shannon was a very healthy and bright child until shortly after her first birthday. At this time she developed a number of disturbing behavior patterns including repetitive body rocking, hand wringing, humming, and hair pulling. Even more disturbing, she seemed to be moving backward rather than learning new skills. For example, her walking gait became more awkward and her increasingly skillful use of toys and other objects became more and more primitive. Formerly a very social child, she would now often ignore or avert her gaze when someone spoke to her. She quit calling her mother and father "mama" and "dada" and meaningful back and forth gestural or vocal communication became less and less frequent. Shannon's family consulted with medical experts who initially believed she might have autism. After additional tests and observation Shannon was diagnosed as having Rhett Syndrome, a rare degenerative neurological disease.

Shannon and her family participated in an early intervention program. Shannon's goals focused on trying to maintain and improve the quality and usefulness of her existing skills (e.g., walking, some use of her hands, some social responsiveness, an apparent enjoyment of noise, motion, light, and sound) and on including Shannon as a part of her family and community. After the family had a chance to grieve over the changes in Shannon's life and their own, they resumed their many activities and interests. They also became actively involved in advocacy activities intended to improve the lives of individuals with disabilities.

While a toddler Shannon stayed with a babysitter three afternoons a week. Shannon did not show a lot of reaction to being around other children or to new and stimulating situations. However, her babysitter did notice that she would walk over to other children, and stand by them and rock. Sometimes Shannon would put her face close to the other children's and breathe in and out quickly and loudly. These were the same patterns that her family observed at home. While it was difficult to say for sure, her family interpreted these behaviors as Shannon's attempts to be near and interact with others. If she didn't enjoy others why didn't she just stay still or walk away from them?

When Shannon was old enough to begin preschool her family wanted to enroll her in the Jefferson County Community Preschool, which was located at the elementary school her brother and sister attended. Two other children receiving special education services already attended this preschool. Both were children with mild-moderate developmental delays. The school district placement committee was puzzled both by Shannon's parents plans to enroll her in Community Preschool, and by their assumption that she could receive all needed special education and related services within that setting. The district placement committee recommended enrolling Shannon in the Mountain View Preschool Program. It was only a half hour bus ride for Shannon to go to this special education preschool, and because it was located in an elementary school with several special classes it had all of the specialists Shannon would need located right in the building. Some of the children in the special education preschool went into the kindergarten class for about half an hour two-three times a week and if her parents felt like it would make a difference to Shannon this could also be arranged for her.

Point:

The district special education placement team do not believe that Shannon's parents are making the decision that will be in Shannon's best interest. Sure they have district children with devel-

(continued)

POINT AND COUNTERPOINT 6-1   *Continued*

opmental delays that attend "regular" preschool programs but they are almost entirely children with mild-moderate delays who can really benefit not only from regular contact with preschool children without disabilities, but also from the preschool curriculum. While they receive speech therapy and special instruction it is on an itinerant only basis, and wouldn't be sufficient for a child like Shannon. Shannon needs intensive daily instruction and also needs to be seen by a physical therapist at least twice a week. The staff at Jefferson County Community Preschool also cannot be expected to change Shannon's diaper, feed her lunch and snacks, and lead her by the hand to every new group activity. Besides, what's the point? She doesn't imitate or play with the other children and her cognitive level is much like a three-month old. What will she get out of the whole language, Spanish, Children Around the World, and Nature and Science programs which are implemented so well in the community preschool? It just isn't fair to Shannon, the community preschool teachers, or the many children with mild-moderate disabilities who still aren't integrated into regular preschool programs to try to attempt something like this. Maybe sometime in the future there will be enough community preschool placements, and enough specialized support resources to make something like this work.

Counterpoint:

Regardless of her abilities or disabilities Shannon's family believe that she has a basic right to be included within her family and community and to attend the same school as her brother and sister. Maybe Shannon doesn't play or imitate children in the usual way but she does seem to show an interest in her peers in the best way she knows how. Even if she doesn't learn the same things as the other children, all of her educational goals can readily be incorporated within the ongoing preschool activities and she'll probably enjoy it at least as much as she would the more structured and less play oriented special education classroom. Who's to say what really goes on in Shannon's mind, what she is learning, aware of, enjoys? Can a more clear benefit for Shannon really be predicted if she attends the special education preschool? What exactly is a clear educational benefit anyway for a child like Shannon with a degenerative condition? Does she have to make as much progress as the children without disabilities to be viewed as "able to benefit" from the Jefferson County program, and if so, how do we justify making these opportunities available to children with mild-moderate disabilities? If the specialists and resources to support a child like Shannon are not currently available in the Jefferson County preschool is there any reason why they can't be? Let's face it, it does cost more to support and educate a child like Shannon wherever she attends school. It just isn't at all clear that bussing her to a special program will make it any less so.

****

base but the foundation is well laid. As Safford (1989) points out, " The fields of early childhood education and special education have a great deal in common because of their stress on children as individuals, and their recognition of every child's right to an education that is appropriate to individual and developmental needs" (p. xi). (Bredekamp & Rosegrant, 1992).

Preschool children with severe disabilities are clearly a part of this inclusive future, as conceptualized by early childhood educators, as well as by early childhood special educators, related professions, and the children's families.

Focus Review

Focus 1: What types of services have been made available to preschoolers with disabilities and their families?

- If preschoolers with severe disabilities received any services prior to the late 1950s or early 1960s, they were usually provided within institutions.
- Homebased or classroom-based programs for preschoolers became increasingly available from the late 1950s through the 1980s. However, preschool services were not available for all children with disabilities and their families, and services such as transportation were frequently not provided.
- Since 1990, states have been required to provide preschool special education and related services for all eligible three to five year olds.

Focus 2: What is developmentally appropriate practice and how does it apply to preschool children with severe disabilities?

- Developmentally Appropriate Practice (DAP) guidelines are used to define appropriate learning environments and experiences for young children (birth–eight) as distinct from those provided to upper elementary, intermediate, and secondary students. These distinctions include (a) a need for learning activities that are initiated and directed by the child and supported by the teacher, and (b) an emphasis on learning through play, exploration, social interaction, and inquiry, rather than through directive teaching to specific goals.
- Many early childhood special educators believe that developmentally appropriate practice provides an environment that is necessary and desirable for young children with severe disabilities but that it is "not sufficient" to meet all of their educational needs. They would favor implementing intensive individualized intervention within developmentally appropriate settings and doing frequent evaluation to determine whether this intervention is being effective or needs to be modified.

Focus 3: What policy statements have been made about preschoolers with developmental delays and inclusion? How well do these statements correspond to federal regulations related to educating preschoolers with disabilities in the Least Restrictive Environment?

- The Division for Early Childhood of the Council for Exceptional Children has issued a policy statement in favor of supported inclusion for all young children.
- The federal regulations require preschoolers with disabilities to be educated in the Least Restrictive Environment, or to the maximum extent possible with their peers without disabilities. Because this is open to interpretation, at this time, the LRE requirement in effect allows IEP teams and school districts to choose to serve preschool children with disabilities in special school settings or in elementary schools which do not have classes for typically developing preschoolers.

: Describe the major goals of preschool programs for children with disabilities.

ir goals are often stressed by families and educational programs during the preschool years. These goals include:

1. Maximizing the child's development in a variety of important developmental areas
2. Developing the child's social interaction and classroom participation skills
3. Preparing the child for inclusive school placements and providing support for the transition to kindergarten or elementary school
4. Increasing community participation through support to family members and other caregivers

Focus 5: How do interventionists implement ecologically-based curriculum for preschool children with developmental delays?

- Interventionists implement ecologically-based curriculum in the natural play and caregiving routines and activities in which preschoolers participate in home, preschool/childcare, and community settings.
- Family, caregivers, and preschool team members collaborate in assessment and IEP development activities. IEP goals are selected to support the child's performance and participation in valued natural routines. Once priority IEP goals have been developed, the team can collaborate to infuse goal-based intervention into relevant natural settings. One way of carefully planning for quality individualized intervention is to record the methods for carrying out and evaluating intervention in natural settings in an individual intervention plan.

References

Allen, K. A., & Martoz, L. (1989). *Developmental profiles: Birth to six*. Albany, NY: Delmar Publishers.

Bailey, D. B., Jr., & McWilliam, P. J. (1993). The search for quality indicators. In P. J. McWilliam & D. B. Bailey, Jr. (Eds.), *Working together with children and families: Case studies in early intervention* (pp. 3–20). Baltimore: Paul H. Brookes.

Bailey, D. B., Jr., & McWilliam, R. A. (1990). Normalizing early intervention. *Topics in Early Childhood Special Education, 10*(2), 33–47.

Bailey, D. B., Jr., & Simeonsson, R. J. (1988). Home-based early intervention. In S. L. Odom & M. B. Karnes (Eds.), *Early intervention for infants and children with handicaps: An empirical base* (pp. 199–216). Baltimore: Paul H. Brookes.

Bailey, Jr., D. B., & Wolery, M. (1992). *Teaching infants and preschoolers with disabilities* (2nd ed.). New York: Merrill Publishing.

Bailey, E. J., & Bricker, D. (1984). The efficacy of early intervention for severely handicapped infants and young children. *Topics in Early Childhood Special Education, 4*(3), 30–51.

Bennett, T., Raab, M., & Nelson, D. (1991). The transition process for toddlers with special needs and their families. *Zero to Three, 11*, 17–21.

Bredekamp, S. (1986). *Developmentally appropriate practice*. Washington, DC: National Association for the Education of Young Children.

Bredekamp, S. (1987). *Developmentally appropriate practice in early childhood programs serving children from birth through age 8: Expanded edition*. Washington, DC: National Association for the Education of Young Children.

Bredekamp, S., & Rosegrant, T. (1992). *Reaching potentials: Appropriate curriculum and assessment for young children* (Vol. 1). Washington DC: National Association for the Education of Young Children.

Bricker, D. D., & Bricker, W. A. (1973). Infant, toddler, and preschool research and intervention project report: Year III. *IMRID Behavior Science Monograph* (No. 23). Nashville, TN: Institute on Mental Retardation and Intellectual Development, George Peabody College.

Bricker, D., & Kaminski, R. (1986). Intervention programs for severely handicapped infants and children. In L. Bickman & D. L. Weatherford (Eds.), *Evaluating early intervention programs for severely handicapped children and their families* (pp. 51–78). Austin, TX: Pro-Ed.

Bricker, W. A., & Bricker, D. D. (1976). The infant, toddler, and preschool research and intervention project. In T. D. Tjossem (Ed.), *Intervention strategies with high risk infants and young children*. Baltimore: University Park Press.

Caplan, T., & Caplan, F. (1983). *The early childhood years: The two to six year old*. New York: Bantam Books.

Carta, J. J., Schwarz, I. S., Atwater, J. B., & McConnell, S. R. (1991). Developmentally appropriate practice: Appraising its usefulness for young children with disabilities. *Topics in Early Childhood Special Education, 11*(1), 1–20.

Cooke, T. P., Ruskus, J. A., Apolloni, T., & Peck, C. A. (1981). Handicapped preschool children in the mainstream: Background, outcomes, and clinical suggestions. *Topics in Early Childhood Special Education, 1*, 73–83.

Demchak, M., & Drinkwater, S. (1992). Preschoolers with severe disabilities: The case against segregation. *Topics in Early Childhood Special Education, 11*(4), 70–83.

DeStefano, D. M., Howe, A. G., Horn, E. M., & Smith, B. A. (1991). *Best practices: Evaluating early childhood special education programs*. Tucson: Communication Skill Builders.

Diamond, K. E., Spiegel-McGill, P., & Hanrahan, P. (1988). Planning for school transition: An ecological-developmental approach. *Journal of Early Intervention, 12*, 245–252.

Dunst, C. J. (1986). Overview of the efficacy of early intervention programs. In L. Bickman & D. L. Weatherford (Eds.), *Evaluating early intervention programs for severely handicapped children and their families* (pp. 79–148). Austin: Pro-Ed.

Esposito, B. G., & Koorland, M. A. (1989). Play behavior of hearing impaired children: Integrated and segregated settings. *Exceptional Children, 55*, 412–419.

Fink, W. (1982). Education and rehabilitation of the moderately and severely handicapped. In P. T. Cegelka & H. J. Prehm (Eds.), *Mental retardation: From categories to people* (pp. 260–286). Columbus, OH: Charles E. Merrill Publishing Company.

Fredericks, H. D., Baldwin, V. L., Moore, W., Furey, V., Grove, D., Riggs, C., Moore, B., Gage, M. A., Levak, L., Alrick, G., Wadlow, M., Fruin, C., Makohon, L., Lyons, B., Samples, B., Jordan, E., Moses, C., & Rogers, G. (1977). *A data-based classroom for the moderately and severely handicapped* (2nd. ed.). Monmouth, OR: Instructional Development Corporation.

Gentry, D., & Olsen, J. (1985). Severely mentally retarded young children. *Severe mental retardation: From theory to practice* (pp. 50–75). Reston, VA: The Division on Mental Retardation of the Council for Exceptional Children.

Guralnick, M. J. (1990). Major accomplishments and future directions in early childhood mainstreaming. *Topics in Early Childhood Special Education, 10*, 1–17.

Guralnick, M. J. (1991). The next decade of research on the effectiveness of early intervention. *Exceptional Children, 58*(2), 174–183.

Guralnick, M. J., & Bricker, D. (1987). The effectiveness of early intervention for children with cognitive and general developmental delays. In M. J. Guralnick & F. C. Bennett (Eds.), *The effectiveness of early intervention for at-risk and handicapped children* (pp. 115–173). Orlando, FL: Academic Press, Inc.

Guralnick, M. J., & Groom, J. M. (1987). The peer relations of mildly delayed and nonhandicapped preschool children in mainstreamed play groups. *Child Development, 58*, 1556–1572.

Hains, A. H., Rosenkoetter, S. E., & Fowler, S. A. (1991). Transition planning with families in early intervention programs. *Infants and Young Children, 3*(4), 38–47.

Hanline, M. F. (1993). Inclusion of preschoolers with profound disabilities: An analysis of children's interactions. *The Journal of the Association for Persons with Severe Handicaps, 18*(1), 28–35.

Hanline, M. F., & Knowlton, A. (1988). A collaborative model for providing support to parents during their child's transition from infant intervention to preschool special education public school programs. *Journal of the Division for Early Childhood, 12*(2), 116–125.

Hanson, M. J., & Lynch, E. W. (1989). *Early intervention: Implementing child and family services for infants and toddlers who are at-risk or disabled.* Austin: Pro-Ed.

Harbin, G. L. (1993). Family issues of children with disabilities: How research and theory have modified practice in early intervention. In N. J. Anastasiow & S. Harel (Eds.), *At-risk infants: Interventions, families, and research* (pp. 101–114). Baltimore: Paul H. Brookes.

Hayden, A. H., & Dmitriev, V. (1975). The multidisciplinary preschool program for Down's syndrome children at the University of Washington Model Preschool Center. In B. Z. Friedlander, G.M. Sterritt, & G. E. Kirk (Eds.), *Exceptional infant: Assessment and Intervention* (Vol. 3). New York: Brunner/Mazel.

Hayden, A. H., & Haring, N. G. (1976). Early intervention for high risk infants and young children: Programs for Down's syndrome children. In T.D. Tjossem (Ed.), *Intervention strategies for high risk infants and young children.* Baltimore: University Park Press.

Hebbler, K. M., Smith, B. J., & Black, T. L. (1991). Federal early childhood special education policy: A model for the improvement of services for children with disabilities. *Exceptional Children, 58*(2), 104–114.

Jenkins, J. R., Odom, S. L., & Speltz, M. C. (1989). Effects of social integration of preschool children with handicaps. *Exceptional Children, 55,* 420–428.

Johnson, J. E., & Johnson, K. M. (1992). Clarifying the developmental perspective in response to Carta, Schwartz, Atwater, and McConnell. *Topics in Early Childhood Special Education, 12*(4), 439–457.

Kilgo, J. L., Richard, N., & Noonan, M. J. (1989). Teaming for the future: Integrating transition planning with early intervention services for young children with special needs and their families. *Infants and Young Children, 2*(2), 37–48.

Kostelnik, M. J. (1992). Myths associated with developmentally appropriate programs. *Young Children, 47*(4), 17–23.

Linder, T. W. (1990). *Transdisciplinary play-based assessment: A functional approach to working with young children.* Baltimore: Paul H. Brookes.

Mallory, B. (1992). Is it always appropriate to be developmental?: Convergent models for early intervention practice. *Topics in Early Childhood Special Education, 11*(4), 1–12.

McCormick, L., & Kawate, J. (1982). Kindergarten survival skills: New directions for preschool special education. *Education and Training of the Mentally Retarded, 17,* 247–252.

McDonnell, A. (1990). *Selecting play and natural routines as contexts for goal-based interventions for infants, toddlers, and preschoolers with disabilities.* University of Utah, Department of Special Education, Salt Lake City.

McDonnell, A., Berki, P., Hoagland, V., & Kiefer-O'Donnell, S. (1992). *Transdisciplinary team IEP development for preschoolers with disabilities: A peer and family-referenced approach.* Salt Lake City: University of Utah, Department of Special Education, Utah Statewide Preschool Inservice Network.

McDonnell, A., & Freston, J. (1990, May). *A collaborative process for transitioning preschoolers with moderate and severe disabilities to their neighborhood school kindergarten.* Paper presented at the 114th Annual Meeting of the American Association on Mental Retardation, Atlanta, GA.

McDonnell, A., & Hardman, M. (1988). A synthesis of "best practice" guidelines for early childhood services. *Journal of the Division for Early Childhood, 12*(4), 328–341.

McDonnell, J., McDonnell, A., Berki, P., Hightower, J., Kiefer-O'Donnell, R., Mathot-Buckner, C., Milligan, P., & Thorson, N. (1992). *The School and Community Integration Program Curriculum for Students with Severe Disabilities.* Salt Lake City: School and Community Intergration Program, Department of Special Education, University of Utah.

McDonnell, A., Thorson, N., & Freston, J. (1992). *Developing transition plans for elementary students with severe disabilities.* Salt Lake City: University of Utah, Department of Special Education, Utah Elementary Integration Dissemination Project.

McLean, M., & Hanline, M. F. (1990). Providing early intervention services in integrated environments: Challenges and opportunities for the future. *Topics in Early Childhood Special Education, 10,* 62–77.

National Association for the Education of Young Children and the National Association of Early Childhood Specialists in State Departments of Education (1991). Guidelines for appropriate curriculum content in programs serving children ages 3 through 8: A position statement. *Young Children, 46,* 21–38.

Noonan, M. J., & McCormick, L. (1993). *Early intervention in natural environments: Methods and procedures.* Pacific Grove, CA: Brooks/ Cole Publishing Co.

Odom, S. L., & McEvoy, M. A. (1988). Integration of young children with handicaps and normally developing children. *Early intervention for infants and children with handicaps: An empirical base.* Baltimore: Paul H. Brookes.

Rubin, R. R., & Fisher, III, J. J. (1982). *Ages three and four: Your preschooler.* New York: Collier Books.

Rule, S., Fiechtl, B. J., & Innocenti, M. (1990). Preparation for transition to mainstreamed post-preschool environment: Development of a survival skills curriculum. *Topics in Early Childhood Special Education, 9*(4), 78–90.

Rule, S., Stowitschek, J. J., Innocenti, M., Striefel, S., Killoran, J., Swezey, K., & Boswell, C. (1987). The Social Integration Program: An analysis of the effects of mainstreaming handicapped children into daycare centers. *Education and Treatment of Children, 10*(2), 175–192.

Shearer, D. E., & Shearer, M. S. (1976). The Portage Project: A model for early childhood intervention. In T. D. Tjossem (Ed.), *Intervention strategies for high risk infants and young children.* Baltimore: University Park Press.

Simeonsson, R. J., Olley, J. G., & Rosenthal, S. L. (1987). Early intervention for children with autism. In M. J. Guralnick & F. C. Bennett (Eds.), *The effectiveness of early intervention for at-risk and handicapped children* (pp. 275–296). Orlando, FL: Academic Press, Inc.

Strain, P. S. (1990). LRE for preschool children with handicaps: What we know, what we should be doing. *Journal of Early Intervention, 14*(4), 291–296.

Striefel, S., Killoran, J., & Quintero, M. (1991). *Functional integration for success: Preschool Intervention.* Austin: Pro-Ed.

Taylor, S. (1988). Caught in the continuum: A critical analysis of the principle of the least restrictive environment. *Journal of the Association for Persons with Severe Handicaps, 13*(10), 41–53.

Thurman, S. K., & Widerstrom, A. H. (1990). *Infants and young children: A developmental and ecological approach* (2nd ed.). Baltimore: Paul H. Brookes.

Vincent, L. J., Brown, L., & Getz-Sheftl, M. (1981). Integrating handicapped and typical children during the preschool years: The definition of best educational practice. *Topics in Early Childhood Special Education, 1*(1), 17–24.

Vincent, L. J., Salisbury, C., Walter, G., Brown, P., Gruenewald, L., & Powers, M. (1980). Program evaluation and curriculum development in early childhood/special education: Criteria of the next environment. In W. Sailor, B. Wilcox, & L. Brown (Eds.), *Methods of instruction for severely handicapped students* (pp. 303–328). Baltimore: Paul H. Brookes.

Walsh, S. (1993). Head Start disability regulations released. *DEC Communicator, 19*(3), 3.

Walter, G., & Vincent, L. J. (1982). The handicapped child in the regular kindergarten classroom. *Journal of the Division for Early Childhood, 6,* 84–95.

Willer, B., Hofferth, S. L., Kisker, E. E., Divine-Hawkins, P., Farquhar, E., & Glantz, F. B. (1991). *The demand and supply of child care in 1990: Joint findings from The National Child Care Survey 1990 and A Profile of Child Care Settings.* Washington DC: National Association for the Education of Young Children.

Wolery, M., Holcombe, A., Venn, M. A., & Werts, M. G. (1992, December). *Finding the balance: Developmentally appropriate practice and instruction of young children with special needs.* Preconference workshop presented at the International Early Childhood Conference on Children with Special Needs, Washington DC.

Wolery, M., Strain, P. S., & Bailey, Jr., D. B. (1992). Reaching potentials of children with special needs. In S. Bredekamp & Teresa Rosegrant (Eds.), *Reaching potentials: Appropriate curriculum and assessment for young children, Vol. I* (pp. 92–112). Washington DC: National Association for the Education of Young Children.

Chapter *7*

Elementary School Programs

Many of our best childhood memories originate from the time spent in elementary school. For most children, life there is fun, challenging, and rewarding. School environments provide a perfect opportunity to make friends, learn new games, and perhaps, even become the captain of a favorite team. It is there that future computer specialists, bank managers, and electricians learn the essentials of living. Students learn to multiply fractions, write poems, use maps, and problem-solve with computers. Equally important, they become sympathetic counselors for a buddy who failed the spelling quiz, and adept at the art of negotiation while preventing a fight on the playground. Through elementary schools, young children begin to experience an exciting new life—one that takes them to a step beyond the family activities and relationships of home and the play routines of preschool.

Educational opportunities from this period shape the character and skills of young children, preparing students for the rising expectations of adolescence and later, young adulthood. These demands, which have grown in complexity as the character of our communities has changed, have compelled elementary programs to re-assess its standards and adjust its programs to meet the expanding needs of the students that it serves. As a nation, we have become increasingly aware of this new shift in focus, and have taken significant steps to restructure our schools in a way that allows them to adapt to the individual student and local differences (Bacharach, 1990; Kirst, 1988; McDonnell, & Kiefer-O'Donnell, 1992; Murphy, 1991; Odden & Marsh, 1990).

The same challenge holds true for the role that elementary schools play for children with severe disabilities. These programs, like those for secondary services, must also prepare their young students to face the hurdles of everyday community life. The instructional routines, support, and ultimately, risks experienced regularly by these children will directly affect the quality of their later life. Establishing meaningful friendships, meeting one's personal needs, communicating effectively, moving independently throughout the school and neighborhood, and accessing help when needed are true daily concerns for these students while in their elementary years. How schools have met the challenge to meet these needs since the enactment of PL 94-142 has changed

WINDOW 7-1   A New Day for the Fifth-Grade Homeroom

As students in Ms. Nelson's fifth-grade class begin a second day's work on team projects in science, their teacher temporarily interrupts them to introduce two new pupils in the class.

"Girls and boys, I would like you to stop your work for a moment. We have two new students in our class who I would like to introduce."

One girl, Joanne, has just moved into the community from the Philippines. She's lived there for two years. Prior to that time, she lived in California, where she attended a school on base. She has recently returned to the states with her parents with the closure of the island military base.

"I would like to introduce Joanne Wilson. She just moved back to the United States from the Philippines, where she saw that volcano erupt! Her parents were stationed there, and left just two days before the mountain totally exploded. I bet she has quite a bit to tell us about living and going to school there. Marsha, will you move those books on the empty desk next to you? Joanne will join in with your team, and work with you on the science project."

Students in Marsha's group are excited about having the new student be part of their team. As Joanne takes her seat, each of her teammates simultaneously begin to ask her questions about her experience with the volcano.

"All right children, settle down for a moment. We have another new student to introduce."

The second girl is also new to the school. Different than Joanne however, Jennifer has lived in town all of her life. Actually, she has lived a block from school for the past four years. She has always attended a special school for children with severe disabilities.

"Class, this is Jennifer McCarthy. As you can see, she uses a wheelchair to move through school. Jennifer had been attending Middleton School, across town, but will now be going to our school. We'll have to make sure to keep the aisles clear so that Jennifer can get in and out. Tom, can you help her back by you? Her aide will be here soon to help her with her math."

Within several minutes, the period ends and it's time for lunch. The special education aide has not yet arrived, so Tom helps Jennifer out of class and to the gym for lunch. He pushes her to an open table, where Ms. Nelson asks if she'll be okay until the aide comes with her lunch. Jennifer nods indicating "yes," and Tom and his teacher leave. Joanne has taken a seat at another table with a number of other classmates, and is already busy with lunch. Girls from Marsha's group have joined her and have begun to ask about "seeing that volcano."

After about 10 minutes, Jennifer's aide arrives with lunch, apologizing for her tardiness. She gives Jennifer her lunch, and begins her own meal, as the student does the same. The meal proceeds quietly, until both are done. The aide, knowing that she failed to complete the math assignment, wheels Jennifer to her homeroom, where they spend the remainder of lunch doing addition problems.

As children with severe disabilities are given the opportunity to attend neighborhood schools and be included within homerooms, a number of new questions must be asked. In closing this Window, consider,

- How do we best prepare new teachers and students for the placement of students with disabilities in homerooms?
- How is support planned for them in these settings (especially, so that social relationships with peers can develop)?
- What function do the instructional activities and routines of the homeroom serve for these students?
- Do current practices of instruction and support from special education apply to these new settings?
- And finally, what steps can we take to establish positive attitudes toward the new student as a full member of the class and school?

substantially through the last two decades. This chapter will discuss the status of those services through review of the structural elements of school programs, effective organizational strategies, and best instructional practices that are currently employed within elementary programs for students with severe disabilities.

Structure of Elementary Programs

The contemporary history of the education of students with severe disabilities, and particularly that of young children, is striking in its degree of change and transition. Like other vulnerable and under-served individuals in our society, change for these students has come, at times, rather painfully. The reform that has taken place over nearly the last 20 years in services for these students has resulted in a dramatic shift in the school-based programs for children six through twelve years of age. This change, continuing now, and its resulting impact on children and their families, contributes greatly to the shape and quality of elementary-school programs. Four features of these programs act as the basis for the structure of these elementary services. They are the location of the service programs, the staffing patterns employed to educate children, the educational resources that they use, and the goals that these programs are trying to achieve.

Focus 1:

How are elementary programs for students with severe disabilities structured?

Service Location

Services for elementary children with severe disabilities were vastly different across the states prior to the institutionalization of special education nationwide through P.L. 94-142. As states began to take responsibility for the education of these children, services operated by private, non-profit programs and staffed mainly by uncertified personnel, were often absorbed by publicly-operated, school districts. Initially, many local educational agencies opted to institute multi-district cooperatives that served large geographical regions. The collaborative arrangements were located in a central site, such as an older school building that was no longer in use, and commonly educated all students with severe disabilities from the cooperating school districts. These cross-age programs appeared necessary given the shortage of certified personnel, high costs for related services, and the apparent similarity in student service needs. But most important, this centralized format met the recognized educational need for these young children—they functioned as an available and reliable day treatment program.

Though some of these cooperatives continue to exist, the majority of elementary students now receive services directly from their home districts. However, the location of these school programs for these students may differ greatly from that of their nondisabled neighbors and friends. Often, districts employ as many as four different site options for elementary programs for students with severe disabilities.

Special schools are separate buildings or units dedicated solely to provision of services for students with disabilities. They typically house a full array of educational and therapy staff. Students are bussed to this centralized site from throughout the district to receive services. The size of the student population there may be as large as a typical elementary school.

Clustered arrangements are special, districtwide programs that are located within a regular elementary school. Often, a wing of the school is set aside, with the entire group of classes dedicated (or, "clustered") for district students with severe disabilities. This option may have the full same contingent of professionals found within a special school arrangement. It differs though from the special school in several ways. First, nondisabled students also are in attendance at the school. These programs may also serve fewer students than the first school arrangement. And finally, the length of the bus ride that children have to school may for particular students be shorter.

Local or *neighborhood schools programs* are alternatives which offer student services within the natural school catchment area for the family. Students attend the school that their neighbors and friends attend, with professional staff working in the school on a full, part-time, or itinerant basis. The size of the population of students with severe disabilities in attendance is normally much less than that of the first two options, being based on the natural distribution of children with disabilities for the area. Students may be bussed or walk to school.

A fourth structure, *homebound services*, is offered for students who commonly have special health or behavioral needs that prohibit regular school attendance. Services are provided jointly by a special educator who travels to the home and the child's caregivers. With a change in the student's status, the child is transferred to a school-based program.

The diversity of educational sites for elementary-school programs exists to meet two distinctly different needs for districts. First, local educational agencies employ the different school options in partial fulfillment of the legal mandates of IDEA (Bararach, 1985; Biklen, 1982; Brown, et al., 1989; Taylor, 1988). These rules define the student's right to equal protection and access to education, free and appropriate public education (FAPE), and the right to services within one's least restrictive educational environment (LRE). Together, these tenets guide and manage services for these children, affecting the location of educational services, its organization, and the expected benefit from instruction.

While each is critical to the quality of education for young children with disabilities, the LRE provision of P.L. 94-142 is the rule most commonly referenced as the basis for an array or continuum of different school sites. Specifically, when the educational needs of a particular child with severe disabilities cannot be satisfactorily met in a regular class with the use of supplemental aides or services, an alternate environment must be considered. Federal regulations for LRE stipulate that:

(a) *Each public [educational] agency shall ensure that a continuum of alternative placements is available to meet the needs of handicapped children for special education and related services.*

(b) The continuum required under paragraph (a) of this section must (1) include the alternative placement listed ... and, (2) make provision for supplementary services (such as resource room or itinerant instruction) to be provided in conjunction with regular class placement (34 C.F.R. Sec. 300.551, 1988).

The legal intent for the provision of a continuum is the prevention of temporary or permanent misplacement of a student with disabilities in a more restrictive school site than needed, due to a gap in the service system (Tucker & Goldstein, 1991). Districts, in structuring services, employ the array of locations as part of a decision-making process to ensure individualized services, matching the particular student need to the efficient organization of available resources at the different placement sites.

A second argument often raised in support of the continuum is that the mission of special education programs, especially those for young children, is to fix, cure, treat, or maintain students with disabilities, as dictated by the medically-oriented, developmental model (Skrtic, 1991). Serving in a role analogous to an outpatient clinic, the school sites are centrally arranged for expedient access to professional remediation services. As students' needs require more intensive treatment, special educators, related servers, and equipment are further concentrated, as one might do in a hospital or specialized treatment center.

Much debate has taken place over the actual practice of developing and maintaining a diversity of service placement sites for elementary students. The U.S. Department of Education (1986), in its standards, clearly stipulates that placements may not be based on (1) the student's category of disability condition, (2) configuration of service delivery system, (3) the availability of educational or related services, and (4) the availability of space (p. 376). In lieu of placement within regular education, students, however, immediately find themselves in homogeneous programs for children with the same disability, or in a cross-age class for all students with significant handicaps from within the local education agency (Sailor, et al., 1989; Stainback & Stainback, 1990). Placements are frequently driven, not as a consequence of team consideration of attainment of the appropriate I.E.P., but rather, because "slots" are open within particular programs. And movement upward within the continuum occurs only when it is demonstrated or earned by the student (TASH, 1986).

Additionally, the educational role and importance of the location of services for these children has also become increasingly more evident. Just as it is for nondisabled neighbors and friends, an elementary school is more than simply a building to access professional services for the student with severe disabilities. Serving a pivotal role in the student's childhood development, the school's location may positively influence the nature of the student's curriculum. Goals related to learning routes to school, using specific playground equipment before, after, and during school, or participating as a member of the school newspaper staff are directly linked to the school's location. Similarly, the school location determines who may become the student's friend. Friends from across town are difficult to access after school and on weekends, while other children from within one's own neighborhood have the potential for regular contact. Lastly, the arrangement selected for the school program can define the role that families may play in participating in the overall school experience. Parents of children in clustered arrangements often do not relate to the school as other than a visitor for meetings while local school parents have the opportunity for a great variety of roles and social activities.

As such, many parents and educators support only one placement option for children with severe disabilities (Brown, et al., 1989; McDonnell, et al., 1991; Sailor, et al., 1989; Stainback & Stainback, 1990). More and more, a call for placement only within a student's local or neighborhood school is heard. Defined as the school that "a student would attend if he or she were neither attending a private school nor requiring special education services" (Sailor, et al., 1989, p. 3), neighborhood school placement, together with the child's home and local community, are seen by a growing number of professionals and parents as the three primary educational contexts for instruction.

A number of crucial points can be offered in support of neighborhood school placement. Of significant importance are those that pertain to the quality of the educational experience (Brown, et al., 1989; Sailor, et al., 1989). Through these settings, the child with severe disabilities can experience and learn the real expectations for an elementary-aged student rather than the ones simulated within special schools or classes. Likewise, the child will have much less difficulty transferring skills that are acquired in that the setting of instruction when it is the real setting for performance. And finally, and equally important, students with severe disabilities in local schools have more frequent opportunities to establish meaningful friendships and other social relationships that can easily be continued outside the school environment. As the research on effective instruction grows, and the full benefits of local school placement become realized, a leading question in educational reform is shifting from "should students with severe disabilities be educated within regular schools?" to "what are the best methods for teaching these students within their own neighborhood school and other valued settings?"

Service Delivery Staffing Patterns

The variety of educational needs of the general population of young students with severe disabilities is very broad. A program's staffing pattern is therefore composed of those personnel who have day-to-day contact with children and related servers who are needed to support planning and instruction. Direct instructional staff are usually led by the special educator whose primary duties are either as a teacher or as an instructional manager who assigns most teaching responsibilities to others (i.e., teaching assistants, regular educators, peer tutors, or volunteers). Further, smaller or rural districts often assign educators who work within a "teacher as manager" role as itinerant special educators, serving two or more school sites. Regardless of the role, however, the special educator must develop instructional programs, facilitate the training of paraprofessionals, and ensure quality through the supervision of all instructional delivery.

P.L. 94-142, and now IDEA has defined the wide range of other personnel who may be needed to effectively plan and implement instructional services. In the state of Utah, for example, 14 categories of related services exist that may be called upon to support the core services provided through the elementary school special educator. In addition to the motor and speech therapies, these may include (1) assistive technology,

(2) parent training, (3) vision and audiological services, (4) social work support, and (5) counseling (Utah State Office of Education, 1993). Which services are needed and how the professionals are employed vary dramatically and should be a decision of the I.E.P. team. The method by which professionals are linked together to meet the these needs is called the program's team model.

Traditionally, one of three types of teaming models is used by elementary professionals to plan and deliver services to these children (Orelove & Sobsey, 1991). The primary factor that differentiates these patterns of service delivery is the extent to which professionals work together to develop and then implement instruction. The first, *multidisciplinary teaming*, is a direct offshoot of the professional team approach developed for medical services. Each professional is responsible for their own evaluation and, in essence, plan development. The individual segments are merged together as the Individual Education Plan with each team member responsible for the implementation of their own treatment or instruction.

Under an *interdisciplinary teaming model*, more collaboration between the various team members takes place. Certain decisions, such as which evaluations are to be completed and the selection of goals, are done jointly. While individual team members may still be responsible for their own service delivery, they also are expected to assist other team members, especially the special educator. A speech and language therapist for example may, following an observation of the special educator's instruction of personal hygiene, provide input as to how student requests for soap, assistance with the water, and the towel may be facilitated.

Transdisciplinary teaming takes the cooperative role several steps further. Here, only one unified plan is developed, as opposed to the multidisciplinary team approach which generates a number of small "mini-plans." A major emphasis of the model is placed on the sharing of information and skills rather than on independent service. Each team member provides input as to how coordinated goals may be identified and achieved. Often, the related service professional does not do direct instruction or therapy, but rather, trains other professionals or teaching assistants how to incorporate techniques across the entire day's routine.

The model of service delivery and professional teaming that is employed for elementary services has a dramatic impact on services and their outcomes. Oftentimes, districts will define the teaming model based on the availability of professional resources and the types of school placements offered. For example, special schools, with their full complement of related servers located on-site, often use their professionals in a direct instruction or therapy roles. While in other types of placements, students may receive the same services through the special educator, a paraprofessional, or perhaps a peer tutor. Research and a number of instructional models have demonstrated the impact of the skills and training of different providers on the quality of instruction (Giangreco & Meyer, 1988; Jorgensen, 1992; Kohl, Moses, & Stettner-Eaton, 1984; Rainforth, & York, 1987; Thousand, & Villa, 1990). This issue of the school placement role as a factor in determining the services a student receives has emerged as a major controversy over the last decade.

Taylor (1988), in a discussion of this practice, stated that the requirement of various types of placements under LRE, *as a mechanism for decision-making,* has resulted in a number of significant pitfalls. The perpetuation of the concept of continuums has changed the original intent of LRE, resulting in a functionally different application of the principle. Four problems, related to student services, have emerged from the use of continuum of placements for planning. They are that this process (1) supports the primacy of professional decision-making over the recommendations of parents or the individual needs of students, (2) directs attention to the physical setting over the services and supports people need to be integrated in the community, (3) is based on and promotes a "readiness model," and (4) implies that people must move as they grow and change (Taylor, 1988, pp. 45-48).

As an alternative to the cascade of placements for these students, Taylor (1988) suggests that the LRE principle be redefined. The services, and not the student placement, should be moved as necessary, to allow the child to experience the natural duration of full regular school placement. The intensity of services should be adapted and adjusted within this core location as needs increase or decrease. As such, planning for individual instruction within a placement should be understood as a balance between two dimensions, need for specialized instructional programming and the provision of support.

Giangreco and Putnam (1991) have suggested a model based on these parameters to describe the planning role for the team for successful instruction within inclusive educational settings. Figure 7-1 summarizes this model. As the student's educational needs differ from those presented within the regular education setting, team members must increase accommodations or adaptations for the student within that setting. Like-

SUPPORTS

	Supports similar to those typically available in regular education	Supports that are extended, modified, or individualized
PROGRAMS — Educational program similar to regular education	A No accommodations required	B Support accommodations required
Educational program that is extended, modified, or individualized	C Program accommodations required	D Program and support accommodations required

FIGURE 7-1   Dimensions of Instructional Services

Taken from, Giangreco, M., & Putnam, J., (1991). Supporting the education of students with severe disabilities in regular education environments. In L. Meyer, C. Peck, & L. Brown (Eds.) *Critical Issues in the Lives of People with Severe Disabilities,* p. 247, Baltimore, MD: Paul H. Brookes.

wise, as performance and participation expectations increase, accommodations for support must also increase (Giangreco & Putnam, 1991, pp. 246–247).

Successful application of this alternate model to organization and use of staff has been achieved by various school programs (c.f., Brown et al., 1983; Biklen, 1985; Ford et al., 1989; Giangreco & Meyer, 1988; McDonnell et al., 1991; Sailor et al., 1989; Stainback & Stainback, 1990). Often initially focusing on the organization and methods for those non-school instructional settings that are important for elementary-aged students (i.e., home, stores, community parks, and centers, etc.), the emphasis has now shifted to fully address services within included school settings. Flexible and adapted staffing patterns for educators and related servers promote the individualized delivery and modification of services (e.g., direct instruction, physical and occupational therapy, behavioral support, etc.) within normal classroom settings while also being compatible with educational services of other children.

Utilizing Inclusive Educational Resources

Homerooms that extend from kindergarten to sixth grade, a gymnasium, playgrounds with swings and monkey bars, the long hallway leading to the principal's office, rooms for art and music, and children, many smiling children—this is the image that many of us remember when we think of elementary schools. A fully rounded education requires contact with a variety of school settings, students, and professionals. Each serves as a resource for teachers, and ultimately, for young students. However, this vision is not a view that most students with severe disabilities have experienced. Rather, it has only been within this generation of elementary students that the trend away from full-time education in segregated environments is truly beginning to take hold.

A number of educational resources can be used by special educators to structure the educational day of elementary students with significant disabilities. Perhaps the most important is the classroom. Teachers have used variations from among three types of classroom placements. The student may be educated full-time within a *self-contained classroom*. Many students spend the entire day there receiving instruction in fulfillment of the IEP. Therapy by related servers may be completed there or within a second dedicated area, such as a speech or physical therapy room. Commonly, the student has contact solely with special education personnel or other students with severe disabilities (Ford & Davern, 1989).

An elementary student with significant disabilities may receive part-time instruction within a *resource classroom*. The student may then spend time in either the self-contained class, or elsewhere within the school. Instructional services there are similar to those found within the self-contained class. One difference found there, however, is that the student has the potential to interact with a wider array of students from the school. The third classroom placement is within the student's grade level *homeroom class*. Core instruction is provided within that setting and worked into the regular education routines. The child may have little or no contact with other students with disabilities, and less direct interaction as a rule with special education personnel.

By the mid-1980s, the need to educate students with severe disabilities in other than self-contained environments had become evident (Schnoor, 1990; Stainback & Stainback, 1990). With the operational costs of separate facilities and services for a relatively small number of students increasing, and pressure from parents and educators to employ homerooms and other school settings as educational resources, public educational agencies have made more regular classroom placement options available. The status of this trend can be seen through Table 7-1, which summarizes classroom placement information from 1987–88 for four student groups commonly associated with severe disabilities (U. S. Department of Education, 1990). These data compare very favorably to the status of placements prior to 1983, when most young children with significant disabilities rarely or never interacted with included school environments.

Other school and community settings can used as educational resources and opportunities for students (Ford & Davern, 1989; McDonnell et al, 1991; Stainback & Stainback, 1990). *Content area classes*, such as music and art rooms or the gymnasium, provide opportunities to access routines, materials, and students in support of the child's IEP. Likewise, areas such as the lunchroom, school restrooms, and the playground may be designated for instructional use. Additional educational opportunities may be found through participation in the school's *extracurricular and after-school activities*. Though these formal groups are less common in elementary school than with older students, clubs and teams are a valuable resource for all children in kindergarten through sixth grade. These may include class newspapers, action groups for the homeless, soccer and basketball teams, and recycling, science, and environmental clubs. *Community and home-based instruction* has been shown to be both effective and critical for these young students (Ford et al, 1989; McDonnell et al, 1992). Different than secondary programs, where there is a need to emphasize vocational training in regular job settings, this instruction for elementary students is often based on the lifestyle choices of the family (e.g., chores from home, recreational preferences, or family rou-

TABLE 7-1 **Type of Educational Placement for Selected Students Served Under Chapter 1 of ESEA and Part B of EHA for 1987–1988[1]**

Disability condition	Total	Regular class[2]	Resource class[2]	Special class[2]	Special school, home, or other setting
Intellectually Disabled	593,796	5.7%	24.0%	57.6%	12.7%
Orthopedically Disabled	47,222	27.7%	18.0%	31.8%	22.5%
Multiply Disabled	75,637	6.4%	13.3%	45.9%	34.3%
Dual Sensory Impaired	1,556	8.9%	7.2%	35.1%	48.9%
Total	718,211	51,916	161,193	392,337	112,765
Percentage	100%	7.2%	22.4%	54.7%	15.7%

[1]Data taken from, U.S. Department of Education (1990). *Twelfth annual report to Congress on the implementation of the Education of the Handicapped Act (EHA)*.

[2]Placement is within a regular school, but not necessarily the student's neighborhood school.

tines with siblings), and the natural community settings (e.g., grocery, church, mall, or park) that they frequent with their child.

Focus 2:

What is the emerging mission of elementary school services for students with severe disabilities?

Meaningful Educational Benefit

Perhaps the most critical question that an elementary program must answer pertains to its mission for these young children with disabilities. Excellence and equity—for years, these were the guiding principles that shaped regular elementary school programs (Greer, 1972). In practice, their fulfillment has truly challenged school professionals. Similarly, educators who teach young students with severe disabilities have had to re-examine their goals and the projected outcomes for their services. But different than services for older children, which focused on job training and community living skills, elementary teachers initially had little clear direction. As Tawney & Sniezek (1985) stated,

> *An analysis of the literature reveals little of substance that is directly referenced to elementary programs . . . [However,] the task for the teacher of elementary school-age [children with severe disabilities] is essentially the same as that of the regular grade teacher—to take the child from the present level . . . to the next level (p. 80–81).*

Programs for these children have traditionally used the standard of quality conveyed through FAPE as the basis for planning and evaluating Individual Educational Programs. An IEP must be "appropriate" for the child's educational needs. This standard however, gave professionals little functional direction for planning, and provided less assistance for evaluation. Likewise, the degree of appropriateness and the extent of district responsibility to meet the student's needs, through support, adaptive equipment, and medical or therapy service could not be gauged using this guide as a criterion. However, the rulings of the U.S. Supreme Court, from *Board of Education of H. Hudson School District v. Rowley* (1982), have begun to clarify this standard. Through the court's action, educational teams have been directed to focus on individually meaningful outcomes or benefits as a measure of "appropriate."

Implications of this definition of appropriate are rather significant as it applies to the mission of educational programs. Rather than simply seeking to fix or cure students (Skrtic, 1991), services are now beginning to focus on achieving those outcomes that impact the quality of the child's life as a functional indicator of their "appropriateness" of the service (Kiefer-O'Donnell, 1991; Osborne, 1992; Villa & Thousand, 1993). To understand how meaningful educational benefits may be achieved for students, one need only look to a common day-to-day experience for a typical young child.

A vivid memory for most adults is first learning, as a young child, to ride a bike. Thoughts about the experience, for many, center around bruised knees, elbows, and feelings. But with time, other very important memories of the event come to mind. For many children, the desire to ride a "two-wheeler" was stimulated by seeing other friends in the neighborhood race down the block, hopping over potholes. Buddies, more "motorically-inclined," perhaps had developed the skill weeks before. To use training wheels, when everyone else had mastered the necessary balance and coordination with little effort (or pain), was more uncomfortable than the thought of bruised knees. A decision was made and help was recruited, from one's parent, big brother or sister, or best friend, to take on the challenge that had to be mastered. With time and support, the task was accomplished. Our memory often ends with the entire group of friends on their first adventure together. And with that begins thoughts of another rewarding experience.

The valued benefits of this experience for individual children are clearly evident. It demonstrates how functional tasks can take on meaning only through their application within normal social contexts. Similarly, this same natural environment is an excellent starting point to establish performance expectations and identify natural resources for support. And as effort and competence increase, opportunities are opened for increased learning, friendships, and quality of living experiences.

These benefits may also act as valued overall goals or mission of services for students with severe disabilities. Research and successful practice over the last ten years has identified a number of key outcomes that can act as the basis of the school's mission. Services should be structured to ensure:

1. Meaningful participation and performance by the student in activities of normal, age-based routines (Baumgart et al., 1982; McDonnell et al., 1991; Nietupski, & Hamre-Nietupski, 1987; Snell, 1989)
2. The establishment of supportive, social relationships with peers, adults, and neighbors (Forest & Pierpoint, 1992; O'Brien & Lyle-O'Brien, 1992; Perske, 1988; Vandercook, York, & Forest, 1989)
3. The acquisition of collateral, enrichment, or extension skills (e.g., communication, motor, choice, money, functional math, mobility, etc.) through integrated, activity-based planning and instruction (Brown, et al., 1987; Campbell, 1987; Helmstetter & Guess, 1987; McDonnell et al., 1992; Orelove & Sobsey, 1991; Rainforth & York, 1987; Rainforth, York, & Macdonald, 1992)
4. The inclusion of student's, parents', and family members' choices as the linchpin for all team planning (Hamre-Nietupski, Nietupski, & Strathe, 1992; Giangreco et al., 1991; Singer & Irvin, 1991)
5. The utilization of a performance criterion for an activity goal that is based on normal expectations and conditions (Brown, et al., 1976; White, 1988).

With these goals as the basis for the mission for elementary services, systematic planning, and selection of specific organizational and instructional strategies for services for young children can occur. While serving as a guide for individual student's educational program, they also act as standards by which the IEP may be evaluated.

WINDOW 7-2   The Beginning of a New Circle of Friends

Both Joanne and Jennifer are new students in the fifth-grade homeroom. It's mid-afternoon of their first day at the new school, and time for recess. The special education aide has break now, so Tom and Maria, two students in the homeroom, volunteer to help Jennifer outside to the playground. Halfway down the hall, Jennifer begins to wheel her chair—slowly, but by herself. Tom lights up.

"Hey, I didn't know that you could do that. Why didn't you tell me before?"

Jennifer first smiles, and then lets out a full laugh. The two other fifth graders join in. They continue slowly outside, where Tom leaves to play softball. Joanne, the other new student, has been invited to join an impromptu soccer game, serving because of her height, as goalie. Maria, not wanting to leave Jennifer simply sit by herself during recess, asks,

"Do you want to play jump rope?"

Again, Jennifer smiles, and looks toward the group of girls next to the building who have already begun to play jump rope. Maria understands, and helps Jennifer over a curb, as the two girls move on to the game. Once there, Maria asks,

"Do you know how to twirl?"

Jennifer shakes her head, "no," so Maria places the end of the rope in her hand, and holding it together, says,

"Okay, hold it like this, and go round this way," guiding her movements with her hand.

Soon, Jennifer gets the hang of it, and Maria is able to let go. It's her turn to jump, so she leaves Jennifer's side, and begins her routine. She is able to jump longer than any of the other girls. As she spins around to complete a maneuver, she faces Jennifer as she jumps. Seeing her twirl, Maria sticks out her tongue and both girls laugh. Unfortunately, the twirling stops, ending Maria's turn. It doesn't really matter, because a new game will start again tomorrow and Maria usually wins anyway.

In a moment Ms. Nelson calls to the students to return to class, and Maria and Jennifer come in together. As they enter the room, Ms. Nelson asks the classmates to take out their library books and use the remaining time to read silently. Marsha, who had been playing soccer with Joanne asks her teacher if she could loan her one of her books to read. Ms. Nelson approves, and the girls go to the reading corner of the room to choose among Marsha's three books.

The special education aide, in seeing Jennifer enter the class, takes her chair and moves her to the side of the room to work on her communication board. Maria asks her teacher,

"Ms. Nelson, is it okay if I give Jennifer one of my books to look at?"

The special education aide hearing the requests interrupts, saying,

"Honey, Jennifer really can't read your books. But thanks anyway."

"Well, what if we read together?"

Both her teacher and the aide think for a second, and simultaneously give their approval. Together, Maria and Jennifer spent the remainder of class reading her two books, one on raising tropical fish, and the other, about a girl on a ranch and her pet horse. Class ends, and the special education aide helps Jennifer place her papers in her backpack and out to the special education bus.

From a young child's perspective, establishing friends is one of the more important activities of school. Taking advantage of natural opportunities that occur at school is crucial for all students, including those with severe disabilities. Learning to communicate, including new ways to listen, is all part of the process of building bonds. With positive experiences come new opportunities. Often, the best action on the part of team members is to not act and let the natural events and efforts of peers begin to evolve. In closing this Window, consider,

- Could this experience have as easily occurred in a special school, or if Jennifer had been served solely a self-contained classroom?
- How can this relationship be continued? possibly expanded outside of school?
- Under what conditions is it appropriate to change scheduled instruction (e.g., working on a communication board) for more spontaneous opportunities?
- What role does being a "member" of the homeroom have on children establishing relationships and supporting peers?

Likewise, and as important, they function as a tool for educational professionals in the program planning and evaluation of the comprehensive services for these children.

Effective Organizational Strategies of Elementary-School Programs

Elementary programs for young children with severe disabilities operate most effectively when the service system utilizes planning strategies that maximize use of the school's resources toward realization of the program's goals. Four organizational strategies for the school's structure have emerged as innovative practices in the delivery of services to elementary-aged children. These approaches promote more effective identification and use of educational resources for these students with severe disabilities, and focus services on the attainment of the five valued outcomes. Though these strategies may be clearly applied as a measure of the achievement of specific IEP goals, they are perhaps better discussed here as part of the overall structure for the school program.

Focus 3:

What organizational patterns and practices help elementary teams to achieve the valued outcomes for students with severe disabilities?

Family Support, Choice, and Partnerships

Effective individual service delivery begins with the establishment of a student IEP that is supported by the mission of the school. Past processes to determine this plan provided parents with only a nominal role. As schools have changed, so has the orientation that programs have taken toward parental participation and family support (Dokecki & Heflinger, 1989; Singer & Irvin, 1991). Over the course of the nearly two decades that PL 94-142 has been in effect, the part that parents play in cooperatively planning the services for their child has increased significantly. This has been due, in part, to a shift in the perspective of professionals.

Past "models" for working with parents of children with disabilities emphasized family dysfunctioning, stress and coping, and inadequate parenting skills. These attitudes and approaches have left educators with what at times is no more than myths about the impact of having a child with severe disabilities in a family. As "family-need fables" (Barber, et al., 1988), they overlooked the individual nature of families and the normal functions that they serve for all members, including a son or daughter with disabilities. When a family is considered a "family first," through a family system orientation, their ability to determine and plan a direction for services becomes apparent, let alone not questioned.

Educators are beginning to recognize and incorporate this new perspective, and focus first on supporting the ability of families to make their own best decisions. As Salisbury (1992) states,

Over the past century, a number of role changes have emerged for parents of children with disabilities. Parents have moved from being perceived as the source of their child's problems to more proactive roles as service developers, learners, teachers of their child, advocates, and educational decision-makers. Unfortunately, in our zealousness to create more sub-stantive roles and responsibilities for parents within the educational con-text, we have forgotten the primary role of these individuals—parents as family members . . . It is therefore incumbent upon professionals to engage in a consensus-building within the team and acknowledge the acceptability of differences among families, and between professional and parent agen-das (pp. 43–44).

A first key issue for many families is to be assured of the quality and safety of the ser-vices delivered (McDonnell, 1987). Concurrently, many desire to have a more active voice in the direction of educational services for their son or daughter. Implementa-tion of a decision-making process that acknowledges preferences and provides parents a meaningful team role requires a clear, positive relationship.

Establishing a partnership between a family and schools begins with building trust. As with any cooperative arrangement that relies on volunteer participation, a home-school partnership should first begin with establishing mutually agreed-upon goals for activities (Brightman, 1988; Salisbury, 1992; Walker, 1989). Accepting parent and family priorities as a critical concern for the IEP is a major first step in establishing that bond and building the partnership. A tangible indication of that acceptance is the incor-poration of procedures which recognize and award high-priority status to parental choice in the selection of IEP goals and objectives (Ford et al, 1989; McDonnell et al., 1991).

A variety of educational models have begun to use parent choice as a key factor in the selection of IEP goals (Malette et al., 1992; McDonnell et al., 1991; Vander-cook & York, 1989). Consistent with an overall ecological or lifestyle planning process, this empowerment promotes consideration of ethnic or cultural preferences within the planning process. Parental choices may include consideration of the over-all location of the placement, time spent within homeroom settings, role that social relationships play as goals, incorporation of functional academic skills within regu-lar activities, and emphasis for transition planning (Halverson, et al., 1989; Hamre-Nietupski, Nietupski, & Strathe, 1992). One approach, McGill Action Planning System (MAPS), also solicits input from the student's friends, neighbors, or relatives to plan and structure the daily routine. By doing so, it is recognizing that the people who are part of the student's daily life are the individuals best able to shape the child's lifestyle.

The movement to redefine the role of families within schools has also impacted educational for typical students. Consumer-driven structures within school boards, community-school task forces, and planning committees, non-graded planning processes such as Individual Student Learning Plans, and partnerships with local agen-cies and businesses are building school resources to meet changing community needs (Boyer, 1990; Kirst, 1988; Metz, 1990).

Collaborative Approach to Teaming

As special education programs were first developed within regular schools, the model of service delivery that was often employed mirrored the contemporary values and attitudes of professionals about students with severe disabilities. Past school missions were simply to provide a reliable day treatment program. Children with disabilities needed to be cured, treated, and cared for. Given the depth and variety of these needs for most students, the best approach for services, that also satisfied these values, was to implement an individual expert model. Similar to the approach used within health services, needs were addressed through a schedule of individually delivered sessions for therapy and instruction, with each specialist responsible for only a small phase of the child's educational plan. Today, the "pull-out" approach, based on the multidisciplinary team model, continues to serve as a frequently utilized method of therapy planning and delivery.

Support of the five valued educational outcomes for elementary students, however, requires more effective use of available educational resources. It requires service delivery to be integrated within natural, age-based routines, and assessed using standards tied to normal life. The model that has evolved as effective in achieving these outcomes is a transdisciplinary approach that is implemented through a collaborative team process (Dunn, 1991; Rainforth, York, & Macdonald, 1992; Orelove & Sobsey, 1991; Snell, 1991b; Stainback & Stainback, 1990). The two elements, transdisciplinary roles and collaborative problem-solving, work together to focus the team's effort toward more effective resource identification and usage.

Role definition and process

As previously stated, the first component, *transdisciplinary approach*, guides team members in the use of information, skills, and methods from each discipline. Like the musicians of a symphony orchestra, each field represented on the team contributes to the single, instructional service plan for the student. The team, therefore, is jointly responsible for the entire plan. Every aspect of the process, including assessment, IEP development, transition planning, and instructional program planning, is done with one outcome in mind—the "sharing, or transferring of information and skills across traditional disciplinary boundaries," establishing a unified service plan (Orelove & Sobsey, 1991, p. 11).

Successful implementation of a transdisciplinary approach results in a significant change in the traditional roles of most team members. This process suggests activities that require (1) role release, or the sharing of techniques from one discipline to another, (2) role expansion, or the acquiring of new information and skills from other disciplines, and (3) role support, or the training and encouragement of other disciplines who are engaged in new skill activities (Garland et al., 1989). By sharing skills through formal staff development activities or ongoing consultation, transdisciplinary team members furnish each other with the tools to make the individual strategies from any one discipline more effective.

The collaborative element to this model defines how professionals and parents will work together to achieve this unified service plan. Collaboration refers to "a nonhierarchical relationship in which all team members are seen as equal contributors, [with] each adding his or her own expertise or experience to the problem-solving process" (Stainback & Stainback, 1990, p. 96). As a framework for day-to-day teaming, collaboration operates with mutually-agreed goals, planning and communication systems, and conflict resolution strategies. Rainforth, York, & Macdonald (1992) have suggested ten core assumptions for collaboration, found in Table 7-2, that link valued educational outcomes for students with severe disabilities to this daily team process, and aid in defining team and member roles.

Effective school programs commonly use a two-level system of team organization and functioning to projected outcomes. The day-to-day planning and problem-solving group, which includes the special educator, homeroom teacher, parent, individual related servers, perhaps the principal, and *the student*, serves as the *core team*. Nontraditional members, such as school janitors or cooks, relatives of the student, and student friends, may also be part of this group, on an as-needed basis. This smaller group differs from the *extended team*, which meets less frequently, and is made up of the parents, student and entire array of professionals designated on the IEP (Giangreco, Cloninger, & Iverson, 1993). Their role is broader, conducting transdisciplinary-based assessments, collaborating on decisions for annual goals and objectives, and drafting integrated instructional plans.

TABLE 7-2   Requirements of a Collaborative Teamwork Approach to Education and Related Services for Students with Severe Disabilities[1]

- All students can learn given the opportunity and appropriate support.
- The desired educational outcomes for all students are participation in, contribution to, and enjoyment of family, school, and community life, now and in the future.
- All students, regardless of abilities, interests, and needs, must grow up and learn together in the same school and community environments in order to achieve desired educational outcomes.
- It is the explicit responsibility of the collaborative educational team to assist students in achieving desired educational outcomes.
- The collaborative team is comprised of the student, significant family members, friends, and the education and related services personnel required to assist students in achieving desired educational outcomes.
- Positive social interdependence among team members must be structured to realize the benefits of collaborative teamwork.
- Discipline-referenced knowledge and skills are shared among team members so that relevant expertise is available to students in all aspects of their educational program.
- An ecological curricular design is required to assist students in achieving desired educational outcomes.
- An Individualized Educational Program (I.E.P.) is developed jointly by the collaborative educational team and reflects an integrated approach to service, design, and provision.
- Collaborative teamwork strategies must remain flexible in order to meet changing needs of students and their families.

[1]Taken from, Rainforth, B., York, J., Macdonald, C. (1992) *Collaborative teams for students with severe disabilities: Integrating therapy and educational services.* p. 37.

Outcomes of collaborative teaming. Incorporation of transdisciplinary and collab-orative strategies for teaming produces significant benefit for elementary children with severe disabilities. These include improved skill acquisition (Campbell, McInerney & Cooper, 1984; Giangreco, 1986), defragmentized services (Albano et al.,1981; Camp-bell, 1986), and increased overall instructional time for students (McCormick, Cooper, & Goldman, 1979). These more integrated methods promote planning from student strengths (Campbell, 1989), emphasizing assessment and planning from real context performance (Downing & Bailey, 1990). Parent satisfaction, especially in the area of assessment is enhanced through its application (Wolery & Dyk, 1985). Teams use their time more efficiently to achieve valued outcomes for students (Thousand & Villa, 1990), and make better decisions (Thousand & Villa, 1992).

Shared Ownership by School Team to Achieve Membership

In the past, elementary services for students with significant and multiple disabilities were delivered in a way that typified what Skrtic (1991) has described as the phenom-enon called "the special education paradox" (p. 210). Functioning as an add-on to the mission of the school, special education programs and children would come and go with little or no impact on the operation of services for the remaining student body. Likewise, changes in their services were rarely done with any attention to the impact on the entire site, and, equally important, as part of an overall plan for the school. As such, a major barrier to the achievement of the true mission for the whole school existed. Resolution of this problem can begin only when students with severe disabili-ties fully *belong in the school*. Belonging demands that faculty, administrators, and peers of these children accept them as full members of homerooms, the grade, and the school as a whole.

A growing number of educators believe that this focus for programs is the most important first step to be taken in the planning of effective regular school services (McDonnell et al., 1991; Thousand et al., 1986; Williams et al., 1989). Moving beyond the self-contained classroom, it is the first step to making the school as a whole the stu-dent's classroom. It begins with an informal analysis of the school environment. Iden-tifying attitudes toward homeroom placement, barriers to participation and access, and needs of teachers, peers, parents, and administrators for information on disabilities and services aid the team in establishing membership. Activities should guarantee that regular teachers, parents, administrators, and peers (1) are part the decision process for homeroom placement, (2) receive pre-placement and then ongoing support and inservice training, and (3) are participants in ongoing planning and problem-solving of placement issues. These may include the removal of barriers to participation in nor-mal homeroom and school activities, identification of methods to increase friend-ships, and the modification of routines that create perceptions of the student as a visitor (McDonnell et al.,1991).

Programs that have achieved an atmosphere of "shared ownership" engage in a number of similar organizational activities. Some schools have found the establish-ment of grade-level placement teams to be an effective mechanism to guarantee participation on the part of entire faculty and administration. Inservice training for regular educators and students within the homeroom can be a productive tool to ensure a positive, brain-storming orientation. Often this orientation emphasizes the specific strengths and abilities of particular children, and the role that class members may play in supporting the student. Key to the effective organization of included education is the role of the special educator as facilitator. This role-player must be able to engage in regular visits to the homeroom and be given sufficient opportunity to discuss with the regular teacher the status of the student's services and education there.

Successful implementation of these activities results in changes in the role for the homeroom teacher in the student's team, and the increased participation by the student in the various duties and informal routines of the homeroom (e.g., as leaders, helpers, planners, builders, etc.). Tangible indicators of "shared ownership" for the new homeroom student can be seen when the homeroom teacher co-facilitates IEP meetings, and invites the child's parents to regular parent-teacher conferences. These teachers may also "demand" more time for the student in the homeroom, and take the initiative to brainstorm and implement alternate, more natural means of support throughout the day. However, without positive attitudes conveyed in words and action by the regular educator, the child with disabilities will continue to be just someone who "comes and goes," and not a student who belongs in the homeroom. Nor will the homeroom or school be one that belongs to that student (Schnoor, 1990; Giangreco, et al., 1993).

Utilization of Natural Supports

A day in the life of a typical fourth-grade student with severe disabilities in the 1980s would reveal an interesting fact about relationships and how society perceived its role in teaching social skills. Much of the school day was spent interacting with only individuals who were paid (and therefore required) to do so. Teachers, aides, and therapists made up the typical, daytime social network for many students. Little time was spent either with friends, or benefiting from the modeling from peers. Communication, under these conditions, is primarily one directional, so that most interactions with adults were in response to cues or directions, and not as part an interactive and evolving conversation (Rowland, 1990). Likewise, real choices were rarely afforded (Houghton, Bronicki, & Guess, 1987). As such, most opportunities to build spontaneous communication were lost (Halle, 1987; Reichle, 1991).

An alternate organizational strategy that builds friendships, provides frequent opportunities for learning from participation and effective models, and strengthens interactive and spontaneous communication is to take advantage of natural supports. This approach for elementary students has been defined as any person, technology, or resource that "enables all students to be fully participating members of regular classroom[s], school, and community life . . . [and] brings children closer together as friends and learning partners rather than isolating them" (Jorgensen, 1992, p. 183). As Nisbet (1992) states,

> The concept of natural supports is based on the understanding that relying on typical people and environments enhances the potential for inclusion more effectively than relying on specialized services and personnel. Though appar-

ently simple, this concept forces reconceptualization of service delivery models and options, and at the same time, forces us to disassemble some of our thinking (p. 5).

Goals for the provision of support

Key to the effective use of natural supports is understanding its two crucial objectives: the provision of assistance in the least intrusive manner, and the facilitation of meaningful social relationships. Assistance is most effective when it is linked to the natural conditions for performance of the routine activity, using the normal resources from the setting. As demands increase, support may need to also increase to ensure ongoing participation in the routine by the student. And as demands decrease, support should be lessened, to provide a natural opportunity for the student to demonstrate competence and decrease the potential for dependency on support mechanisms. Organizational practices that begin by permanently scheduling instructional assistants or one of the team's professionals as "support" are inefficiently over-using educational resources and creating a perfect condition to maintain the visitor, non-member role for the student (i.e., "Johnny? Oh, he's the one who always has the aide hovering over him").

The facilitation of significant social relationships and friendships, as the second goal to the employment of natural supports, is clearly a new role for special education. Remediation of maladaptive behaviors, teaching requesting skills in isolation, and expansion of semantic or syntactic skills more commonly served in the past as goals for instruction. These have proven to be insufficient in meeting the valued outcomes for education and the specific needs of students. Haring (1991), in an analysis of the research on relationships, found that its inclusion as a valid educational outcome was clearly justified as having a number of positive benefits. Social relationships contribute substantially to the quality of life of all children. Social skill instruction, ideally produced within the context of an ongoing relationship with another person, is necessary for functional participation in many critical activities. Many critical skills are maintained over time by complex, remote schedules of reinforcement, but are maintained on an immediate basis by the socially reinforcing aspects of interacting with people with whom you have a relationship. And lastly, there is a relationship between social skills use and a lessening of a need for programming based on behavioral control (Haring, 1991, p. 197).

Alternatives for the provision of support

Three organizational approaches to the planning and provision of natural support been shown to be effective with the establishment of non-intrusive forms of assistance and lasting social relationships. The first, based on the consideration of individual routines targeted for instruction or participation, begins with a review of the typical ways that peers share, teach, and support each other for any particular activity. Cooperative learning, and peer tutor, model, and buddy systems (Gartner & Lipsky, 1990; Jenkins & Jenkins, 1981; Kohl et al., 1984; Sapon-Shevin, 1990) incorporate this technique. Emphasis is placed on the peer support of ongoing and meaningful participation and performance by the student during the activity, with the establishment of relationships naturally being a positive offshoot of the structured interactions.

A second system looks at the goals of assistance and social relationships equally, and attempts to address the more comprehensive needs for the student. Groups of concerned peers and family provide a "circle" from which the provision of support and advocacy emanates for the child (Forest, 1991; Perske, 1988). Through formalized circles of friends, support is established to provide a long-term commitment for assistance and friendship, continuous problem-solving, and nurturance (Forest & Pierpoint, 1992, p. 85). Though not sufficient to meet all the needs of students with severe disabilities, this strategy has successfully dismantled old notions of the quality of professional

---

WINDOW 7-3   Neighborhood Volunteers Lead the Way

Both Jennifer and Joanne have been members of the fifth-grade homeroom for a month. One of the parents of a classmate, Monica, approaches them as school ends one day to ask if they are interested in joining the Girl Scouts. Girls in the neighborhood are all members of the same pack. Monica's mother suggests that they come over on Saturday to see what it's like. It will be the first day of the annual "pop-can recycling drive," and the pack could use their help.

The two girls both get permission and, with the help of their parents, get a ride over to Monica's on the day of the recycling drive. Things begin with a door-to-door collection. Maria, who has become a pal of Jennifer, walks with her and 3 other girls. Each carry a plastic bag for the pop cans. Jennifer's bag is a pouch with handles, and has to be attached to the back of her chair. At each home, they introduce themselves, explain the purpose of their visit, and ask if the neighbors have any empty pop cans to recycle. They take turns retrieving them from the adult. That way, if they do, no one will have more than anyone else to carry.

By noon, each of the girls have filled their bags. They return home to Monica's where lunch is ready. At lunch, it's decided that they all have a "smashing party", collapsing the cans while they eat. Jennifer volunteers to try first. Grasping the handle, she pulls down on the lever, smashing the can that Monica has inserted. In a short while, they switch, with Jennifer loading the fresh can in the slot to be smashed. Later, when all the cans

have been smashed and lunch is over, Monica and Jennifer's mothers drive the pack over to the recycling center to see what happens with the bags of smashed cans. As they arrive home, both Jennifer and Joanne agree that they'll ask their parents if they could be regular members of the Girl Scout pack.

Friendships provide the best justification for support and participation. Both Joanne and Jennifer were invited to joint in on the Scout's recycling drive because of the relationships that they had established at school. The homeroom, a natural social network, has provided access to a new group, the neighborhood Girl Scouts. As more and more social networks are joined, inclusion and support become easier, and social competence increases. In closing this Window, consider,

- If the two girls had not been attending school within their own neighborhoods, would access to the Scouts have been as easy? What logistical problems would arise?
- What are other typical social groups, formal or informal, that may serve as accessible social networks for fifth-grade students?
- If Jennifer hadn't the skills to smash the cans, push her chair, or collect cans, would her participation have been different? How? What natural adaptations could have been employed to ensure full participation in the different activities of the pop-can drive?

support, and has played a major role in redefining the scope of educational services for these children. "To have supportive and meaningful friends" not only has become a valued outcome for services, but has taken a legitimate place within Individual Educational Programs as a goal for many children with severe disabilities.

Similar to the establishment of a circle of friends is the facilitation of inclusion into social networks. A social network is any formal or informal group of people with whom a person has repeated contact, and who are identified as socially important (Horner, et al., 1987). A social network can be any group of individuals that meet for a specific function, be it play, work, or personal management. Membership in a social network, such as scouts, a softball team, the newspaper club, or "the group of children who always jump rope in the back corner of the playground during recess" provides natural means of support, friendship, and access to other groups. For example, by being a member of the scouts, a student with severe disabilities is given the opportunity to meet and become friends with another student who, in turn, encourages membership in their school's pep club. The new friend then introduces her to the group of cheerleaders, and offers assistance with critical group activities. As membership is maintained, support expands from throughout the group, with a variety of participants providing regular and valuable assistance.

Effective Instructional Practices for Elementary School Programs

Instructional planning and delivery for individual students should have as a primary goal the achievement of meaningful benefit for each child. That is, the individualized selection of curriculum and teaching methods for a student should be based on a match between the skills of the student and educational resources. It should be done in a manner that assures achievement of the identified valued outcomes as applied through the child's IEP. Research has determined that three approaches to individualized instruction support these valued outcomes. They include: (1) goal selection based on meaningful performance and participation in valued routines and activities (Ford, et al., 1989; McDonnell et al., 1992; Rainforth, York, & Macdonald, 1992; Vandercook, York, & Forest, 1989; Wilcox & Bellamy, 1987); (2) the inclusion of the student within supported, age-appropriate settings as a mechanism to maximize performance (Giangreco, Dennis et al., 1993; McDonnell & Hardman, 1989; McDonnell et al., 1991; Stainback & Stainback, 1990); and (3) the integration of instructional methods within and across functional activities (Campbell, 1987; Goetz et al., 1987; Helmstetter & Guess, 1987; Orelove & Sobsey, 1991; Rainforth, York, & Macdonald, 1992). Each approach will be described in detail.

Focus 4:

What are individual, student-based strategies that have been shown to be effective in achieving valued educational outcomes for elementary students with severe disabilities?

Curriculum and Educational Planning

Perhaps the most visible change in the delivery of services for children with significant and multiple disabilities has come in the process of curriculum selection. "What should be taught" has been answered through numerous approaches and tools, many of which were built from developmentally-based sequences, modified pre-academic and academic skills, custodial or passively-oriented services, or checklists of daily living skills arranged by topical focus. While each may have resulted in some form of "success" (i.e., instructional strategies did facilitate the attainment of targeted objectives), they all had shortcomings that minimized the student's potential for generalized performance within home, school, and community settings.

These early efforts demonstrated little or no relationship between the selection of the instructional target and actual performance expectations. Most often, they emphasized the acquisition and performance of skills under isolated or simulated conditions rather than as part of meaningful and functional activities. Individual choice by students or parents was rarely if ever considered as a factor in the selection of goals and activities. And lastly, these curricula ignored, for the most part, the role of friendships and social relationships as a valid curricular focus for services.

As a response to the inadequacies of these approaches, planning methods were developed to determine the "criterion of ultimate functioning" for the individual student (Brown, Nietupski, & Hamre-Nietupski, 1976). That is, instruction was arranged from the results of an ecological or environmental inventory of the natural routines and activities of the student's frequently contacted or future settings. So, if the elementary student regularly used home kitchen and school lunchroom facilities to have meals, teachers used routines from those settings as the basis of curricular planning and assessment. The ecological process specifies:

1. The age-appropriate environments and settings where performance and participation occur
2. The routines and activities that normally take place there
3. A short description of the natural sequence of steps for an activity
4. Descriptive features of the activities, such as its duration, social or communicative demands, natural mechanisms of support, materials that are needed, and natural signals or cues
5. Mobility requirements for the activity and stimulus dimensions of the setting, commonly collected through the use of a teacher-drawn map

The inventory may also differentiate the components or critical phases of the activity, including preparation, initiation, continuation, closure, and transition (Brown, et al., 1987).

Perhaps the only major drawback to the ecological approach was the fact that analysis of critical current and future environments produced too many possible targets for instruction. Teachers and parents could easily be overwhelmed with options suggested from such a review, and were given little guidance in how to prioritize goals for the student. As a result, the early community-referenced curriculum process was modified to include decision processes linked to lifestyles and participation in valued routines of the home, school, and community settings (Ford et al., 1989; Malette et al., 1992; McDonnell et al, 1992; Vandercook, York, & Forest, 1989; Wilcox & Bellamy, 1987).

The prioritization and selection of goals begins with the team members' review of current or preferred settings, and the valued routines, activities, and skills that naturally take place within those environments. When collected and summarized, choices are weighed by the team, considering (1) preference by the student to participate in the activity, (2) regular frequency of performance of the activity, (3) opportunities for social interaction with peers during the activity, (4) level of support or assistance needed, (5) age-appropriateness of the activity, and (6) degree of inclusion afforded by the context and routines (McDonnell et al., 1991, Rainforth, York, & Macdonald, 1992; Wilcox & Bellamy, 1987).

An alternate process for decision-making, based on the results of ongoing discussion by a student's family, circle of friends, and supportive team members has been developed through the McGill Action Planning System, or MAPS (Vandercook, York, & Forest, 1989). This approach utilizes seven questions as the first stage of a vision planning process (Malette et al., 1992). Team members use the structure to focus on key issues of inclusion, support, participation, and choice to aid in the establishment of meaningful routines for the child, and ultimately, targeted goals for the student's IEP.

The outcome from the different routine-based approaches is the development of a functional and meaningful curricular base for the IEP. As such, it serves as an individualized technique for planning regular and ongoing participation and performance within normal, age-based activities. It is preferred that "activities" are chosen as the basis of instruction and act as targets for the IEP. Activities are a combination or sequence of skills, performed at prescribed periods of the day. Completing morning hygiene, making lunch, or purchasing school supplies are examples of typical activities for elementary students. The nature of this instructional unit is that it is, when properly chosen, inherently functional and usually meaningful for the student.

If skill-based performance is considered as an appropriate unit of instruction and acquisition for the student (i.e., the task is a single behavior or short chain of behaviors, reflecting less complexity than an activity), the target skill must be taught across multiple times and settings of the day in order for function and meaning to be established. This requirement can be seen through the instruction of a motor/mobility skill, "transfers out of chair or wheelchair to a walker." Considered in isolation, the skill has little real meaning for the student. Over time, if taught repeatedly, out of context, it would result in both fatigue and resistance on the part of the student. However, if incorporated naturally as part of a transition to lunch, recess, P.E., and music, the skill is given meaning and more likely to be acquired.

Goals and objectives that are selected by the team from this process should reflect the integration of recommendations and methods from the team into a coordinated and unified instructional plan. It is preferred that goals are defined using an activity as a base. The focus of the goal should be the student's full or partial performance of an age-based activity within two or more natural settings and regular routine(s). Objectives may then be drafted to address one or more of five aspects of performance:

1. Increasingly more independent or complex performance of activity-goal, across required settings
2. Performance of extension skills in support of the goal, or those skills that focus specifically on components or critical phases (i.e., preparation, initiation, continuation, closure, and transition) of the activity (Brown et al., 1987)
3. Performance of naturally required enhancement or collateral skills, such as communication, motor, mobility, or practical academic skills that are required as part of the activity
4. Performance of an alternate performance strategy as part of the activity (including use of adaptive equipment)
5. Increased performance of the activity or critical extension or enhancement skill in simulation when the actual frequency of performance in the natural setting is insufficient to meet the targeted criteria

Rainforth, York, & Macdonald (1992) suggest that skill performance may serve as the emphasis of goals for the IEP when the targeted skill is defined with a specific function, and performance is required over multiple activities and setting from the student's natural routine. Objectives then serve one of two functions. They may be drafted to specify the increasing number or complexity of contexts for performance of the objective, with a secondary emphasis on the student's full or partial participation or full or partial independence. Objectives may also serve as the means to integrate specific transdisciplinary procedures for the performance of the skill (e.g., decreasing support, with use of adaptive equipment, for increasing duration, etc.). Examples of the two formats for IEP formation have been included in Figure 7-2.

Instruction within Natural Performance Settings

Inclusion of elementary students within homeroom and other regular school settings is perhaps the greatest planning and delivery challenge for educational teams. Concerns often voiced include its impact on the operation of the homeroom, quality of services received there, effect on the services provided to other students, physical and emotional threats to students with disabilities, teacher support needs, and adequacy of staffing ratios within the regular setting. Placement of students there, however, can result in positive outcomes for all students and teachers if planned and managed properly. Research has demonstrated that placement of students within included settings can result in successful and increase achievement of IEP objectives (Brinker & Thorpe, 1984; Hunt, Goetz, & Anderson, 1986), gains in adaptive behavior (McDonnell et al., 1991), positive attitudes and interactions with nondisabled peers (Brinker & Thorpe, 1986; Haring, et al., 1987; Voeltz, 1980, 1982), and positive homeroom teacher satisfaction with support services (Giangreco et al., 1993; McDonnell et al., 1991). Attainment of these positive outcomes and avoidance of the problems that may result can only be accomplished through cooperative and ongoing planning between regular and special education.

Homeroom as an effective instructional resource

The natural routines and activities of a regular education homeroom and other school settings can act as a basis for effective planning and implementation of instruction for

Format	Annual Goal	Short-term Objectives
Activity-based goal	Susan will participate for at least hour per session in a twice-weekly swim class in the regular Sandy City Park and Recreation after-school program.	While traveling with her friend and sister, Susan will complete the required activities for use of the city bus to go to the swimming pool center (i.e., walk, wait, enter, seat self, rise when "announced", exit, and walk), on each of 5 consecutive probes.
Objectives transition preparation communication, choice, and increasing duration communication		Susan will independently use the locker room before and after swimming (i.e., get key/lock, locate locker, unlock key-style lock, change, lock/remove key, find locker, unlock, undress/shower, dry/dress, return key/lock) over each of 5 consecutive probes.
		When shown her communication book, Susan will choose and engage in at least 1 of 5 typical pool activities for at least 15 minutes during the 45 minute open swim period over each of 5 consecutive probes.
		When shown her communication book in class (prior to leaving for the pool), Susan will first choose "pool vs. non-pool" for any of 20 activity pictures (10/10 correct over 4/5 pre-travel sessions), and then point to the pool activity signed to her when shown three pool activity pictures (same criteria).
Activity-based goal	Tony will independently purchase and eat lunch at school, Wendy's, and Eat-a-Burger at least weekly.	Tony will use tactile signing and his communication flip-card book to order different lunch on each 5 different consecutive opportunities in the school cafeteria, Wendy's, and Eat-a-Burger.
Objectives Communication and initiation Alternate perform. strategy Continuation/ closure and mobility		Tony will chose correctly from three envelopes holding $1, $3, or $5 (marked with a textured value), based on the cash register/cashier stated amount tactually signed to him, and purchase lunch, on 10 consecutive probes in the school cafeteria, Wendy's, and Eat-a-Burger.
		When guided at the elbow by a peer buddy, Tony will independently carry his food and communication book to a preferred, vacant table/chair, sit down, complete his meal, and dispose of his trash/tray, on 10 consecutive probes in the school cafeteria, Wendy's and Eat-a-Burger.

FIGURE 7-2   Sample IEP goals and objectives

elementary students with severe disabilities. Generally, instructional strategies for use there can be broken into two broad categories though, in practice, they may be combined or actually used interchangeably. They are those strategies that modify the existing class curriculum activities to facilitate participation and performance, and the infusion of instruction in critical IEP targets within the homeroom educational routines.

A number of promising approaches have been applied to the modification of classroom curricular instruction. *Cooperative learning* is a strategy that structures activities "so that students work *together* to accomplish goals, accommodating [to] each other's differences and finding ways to encourage and nourish high levels of achievement and positive social interaction" (Sapon-Shevin, 1990, p. 65). It is accomplished through a combination of classroom modifications (e.g., removal of competitive images and practices within the classroom, infusion of readings that support cooperation, etc.) and the use of specific cooperative learning techniques. Three effective alternatives for cooperative learning are the (1) the "jigsaw method," where students divide the activity into independent or small team tasks, (2) "learning together" formats, with each member of the team participating in all tasks of the project, and (3) "group investigation," where the team subdivides the study of a topic into small team projects (Sapon-Shevin, 1990).

A second strategy, that has been applied successfully to both classroom and community instruction, is *partial participation* (Baumgart, et al., 1982; Ferguson & Baumgart, 1991). Through partial participation, expectations on student performance are changed. Based on the rejection of developmental readiness, independent performance, prerequisite skill, or "all or nothing" notions of participation, partial participation promotes the full inclusion of students in classroom activities through the modification of one or more of four features of the task. These adaptations include changing rules for participation, adjusting the support or assistance needed, changing the sequence of steps for the activity, or adapting materials or equipment commonly used within the task (Baumgart et al., 1982; Ferguson & Baumgart, 1991).

Educators may opt to employ *curricular adaptations* to promote more active participation and performance within regular homeroom instruction. Similar to partial participation, curricular adaptations modify or adapt the specific requirements or assignments of a classroom task to be consistent with student needs. This may include the utilization of adaptive or assistive technology in lieu of traditional classroom materials (i.e., computer enlargement programs and Braille-based input as opposed to books, paper, and pencils), or be facilitated by the establishment of alternate goals for an assignment. For example, a lesson on the local community economy for fifth graders may emphasize the diversity of different small stores and businesses for the typical students. For a student with severe disabilities, emphasis may be placed on the activity of shopping and the function of money to make preferred purchases.

Educational teams may use the homeroom routines as a natural opportunity to distribute performance of targeted IEP activities and skills. Research has shown that instruction of skills on a schedule based on their natural dispersal across the day and within activities is a highly effective method to establish meaning for them (Koegel & Koegel, 1986; Mulligan et al., 1982). Two methods have been developed to achieve this end. *Skill scheduling matrix* (Giangreco et al., 1993; Helmstetter & Guess, 1987) and

WINDOW 7-4   Cooperating to Write a Newspaper

One more week and school will be out for the summer! And language class has a new project. Students, as part of cooperative learning teams, will each develop a school newspaper article, interviewing students from different grade levels. Jennifer's group has chosen the fourth-grade classes, while Joanne's team will report on the activities of the third grade. The purpose of the interviews is to find out what plans students have for the summer.

Each team is to plan the project together, including (1) identification of who will be interviewed (four students from each of the three classes in a grade), (2) arrange, schedule, and conduct the interviews, (3) write the articles, (4) draw, take, or collect pictures, and (5) print and reproduce the newspaper for the class.

Jennifer's team has a total of four members on it. Her skills do not include being able to write or speak orally. She can use her communication board to ask basic questions, uses a tape recorder independently, and gets around the school by herself. All the children will have different duties, based on both individual and group agreement. Roles that the team have jointly decided for Jennifer include:

• Taking a written message down to each fourth-grade teacher to request a time and volunteers for the interview
• Initiating the interview with her tape recorder, playing a pre-made tape for the student about the newspaper article
• Recording the interview with her tape recorder
• Jointly choosing with other team members, segments of the interview to write and pictures to include

• Printing the complete article and newspaper from the computer
• Jointly distributing the completed newspaper

The activity proceeded as planned without many glitches. The tape recorder batteries did run out in the middle of the second interview, so it had to be started over. Students from the fourth-grade class asked if they could have their tapes to play for their parents. All in all, it was a good way to end the school year and jump into summer.

Cooperative learning is one of the more effective tools that teachers can employ for all students. In this case, minor adaptations were brainstormed by the team that served the overall purpose of the project. Artificial roles and activities, which really do not contribute to the outcome of the project, are not considered. Jennifer had equal membership in the project, performing critical and required functions for the team. They in turn did the same for each other and for her. In closing this Window, consider,

• What "non-interview" benefits were to be gained from participating in this activity?
• What support do homeroom teachers need from special educators to implement cooperative learning or peer buddy and tutor systems?
• How do you best teach students to work within a cooperative format so that all students have valued roles in the completion of projects?

the *Individual Curriculum Sequencing Model* (Guess & Helmstetter, 1987) are strategies that begin by identifying the natural occurrence of targeted skills and activities within the typical homeroom schedule. The combination of these then, for any particular class period, becomes the instructional focus for the student. Painting with a peer buddy during an art period, for example, may serve as a natural opportunity for a student to take turns, indicate choices, use a pincher grasp to hold objects, request help as needed, and move objects across midline.

Homeroom as a meaningful and supported social environment

As previously discussed within this chapter, the establishment of lasting social relationships is becoming a major focus for special education and role for placement within homerooms. Regular access to peers, in a way that promotes and support friendships, is denied to most elementary students if placement is restricted to self-contained classes or special schools. These new relationships, besides being a sufficient outcome in themselves, provide the best mechanism for the development of social skills (Haring, 1991; Haring & Lovinger, 1989) and functional communication (Downing & Siegal-Causey, 1988; Houghton, Bronicki, & Guess, 1987; Hunt, Alwell, & Goetz, 1988)

Oftentimes, educational teams may need to augment the efforts provided through natural support mechanisms (i.e., peer tutor and buddy relationships, circle of friends, inclusion of social networks) to teach specific social, communicative, or behavioral skills. Instructional planning and strategies related to these needs are diverse and require a depth of presentation beyond what is available through this chapter. However, certain key elements about effective social and behavioral support have emerged in research and practice. They include (1) the utilization of a functional analysis process as a tool for assessment and intervention decision-making (Donnellan et. al., 1984; Durand, 1992; O'Neill et. al. 1987), (2) the ongoing student, peer, and parent review of the support plan to ensure its acceptability (Sprague & Horner, 1991), (3) limitations on the utilization of compliance-oriented procedures, especially when student choice is possible (Guess & Siegal-Causey, 1985; McDonnell, 1993), and (4) the prohibition of highly aversive procedures as part of the treatment plan (Meyer & Evans, 1989; Turnbull & Guess, 1986). Readers interested in more information in this area are encouraged to consider Durand (1992), or Meyer and Evans (1989) for a more thorough presentation of behavioral support issues and methods.

Integrated Instructional Delivery

The most effective, yet challenging role for members of transdisciplinary teams is the coordination of methods across the key instructional activities, including assessment, IEP development, and instructional planning. To do so is the first step in assuring that the diverse needs of students are addressed thoroughly, naturally, and as non-intrusively as possible. Achievement of this goal first requires the joint planning of a functional, transdisciplinary assessment (Goetz & Gee, 1987; Orelove & Sobsey, 1991; Rainforth, York, & Macdonald, 1992).

Functional assessment for students with severe disabilities determines the current level of student performance of regular routines, as compared to the expected performance of peers. This procedure, called *discrepancy analysis*, structures assessment from an ecological inventory or informal review of the typical performance expectations (i.e., routines, activities, and skills that are required for participation within regular settings), (Browder, 1991; Brown, et al., 1976; Falvey, 1986). Transdisciplinary assessment procedures are then incorporated to further analyze features of the environment and student's performance, such as the stimulus dimensions of the setting (i.e., those natural features under which sensory input must take place), motor characteristics of the various required responses, and social or communication demands associated with the tasks of the routine. Team members convene to plan the implementation of the assessment, incorporating methods of formal evaluation into the discrepancy analysis to determine specific performance and error categories relevant to targeting adaptive instructional strategies.

Integrated instructional methods

Performance of and participation in these integrated goals and objectives within natural homerooms and other school, home, or community contexts also require that team members integrate mutually-accepted methods into practice. The different opportunities to perform activities and skills may be taught through specific instructional procedures associated with a particular educational program, or facilitated with more generic procedures that guide teacher assistance across the different times and settings. These methods may include the designation of procedures related to (1) a specific response prompt hierarchy, (2) the use of a stimulus shaping, fading, or alternate discrimination techniques, (3) systematic fading or modification of motor performance, (4) reinforcement, and (5) assessment of progress toward achievement of the targeted objective across routines and settings.

An emerging procedure related to integrated data collection is *error analysis*. Reflecting the student's response to the particular integrated instructional methods, error analysis allows for the collection of specific data about the quality of instruction. Data are collected on various aspects of non-successful responses by the student. These may include failure to initiate the targeted skill, demonstration of a discrimination or response error, and extremes in the latency or duration of response. Analysis of the information is conducted not from the perspective of student failure, but rather, inadequacies in the designation or implementation of integrated instructional methods, and is best done with the resources of the extended transdisciplinary team.

Conclusion

This chapter has focused on those issues associated with effective and innovative service delivery within elementary schools for children with significant and multiple disabilities. It has reviewed practices on three levels of service planning, namely, the structure of elementary programs, effective organizational strategies, and best instructional practices. Clearly, they overlap in their application and serve a variety of purposes for students. Of more importance than the level of implementation of the practice is the actual incorporation of the strategies for the children who are served. Perhaps the first and best starting point for that implementation is the application of those valued meaningful outcomes for these students into the missions of schools and districts. Agreeing on the "destination" before setting out on the trip is always a wise course of action.

These meaningful benefits can have a highly significant impact on the quality of life for children with severe disabilities. Their application means daily participation in the routine activities of the school. These students then have the chance to become true members of the school—a condition that many of us take for granted. Often, we only briefly recognize its impact, especially when we see children who move quickly in and out of a community. Not staying long enough to impact the lives of others, they themselves only minimally experience the real benefits of elementary school. When children with disabilities *belong*, they then have the opportunity to start lasting friend-ships—ones that continue after school, on weekends, and during vacations. And through these friends, they gain access to a greater number of life experiences than school and IEPs will ever have a chance to provide them.

One can ask, "why haven't these practices been universally accepted?" A number of educators consider that question on a daily basis. Meyer (1991) has identified three typical reasons. They begin with disinterest on the part of the district, school, or pro-fessionals. Laws and regulations will not change all behavior. Secondly, real limits in fiscal, economic, and social-political resources exist. Current allocations may both be distributed incorrectly and insufficiently to get this job done. And finally, we still do not have the full capacity to achieve these valued outcomes. Preservice and inservice resources need to be improved and expanded to fully address this challenge.

Perhaps images from the past are the best pictures for the future. The significant changes that have taken place over the last 20 years reflect a true picture and predictor of the future. In this picture, education has seen a 180-degree reversal in how the field perceives children with disabilities, the attitudes that professionals have about families, and the roles that schools play in meeting their needs. Clearly, the next two decades will be years of continued change. However, as we achieve membership for students through further family participation and team support, the image of this future looks promising.

Focus Review

Focus 1: How are elementary programs for students with severe disabilities structured?

Elementary programs are offered in a variety of service locations. These include:

- *Special schools* are separate buildings or units dedicated solely to provision of ser-vices for students with disabilities.
- *Clustered arrangements* are special, districtwide programs located within a regular elementary school. Often, a wing of the school is set aside, with the entire group of classes dedicated (or, "clustered") for district students with severe disabilities.
- *Neighborhood schools programs* are alternatives which offer student services within the natural school catchment area for the family. Students attend the school that their neighbors and friends attend, with professional staff working in the school on a full, part-time, or itinerant basis.
- *Homebound services* are offered for students who commonly have special health or behavioral needs that prohibit regular school attendance. Services are provided jointly by a special educator who travels to the home and the child's caregivers.

Elementary programs may be staffed using a variation from three teaming mod-els, including:

- *Multidisciplinary teaming* is a direct offshoot from the professional team ap developed for medical services. Each professional is responsible for their own uation and, in essence, plan development. The individual segments are mer together as the Individual Education Plan with each team member responsible f the implementation their own treatment or instruction.
- *Interdisciplinary teaming model* suggests more collaboration among the various team members. Certain decisions, such as which evaluations are to be completed and the selection of goals, are done jointly. While individual team members may still be responsible for their own service delivery, they also are expected to assist other team members, especially the special educator.
- *Transdisciplinary teaming* takes the cooperative role several steps further. Here, only one unified plan is developed, as opposed to the multidisciplinary team approach which generates a number of small "mini-plans." A major emphasis of the model is placed on the sharing of information and skills rather than independent service. Each team member provides input as to how coordinated goals may be identified and achieved. Often, the related service professional does not do direct instruction or therapy, but rather, trains other professionals or teaching assistants how to incorporate techniques across the entire day's routine.
- Special educators may serve in primarily a teaching role, or as an instructional manager, delegating teaching duties to others. Regardless of the role, however, the special educator must develop instructional programs, facilitate the training of paraprofessionals, and ensure quality through the supervision of all instructional delivery.

Services may use a variety of educational resources to use as a base for service delivery. They include:

- *Self-contained classroom*, or classes dedicated to the instruction of only those students with disabilities. Many students spend the entire day there receiving instruction in fulfillment of the IEP. Therapy by related servers may be completed there or within a second dedicated area, such as a speech or physical therapy room. Commonly, the student has contact solely with special education personnel or other students with severe disabilities.
- An elementary student with significant disabilities may receive part-time instruction within a *resource classroom*. The student may then spend time in either the self-contained class, or elsewhere within the school. Instructional services there are similar to that found within the self-contained class. One difference found there, however, is that the student has the potential to interact with a wider array of students from the school.
- The third classroom placement is within the student's grade level *homeroom class*. Core instruction is provided within that setting, and worked into the regular education routines. The child may have little or no contact with other students with disabilities, and less direct interaction as a rule with special education personnel.
- *Content area classes*, such as music and art rooms or the gymnasium provide opportunities to access routines, materials, and students in support of the child's

, areas such as the lunchroom, school restrooms, and the playground
ited for instructional use.
.ucational opportunities may be found through participation in the
extracurricular and after-school activities. Though these formal groups
e less common in elementary school than with older students, clubs and teams are
a valuable resource for all children in kindergarten through sixth grade. These
may include class newspapers, action groups for the homeless, soccer and basketball teams, and recycling, science, and environmental clubs.

- *Community and home-based instruction* has been shown to be both effective and
critical for these young students . Different than secondary programs, where there
is a need to emphasize vocational training in regular job settings, this instruction
for elementary students is often based on the lifestyle choices of the family (e.g.,
chores from home, recreational preferences, or family routines with siblings), and
the natural community settings (e.g., grocery, church, mall, or park) that they frequent with their child.

Focus 2: What is the emerging mission of elementary school services for students
with severe disabilities?

Five values of educational outcomes have emerged that may serve as the mission
for programs. They include:

- Meaningful participation and performance by the student in activities of normal,
age-based routines (Baumgart et al., 1982; McDonnell et al., 1991; Nietupski &
Hamre-Nietupski, 1987; Snell, 1989)
- The establishment of supportive, social relationships with peers, adults, and neighbors (Forest & Pierpoint, 1992; O'Brien & Lyle-O'Brien, 1992; Perske, 1988; Vandercook, York, & Forest, 1989)
- The acquisition of collateral, enrichment, or extension skills (e.g., communication, motor, choice, money, functional math, mobility, etc.) through applied and
integrated, activity-based planning and instruction (Brown et al., 1987; Campbell,
1987; Helmstetter & Guess, 1987; McDonnell et al., 1992; Orelove & Sobsey,
1991; Rainforth & York, 1987; Rainforth, York, & Macdonald, 1992)
- The inclusion of student's, parents', and family members' choices as the linchpin
for all team planning (Hamre-Nietupski, Nietupski, & Strathe, 1992; Singer &
Irvin, 1991; Giangreco et al., 1991)
- The utilization of a performance criterion for an activity goal that is based on normal expectations and conditions (Brown et al., 1976; White, 1988).

Focus 3: What organizational patterns and practices help elementary teams to achieve
the valued outcomes for students with severe disabilities?

- Family support and partnership through trust building, empowerment, and choice
- Collaborative approach to transdisciplinary teaming to improve the efficiency and
effectiveness of use of educational resources

- Shared ownership by school team to achieve membership by the student in the homeroom and the school
- Utilization of natural supports as a mechanism to provide assistance and long-lasting and meaningful relationships

Focus 4: What are individual, student-based strategies that have been shown to be effective in achieving valued educational outcomes for elementary students with severe disabilities?

- Routine-based curriculum and educational planning through
  (1) ecological assessment
  (2) values-based decision making reflecting parental choice and lifestyle preferences
- Supported inclusion of students within homerooms and other natural school and community settings, allowing
  (1) the effective use of homeroom routines as a base for instruction
  (2) establishment of meaningful social relationships through facilitated homeroom experiences
- Integration of team recommendations for service planning and delivery into one unified plan as a result of
  (1) transdisciplinary assessment
  (2) integrated and activity-based IEP development
  (3) integration of methodology into natural routines
  (4) use of cooperative learning, partial participation, curricular adaptation, and distributed instructional methods

References

34 Congressional Federal Regulations: Sec. 300.551, (1988).

Albano, M., Cox, B., York, J., & York, R. (1981). *Educational teams for students with severe and multiple handicaps.* In R. York, W. Schofield, D. Donder, R. Ryndak, & B. Reguly (Eds.), *Organizing and implementing services for students with severe and multiple handicaps* (pp. 23–44). Springfield, IL: State Board of Education.

Bacharach, S. B. (1990). Education reform: Making sense of it all. In S. B. Bacharach (Ed.), *Educational reform: Making sense of it all* (pp. 1-6). Boston: Allyn & Bacon.

Bararach, L. (1985). Deinstitutionalization: The meaning of the least restrictive environment. In R. Bruininks & K. Lakin (Eds.), *Living and learning in the least restrictive environment* (pp. 23–36). Baltimore, MD: Paul H. Brookes.

Barber, P., Turnbull, A., Behr, S., & Kerns, G. (1988). A family systems approach on early childhood special education. In S. Odom & M. Karnes (Eds.), *Early intervention for infants and children with handicaps: An empirical base* (pp. 179–198). Baltimore, MD: Paul H. Brookes.

Baumgart, D., Brown, L.; Pumpian, I.; Nisbet, J.; Ford, A.; Sweet, M.; Messina, R.; & Schroeder, J. (1982). Principle of partial participation and individualized adaptations in educational programs for severely handicapped students. *Journal of the Association for Persons with Severe Handicaps, 7*(2), 17–27.

Biklen, D. (1982). The least restrictive environment: Its application to education. In G. Melton (Ed.),

Child youth and services (pp. 121–144). New York, NY: Hayworth.

Biklen, D. (1985). *Achieving the complete school: Strategies for effective mainstreaming.* New York: Teachers College Press.

Board of Education of H. Hudson School District v. *Rowley,* 458 U.S. 176 (1982).

Boyer, E. L. (1990). The new agenda for the nation's schools. In S. B. Bacharach (Ed.), *Educational reform: Making sense of it all* (pp. 30–37). Boston: Allyn & Bacon.

Brightman, H., (1988). General strategies for improving team effectiveness. In H. Brightman, *Group problem solving: An improved managerial approach* (pp. 57–90). Atlanta, GA: Georgia State University Business Publishing Division.

Brinker, R. P., & Thorpe, M. E. (1984). Integration of severely handicapped students and the proportion of IEEE objectives achieved. *Exceptional Children, 51,* 168–175.

Brinker, R. P., & Thorpe, M. E. (1986). Features of integrated educational ecologies that predict social behavior among severely mentally retarded and nonretarded students. *American Journal of Mental Deficiency, 91,* 150–159.

Browder, D. (1991) *Assessment of individuals with severe handicaps: An applied behavioral analysis approach to life skills assessment* (2nd Ed.). Baltimore, MD: Paul H. Brookes.

Brown, F., Evans, I., Weed, K., & Owen, V., (1987). Delineating functional competencies: A component model. *The Journal of the Association for Persons with Severe Handicaps, 12*(2), 117–124.

Brown, L., Ford, A., Nisbet, J., Sweet, M., Donnellan, A., & Gruenewald, L. (1983). Opportunities available when severely handicapped students attend chronological, age appropriate regular schools. *The Journal of the Association For Persons with Severe Handicaps, 8*(1), 16–24.

Brown, L, Long, E., Udvari-Solner, A., Davis, L., Pat VanDeventer, P., Ahlgran, C., Johnson, F., Gruenwald, L., & Jorgensen, J. (1989a). The home school: Why students with severe intellectual disabilities must attend the schools of their brothers, sisters, friends, and neighbors. *The Journal of the Association For Persons with Severe Handicaps, 14*(1), 1–7.

Brown, L., Long, E., Udvari-Solner, A.,, Schwarz, P., VanDeeventer, P., Ahlgren, C., Johnson, F.,

Gruenewald, L., & Jorgensen, J. (1989b). Should students with severe intellectual disabilities be based in regular or in special education classrooms in home schools? *The Journal of the Association For Persons with Severe Handicaps, 14*(1), 8–12.

Brown, L., Nietupski, J., & Hamre-Nietupski, S. (1976). Criterion of ultimate functioning. In M. A. Thomas (Ed.), *Hey, don't forget about me!* Reston, VA: Council for Exceptional Children.

Brown, L., Stewards, Udvari-Soner, A., Kampschroer, E. E., Johnson, F., Jorgensen, J., Gruenwald, L. (1991). How much time should students with severe intellectual disabilities spend in regular education classrooms and elsewhere? *The Journal of the Association for Persons with Severe Handicaps, 16,* 39–47.

Brown v. *State Board of Education of Topeka, KA* 347 U.S. 483 (1954).

Campbell, P. (1986). The application of neurodevelopmental treatment procedures with children with severe handicaps. In *Selected Proceedings from the Babro Salek Memorial Symposium* (pp. 81–112). Chicago, IL: NDTA, Inc.

Campbell, P.H. (1987). The integrated programming team: An approach for coordinating professionals of various disciplines in programs for students with severe and multiple handicaps. *The Journal of the Association for the Severely Handicapped, 12*(2), 107–116.

Campbell, P. (1989). Dysfunction in posture and movement in individuals with profound disabilities: Issues and practices. In F. Brown & D. Lehr (Eds.), *Persons with profound disabilities: Issues and practices* (pp. 163–189). Baltimore, MD: Paul H. Brookes.

Campbell, P., McInerney, W., & Cooper, M. (1984). Therapeutic programming for students with severe handicaps. *American Journal of Occupational Therapy, 38,* 594–602.

Dokecki, P., & Heflinger, C. (1989). Strengthening families of young children with handicapping conditions: Mapping backward from the "street level." In J. Gallagher, P. Trohanis, & R. Clifford (Eds.), *Policy implementation and PL 99-457: Planning for young children with special needs* (pp. 59–84). Baltimore, MD: Paul H. Brookes.

Donder, D., & York, R. (1984). Integration of students with severe handicaps. In N. Certo, N.

Haring, & R. York (Eds.) *Public school integration of severely handicapped students: Rationale issues and progressive alternatives.* (pp. 1–14). Baltimore: Paul H. Brookes.

Donnellan, A., Mirenda, P., Mesaros, R., & Fassbender, L. (1984). Analyzing the communicative function of aberrant behavior. *Journal of the Association for the Severely Handicapped, 9*(3), 201–212.

Downing, J. & Bailey, B., (1990). Sharing the responsibility: Using a transdisciplinary team approach to enhance the learning of students with severe disabilities. *Journal of Educational and Psychological Consultation, 1*(3), 259–278.

Downing, J. & Siegal-Causey, E., (1988). Enhancing the nonsymbolic communicative behavior of children with multiple disabilities. *Language, Speech, and Hearing Sciences in Schools, 19,* 338–348.

Dunn, W. (1991). Integrated related services. In L. H. Meyer, C. A. Peck, & L. Brown (Eds.), *Critical issues in the lives of people with severe disabilities* (pp. 353–377). Baltimore: Paul H. Brookes.

Durand, M. (1992). *Severe behavior problems: A functional communication training approach.* New York, NY: The Guilford Press.

Espino v. *Besteiro,* 520 F. Supp. (S.D. Tex, 1981).

Falvey, M. (1986). Assessment strategies. In M. Falvey, *Community-based instruction: Instructional strategies for students with severe handicaps* (pp. 13–30). Baltimore, MD: Paul H. Brookes.

Ferguson, D., & Baumgart, D. (1991). Partial participation revisited. *Journal of the Association for the Severely Handicapped, 16*(4), 218–227.

Ford, A., & Davern, L. (1989). Moving forward with school integration: Strategies for involvement with students with severe handicaps in the life of the school. In R. Gaylord-Ross (Ed.) *Integration strategies for students with severe handicaps.* pp. 11–31. Baltimore, MD: Paul H. Brookes Publishing Co.

Ford, A., Schnorr, R., Meyer, L., Darvern, L., Black, J., & Dempsey, P. (1989). *The Syracuse community-referenced curriculum for students with moderated and severe disabilities.* Baltimore, MD: Paul H. Brookes.

Forest, M. (1991). It's about relationships. In L. H. Meyer, C. A. Peck, & L. Brown (Eds.), *Critical issues in the lives of people with severe disabilities* (pp. 399–407). Baltimore: Paul H. Brookes.

Forest, M. & Pierpoint, J., (1992). Families, friends, and circles. In J. Nisbet (Ed.). *Natural supports in school, at work, and in the community for people with severe disabilities.* Baltimore: Paul H. Brookes.

Garland, C., McGonigel, M., Frank, A., & Buck, D. (1989). *The transdisciplinary model of service delivery.* Lightfoot, VA: Child Development Resources.

Gartner, A., & Lipsky, D. (1990). Students as instructional agents. In W. Stainback & S. Stainback (Eds.), *Support networks for inclusive schooling: Interdependent integrated education.* 81–94, Baltimore: Paul H. Brookes.

Giangreco, M. (1986). The effects of integrated therapy: A pilot study. *Journal of the Association for Persons with Severe Handicaps, 11*(3), 205–208.

Giangreco, M., Cloninger, C., & Iverson, V. (1993). *Choosing options and accommodations for children: A guide to planning inclusive education,* Baltimore, MD: Paul H. Brookes.

Giangreco, M., Cloninger, C., Mueller, P., Yuan, S., & Ashworth, P. (1991). Perspectives of parents whose children have dual sensory impairments. *Journal of the Association for Persons with Severe Handicaps, 16*(1), 14–24.

Giangreco, M., Dennis, R., Cloninger, C., Edelman, S., Schatman, R. (1993). "I've counted Jon": Transformational experiences of teachers educating students with disabilities. *Exceptional Children, 59*(4), 359–372.

Giangreco, M. & Meyer, L. (1988). *Expanding service delivery options in regular schools and classroom for students with severe disabilities.* In J. Graden, J. Zins, & M. Curtis (Eds.), *Alternate educational delivery systems: Enhancing instruction options for all students* (pp. 241–267). Washington, D.C.: National Association of School Psychologists.

Giangreco, M. F. & Putnam, J. W. (1991). Supporting the education of students with sever disabilities in regular education environments. In L. H. Meyer, C. A. Peck, & L. Brown (Eds.), *Critical issues in the lives of people with severe disabilities* (pp. 245–270). Baltimore: Paul H. Brookes.

Goetz, L. & Gee, K., (1987). Functional vision programming: A model for teaching visual behaviors in natural contexts. In L. Goetz, D. Guess, & K. Stremel-Campbell (Eds.) *Innovative program design for individuals with dual sensory impairments*. Baltimore, MD: Paul H. Brookes.

Goetz, L., Guess, D., & Stremel-Campbell, K., (1987). *Innovative program design for individuals with dual sensory impairments*. Baltimore, MD: Paul H. Brookes.

Greer, C. (1972). *The great school legend: A revisionist interpretation of American public education*. New York, NY: Basic Books.

Guess, D. & Helmstetter, E. (1986). Skill cluster instruction and the Individualized Curriculum Sequencing Model. In R.H. Horner, L.H. Meyer, & H.D. Fredericks (Eds.), *Education of learners with severe handicaps: Exemplary service strategies* (pp. 221–250). Baltimore: Paul H. Brookes Publishing Company.

Guess, D. & Siegal-Causey, E. (1985). Behavior control and education of severely handicapped students: Who's doing what to whom? And why?. In D. Bricker & J. Fuller (Eds.) *Severe mental retardation: From theory to practice* (pp. 230–244). Reston, VA: Division of Mental Retardation, Council on Exceptional Children.

Halle, J. (1987). Teaching language in the natural environment: An analysis of spontaneity. *Journal of the Association for Persons with Severe Handicaps, 12*(1), 28–37.

Halverson, A., Doering, K., Farron-Davis F., Usilton, R., & Sailor, W. (1989). The role of the parents and family members in planning severely disabled students' transitions from school. In G. Singer & L. Irvin, (Eds.). *Support for caregiving families* (pp. 253–268). Baltimore, MD: Paul H. Brookes.

Hamre-Nietupski, S., Nietupski, J., & Strathe, M. (1992). Functional life skills, academic skills, and friendship/social relationship development: What do parents of students with moderate/ severe/profound disabilities value? *Journal of the Association for Persons with Severe Handicaps, 17*(1), 53–58.

Hardman, M. L., McDonnell, J., & McDonnell, A. (1989). *The inclusive school: Serving students with severe disabilities in the least restrictive environment*. Salt Lake City, UT: University of Utah, School and Community Integration Program.

Haring, N., & Billingsley, F., (1984). Systems change strategies to ensure the future of integration. In N. Certo, N. Haring, & R. York (Eds.) *Public school integration of severely handicapped students: Rationale issues and progressive alternatives* (pp. 83–107). Baltimore: Paul H. Brookes.

Haring, T. (1991). Social relationships. In L. Meyer, C. Peck, & L. Brown (Eds.), *Critical issues in the lives of people with severe disabilities* (pp. 195–218). Baltimore, MD: Paul H. Brookes.

Haring, T. G., Breen, C., Pitts-Conway, V., Lee, M., & Gaylord-Ross, R. (1987). Adolescent peer tutoring and special friend experiences. *Journal of the Association for Persons with Severe Handicaps, 13*(4), 280–286.

Haring, T., & Lovinger, L. (1989). Social interaction through teaching generalized play initiation responses to children with autism. *Journal of the Association for Persons with Severe Handicaps, 14*(1), 58–67.

Helmstetter, E. & Guess, D., (1987). Application of the Individualized Curriculum Sequencing Model to Learners with severe sensory impairments. In L. Goetz, D. Guess, & K. Stremel-Campbell (Eds.) *Innovative program design for individuals with dual sensory impairments*. Baltimore, MD: Paul H. Brookes

Horner, R., Newton, S., LaBaron, J., Stoner, N., & Ferguson, P. (1987). *The community network project: Strategies for supporting the social network of people with severe disabilities* (Contract 84. 158J), Washington, D.C.: U. S. Department of Education.

Houghton, J., Bronicki, G. J., & Guess, D., (1987). Opportunities to express preferences and make choices among students with severe disabilities in classroom settings. *Journal of the Association for Persons with Severe Handicaps, 12*(1), 18–27.

Hunt, P., Alwell, M., & Goetz, L. (1988). Acquisition of conversational skills and the re-education of inappropriate social interaction patterns. *The Journal of the Association for Persons with Severe Handicaps, 13*, 280–286.

Hunt, P., Goetz, L., & Anderson, J. (1986). The quality of IEP objectives associated with placement on integrated vs segregated school sites. *The*

Journal of the Association for Persons with Severe Handicaps, 11, 125–130.

Jenkins, J. & Jenkins, L. (1981). *Cross age and peer tutoring: Help for children with learning problems*, Reston, VA: The Council for Exceptional Children.

Jorgensen, C., (1992). Natural supports in inclusive schools. In J. Nesbit, (Ed.). *Natural supports in school, at work, and in the community for people with severe disabilities* (pp. 179–215). Baltimore, MD: Paul H. Brookes.

Kiefer-O'Donnell, R., (1991). Redefining the role of special education: Participation and success in one's community and culture. *Journal of Navajo Education, 7*(3), 23–27.

Kirst, M. W. (1988). On reports and reform: Nation at Risk assessed. *Educational Evaluation and Policy Analysis, 7*, 40.

Koegel, L., & Koegel, R. (1986). The effects of interspered maintenance tasks on academic performance in a severe childhood stroke victim. *Journal of Applied Behavior Analysis, 19*, 425–430.

Kohl, F., Moses, L., & Stettner-Eaton, B. (1984). A systematic training program for teaching nonhandicapped students to be instructional trainers of severely handicapped schoolmates. In N. Certo, N. Haring, & R. York (Eds.) *Public school integration of severely handicapped students: Rationale issues and progressive alternatives*. Baltimore: Paul H. Brookes.

Malette, P., Mirenda, P., Kandborg, T., Jones, P., Bunz, T., & Rogow, S. (1992). Application of a lifestyle development process for persons with severe intellectual disabilities: A case study report. *The Journal of the Association for Persons with Severe Handicaps, 17*(3), 179–191.

McCormick, L., Cooper, M., & Goldman, R. (1979). Training teachers to maximize instructional time provided to severely and profoundly handicapped children. *AAESPH Review, 4*, 301–310.

McDonnell, A. (1993). Ethical considerations in teaching compliance to individuals with mental retardation. *Exceptional Children, 28*(1), 3–12.

McDonnell, A., McDonnell, J., Hardman, M., & McCune, G. (1991). Educating students with severe disabilities in their neighborhood schools: The Utah Elementary Integration

Model. *Remedial and Special Education.12*(6), 34–45.

McDonnell, A., Thorson, N., Sweezy, K., McCune, G., Kiefer-O'Donnell, R., (1991). *Integration of elementary-aged students with severe disabilities in neighborhood schools*. Utah Elementary Integration Dissemination Project (UEID), University of Utah, Department of Special Education, Salt Lake City, UT.

McDonnell, A., & Hardman, M. (1989). The desegregation of America's special schools: Strategies for change. *Journal of the Association for Persons with Severe Handicaps, 14*(1), 68–74.

McDonnell, J. (1987). The integration of students with severe handicaps into regular public schools: An analysis of parents perceptions of potential outcomes. *Education and Training in Mental Retardation, 22*(2), 98–111.

McDonnell, J. & Kiefer-O'Donnell, R. (1992). Educational reform and students with severe disabilities. *Journal of Disability Policy Studies, 3*(2) 53–74.

McDonnell, J., McDonnell, A., Hightower, J., Kiefer-O'Donnell, R., Mathot-Buckner, C., Milligan, P., & Thorson, N., (1992). *The School and Community Integration Project curriculum for students with severe disabilities* (pp. 1–18 and Appendix for elementary school routines). University of Utah, Department of Special Education, Salt Lake City, UT.

Metz, M. H. (1990). Some missing elements in the educational reform movement. In S. B. Bacharach (Ed.), *Educational reform: Making sense of it all* (pp. 141–154). Boston, MA: Allyn & Bacon.

Meyer, L. (1991). Advocacy, research, and typical practice: A call for the reduction of discrepancies between what is and what ought to be, and how to get there. In L. Meyer, C. Peck, & L. Brown (Eds.), *Critical issues in the lives of people with severe disabilities* (pp. 629–649). Baltimore, MD: Paul H. Brookes.

Meyer, L., & Evans, I. (1989). *Nonaversive intervention for behavior problems: A manual for home and community*, Baltimore, MD: Paul H. Brookes.

Mulligan, M., Lacy, L., & Guess, D. (1982). Effects of massed, distributed, and spaced trial sequencing on severly handicapped students' performance. *Journal of the Association for the Severely Handicapped*, 5, 325–336.

Murphy, J. (1991). The educational reform movement of the 1980s: A comprehensive analysis. In J. Murphy (Ed.), *The Educational Reform Movement of the 1980s: Perspectives and Cases* (pp. 3–55). Berkeley, CA: McCutenhan Publishing Corporation.

Nietupski, J., & Hamre-Nietupski, S. (1987). An ecological approach to curriculum development. In L. Goetz, D. Guess, & K. Stremel-Campbell (Eds.) *Innovative program design for individuals with dual sensory impairments*. Baltimore: Paul H. Brookes.

Nisbet, J. (1992). Introduction. In J. Nisbet (Ed.), *Natural supports in school, at work, and in the community for people with severe disabilities* (pp. 1–10). Baltimore, MD: Paul H. Brookes.

O'Brien, J., & Lyle-O'Brien, C., (1992). Members of each other: Perspectives on social support. In J. Nisbet (Ed.). *Natural supports in school, at work, and in the community for people with severe disabilities*. Baltimore: Paul H. Brookes.

Odden, A., & Marsh, A. (1990). Local response to the 1980s state education reforms: New patterns of local and state interaction. In J. Murphy (Ed.), *The Educational Reform Movement of the 1980s: Perspectives and Cases* (pp. 167–186). Berkeley, CA: McCutenhan Publishing Corporation.

O'Neill, R., Horner, R., Albin, R., Storey, K., & Sprague., J. (1987). *Functional analysis: A practical assessment guide*. Eugene, OR: Specialized Training Program, University of Oregon.

Orelove, F. P., & Sobsey, D. (1991). *Educating children with multiple disabilities: A transdisciplinary approach*. Baltimore: Paul H. Brookes.

Osborne, A., (1992). Legal standards for an appropriate education in the post-Rowley era. *Exceptional Children*, 58(6), 488–494.

Perske, R. (1988). *Circles of friends: People with disabilities and their friends enrich the lives of one another*. Nashville, TN: Abingdon Press.

Rainforth, B., & York, J. (1987). Integrating related services in community instruction. *Journal of the Association for Persons with Severe Handicaps*, 12(3), 190–198.

Rainforth, B., York, J., & Macdonald, C., (1992). *Collaborative teams for students with severe disabilities: Integrating therapy and education services*. Baltimore, MD: Paul H. Brookes.

Reichle, J., (1991). Developing communicative exchanges. In J. Reichle, J. York, & J. Sigafoos, *Implementing augmentative and alternative communication: Strategies for learners with severe disabilities* (pp. 89–114). Baltimore, MD: Paul H. Brookes, Inc.

Rothstein, L. (1990). *Special education law*. New York, NY: Longman.

Rowland, C. (1990). Communication in the classroom for children with dual sensory impairments: Studies of teacher and child behavior. *Augmentative and Alternate Communication*, 262–274.

Sailor, W. (1991). Special education in the restructured school. *Remedial and Special Education*, 12(6), 8–22.

Sailor, W., Anderson, J. L., Doering, K., Filler, J., & Goetz, L. (1989). *The comprehensive local school*. Baltimore: Paul H. Brookes.

Salisbury, C., (1992). Parents as team members: Inclusive teams, collaborative outcomes. In B. Rainforth, J. York, & C. Macdonald, *Collaborative teams for students with severe disabilities: Integrating therapy and educational services* (pp. 43–66). Baltimore, MD: Paul H. Brookes.

Sapon-Shevin, M. (1990). Student support through cooperative learning. In W. Stainback & S. Stainback (Eds.), *Support networks for inclusive schooling: Interdependent integrated education* (pp. 65–80). Baltimore: Paul H. Brookes.

Schnoor, P. (1990). "Peter? He comes and goes. . . ." First graders' perspective on a part-time mainstream student. *Journal of the Association for Persons with Severe Handicaps*, 15(4), 231–240.

Singer, G., & Irvin, L., (1991). Supporting families of persons with severe disabilities: Emerging findings, practices, and questions. In L. Meyer, C. Peck, & L. Brown (Eds.), *Critical issues in the lives of people with severe disabilities*. Baltimore: Paul H. Brookes.

Skrtic, T. (1991). *Behind special education: A critical analysis of professional culture and school organization*. Denver, CO: Love Publishing Co.

Snell, M. (1988a). Curriculum and methodology for individuals with severe handicaps. *Education and Training in Mental Retardation, 23*(4), 302–314.

Snell, M. E. (1989b). *Systematic Instruction for the Moderately and Severely Handicapped (3rd Edition)*. Columbus, OH: Merrill.

Sprague, J., & Horner, R., (1991). Determining the acceptability of behavior support plans. In M. Wang, M. Reynolds, & H. Walberg (Eds.) *Handbook of Special Education: Research and practice, Vol. 4: Emerging Programs* (pp. 107–123). New York: Pergamon Press.

Stainback, W., & Stainback, S., (1990). *Support Networks for Inclusive Schooling: Interdependent integrated education*. Baltimore: Paul H. Brookes.

Tawney, J. & Sniezek, S., (1985). Educational programs for severely mentally retarded elementary-aged children: Progress, problems, and suggestions. In D. Bricker & J. Filler (Eds.) *Severe mental retardation: From theory to practice* (pp. 76–96). Reston, VA: Council for Exceptional Children.

Taylor, S. J. (1988). Caught in the continuum: A critical analysis of the Principle of the Least Restrictive Environment. *The Journal of the Association for Persons with Severe Handicaps, 13*, 41–53.

The Association for Persons with Severe Handicaps (TASH), (1986). Resolution on the redefinition of the continuum of services (Original resolution "I.Q. Tests"). In L. H. Meyer, C. A. Peck, & L. Brown (Eds.), *Critical issues in the lives of people with severe disabilities* (pp. 241–242). Baltimore: Paul H. Brookes.

Thousand, J., Fox, T., Reid, R., Godek, J., Williams, W., & Fox, W. (1986). *The Homecoming Model: Education students who present intensive educational challenges with regular education environments*. Burlington, VT: University of Vermont, Center for Developmental Disabilities.

Thousand J., & Villa, R. (1990). Sharing expertise and responsibilities through teaming teams. In W. Stainback & S. Stainback (Eds.), *Support networks for inclusive schooling: Interdependent integrated education* (pp. 151–166). Baltimore: Paul H. Brookes.

Thousand, J. & Villa, R., (1992). Collaborative teams: A powerful tool in school restructuring. In R. Villa, J. Thousand, W. Stainback, & S. Stainback, *Restructuring for caring and effective education: An administrative guide to creating heterogeneous schools* (pp. 73–108). Baltimore, MD: Paul H. Brookes.

Tucker, B., & Goldstein, B. (1991). *The educational rights of children with disabilities: A guide to the federal law*. Horsham, PA: Legal Rights of Persons Publications

Turnbull, H. R., & Guess, D. (1986). A model for analyzing the moral aspects of special education and behavioral interventions. In P. Dokecki & R. Zaner (Eds.) *Ethics of dealing with persons with severe handicaps: Toward a reseach agenda* (pp. 167–210). Baltimore, MD: Paul H. Brookes.

U.S. Department of Education (1986). Standards and guidelines for compliance with federal requirements for the education of the handicapped. Washington, D.C.: U. S. Department of Education.

U. S. Department of Education (1990). *Twelfth annual report to Congress on the implementation of the Education of the Handicapped Act (EHA)*, Washington, D.C.: U.S. Department of Education.

Utah State Board of Education, (1993). *Special education rules*. Salt Lake City, UT: Utah State Office of Education.

Vandercook, T., & York, J., (1989). The McGill Action Planning System (MAPS): A Strategy for building the vision. *Journal of the Association for the Severely Handicapped, 14*(3), 025–215.

Vandercook, T., York, J., & Forest, M. (1989). The McGill Action Planning System (MAPS): A strategy for building the vision. *Journal of the Association for the Severely Handicapped, 14*(3), 025–215.

Villa, R., & Thousand, J., (1993). *One divided by two or more: Redefining the role of the special educator and other support personnel as co-equal members of a cooperative education team*. Burlington, VT: Center for Developmental Disabilities, University of Vermont.

Voeltz, L. M. (1980). Children's attitudes toward handicapped peers. *American Journal on Mental Deficiency, 84*, 455–464.

Voeltz, L. M. (1982). Effects of structured interactions with severely handicapped peers on children's attitudes. *American Journal of Mental Deficiency, 86,* 380–390.

Walker, B. (1989). Strategies for improving parent-professional cooperation. In G. Singer & L. Irvin, (Eds.). *Support for caregiving families* (pp. 103–121). Baltimore, MD: Paul H. Brookes.

White, O. (1988). Probing skill use. In N. Haring (Ed.), *Generalization for students with severe handicaps: Strategies and solutions* (pp. 131–141). Seattle: University of Washington Press.

Wilcox, B., & Bellamy, G. T. (1987). *The Activities Catalog: An alternative curriculum for youth and adults with severe disabilities.* Baltimore: Paul H. Brookes.

Williams, W., Fox, T., & Thousand, J., (1989). Level of acceptance and implementation of best practices in the education of students with severe handicaps in Vermont. *Education and Training in Mental Retardation, 25*(2), 120–131.

Chapter *8*

Secondary Programs[1]

Adolescence is a time when we establish long-term goals for our careers and life in the community (Gould, 1978; Havighurst, 1972; Levinson, 1978). Students' educational experiences during middle-school, high-school, and post-secondary programs help them to develop the skills necessary to achieve future goals, establish their identity as an adult, and develop social relationships that will support participation in community life (Gould, 1978; Havighurst, 1972; Levinson, 1978; Selman, 1980). As such, secondary programs play an important role in enhancing the quality of life experienced by youth once they leave school.

Effective secondary programs are no less critical for students with severe disabilities. Over the last decade it has become clear that middle-school, high-school, and post-secondary programs have had a significant impact on what happens to students once they leave school. Secondary programs provide students with (1) the educational experiences necessary to obtain meaningful employment and use community resources, (2) the structure necessary to ensure that they access needed community service programs upon graduation, and (3) the opportunities to establish social relationships with friends, family, coworkers, and neighbors (McDonnell, Wilcox, & Hardman, 1991; Wehman, 1992; Nisbet, 1992).

This chapter examines the role of secondary programs in preparing youth with severe disabilities for life in the community. We will give an overview of federal legislation which governs transition programming for students with disabilities and discuss program practices that research has shown to be predictive of successful post-school adjustment by students with severe disabilities.

---

[1] This chapter was written with Van Padjen, School and Community Integration Program, Department of Special Education, University of Utah, Salt Lake City, Utah.

WINDOW 8-1

Carla is 18 years old and has severe mental retardation. She is in her last year of high school and next year will be going to the program administered by the school district at the local community college. Last spring, Carla and the other members of her Individualized Education Program (IEP) team met to discuss her program for her last year. They began by examining what Carla wanted to do after she got done with school. They talked about what kind of job she would like, where she might want to live, what kinds of things she wanted to do in her free time, and so on. Based on that discussion, they developed a transition plan in her IEP that matched Carla's long-term goals and her personal interests.

Carla currently has a work experience job at a local pet store. She really likes her job because she enjoys working with animals. She works at the pet store about three hours a day in the morning. One of the paraprofessionals who works at the high school trained her to do her job and now provides support to make sure she gets the job done right. After her job she goes back to school and has lunch with her friends Mindy, Rachel, and Karen. They are also seniors at Carla's high school. Mindy and Karen are going out of state for college but Rachel will be going to the community college in town. Carla and Rachel often talk about the things they will be able to do together next year as college students. Like most high-school students Carla, Mindy, Rachel, and Karen do lots of things together after school and on the weekends.

After lunch, Carla goes to her home economics class and physical education. In home economics, she works as part of a team of four students on each of the assignments. The team members, with the help of their teacher, decide what each person will do in completing the day's assignment. In physical education, Carla is doing aerobics. She really enjoys it and wants to enroll in a class next year when she goes to the community college. Carla also is also learning to use an automatic teller machine, ride the bus to the mall, and shop for groceries. She gets help from a peer tutor named Vickie when she works on these activities. They travel together to these activities and Vickie provides assistance as necessary to ensure that Carla completes the activities correctly. Even though Vickie helps her learn these activities they also talk a lot about upcoming games or dances, what they watched on TV the night before, or what they are going to do this summer. Carla and Vickie have become really good friends. They spend time together after school and going to the mall to shop on the weekends.

Over the last several years, Carla's educational program has been structured to prepare her for her transition to adulthood and community life. Her program has been focused on developing the skills she will need to work and live in the community. Like many of her peers, over the next three years she will direct these experiences toward achieving specific employment and personal goals.

Statutory Foundations of Secondary Programs

Secondary special education programs became a main focus of federal initiatives in the 1980s. During this time, the federal Department of Education's Office of Special Education and Rehabilitation Services (OSERS) was authorized by Congress to offer grant initiatives (The Education Amendments of 1983, P.L. 98-199) to support research and program development in the areas of transition planning and service delivery. These initiatives were prompted by the dismal post-school outcomes achieved by individuals with disabilities. Graduates with severe disabilities for example, experienced high rates of unemployment, limited-use community resources, and frequently were served in service programs which restricted rather than promoted their participation in the community (Wehman, 1992). Research attributed such bleak post-school outcomes to a lack of coordinated, clearly defined transitional services for youth with disabilities (McDonnell, Wilcox, & Boles, 1986; Wehman, 1992).

Focus 1:

How are transition services defined in the 1990 amendments of IDEA?

In 1990, The Individuals with Disabilities Education Act (IDEA) of 1990 (P.L. 101-476), formerly known as The Education of the Handicapped Act Amendments, was amended to specifically address the transition of youth with disabilities from secondary educational settings to the dynamic environments of adult life. Today, students with disabilities have a "statutory" provision enabling them access to transition services. The statutory term "transition services" is defined as:

> *A coordinated set of activities for a student, designed within an outcome-oriented process, which promotes movement from school to post-school activities, including post-secondary education, vocational training, integrated employment (including supported employment), continuing education, adult services, independent living, or community participation." (Individuals with Disabilities Education Act Amendments, 1990, Section 602 [A], 20 U.S.C. 1401 [A]).*

The transition provision of IDEA clearly provides for a set of comprehensive transition services designed to enhance the quality of life for *all* students with disabilities. Transition services are implemented through the Individualized Education Plan (IEP) as mandated by IDEA. The IEP must include:

> *. . . a statement of the needed transition services for students beginning no later than age 16 and annually thereafter (and, when determined appropriate for the individual, beginning at age 14 or younger), including when appropriate, a statement of the interagency responsibilities of linkages (or both) before the student leaves the school setting. (Individuals with Disabilities Education Act Amendments, 1990, Section 602[A], U.S.C. 1401 [A]).*

Related legislation which can enhance and facilitate transition services is provided by the Carl D. Perkins Vocational and Applied Technology Education Act of 1990 (P.L. 98-524) and the Americans with Disabilities Act (ADA) of 1990 (P.L. 101-336) (Rusch et al., 1992). The Carl Perkins Act provides students with disabilities increased access to vocational education services which can greatly assist disabled youth towards achieving transitional goals. ADA guarantees equal access for individuals with disabilities to critical transition target settings such as: (1) employment, (2) public accommodations, (3) state and local government services, (4) transportation, and (5) telecommunications. Together, IDEA, ADA, and the Carl Perkins Act provide a statutory foundation for comprehensive and flexible transition services for youth with severe disabilities. The challenge facing school districts is how to organize secondary programs so that meaningful post-school outcomes are achieved for students.

Structure of Secondary Programs

While the administrative organization of secondary programs for students with severe disabilities may vary slightly across school districts, they are usually designed to provide services to students in three distinct age groups. Middle-school or junior high-school programs typically serve students between the ages of 11 or 12 and 14 or 15 years old. High-school programs serve students between the ages of 15 or 16 through age 18. Post-secondary or transition programs typically serve students 19 years of age and older. These age levels not only provide convenient administrative divisions for school districts, they also recognize the dramatic differences in the educational and social needs of these groups of students (Gould, 1978; Selman, 1980). A number of researchers have suggested that middle-, high-, and post-high-school programs should be designed to cumulatively develop the student's capacity to function competently in the community as an adult (Bates, 1986; Berkell & Brown, 1989; Brown et al, 1988; McDonnell, Wilcox, & Hardman, 1991; Sailor et al, 1989; Udvari-Solner, Jorgensen, & Courchane, 1992; Wehman, 1992). For example, it is generally recommended that the educational program of middle-school age students focus on the development of basic academic, social, and self-care skills. In contrast, the educational program of a student who is 20 years old should concentrate on achieving specific career and life goals. Table 8-1 sum-

TABLE 8-1   Educational Outcomes for Secondary Programs

Middle School	High School	Transition Program
Build basic academic, communication, social, and self-help skills	Explore employment, leisure, and living options available to nondisabled adults in the local community	Establish employment and living options
Establish performance of age-appropriate leisure and personal management activities	Establish performance of age-appropriate leisure and personal management activities	Establish performance of employment, leisure, and personal management routines
Promote the development of supported relationships with school mates and neighbors who are not disabled	Promote the development of supported relationships with school mates, neighbors, co-workers, and other community members	Promote the development of supported relationships with co-workers, neighbors, and other community members
Encourage participation in school and community social activities and organizations	Encourage participation in school and community social activities and organizations	Encourage participation in work and community social activities and organizations

marizes the recommendations of researchers about the expected outcomes of educational programs for students at each of these age levels.

While the underlying goals of middle-school, high-school, and post-secondary or transition programs are the same, the functions of each program in preparing students for community life vary. The content of the educational program at each age level changes in order to cumulatively build the skills and supports necessary to promote the student's successful adjustment to community life. During middle school, emphasis is placed on the development of basic skills and social relationships with peers. At this time, educational programs should be designed to help students develop their social identity and the skills necessary to establish and maintain friendships (Selman, 1980). During high school, the emphasis is placed on exploration of adult life. Students must be provided opportunities to "sample" the range of work and living options available to adults in the community in which they live. Students also must develop the skills necessary to begin to use the resources of the community. Finally, the focus of transition programs should be on achieving specific employment and living outcomes for students. These outcomes include obtaining paid employment, developing a cohesive network of friends, and establishing the student's reliable performance of the daily routines that will make up their life in the community following graduation.

Effective Practices

> **Focus 2:**
>
> What variables of secondary programs has research shown to be associated with the successful post-school adjustment of students with severe disabilities?

Research over the last decade has identified a number of program practices which are associated with the successful post-school adjustment of students with severe disabilities. These practices include: (1) outcome-based program evaluation, (2) inclusion in the school and community, (3) community-referenced curriculum and instruction, (4) person-centered transition planning, (5) job placement prior to graduation, and (6) family involvement. Each of these factors are discussed in detail below.

Outcome-Based Program Evaluation

Historically, the effectiveness of secondary programs for students with severe disabilities have been defined simply in terms of the number of skills that students learned to perform in the classroom. Unfortunately, this outcome has not allowed most individuals with severe disabilities to achieve a quality of life that is comparable to their nondisabled peers. As a result, advocates, professionals, and policy makers have suggested that the expected outcomes of secondary programs for students with severe disabilities should be defined more broadly to reflect the actual demands of living successfully in the community (Bates, 1986; Brown et al., 1988; Wehman, Moon, Everson, Wood, & Barcus, 1988; Wilcox & Bellamy, 1982; Will, 1984).

Although successful community living is an extremely broad term that can mean different things to different people, we would probably all agree that four general outcomes are universally important: (1) establishing a network of friends and acquaintances; (2) developing the ability to use community resources on a regular basis; (3) securing a paid job that supports the use of community resources and interaction with peers, and (4) establishing independence and autonomy in making lifestyle choices (McDonnell, Wilcox, & Hardman, 1991). An evaluation system referenced to these outcomes would go beyond the question of "How many skills did the student learn?" to include questions such as: How many people are included in the student's social network? What kinds of relationships does the individual have with members of his or her social network? How often do they interact with members of their social network? How often does the individual access community environments? How much support is required by the individual to use community resources? How much money does the person earn? Is the individual satisfied with his or her job? Does the individual make her own choices about what leisure activities she completes? and many others. Obviously, such an evaluation system would redirect staff and material resources away from a focus on developing basic academic and developmental skills to enhancing each student's performance in the community.

Inclusion in the School and Community

Living successfully in the community requires that we develop and maintain social relationships with a number of different people. These individuals may include friends, family members, neighbors, and co-workers. The quality of the relationships that we develop with each of these groups of people significantly influences our satisfaction with our lives (Belle, 1982). These relationships also provide important sources of support in meeting the demands and challenges of adult life (Unger & Wandersman, 1985). This support can range from having someone to talk to after a tough day at work to giving us a ride to the store when our car is in the shop. Although we often do not think about the impact that these relationships have on our lives, ultimately they may be the most important factor in promoting successful community living (O'Brien & O'Brien, 1992). For most adolescents, the skills necessary to develop and maintain such relationships are learned between the ages of 12 and 22 (Selman, 1980).

Focus 3:

Why is the inclusion of high-school students with severe disabilities in school and community settings so important?

Research has shown that regular and frequent opportunities to interact with nondisabled peers in school and community settings is one of the most important things that secondary programs can do to promote the post-school adjustment of students with severe disabilities (Hasazi et al, 1989; Rusch et al, 1992; Wehman, 1992). The opportunity to interact with nondisabled peers allows students with severe disabilities to develop the communication and social skills and the relationships that are so important to successful community living (Haring, 1992). These interactions also allow students without disabilities to develop more positive attitudes about people with disabilities, to develop the skills necessary to effectively support persons with disabilities in school, work, and neighborhood settings, and establish meaningful friendships with people with disabilities (Giangreco & Putnam, 1991). Such outcomes will improve the acceptance of persons with severe disabilities by their nondisabled peers in work and neighborhood settings as adults (see Newsworthy 8-1).

The growing body of research on the benefits of inclusion has prompted a number of authors to suggest that students with severe disabilities should be served in the school that they would attend if they were not disabled; as opposed to the more common model in which students are bused to centralized programs (i.e., self-contained programs located on regular school campuses or separate schools). Recent research suggests that neighborhood school programs are as effective as centralized programs in meeting the social and educational needs of children with severe disabilities (Biklen, 1985; McDonnell, Hardman, Hightower, & Kiefer-O'Donnell, 1991; McDonnell, McDonnell, Hardman, & McCune, 1992).

Neighborhood school models have at least two potential advantages over centralized programs for secondary age students. First, the proximity of the student's educational program to their home increases the relevance of the instruction and training they receive. There is agreement among professionals that the educational programs provided to students with severe disabilities should be focused on establishing performance in the environments that they access every day (Brown et al, 1986; Falvey, 1989; Ford et al., 1989; Horner, McDonnell, & Bellamy, 1986; Sailor et al., 1986; Wilcox & Bellamy, 1987). From a logistical perspective, this is more easily accomplished if students attend the school that is located in their own neighborhood.

Second, close proximity of the student's educational program to their home supports the development and maintenance of social relationships with nondisabled peers. Friendships are unlikely to develop between students unless they have the opportunity to interact during *and* after school hours. When a student with a severe disability does not attend their neighborhood school, the opportunities for social relationships to extend beyond the walls of the school building are drastically diminished. This occurs because the students or their friends must often travel a considerable distance to see each other. They become dependent on family members or school staff to schedule social contacts and provide transportation to and from these activities. The result is that the student's social network is only functionally intact from 8:00 AM to 3:00 PM.

Once students with severe disabilities attend their neighborhood school, teachers must actively encourage the development of social relationships with nondisabled peers. To accomplish this aim, teachers should design their programs to (a) promote the development of supported relationships with peers at school *and* in other community settings, (b) support participation in content-area classes that allow students to meet IEP goals and objectives, (c) encourage student participation in extracurricular activi-

NEWSWORTHY 8-1

A boy found home at last, then the joy of friendship

By Marianne Funk
Deseret News staff writer

Daniel King practiced his short nomination speech over and over during those campaign weeks in April.

"He said it to anyone who would listen," his mother laughed. When there was no one around to listen, he said it softly to himself.

But when Daniel, 15, stepped up to the podium in the auditorium of Viewmont High School to nominate David Barlow as student body president, he froze.

It was the microphone, Daniel is afraid of microphones. Microphones and video cameras remind him of all those times people with cameras, microphones and lights would come to one of the foster homes and have him talk about how much he wanted a real home.

Daniel was a "Wednesday's Child," featured repeatedly on television stations in Oregon. This boy, the reporter would say, is a severely abused child with mental and emotional handicaps who badly needs a home.

Then Daniel would get a home for awhile. He was adopted when he was 7. But the family decided Daniel wasn't quite what they wanted, so they gave him back to the state when he was 8.

The video cameras and microphones came out to another foster home and Daniel again told the camera how much he wanted a home.

Once again, he was adopted. And once again, Daniel wasn't what the family had in mind. His second adoption also was "terminated"—the term used by the state's social services department.

The cameras and microphones

came back to try again.

Even though Daniel was adopted for the third time when he was 11 and has been happily ensconced in the King family ever since, he panicked when he saw the microphone.

Daniel came out onto the stage twice to give his speech. Twice he saw the microphone and backed away.

David Barlow stepped off the stage and stood below the podium. Don't think about the mike or all of

"After Daniel gave his speech and got the ovation, he gave me our handshake. . . . Then he gave me a big hug. The love was so real I couldn't help it. I just started crying."

David Barlow

the people, David said quietly. Just give your speech to me.

Daniel asked someone to push the mike out of the way, then he said his speech to David.

"I nominate David Barlow for student body president," he said. "I'm Daniel King and I'm David Barlow's campaign manager. And I'm wearing a tuxedo," he added. "I think David would be a good president because he's my friend. And besides that, he's also my bud."

"Bud" is the nickname the two boys have for each other. David met Daniel when David signed up for the peer tutoring class last fall. "Daniel is really responsive," David said. "Right off the bat we were instant best friends."

When David decided to run for student body president this spring, he thought of Daniel.

"I was trying to find someone who was really outgoing and would talk to everyone. Daniel just kept coming to my mind. He talks to everybody."

"David, tell her about the part where I went up there," Daniel prompted as the two boys sat on a bench in south hall of Viewmont recounting their victory.

So David explained all about

Daniel's nomination speech. "He got a standing ovation from the school," David said. "That's what I wanted. That's why I wanted him to be my campaign manager."

"Tell her about the part where you were crying," Daniel urged.

"I wanted them to feel the love," David continued. "I wanted people to know that handicapped people have feelings just like everyone else and they want to be accepted. That's exactly what I got."

"When are you going to tell her?" Daniel whispered. "Will you tell her now?"

So David told about the part when he cried. "After he gave his speech and got the ovation, he gave me our handshake." The boys demonstrated the special handshake they share. "Then he gave me a big hug. The love was so real I couldn't help it. I just started crying."

"Tell her about the time I decorated for the convention," Daniel suggested.

"Can I get a drink?" he asked as David started to tell about the decorating. "Talk loud so I can hear you." Daniel pleaded as he dashed down the hall to the drinking fountain.

Daniel's adoration for David radiates from him. Every time David calls him

"Bud," Daniel repeats the name right back to him.

"Do your best, Bud," David encouraged when Daniel was struggling to answer a question.

"OK, Bud," Daniel said.

Daniel watches David's face avidly when David talks. When his attention wanders from his own conversation, a soft word from David brings it back again.

He is especially pleased with their handshake.

Daniel is proud that David is student body president and he never tires of hearing David recount their campaign adventures, especially the part about his own speech.

But he loves David the most for just wanting him around. When asked why David was his friend, Daniel passed over the applause, the fliers and the decorations.

"For taking me out to his mother's."

ties sponsored by the school, (d) encourage after-school interactions with peers without disabilities, and (e) develop the communication and social skills necessary for students to function successfully in various social contexts. An underlying theme of inclusion efforts in secondary programs should be to assist the student to learn how to adjust their social behavior and interactions with peers to the various contexts that they will ultimately be expected to perform in as an adult.

There are a growing number of strategies available to practitioners to achieve these outcomes for students (Giangreco & Putnam, 1991; Jorgensen, 1992). For example, strategies shown to be effective in developing supported relationships between students with severe disabilities and nondisabled peers include (a) circles of friends which encourage the development of friendships between a student with severe disabilities and a small group of peers without disabilities who share common interests, (b) buddy programs which encourage nondisabled peers to provide assistance to students with severe disabilities in specific situations like opening their lockers or getting their wheelchair into an elevator, and (c) peer tutoring programs in which nondisabled peers provide assistance to students in learning important skills in school and community settings. These strategies create systematic opportunities for students to interact with one another. In addition, such relationships provide the natural supports necessary to promote each student's participation in the typical activities of the school and community. Without systematic attempts by secondary programs to encourage interactions between students with and without disabilities, it is highly unlikely that meaningful relationships can or will develop (Haring, 1992).

Other strategies which can support the inclusion of students in content-area classes are also available to secondary teachers. These include (a) cooperative learning which allows students to participate as part of a heterogeneous student group in a content-area class (e.g., participating as a member of "team" in a home economics class in preparing meals), (b) adapted instruction in which a student works on different skills within the same content area (e.g., the student learns to type their name, address, and telephone number during a computer class), and (c) parallel instruction in which students works on skills from different content areas (e.g., the student learns to use a jig saw in woodshop while other students work on building projects). Together these strategies can support the inclusion of students in a wide variety of content-area classes in the regular curriculum, thus increasing the opportunities for students with severe disabilities to develop the communication and social skills and relationships necessary to live successful in the community.

Community-Referenced Curriculum and Instruction

Increasingly, researchers who study secondary programs for students without disabilities have realized that the traditional curriculum and instructional approaches used in most high schools are inadequate to prepare students for community life (Berryman, 1993). This has led to a call by a number of educational reformers for the expansion of the learning opportunities and learning environments that students access in their educational program. These reformers seek to increase the relevance of the curriculum for students in meeting the demands of living and working in the community and to use instructional strategies that will allow students to transfer skills learned in school to everyday activities (Berryman, 1993; Lave, 1991; Resnick, 1987).

A similar movement has evolved in programs serving students with severe disabilities. A number of researchers have suggested that the curriculum for this group of students must be organized to focus on increasing each student's capacity to use the resources of the community independently (Bates, 1986; Berkell & Brown, 1989; Brown et al., 1988; Falvey, 1989; Ford et al., 1989; McDonnell et al., 1991; Udvari-Solner et al., 1992; Wehman, 1992; Wilcox & Bellamy, 1987). The goal is to link curricular content to the demands of living and working in the community as an adult. Community-referenced curricula for students with severe disabilities are different from more traditional academic and developmental curricula in two distinct ways:

1. *The instructional units in the curriculum are activities rather than isolated skills.* An activity is a chain of behavior which, if performed under natural circumstances, results in a functional outcome for the individual (Wilcox & Bellamy, 1982). The outcome, or effect, is the same whether or not the individual performing the activity happens to be disabled.

An activity has three distinct components or phases: preparation or "getting ready"; execution or "doing," and resolution or "ending" the activity and going onto the next. An activity is something you can actually see yourself doing under natural circumstances. "Buying groceries," "paying bills," "attending aerobics class," or "calling friends on the phone" all represent activities, things that we actually do on a day-to-day basis. By contrast, "naming the four food groups," "stating coin values," "forming mental maps of frequented buildings," or "labeling the parts of a telephone" do not.

2. *The overall structure of curriculum content reflects the domains of adult life.* Today there is general agreement that the best approach to designing curriculum for secondary students with developmental disabilities is one that addresses the demands of adult life. This "top-down" approach to guiding what students should learn reflects the fact that adult life cannot be neatly segmented to reflect traditional content or curriculum domains (such as reading, math, communication, social, or motor skills). Instead, most of us work a full- or part-time job, try to find some time for leisure activities, and spend what remains of the week shopping, cooking, cleaning, or otherwise managing our affairs. By organizing the secondary curriculum to reflect the basic functions of adult life—work, leisure, and personal management—we emphasize that the goal of secondary programs is to prepare students for life in the community.

One example of a community-referenced curriculum for students with severe disabilities is *The Activities Catalog* (Wilcox & Bellamy, 1982, 1987). *The Activities Catalog* is a comprehensive listing of "activities" done by people without disabilities who live in a given community. It divides activities into three broad content domains: leisure, personal management, and work. Each domain represents a different function for the individual. Leisure can be viewed as the opportunities presented by an environment, while personal management activities reflect the demands of that environment, and work represents those activities required to generate personal financial resources.

The *leisure domain* includes the variety of activities that can occupy one's discretionary time. Leisure refers to activities chosen by the individual when she or he is not engaged in work or personal management activities (Voeltz, Wuerch, & Wilcox, 1982). Leisure activities include such things as chatting with friends during work breaks, going to a movie, managing an intermural basketball game, and cutting out pictures for a scrapbook of antique cars.

The *personal management* domain includes activities necessary to care for one's personal being and belongings, and to manage one's time, money, and possessions. Personal management activities include such things as cleaning one's bedroom, preparing dinner, depositing payroll checks, shopping for personal items, and using public restrooms.

The *work* domain includes those activities that might represent an individual's claim on wages. Carrying a paper route, volunteering at the local library, receiving training on a high-school work crew, cutting a neighbor's lawn, and inserting components on printed circuit boards for a local manufacturer are all legitimate work activities.

Activities in each domain have been further organized by a set of *categories*. These categories reflect common sense groupings. The categories within each domain were developed to be exhaustive and mutually exclusive. That is, all activities within the content domain could be assigned to one and only one category, while the categories encompassed all possible activities. Table 8-2 presents the overall structure of the catalog.

Obviously, such a curriculum structure also affects the way in which instruction is designed and implemented. The most significant effect is that instruction must occur in actual performance settings (i.e., stores, banks, theaters, restaurants) rather than in the classroom or school. Community-based instruction is necessary because research has shown that students with severe disabilities do not readily generalize skills learned in school settings to natural settings without substantial training (Horner, McDonnell, & Bellamy, 1986). Effective secondary programs are those which are organized to provide students with regular and frequent opportunities to receive instruction in natural settings.

Focus 4:

What outcomes should community-based instruction achieve for students with severe disabilities?

Community-based instruction provides several important outcomes for students, teachers, and families. First, students should learn to perform personal management and leisure activities that will enhance their immediate participation in their home, school, and community. A critical variable in selecting activities is whether they will become part of the student's day to day life. In other words, will the student have the opportunity to perform these activities on a regular basis and can the student's participation in the activities be adequately supported by peers, family, or other community members?

TABLE 8-2   Structure of the Activities Catalog

CATEGORIES IN THE LEISURE DOMAIN

Category	Definition	Examples	Non-examples
1-1 Exercise	Includes any group or individual activity that is characterized by some physical exertion by the participant(s). Exercise may or may not involve equipment.	Attending aerobics class Playing on a baseball team Riding an exercise bike	Playing darts (Game) Playing cards (Game)
1-2 Games, Crafts, and Hobbies	Includes activities that have rules, require special manual skills, or are hobbies. Such activities may or may not involve equipment or scoring. They do not involve strenuous physical participation. (Games or hobbies that involve physical exertion are categorized as exercise.)	Playing video games (both at home and in arcades) Pasting stamps in an album Hooking a rug Attending a craft class at the community college	Going to a football game (Event) Playing in a baseball game (Exercise)
1-3 Events	Includes any activity that is available only on a scheduled basis. Events are structured and often sponsored by a business or formal organization. Such activities may involve any number of participants and require active or passive involvement.	Attending church Going to a movie Watching a track meet Going to a dance Attending club meetings	Going to the Zoo (Other)
1-4 Media	Includes any variety of activities that depend primarily on auditory materials. Such activities may involve equipment and typically require minimal interaction with the materials.	Playing records Watching television Listening to radio	Attending a concert (Event) Playing an instrument (Hobby)
1-5 Other	Includes free-time activities not specifically included in above categories, and accessing any specialized or community environments that are available continuously.	Going to the park Visiting a relative Relaxing	Playing the guitar (Hobby)

CATEGORIES IN THE PERSONAL MANAGEMENT DOMAIN

Category	Definition	Examples	Non-examples
2-1 Self	Includes any activity where primary focus is on basic care and maintenance of the body. There are four clusters of activities in this category: (1) dressing, (2) grooming, (3) bathing, and (4) toileting.	Taking a bath Dressing for work Using public restrooms Getting hair cut	Eating (Food) Ironing clothes (Space and Belongings) Purchasing grooming supplies (Space and Belongings)

TABLE 8-2 *Continued*

Category	Definition	Examples	Non-examples
2-2 Food	Includes all activities that relate to the selection, purchase, preparation, and consumption of food. Such activities may occur either at home or in the community.	Planning meals Using fast food restaurants Preparing breakfast Storing groceries	Doing the dishes (Space and Belongings)
2-3 Space and Belongings	Includes all those activities that focus on the organization and management of personal space and belongings. Such activities include: (1) purchasing and storing materials, (2) cleaning and straightening the environment, and (3) caring for possessions.	Feeding a pet Shopping for groceries Washing clothes Raking the yard Cleaning the bathroom	Setting the table (Food)
2-4 Personal Business	Includes all those activities that relate to maintaining contacts with friends and service providers, handling the health and social emergencies, self-advocacy, and money and time management.	Having an intimate relationship Following a personal schedule/calendar Taking medications Attending a meeting of People First	Purchasing items of apparel (Space and Belongings)

JOB CLUSTERS IN THE WORK DOMAIN

Category	Definition	Examples	Non-examples
3-1 Agriculture and Natural Resources	Includes activities concerned with propagating, growing, caring for, and gathering plant and animal life and products. Also includes caring for parks, gardens, and grounds.	Fruit packer Farm helper Stable attendant Greenhouse worker Groundskeeper Animal care provider Tree planter	Food processor (Distribution)
3-2 Distribution	Includes any activities concerned with handling, processing, or retailing materials. Machinery may be involved in handling or processing operations.	Vegetable processor Fish packer Shelf stocker Bottle sorter Materials receiver Sales clerk Packager	Kitchen helper (Food preparation and Services)
3-3 Domestic and Building Services	Includes activities concerned with providing domestic services in private households or lodging establishments, maintaining and cleaning clothing/apparel in a commercial establishment, and performing cleaning or maintenance services to the interiors of buildings.	Janitor Maid Laundry worker Dry cleaning worker Window washer Furniture cleaner	Busperson (Food Preparation and Services)

(continued)

TABLE 8-2 *Continued*

Category	Definition	Examples	Non-examples
3-4 Food Preparation and Services	Includes activities concerned with preparing food and beverages and serving them to patrons of such establishments as hotels, clubs, restaurants. Also includes activities that maintain kitchen work areas and equipment or that maintain customer eating areas.	Food preparation worker Busperson Dishwasher Food counterperson Kitchen helper	Fruit picker (Agriculture and Natural Resources)
3-5 Office and Business Services	Includes activities concerned with recording, transcribing, reproducing, organizing, and distributing data, records, and communications. Also includes activities related to receiving, storing, and shipping goods and materials from an office/business.	Shipping worker Record filer Mailroom worker Messenger Copy machine operator	Shelf stocker (Distribution)
3-6 Construction	Includes any activities concerned with fabricating, erecting, installing, paving, painting, and repairing structures such as buildings or roads.	Construction worker Road construction worker Painter's helper	Yard maintenance worker (Agriculture and Natural Resources)
3-7 Health Occupations	Includes any activities concerned with maintaining the health, comfort, or safety of individuals. Also includes activities that involve the handling of medicine or materials that are used in hospital care.	Day care attendant Nurse's assistant Nursing home volunteer Child care helper	Hospital kitchen worker (Food Preparation and Services) Hospital laundry worker (Domestic and building Services)
3-8 Manufacturing and Machine Operations	Includes activities concerned with using tools and machines to fabricate, inspect, or repair products.	Dryer operator Assembler Heat-seat machine operator Quality controller Printing press worker	Packager (Distribution)
3-9 Miscellaneous Occupations	Includes a variety of activities that fall outside the other eight categories.	Car wash worker Usher Mover's helper	Child care helper (Health Occupations)

Second, students should have access to community-based instruction that exposes them to the range of employment alternatives available to them following graduation (McDonnell et al., 1991; Wehman, 1992). This "sampling" of work alternatives in non-paid job placements provides students with the opportunities to learn work and work-related skills that will be important to their future employment and to identify their own personal employment strengths and interests. These experiences will provide the infor-

****

POINT-COUNTERPOINT 8-1

Although community-based instruction has become an accepted practice in secondary programs for students with severe disabilities, debate about its role in preparing students for adulthood has increased as the field has begun to emphasize the full inclusion of students in school environments. The question is how much time should students spend outside grade-level or content-area classes learning to complete leisure, personal management, and employment activities in community settings?

Point

In discussing their experiences in supporting their daughter Shawntell during high school Jeffery and Cynthia Strully argue that school friendships are the most important component of high school educational experience:

> *We have learned that Shawntell must be a part of her school in order to have relationships with her schoolmates. If she goes out with adults into other environments (i.e., community-referenced instruction) during her school day then she will not have the opportunity to come to know and be known by her schoolmates. This raises some difficult and troubling questions for families and professionals who have worked to have young people leave school and go into different environments (e.g., domestic, vocational, or leisure environments) during school hours. It is our firm opinion that all young people need to be in school alongside their peers. This does not mean that young people should not work to make their beds, purchase items in stores, and so forth, but activities must take place at appropriate times with the appropriate people. (p. 167; Strully & Strully, 1992).*

Counterpoint

Lou Brown and his colleagues have argued that the practices of full inclusion and community-based instruction should not be presented as an either/or issue:

> *All of our resources could be spent developing social relationships with nondisabled peers in regular education classrooms, but we would be sacrificing teaching what is necessary for effective functioning in real buses, streets, workplaces, parks, and stores. If we devote all our resources to teaching functional skills we would be trading away important social relationships with nondisabled peers and critical recreation/leisure repertories because these do not meet our definition of functionality. . . .*
>
> *The [educational] careers of students who are severely intellectually disabled must be balanced across environments, persons, activities, attitudes, values, and skills. One or two components cannot be allowed to dominate. Although we may emphasize something for a period time, over a 21-year career we must provide services that truly prepare for comprehensive functioning in integrated postschool life. No parent, student or professional should have the power to impose imbalanced or disproportionate educational services. (pp. 45–46, Brown et al., 1991).*

****

mation base necessary for the student and their family to select the student's initial job following graduation.

Finally, community-based instruction creates the conditions necessary for teachers and parents to develop alternative performance strategies and to identify the level of program support that will ensure that students are able to successfully participate in home, school, work, and other community settings. This information will ultimately assist the student and the family to select employment and residential programs that will meet individual needs and preferences.

Person-Centered Transition Planning

Federal law now requires that school districts conduct formal transition planning for each student. These planning efforts should be person-centered and focused on identifying each student's post-school goals and the supports that will be necessary to ensure these goals are met (Mount & Swernick, 1988; O'Brien & O'Brien, 1992; Vandercook et al., 1989). Person-centered transition planning strategies have several common features. First, planning is based on the student's "vision" of life in the community following graduation. This vision is based on the students' personal hopes and dreams including the kind of job the student would like, where they want to live, and the relationships that they want to maintain or develop. Second the vision is shaped by the needs, interests, and abilities of each person, as well as the opportunities that will be available to them in home, school, work, and community settings. Third, the activities necessary to meet the goals are identified. Finally, the people who will assist students in carrying out their plan are identified and their responsibilities are assigned. These individuals could include students, their parents or other family members, peers, community members, and as necessary representatives of educational and community service agencies. The planning process attempts to blend all of these potential sources of support as students move into the community.

The development of a formal transition plan as part of each student's Individualized Educational Program (IEP) is important for several reasons. A formal plan serves to: (1) establish a working relationship between parents and post-school case managers and service providers, (2) identify the services and resources that will ensure meaningful employment and community participation, (3) ensure access to services prior to graduation, and (4) identify systems that will facilitate the maintenance of needed services. A sample transition planning format is presented in Figure 8-1.

At a minimum, the transition planning team should include the student, parent, teacher, adult services case manager(s) (i.e., the vocational rehabilitation counselor if appropriate), and representatives from community service programs. In addition, the transition planning team may be expanded to include friends, co-workers, or neighbors who provide support to the student in home, school, work, or other community settings. Successful implementation of the transition plan will also require the establishment of interagency agreements that combine the resources and staff to accomplish the proposed activities. For example, the secondary program and local supported-employment program provider may need to coordinate staff in order to ensure that students will have access to appropriate training personnel and resources. The transition plan may call for the school to train the student on a specific bus route to an employment site, while the vocational program (e.g., vocational rehabilitation) may provide staff to train specific job skills once the student has arrived.

Student: ___Sally_____   Date of IEP/ITP Development: ___August 27, 1989___

PLANNING AREAS: 1. Employment   2. Residential/Personal   3. Social/Recreational   4. Transportation
                                              Management
                          5. Guardianship   6. Insurance/Health Care   7. Long-Term Support   8. Other

Area: ___Employment___   Annual Goal/Outcome: _Sally will work in a janitorial job for a minimum of 20 hours_
                                                      per week at a commensurate wage.

| Q1 | Q2 | Q3 | Q4 | SHORT-TERM OBJECTIVES | | RESPONSIBLE | WHEN | COMP/MODIFIED |
				LOGISTICAL	INSTRUCTIONAL			
1				1. Sally will be placed on Supported Employment waiting list		Mary Davis, DSH	12-1-89	
2				2. A janitorial position will be obtained for Sally in the Ogden area.		Bill Bailee, Teacher	12-1-89	
3					3. At temporary placement Sally will perform vacuuming, sweeping, and restroom cleaning tasks at public library. Criteria: Independent performance on all tasks on 3 consecutive days and across 3 monthly probes.	Bill Bailee, Teacher, Assigned job coach	12-1-89	
4					4. Sally will purchase lunch from deli-wagon at library. Menu cards will be developed for Sally to use. Money will come from parent. Criteria: Independent purchases for one week.	Bill Bailee, Teacher, Assigned job coach	12-1-89	
5					5. Sally will ride bus to and from library independently for one week.	Bill Bailee, Teacher, Assigned job coach	12-1-89	

FIGURE 8-1   Illustration of Individualized Education Plan/Transition Plan

---

Focus 5:

What aspects of community life should a student's transition plan address?

A student's transition plan should address all of adult life including:

1. *Employment.* The planning should specify the type of placement or program that will be most appropriate for the student. It should also determine how the resources between the school and post-school service programs will be coordinated to ensure that appropriate jobs are identified, and that the student is trained for the placement.

2. *Living Arrangement.* The team should determine which residential alternative is the most appropriate for the student. The parents and student may decide that living at home for a period of time following the school years is their best option. Then the committee should clearly identify for the parents a person whom they may contact at a later date when they are ready for a placement away from the primary family unit.

3. *Leisure Activities.* The committee should identify those leisure alternatives that are most important to the student. Activities should be planned to ensure that the student has the necessary resources or skills to participate in such activities regardless of where the individual chooses to live following school. Such resources or skills may include financing the activity, transportation, establishing a peer to attend the activity with the student, etc.

4. *Income and medical support.* The team should ensure that students are enrolled in social service programs (i.e., Medicaid, Supplemental Social Security Income, etc.) necessary to ensure their financial stability and good health. The committee should also ensure that needed income or medical benefits are not jeopardized by other services that the student may receive.

5. *Transportation.* The specific transportation needs for facilitating access to vocational, residential, and leisure alternatives should be determined. The committee should identify the specific alternatives for each activity, the method of financing transportation, and strategies to coordinate transportation issues between school and adult service providers.

6. *Long-term support and care.* The committee should identify the need for guardianship and/or specific trusts or wills. Specific services or agencies need to be identified that can assist parents in establishing these legal documents (McDonnell, et al., 1986). Prior to the student's leaving school, as many components of the transition plan as possible should be implemented. For example, the student may be placed full time in their target employment setting in order to evaluate performance across several domains. Transportation from home to work should be arranged and potential difficulties examined.

Job Placement

> **Focus 6:**
>
> What are the two functions of employment training for high-school students with severe disabilities?

Research suggests that students who are successful in obtaining and maintaining paid work in community settings following high school are those who (1) receive ongoing opportunities for direct training in community employment sites throughout their high-school career and (2) obtain a paid job before graduation (Hasazi et al, 1985; Hasazi et al., 1989; Wehman et al, 1992). McDonnell, Hardman, & Hightower (1989) have suggested that these outcomes can best be achieved through a differentiated employment curriculum for high-school students which first emphasizes sampling job opportunities available in the local community and then provides specific job training focused on an employment option that matches the student's ability and interests.

For most students with severe disabilities, job sampling would continue throughout high school. Students would be placed in a number of nonpaid positions at actual job sites during this period. The curriculum would be structured to (a) expose them to the actual job options available in the community in which they live, (b) train specific work skills (e.g., use of tools and equipment, staying on-task, soliciting assistance from supervisors and co-workers, etc.), and (c) train work-related skills (e.g., transportation and mobility skills, personal hygiene and dressing skills, self-management skills, etc.). Although the development of work and work-related skills is an important outcome of job sampling, another important purpose is to conduct a comprehensive assessment of the student performance in each training site. The teacher would determine the student's strengths and weaknesses in completing the assigned job tasks and necessary work-related skills, the student's level of satisfaction with the job, and the level of support and assistance that the student needs to be successful in the job. In this way, job sampling provides a cumulative record of the student's performance in a wide range of employment possibilities. Based on this information, the student, the parents, and the teacher can select an employment alternative for the student that matches their interests and abilities.

The second component of the employment preparation program is specific job training and placement. The primary outcomes of this component are to (a) identify a job in the community which matches the interests and needs of the student, (b) train the student to complete assigned job tasks to employer standards, (c) promote the inclusion of the student in the natural social networks of the job site, and (d) resolve logistical issues that might interfere with the student's on-going success in the job placement following school. Achieving these goals for students with severe disabilities may take from several months to several years. Consequently, job training and placement efforts must usually begin several years before the student ages out of school.

Family Involvement

A student's family is one of the most important elements in their adjustment to community life. Research has shown that families play a significant role in (a) securing a student's job after school (Hasazi, Gordon, & Roe, 1985; Hasazi et al., 1989), (b) providing residential support to students (McDonnell, Wilcox, Boles, & Bellamy, 1985), and (c) assisting the student in developing relationships that will support their participation in the community (Nisbet, Covert, & Schuh, 1992). Given this, it is only logical that parents and other family members be directly involved in each student's educational program. Families must have real opportunities to participate in the critical decisions that are made about each student's transition to the community and in supporting the student's efforts to achieve their own goals. Secondary programs must assist family members to identify their role in supporting the student and to obtain the information and develop the skills necessary to effectively play this role.

To accomplish this goal secondary programs must encourage and support family participation in the student's educational program in a number of ways including:

1. *Direct participation in educational planning.* Achieving a student's post-school goals will require active support from their parents and other family members. This support is more likely to be forthcoming if family members have a role in making decisions about the content of the student's educational program. Parents and other family members can provide invaluable information about the student's needs and preferences, the activities that will be the most meaningful to the student in home, school, and community settings, and the resources available to support the student's participation in these activities. It is critical that educational planning be structured to encompass not only the student's needs but their needs as a member of a family.

2. *Providing information.* Because preparing students for life in the community is a cumulative process, families will need access to various types of information as the student progresses toward graduation. Secondary programs should be organized to assist families in gaining access to the information necessary to make wise decisions about their child's post-school life (Turnbull et al., 1989). For example, families may require information about innovative employment and residential programs for persons with severe disabilities, the range of services currently available in the community, how to access social service programs such as Medicaid and the Supplemental Social Security Income Program, and so on. This information will allow families to identify and develop the supports necessary to meet the student's future goals.

3. *Assisting families in defining their role in supporting the student's transition from school to community life.* During the last several years of school, it is critical that families clarify their role in supporting the student in community life (Turnbull et al., 1989). The student and the family must address a number of emotional issues including where the student will live, where he or she will work, how much control the student has over their own lifestyle choices, and so on. As noted earlier, parents and families play a significant role in supporting the transition of many students to community life. Consequently, it is imperative that secondary programs be structured to assist parents in defining the role they will play in supporting their son or daughter as an adult. Strategies that have proven to be effective in addressing these issues are (a) offer workshops to families which are designed to promote a critical examination of these issues (c.f., Turnbull et al., 1989) and (b) create opportunities for families to obtain support from one another in addressing the needs of the student (Everson, Barcus, Moon, & Morton, 1987; McDonnell et al., 1992; Nisbet et al., 1992).

Conclusion

This chapter has examined the role of secondary programs in improving the quality of life experienced by persons with severe disabilities. In the last decade, secondary programs have changed dramatically. These changes have been driven in large part by the clarification of the outcomes that educational programs should achieve for students. It is no longer acceptable that students simply learn more skills. Rather students, families, professionals, and advocates are demanding that secondary programs prepare students for community life. A focus on outcomes dramatically impacts program design and operation. To prepare students for life in the community, schools must ensure that students have regular and frequent opportunities to interact with peers who are not disabled, access instruction which teaches them to use the resources of the community in which they live, receive employment training that results in a paid job, plan educational programs based on the personal goals, needs, and preferences of students, and ensure that families are directly involved in the educational program. Together, these practices allow school districts to provide middle-school, high-school, and transition programs which effectively prepare adolescents with severe disabilities for community life.

Focus Review

Focus 1: How are transition services defined in the 1990 amendments of IDEA?

- They are defined as a "coordinated set of activities" designed to produce meaningful post-school outcomes for students.
- These services may include a variety of traditional and nontraditional training programs ranging from vocational education to supported employment and living.

Focus 2: What variables of secondary programs has research shown to be associated with the successful post-school adjustment of students with severe disabilities?

- Outcome-based program evaluation
- Inclusion in the school and community
- Community-referenced curriculum and instruction
- Person-centered transition planning
- Job placement prior to graduation
- Family involvement

Focus 3: Why is the inclusion of high school students with severe disabilities in school and community settings so important?

- Inclusion creates the opportunities for students to develop the social and communication skills necessary for community life.
- Inclusion allows students with and without disabilities to develop relationships that will support their mutual participation in community life.
- It helps nondisabled individuals to develop attitudes and skills that encourage the acceptance of individuals with disabilities in work and community settings.

Focus 4: What outcomes should community-based instruction achieve for students with severe disabilities?

- Learn personal management and leisure activities necessary for successful community living.
- Sample the range of employment alternatives available to adults living in the community.
- Identify and develop the structural supports necessary to ensure that students have a high quality of life after school.

Focus 5: What aspects of community life should a student's transition plan address?

- Employment, living arrangement, leisure activities, income and medical support, transportation, and long-term support and care
- The specific options or alternatives selected by the student and the IEP team should reflect the student's own "vision" of their life in the community after school.

Focus 6: What are the two functions of employment training for high school students with severe disabilities?

- Sampling employment alternatives to identify the student work strengths and interests
- Placement in a paid job prior to graduation

References

Bates, P. E. (1986). Competitive employment in southern Illinois: A transitional service delivery model for enhancing the competitive employment outcomes for public school students. In F. R. Rusch (Ed.) *Competitive employment: Issues and strategies* (pp. 51–64). Baltimore: Paul H. Brookes.

Belle, D. (1982). Social ties and social support. In D. Doled (Ed.). *Lives in stress*. Beverly Hills: Sage.

Berkell, D. E., & Brown, J. M. (1989). *Transition from School to Work for Persons with Disabilities*. New York: Longman.

Berryman, S. E. (1993). Learning for the workplace. In

L. Darling-Hammond (Ed.), *Review of Research in Education* (pp. 343–404). Washington, DC: American Educational Research Association.

Biklen, D. (1985). *Achieving the complete school: Strategies for effective mainstreaming.* New York: Teachers College Press.

Brown, L, Albright, K. Z., Rogan, P., York, J., Solner, A. U., Johnson, F., VanDeventer, P., & Loomis, R. (1988). An integrated curriculum model for transition. In B. L. Ludlow, A. P. Turnbull, & R. Luckasson (Eds.). *Transitions to adult life for people with mental retardation—Principles and practices* (pp. 67–84). Baltimore: Paul H. Brookes.

Brown, L., Nisbet, J., Ford, A., Sweet, M., Shiraga, B., York, J., & Loomis, R. (1983). The critical need for nonschool instruction in educational programs for severely handicapped students. *The Journal of the Association for the Severely Handicapped, 8,* 71–77.

Everson, J. M., Barcus, M., Moon, M. S., & Morton, L. (1987). *Achieving outcome: A guide to interagency training in transition and supported employment.* Richmond, VA: Virginia Commonwealth University, Project Transition to Employment.

Falvey, M. A. (1989). *Community-based curriculum: Instructional strategies for students with severe handicaps.* Baltimore, MD: Paul H. Brookes.

Ford, A., Schnorr, R., Meyer, L., Davern, L., Black, J., & Dempsey, P. (1989). *Syracuse community-referenced curriculum guide for students with moderate and severe disabilities.* Baltimore, MD: Paul H. Brookes.

Giangreco, M. F. & Putnam, J. W. (1991). Supporting the education of students with severe disabilities in regular education environments. In L. H. Meyer, C. A. Peck, & L. Brown (Eds.). *Critical issues in the lives of people with severe disabilities* (pp. 245–270). Baltimore, MD: Paul H. Brookes.

Gould, R. (1978). *Transformations: Growth and change in adult life.* New York: Simon & Schuster.

Haring, T. G. (1992). Social relationships. In L. H. Meyer, C. A. Peck, and L. Brown (Eds.), *Critical issues in the lives of people with severe disabilities* (pp. 195–218). Baltimore: Paul H. Brookes.

Hasazi, S. B., Gordon, L. R., & Roe, C. A. (1985). Factors associated with the employment status of handicapped youth exiting high school from 1975 to 1983. *Exceptional Children, 51,* 455–469.

Hasazi, S., Johnson, R.E., Hasazi, J., Gordon, L.R., & Hull, M. (1989). Employment of youth with and without handicaps following school: Outcomes and correlates. *Journal of Special Education, 23,* 243–255.

Havighurst, R. J. (1972). *Developmental tasks and education* (3rd ed.). New York: David McKay Co.

Horner, R. H., McDonnell, J. J., & Bellamy, G. T. (1986). Teaching generalized skills: General Case Instruction in simulation and community settings. In R. H. Horner, L. H. Meyer, H. D. Fredericks (Eds.), *Education of learners with severe handicaps: Exemplary service strategies* (pp. 289–214). Baltimore, MD: Paul H. Brookes.

Jorgensen, C. M. (1992). Natural supports in inclusive schools: Curricular and teaching strategies. In J. Nisbet (Ed.), *Natural Supports in School, at Work and in the Community for People with Severe Disabilities* (pp. 179–216). Baltimore, MD: Paul H. Brookes.

Lave, J. (1991). Situated Learning in Communities of Practice. In L. B. Resnick, J. M. Levine, & S. D. Teasley (Eds.), *Perspectives on Socially Shared Cognition* (pp. 63-84). Washington, DC: American Psychological Association.

Levinson, D. J. (1978). *The Seasons of a Man's Life.* New York: Alfred A. Knopf.

McDonnell, A., McDonnell, J., Hardman, M. L., & McCune, G. (1992). Educating students with severe disabilities in their neighborhood school: The Utah Elementary Integration Model. *Remedial and Special Education, 12,* 34–45.

McDonnell, J. & Hardman, M. L. (1985). Planning the transition of severely handicapped youth from school to adult services: A framework for high school programs. *Education and Training of the Mentally Retarded, 20,* 275-286.

McDonnell, J., Hardman, M. L., & Hightower, J. (1989). Employment preparation for high school students with severe handicaps. *Mental Retardation, 27,* 396–404.

McDonnell, J., Hardman, M. L., Hightower, J., & Kiefer-O'Donnell, R. (1991). Variables associated with in-school and after-school integration of secondary students with severe disabilities. *Education and Training in Mental Retardation, 26*, 243–258.

McDonnell, J., Wilcox, B., & Boles, S. M. (1986). Do we know enough to plan for transition? A national survey of state agencies responsible for service to persons with severe handicaps. *Journal of the Association for Persons with Severe Handicaps, 11*(1), 53–60.

McDonnell, J., Wilcox, B., Boles, S. M., & Bellamy, G. T. (1985). Transition issues facing youth with severe disabilities: Parents' perspective. *Journal of the Association for Persons with Severe Handicaps, 10*, 61-65.

McDonnell, J., Wilcox, B., & Hardman, M. (1991). *Secondary programs for students with developmental disabilities.* Boston, MA: Allyn & Bacon.

Mount, B., & Zwernik, K. (1988). *It's never too early, it's never too late. A booklet about personal futures planning.* Minneapolis, MN: Metropolitan Council.

Nisbet, J. (1992). *Natural Supports in School, at Work and in the Community for People with Severe Disabilities.* Baltimore, MD: Paul H. Brookes.

Nisbet, J., Clark, M., & Covert, S. (1991). Living it up! An analysis of research on community living. In L. H. Meyer, C. A. Peck & L. Brown (Eds.). *Critical issues in the lives of people with severe disabilities* (pp. 115–144). Baltimore, MD: Paul H. Brookes.

Nisbet, J., Covert, S., & Schuh, M. (1992). Family involvement in the transition from school to adult life. In F. R. Rusch, L. Destefano, J. Chadsey-Rusch, L. A. Phelps, & E. Szymanski (Eds.). *Transition form School to Adult Life: Models, Linkages, and Policy* (pp. 407–424). Sycamore, IL: sycamore Publishing Company.

O'Brien, J. & O'Brien, C. L. (1992). Members of each other: Perspectives on social support for people with severe disabilities. In J. Nisbet (Ed.). *Natural Supports in School, at Work and in the Community for People with Severe Disabilities* (pp. 11–16). Baltimore, MD: Paul H. Brookes.

Resnick, L. B. (1987). Learning in school and out. *Edcucational Researcher, 16*, 13–20.

Rusch, F. R., Destefano, L., Chadsey-Rusch, J., Phelps, L. A., & Szymanski, E. (1992). *Transition from school to adult life: Models, Linkages, and Policy.* Sycamore, IL: Sycamore Publishing Company.

Sailor, W., Halvorsen, A., Anderson, J., Goetz, L., Gee, K., Doering, K., & Hunt. P. (1986). Community intensive instruction. In R. H. Horner, L. H. Meyer, & H. D. Fredericks (Eds.). *Education of learners with severe handicaps: Exemplary Service Strategies* (pp. 251–288). Baltimore, MD: Paul H. Brookes.

Selman, R. L. (1980). Four domains, five stages: A summary portrait of interpersonal understanding. In R. L. Selman (Ed.). *The Growth of Interpersonal Understanding* (pp. 131-155). New York: Academic Press.

Turnbull, H. R., III, Turnbull, A. P., Bronicki, G. J., Summers, J. A., & Roeder-Gordon, C. (1989). *Disability and the family: A guide to decisions for adulthood.* Baltimore, MD: Paul H. Brookes.

Udvari-Solner, A., Jorgensen, J., & Courchane, G. (1992). Longitudinal vocational curriculum: The foundation for effective transition. In F. R. Rusch, L. Destefano, J. Chadsey-Rusch, L. A. Phelps, & E. Szymanski (Eds.). *Transition from school to adult life: Models, Linkages, and Policy* (pp. 285–320). Sycamore, IL: Sycamore Publishing Company.

Unger, D. G. & Wandersman, A. (1985). The importance of neighbors: The social, cognitive, and affective components of neighboring. *American Journal of Community Psychology, 13*, 139–169.

Vandercook, T., York, J., & Forest, M. (1989). The McGill Action Planning System (MAPS): A strategy for building the vision. *The Journal of the Association for Persons with Severe Handicaps, 14*, 205–215.

Wehman, P. (1992). *Life Beyond the Classroom: Transition Strategies for Young People with Disabilities.* Baltimore: Paul H. Brookes.

Wehman, P., Moon, M. S., Everson, J. M., Wood, W., & Barcus, J.M. (1988). *Transition from school to work: New challenges for youth with severe disabilities.* Baltimore, MD: Paul H. Brookes.

Wilcox, B. & Bellamy, G. T. (1982). *Design of high school programs for severely handicapped students*. Baltimore, MD: Paul H. Brookes.

Wilcox, B. & Bellamy, G. T. (1987). *A comprehensive guide to the Activities Catalog*. Baltimore, MD: Paul H. Brookes.

Will, M. (1984). *OSERS program for the transition of youth with disabilities: Bridges from school to working life*. Washington, D.C.: Office of Special Education and Rehabilitative Services, U. S. Department of Education.

Chapter 9

Adult Service Programs

Most adults with severe disabilities will require ongoing support to live successfully in the community. Ideally, most of this support would be provided by friends, family, co-workers, and neighbors (O'Brien & O'Brien, 1992). These sources of support provide the best framework for meeting each individual's needs and establish a lifestyle that matches their preferences. However, many persons with severe disabilities will also require support from community service agencies to obtain meaningful employment and to develop an appropriate living alternative. This chapter will examine adult service programs for persons with severe disabilities. We will review the administrative structure of adult services and will discuss supported employment and supported living programs.

Structure of Adult Service Programs

The administrative structure of adult services for persons with severe disabilities is quite different than that of school programs. In contrast to educational services which are mandated through a single federal law (i.e., the Individuals with Disabilities Education Act) and administered through a single federal agency (Office of Special Education Programs), adult service programs are authorized through a number of laws and administered across several government agencies (see Chapter 3).

Focus 1:

What are entitlement and eligibility programs?

Another critical difference is that there are two types of adult service programs. The first is called an *entitlement* program. In an entitlement program, all individuals who meet the eligibility requirements *must* be provided service. These services are provide irregardless of the availability of funds. Income support (i.e., the Supplemental

WINDOW 9-1

Robyn is 38 years old and has moderate mental retardation. She has been working in a fast food restaurant for the last several years. She has become good friends with Beth who also works at the restaurant. They spend their breaks and lunches together talking or reading magazines. Three days a week after work they go to the community recreation center to exercise or swim.

A local employment service program found Robyn's job for her. The program also provided her with a job coach who helped her to learn to complete her assignments and now checks in with her each week to make sure she is doing okay. Robyn's employer is very happy with her work and has gradually increased the number of jobs that she does and number of hours she works.

Robyn lives with her friend Vivian in an apartment complex close to her job. She and Vivian have divided up the household chores and plan their weekly menus together. Robyn and Vivian get

assistance from a residential service program that hires staff to assist them to pay their bills and manage their money. The staff also assists them to develop a schedule of activities for the week. Initially, the staff helped Robyn and Vivian to complete basic household chores, do their laundry, and prepare meals. Now they are nearly independent in completing these tasks and the staff simply checks in with them once a day to make sure everything is going alright. Robyn and Vivian have hosted several parties at their apartment with their friends from the apartment complex and their jobs.

Robyn also has a boyfriend name Bill. They see each other several times a week. Sometimes they go out and other times they just stay at home and watch television or listen to music. The staff from the residential program have also helped Robyn get involved in a church and participate in activities sponsored by the women's and single's group.

Social Security Income Program) and medical assistance programs (i.e., Medicaid and Medicare) are the primary entitlement programs available to adults with severe disabilities (see Chapter 3).

The second type of service program is called an *eligibility* program. In these programs, an individual may meet the eligibility requirements for service, but he or she may not be able to receive service because there aren't enough funds to assist all *eligible* people. Most community-based employment and residential services for adults with disabilities are eligibility programs. Under this structure, when an adult with severe disabilities applies for employment or living support, they will only receive service if they are eligible for service *and* the services are available in the local community.

The structure of adult service programs creates several significant problems in developing appropriate community supports for individuals with severe disabilities. The most critical issue is that there is no entitlement to community-based employment and residential service programs. Consequently, the expansion of these support services is often subject to the politics underlying state and local budget processes. Good economic times may see an expansion of these service programs, while in a poor economy these service programs may be cut. The absence of a clear mandate to provide such services has led to significant shortages of appropriate adult service programs for persons with severe disabilities in many states (Biweekly & Bellamy, 1986; McDonnell, Wilcox, & Boles, 1986; Sale, Revell, & Kregel, 1992).

A related problem is that a significant proportion of available federal funding for services for persons with severe disabilities supports programs that segregate them from the community. For example Braddock (1987) reported that during the 1985 fiscal year, 41 percent ($4.68 billion) of all service dollars for persons with disabilities went to supporting the approximately 100,000 individuals living in state-operated institutions. In contrast, the remaining 59 percent of the dollars went to support a vastly larger number of people with disabilities living in the community.[1] This occurs because the entitlement programs available to adults with severe disabilities are structured to support large congregate care facilities rather than community-based alternatives. There is a clear bias in federal policy and funding practices towards segregated programs for adults with severe disabilities.

Finally, the sheer number of federal and state agencies involved in supporting adults with severe disabilities in the community can, and does, create significant problems in developing a cohesive system of community support (Coneley, Elder, & Noble, 1986). In most states, adults with severe disabilities receive services from at least three different federal and state agencies (e.g., Mental Retardation/Developmental Disabilities, Vocational Rehabilitation, and Social Security). Each of these agencies has different purposes and functions, which often conflict with one another. The result is that persons with severe disabilities may find themselves in the undesirable position of compromising personal goals for community participation in order to access necessary support services.

As a field, we have made significant progress in our understanding of how to design service programs support the participation of persons with severe disabilities in the community (c.f., Meyer, Peck, & Brown, 1991). The policy and administrative structure of adult service programs however, is a significant barrier to the development of an effective system. A number of advocacy and professional organizations have recognized the need to address these important issues (Luckasson, et al, 1992; ARC, 1990; TASH, 1987). It is unlikely that improvements in the quality of life of adults with severe disabilities can be achieved until a cohesive federal policy is developed and implemented.

Gerry and Mirski (1992) have suggested that attempts to reorganize federal and state policies underlying adult service programs should be driven by five principles:

1. Services for people with disabilities should be based on the needs and wishes of the individuals themselves and, as appropriate, their families.
2. Services for people with disabilities must empower consumers and be flexible enough to reflect the differing and changing needs of people with disabilities.
3. Every person with disabilities must have a real opportunity to engage in productive employment.
4. Public and private collaborations must be fostered to ensure that people with disabilities have the opportunities and choices that are to be available to all people in the United States.
5. Social inclusion of people with disabilities in their neighborhoods and communities must be a major focus of the overall effort.

---

[1]Braddock estimates that during the 1985 fiscal year there were over 600,000 individuals with disabilities being served in the community-based service system.

Employment Programs

Sustained integrated employment is important for persons with severe disabilities for many reasons. Not only does a job provide monetary rewards, it also supports an adult identity, creates social contacts, and promotes participation in the community. The importance of employment in the lives of adults with severe disabilities prompted the development of an elaborate system of vocational service programs in the late 1960s. This system was based on the concept of a "continuum of service" (see Chapter 3). In spite of the intentions of the "continuum," the actual outcomes of these programs for individuals with disabilities and especially those with severe disabilities have been marginal.

There is, however, reason to be optimistic about employment opportunities for persons with developmental disabilities as we approach the 21st century. Researchers and policy makers are placing a greater emphasis on community employment for persons with disabilities (Ferguson & Ferguson, 1986; Stark & Kiernan, 1986). The result has been the development of alternative employment programs collectively referred to as supported employment (Hill et al., 1987; Mank, Rhodes, & Bellamy, 1986; O'Neill & Stern, 1985; Rusch, Chadsy-Rusch, & Johnson, 1991; Vogelsberg, 1986; Will, 1985). The following sections describe the flow-through model of employment services and supported employment alternatives.

The Continuum of Employment Services

The employment service system for adults with disabilities in most states includes four types of programs: day treatment, work activity centers, sheltered work programs, and transitional employment training programs (Table 9-1). In most communities, these programs are operated by non-profit organizations created to provide services to persons with disabilities. These non-profit organizations contract with state agencies (i.e., Rehabilitative Services and/or the MR/DD agency) to provide day treatment and employment services. Frequently, non-profit agencies are organized to provide all four program alternatives to participants under a single administrative umbrella.

The focus of most day treatment or day activity programs is on teaching basic personal care, communication, motor, and academic skills to program participants. Although day treatment programs are considered to be part of the overall community employment service system, they place little emphasis on development of work or work-related skills. These programs do not typically provide significant amounts of paid work to participants.

The primary focus of habilitation efforts in most work activity centers is to provide "therapeutic" activities designed to increase the individual's capacity for employment. Training usually centers on basic developmental skills and pre-vocational skills. Typically, participants are also provided some paid work. The work that participants complete in most work activity centers is made available through contracts with local businesses and industries. For example, a work activity center may contract with the local Chamber of Commerce to collate and mail their monthly newsletter or contract with a national airline to place dinnerware, napkins, and salt and pepper in hermetically sealed packages for passengers. These contracts are used as a vehicle to teach skills considered to be impor-

TABLE 9-1   Continuum of Employment Services

Program	Description
Day Treatment	Serves persons with disabilities in a separate facility. Program efforts focus on developing basic academic and developmental skills. Little emphasis is placed directly teaching work or work-related skills.
Work Activity Centers	Serves persons with disabilities in a separate facility. Program efforts focus on "therapeutic" activities designed to increase work capacity. Participants are provided a limited amount of paid work.
Sheltered Workshops	Serves persons with disabilities in a separate facility. Program efforts focus on "prerequisite" work and work-related skills necessary for competitive employment. Participants are provided some paid work.
Transitional Employment Training	Serves persons with disabilities in community employment settings. Program efforts focus on training the participant a specific set of job skills and placement in a competitive job. The program provides time-limited follow-up once the individual finds a job.

tant for competitive employment such as staying on-task, basic industrial processes, such as assembly and collation, and interaction with co-workers and supervisors.

Sheltered work programs are structured to develop the work and work related skills necessary obtain a job in community businesses and industries. A second focus of shelter workshop programs is to provide "remunerative" employment or paid work to participants. Typically, the paid work made available to program participants is derived from contracts with local businesses and industries.

Transitional employment training programs are structured to provide up to 12 months of work training in community businesses and industries to program participants. Individuals are placed in a community business or industry to learn the skills necessary to obtain a specific type of job. For example, an individual might be placed in a restaurant to learn the skills necessary to become a dishwasher. Upon graduation from the program, the agency would assist the individual in obtaining a dishwashing job in another restaurant. Transition employment training programs also provide time-limited follow-along to participants until they have made a successful adjustment to their job. Ultimately, however, support to the participants is eliminated and the individual is expected to work independently.

Although the flow-through model of employment services is designed to allow individuals with disabilities to move into competitive employment, research suggests that this outcome is rarely achieved for individuals with severe disabilities. Bellamy, Rhodes, Bourbeau, and Mank (1986) reported that approximately 2.7 percent of all individuals served in day treatment programs graduated to work activity centers, 3 percent of individuals served in work activity centers moved into sheltered workshop programs, and 11.3 percent of individuals served in sheltered workshop programs were successfully placed in competitive employment. These authors also pointed out that individuals with severe disabilities were the least likely to move through the continuum to competitive employment. In essence, an individual placed in a work activity center or sheltered workshop program was likely to remain in that program for the rest of their adult life.

In addition to failing to move people from segregated service programs to community employment, these programs have also been ineffective in producing meaningful employment outcomes for program participants. Research studies indicate that individuals who served in work activity centers and sheltered workshop programs (Buckley & Bellamy, 1985; Rusch, 1990):

1. Earn wages that are significantly below poverty line.
2. Receive less than 20 hours of paid work per week.
3. Have virtually no opportunities to interact or develop ongoing relationships with persons without disabilities.

The ineffectiveness of the existing continuum of employment services has prompted researchers, advocates, and consumers to call for the development of alternative employment programs. In the early 1980s, Congress funded a number of research and model demonstration projects designed to create service alternatives that would provide meaningful community employment for persons with disabilities. These projects led to the development of supported employment programs.

Supported Employment

It is now recognized that virtually all adults with severe disabilities are capable of meaningful employment if they are provide adequate support in work settings (Bellamy & Horner, 1987). A popular approach to providing this assistance is called "supported employment" (Bellamy, Rhodes, Mank, & Albin, 1988; Kiernan & Stark, 1986; Rusch

---

POINT OF INTEREST 9-1

The supported employment initiative has had a significant impact on the community service system for adults with disabilities.*

- In 1990, state vocational rehabilitation agencies nationally reported that 74,657 individuals were participating in supported employment programs. This represented a 43% increase over the 1989 fiscal year.
- Of these individuals, 52.1% were served in individual supported jobs programs, 15.3% were served in enclave programs, 12.8% were served in work crew programs, and 19.8% were served in other alternative models.
- On average, persons participating in supported employment earned $3.87 per hour.
- 80.9% of supported employment participants worked at least 20 hours per week.

Source: West, M., Revell, W. G., & Wehman, P. (1992). Achievements and Challenges I: A five year report on consumer and system outcomes from the supported employment initiative. *The Journal of The Association for Persons with Severe Handicaps, 17,* 226–235.

et al., 1992; Wehman, 1981). Supported employment has proven to be an extremely effective strategy in allowing adults with severe disabilities to work in paid jobs in local businesses and industries (Rusch et al., 1992). Research reports have indicated that supported employment allows persons with severe disabilities to work in a wide range of jobs (Rusch et al., 1992), to earn significant wages and other benefits (Hill et al., 1987; Mank, Rhodes, & Bellamy, 1986; McDonnell, Nofs, Hardman, & Chambless, 1989; Vogelsberg, 1986), and leads to the development of social relationships with peers without disabilities (Hill et al., 1987; McDonnell et al., 1989; Rusch, Johnson, & Hughes, 1990). In addition, supported employment has proven to be as cost-effective as the segregated day treatment and sheltered employment programs currently provided by many states to persons with severe disabilities (Noble & Conley, 1987; Tines et al., 1990).

Definition of supported employment

The effectiveness of supported employment has led to its inclusion in a number of federal laws and programs including the Developmental Disabilities Act, the Home and community Waiver Program of the Health Care Financing Administration, and the Rehabilitation Act. The Developmental Disabilities Act defined supported employment as:

> *Paid employment which (i) is for persons with developmental disabilities for whom competitive employment at or above the minimum wage is unlikely and who, because of their disabilities, need ongoing support to perform in a work setting; (ii) is conducted in a variety of settings, particularly work sites in which persons without disabilities are employed, and (iii) is supported by any activity needed to sustain paid work by persons with disabilities, including supervision, training, and transportation. (Developmental Disabilities Act of 1984, p. 2665)*

Focus 2:

What are the principle characteristics of supported employment programs?

Bellamy, Rhodes, Mank, & Albin (1988) have stressed that supported employment differs markedly from traditional vocational services for persons with severe disabilities. They state that supported employment has four defining characteristics:

1. *Supported employment is paid employment.* Supported employment is intended to be paid employment rather than a vocational training program. The focus of program efforts are on obtaining high wages, job security, job advancement, and acceptance by co-workers. This stands in sharp contrast to traditional vocational services for persons with severe disabilities which emphasize the development of the pre-requisite skills that may allow the person to enter competitive employment.

2. *Continuous versus time-limited support.* Traditional competitive employment services for persons with disabilities have been structured to provide time-limited support to program participants. The emphasis of these programs was on those individuals who could benefit from short-term training and a fixed period of follow-up after job placement. This approach functionally eliminated the participation of persons with severe disabilities, who often require ongoing support to function successfully in community settings. The result is that most adults with severe disabilities are served in day treatment or sheltered employment programs which separate them from the mainstream of community life (Bellamy et al., 1986; Sale et al., 1992).

In contrast, supported employment acknowledges the support needs of persons with severe disabilities and is structured to provide continuous support at the job site. This support may range from monthly telephone contacts with the employer to make sure the person is succeeding to full-time supervision in the job site. Supported employment assumes that the type and level of assistance provided to the person is more critical to work success than his or her functioning level. The obvious policy implication of this assumption is that no person is too severely disabled to participate in paid employment.

3. *Integrated versus segregated service delivery.* A critical feature of supported employment is its emphasis on the integration of persons with disabilities in typical businesses and industries. Supported employment assumes that the opportunity to interact with persons without disabilities is an important outcome of work. These interactions create the opportunities to develop social relationships with peers that will not only support the individual's job performance but their inclusion in other aspects of community life.

4. *Flexibility.* Supported employment is not a single program, rather it is an assortment of strategies that can be used to maintain persons with diverse training and support needs in paid employment. Supported employment is structured to allow program providers to match services to the needs of the individual.

Types of supported employment programs

To date, the most extensively used supported employment programs have been individual supported jobs, enclaves, and work crews (Sale et al., 1992). These models differ from one another in structure and approach. Table 9-2 summarizes the primary characteristics of each model.

The individual supported jobs model is structured to place a single individual with disabilities in a community employment site. The person is provided support in the work setting by a "job coach" or "employment support specialist." The support specialist usually works for a non-profit community service agency which contracts with state agencies to provide employment services to persons with disabilities. The responsibility of the support specialist is to train the person to complete all job tasks, provide the ongoing support necessary to ensure that person continues to perform the job well, promote the individual's inclusion in the social networks of the job site, and assist co-workers and supervisors to support the person in their job (Albin, 1992; Bellamy et al., 1988; Moon et al, 1990).

Enclaves are structured to provide support to a small group of persons with disabilities in a single community employment site. For example, a community service program might place several persons with disabilities in the local hospital. These individuals might all work in the same area (e.g., the laundry) or in different areas of the

TABLE 9-2   Features of Three Supported Employment Models

Feature Model	Number of Workers with Disabilities	Type of Support	Advantages	Disadvantages
Individual Supported Jobs	1	A job coach provides training and on-going support. Support is gradually faded across time. The job coach is hired by an employment service program.	- Allows the employment needs and interests of program participants to be matched to specific jobs - Potential for high wages. - Potential for high rates of interaction and acceptance by co-workers.	- Cost-effectiveness for persons who require continuous support is not known.
Enclave	2–8	Continuous training and on-going support is provided by a job coach. The job coach may be hired by the host company.	- Structure allows for continuous support for program participants when needed. - Potential for high wages. - Potential for high rates of interaction and acceptance by co-workers.	- Employment options are limited by the need to identify a host company large enough to support a small group of persons with disabilities. - Placement of large numbers of people with disabilities in the host business may inhibit interactions and acceptance by co-workers.
Work Crew	2–8	Continuous training and on-going support is provided by a job coach. The job coach is employed by an employment service program.	- Program structure allows for continuous program support when needed. - Potential for high wages.	- Employment outcomes for program participants are linked to the employment service program's ability to obtain work contracts. - Employment options for program participants are limited by the contracts obtained by the employment service program. - Limited opportunities for interaction with people without disabilities.

hospital (e.g., the laundry, the kitchen, the shipping/receiving department). Program participants would receive training and ongoing support from a support specialist. While support specialists most often work for a community service program, the host business may also hire these individuals to support people with disabilities who work for the company (e.g., Rhodes & Valenta, 1985).

Work crews are structured to provide employment opportunities to a small group of persons with disabilities. Unlike enclaves in which participants work in a single business, work crews contract with several different businesses or community members for work. For example, a work crew might complete landscaping services for businesses or community members in the summer and snow removal services in the winter. Work crew participants also receive training and ongoing support from a support specialist who supervises the crew. The participants typically work for a non-profit community service agency rather than for the businesses or individual with whom the work crew has contracts.

Effectiveness of supported employment programs

Although all three of these models have been used effectively to support the employment of persons with disabilities (Rusch et al, 1992), a number of advocates and professionals have criticized the use of enclave and work crews (Brown et al., 1992; Rusch et al., 1990; Thompson, Powers, & Houchard, 1992). These individuals have argued that enclave and work crew models inhibit the inclusion of persons with severe disabilities at the employment site, inhibit the development of the natural supports that are critical to long-term success, and may prevent the individual from selecting employment options which match their own needs and preferences. While additional research is needed on the relative effectiveness of various supported employment models, it is clear that the individual supported jobs model is the most consistent with the outcome of full community participation.

Nationally, the trend has been toward the use of individual supported jobs (West, Revell, & Wehman, 1992). In 1988, 52 percent of people enrolled in supported employment programs were served through individual supported job models. In 1990, this number had grown to 71 percent. At this point, individual supported jobs appear to offer the best possible outcomes for persons with severe disabilities as well as the flexibility necessary to meet the diverse needs and preferences of this group of people.

Residential Programs

Residential programs are a critical component of the community service system for adults with severe disabilities. Perhaps no other element of our lives is more important to our feelings of security, happiness, and well-being than our "home." The 1970s witnessed a significant increase in the number and types of community-based residential alternatives developed for persons with disabilities. As large institutions began to reduce their populations, states were forced to develop community-based alternatives. These programs ranged from large congregate care facilities to personal care in the individual's home. Although the system of residential service programs is less well defined than the employment system (Lakin, Hill, Bruininks, & White, 1986; Landesman & Vietze, 1987; Nisbet, Clark, & Covert, 1991), it also structured around the concept of a "continuum of service."

Although the types of program alternatives included in the current continuum of residential services are quite diverse, the capacity of these programs to provide living arrangements that approximate the opportunities available to community members without disabilities is questionable. Consumers, researchers, and policy makers have begun to advocate for alternative programs for persons with severe disabilities which are structured to provide residential services that are sensitive to needs and preferences of program participants (Boles, Horner, & Bellamy, 1988; Heal, Hanley, Novak & Amado, 1988; Nisbet et al., 1991; Taylor, Biklen, & Knoll, 1987). These alternatives are generally referred to as supported living programs. The following sections describe the current continuum of residential services and the supported living alternatives.

The Continuum of Residential Services

The continuum of community-based residential services in most states is comprised of six program alternatives (Hill, Lakin, & Bruininks, 1988; Taylor et al., 1987). These are nursing home programs, Intermediate Care Facilities for the Mentally Retarded (ICF/MRs), group homes, foster care, semi-independent living, board-and-supervision facilities, and independent living (Table 9-3).

Taylor and colleagues (1987) suggest that nursing home programs represent a "transinstitutionalization" of persons with disabilities. In other words, individuals are transferred from large public institutions to private institutions. The services provided by nursing home programs are typically focused on long-term medical support and personal care rather than training and support for community living. Hill et al., (1987) in their report of a 1982 national survey of residential programs estimated that over 42,000 individuals with mental retardation were living in nursing home programs nationally. Of this group, approximately one-third were 63 years of age or older and over one-third were under 22 years of age. The vast majority of individuals served in this program option have severe and profound mental retardation.

Intermediate Care Facilities for the Mentally Retarded (ICF/MR) are funded under Title XIX of the Social Security Act. ICF/MRs range from small group homes to large private and public institutions. The purpose of the ICF/MR program is to fund residential living and other services to people identified as mentally retarded, and needing 24-hour care. In order to receive reimbursements under the program, the legislation requires states to provide "active treatment" that includes an individual written plan of care, interdisciplinary evaluations, and an annual review. The legislation also allows state-funded institutions for people with mental retardation to receive reimbursements as ICF/MRs. Thus, the government created a strong incentive to states for continuation and expansion of institutional programs. Braddock and Fujiura (1988) report that 87 percent of the funds budgeted under the ICF/MR program in 1986 were ". . . associated with congregate care settings with capacities of 16 beds or larger. Seventy-five percent of these funds supported care in large, state-operated institutions" (p. 262).

TABLE 9-3   Continuum of Residential Services

Program	Description
Nursing Home Programs	Congregate care facility designed to provide 24 hour a day medical care. Little emphasis is placed on providing training that would lead to independent living.
Intermediate Care Facilities for the Mentally Retarded	Designed to provide 24 hour care to program participants. The size of the facility can vary significantly from small group homes to large institutions. These programs are required by federal law to provide "active treatment" based on a individualized assessment of the participant's habilitative needs.
Group Homes	Designed to provide habilitative programming that will lead to independent living. The size ranges from small community residences to large congregate care facilities.
Foster Care	Provides services to the individual in their own home or in the home of another family. These programs provide basic room and board, however, some specialized foster care programs may also provide habilitative programming.
Board-and-Supervision Facilities	Provides room and board to the participant. Typically, the program provides no training or supervision.
Semi-independent Living Programs	Designed to provide the participant with training that will lead to independent living. Participants live in their own residences. Staff are located nearby to provide necessary training and support.

Group home programs include both private and public facilities that can include small community residences to "mini-institutions". In their 1982 national survey of residential facilities, Hill et al. (1987) reported that 84 percent of responding agencies had 15 or fewer participants. Group homes are organized to provide personal care and habilitation programming designed to increase the participant's independence. Most group homes provide training and support in the areas of personal care, maintaining a household, conducting personal business, and leisure/recreational activities.

Foster care providers offer service to one or more persons with disabilities in their own homes. National data suggest that the average number of individuals served in foster care programs is less than 3 persons (Hill et al., 1987). The basic support provided to program participants is room, board, and minimal supervision. In recent years, the development of specialized foster care programs has allowed these programs to provide some habilitative programming designed to enhance the participant's independence at home and in the community.

Board-and-supervision facilities are structured to provide room and board to persons with disabilities. These programs are typically operated by private, for profit organizations. Usually, these programs provide no training or personal care. Hill et al. (1987) reported that only .5 percent of individuals with mental retardation were served in such programs. Most of these individuals were 22 years or older and had mild mental retardation.

Semi-independent living programs are designed to provide training and support that will allow participants to eventually move into their own residence. In these programs, participants share living quarters and program staff are located nearby. Staff provide support to the participants in carrying out activities of daily living, making decisions regarding their personal finances, assist in transportation, and serve as an advocate as necessary. In the national survey conducted by Hill et al. (1987), semi-independent living programs represented less than 2 percent of the residential program options provided to persons with mental retardation.

Research has clearly shown that small community-based residential programs produce superior developmental and quality of life outcomes for persons with severe disabilities than institutional programs (Heal, Haney, & Novak Amado, 1988, Taylor, Biklen, & Knoll, 1987, Nisbet et al., 1991). However, the quality of life experienced by persons with severe disabilities in community-based programs can vary significantly (Nisbet et al., 1991). The success or failure of persons with severe disabilities to adjust to community life appears to be affected more by the philosophical orientation and organizational structure of the residential program than the individual's functioning level. Unfortunately, residential programs are often structured to provide a "service" to program participants rather than creating a "home." Consequently, advocates and researchers have recently begun to promote the development supported living alternatives for persons with severe disabilities.

Supported Living

Many advocates and professionals have embraced the concept of supported living as the basic framework for the design and implementation of residential programs for adults with severe disabilities (Bellamy & Horner, 1987; Nisbet et al., 1991; Taylor, Biklen, & Knoll, 1987). Research has suggested that supported living alternatives can enhance a person's quality of life in a number of ways including promoting interaction with community members, use of community resources, and control over daily activities and lifestyle choices (Boles, Horner, & Bellamy, 1988; Kennedy, Horner, & Newton, 1990; Kennedy, Horner, Newton, & Kanda, 1990).

Focus 3:

What is supported living?

Definition of supported living

The term *supported living* is used to describe living arrangements which (1) are similar in character and structure to the residential options of persons without disabilities living within a particular community and (2) provide the ongoing support necessary to allow a person with disabilities to be successful in the living option that he or she has selected. Bellamy and Horner (1987) state that:

Supported living is defined as persons with disabilities living where and with whom they want, for as long as they want, with the ongoing support needed to sustain that choice." (p. 506).

Boles, Horner, & Bellamy (1988) have suggested that supported living has four critical characteristics:

1. *Accountability for lifestyle outcomes.* In contrast to traditional residential programs which emphasize a readiness approach to the design of service support (see Chapter 2), supported living focuses on achieving significant lifestyle outcomes for program participants. Emphasis is placed on the current quality of life of the persons receiving service rather than some future quality of life implied by skill development. Such lifestyle outcomes include but are not limited to interaction with community members without disabilities, inclusion in the social networks of the neighborhood and community, use of community resources, and empowerment in making lifestyle choices.

2. *Diversity of residential options.* A critical principle of supported living is that people with severe disabilities choose where and how they want to live. Traditionally, the living options available to persons with severe disabilities have been defined by the range of services present in the local community. Supported living is structured to promote personal choice and preference in selecting a living alternative.

3. *Individually determined support.* The level of support required by persons with severe disabilities to live successfully in the community will vary significantly. If persons with severe disabilities are going to have real lifestyle choices then service programs must be flexible enough to accommodate the unique needs of program participants. Supported living is structured to identify and deliver the level of support necessary to ensure each person's participation in the community throughout his or her lifetime.

4. *Broad technology of residential support.* The notion of supporting a person in their residence, as opposed to training for independent living, requires the use of a broad range of technology. Successfully supporting an individuals with severe disabilities in their own home will require the expertise of a number of disciplines including applied behavior analysis, social work, nutrition, physical and occupational therapy, speech and communication therapy, and medicine. Professionals with knowledge in each of these areas must work as a transdisciplinary team to meet the unique needs of each person.

Types of supported living alternatives

A number of supported living options have been reported in the literature within the last several years (Boles et al., 1988; Klien, 1992; Taylor et al., 1987). These alternatives include individuals living in their own homes, living in apartments or houses alone or with other persons with disabilities, and living in apartments or houses with other persons without disabilities. While the settings in which people live are quite diverse, all of these alternatives have several common structural features. These features include a philosophical assumption that the setting is the person's home rather than a service program, consumer and family involvement in planning and quality assurance, the availability of paid staff necessary to meet the needs of each person within their home, the systematic strategies to connect the individual to the social networks of the neighborhood and community.

Conclusion

Employment and residential service programs can play a significant role in enhancing the quality of life of adults with severe disabilities. Advancements in our technology for supporting persons with severe disabilities in the community has created real opportunities for these individuals to become full participants in community life. The challenge currently facing advocates and professionals is to restructure the adult service system so that it becomes more responsive to the individual needs and preferences of the people it serves. Supported employment and supported living programs are critical first steps in achieving this goal. In the future, the role of adult service programs must be designed to supplement, rather than supplant the natural supports available to persons with severe disabilities from friends, family, co-workers, and neighbors.

Focus Review

Focus 1: What are entitlement and eligibility programs?

- In entitlement programs, individuals who qualify must be provided services irregardless of the availability of funds.
- In eligibility programs, individuals are provided service if they qualify for the program *and* funds are available to provide the services.

Focus 2: What are the principle characteristics of supported employment programs?

- Supported employment is paid employment rather than job training.
- Supported employment provides ongoing support as necessary to meet the individual's needs.
- Supported employment recognizes the opportunity to interact with nondisabled peers as a critical outcome of employment.
- Supported employment is flexible, services are tailored around the needs of the individual.

Focus 3: What is supported living?

- Living arrangements which (1) are similar in character and structure to the residential options of persons without disabilities living within a particular community and (2) provide the ongoing support necessary to allow a person with disabilities to be successful in the living option that he or she has selected.

References

Albin, J. M. (1992). *Quality improvement in employment and other human services: Managing for quality through change*. Baltimore: Paul H. Brookes.

Bellamy, G. T., Horner, R. H. (1987). Beyond high school: Residential and employment options after graduation. In M. E. Snell (Ed.), *Systematic Instruction of Persons with Severe Handicaps* (pp. 491–510). Columbus, OH: Charles E. Merrill Publishing Company.

Bellamy, G. T., Rhodes, L. E., Mank, D. M., & Albin, J. M. (1988). *Supported employment: A community implementation guide*. Baltimore: Paul H. Brookes.

Bellamy, G. T., Rhodes, L. E., Borbeau, P., & Mank, D. M. (1986). Mental retardation services in sheltered and day activity programs: Consumer outcomes and policy alternatives. In F. R. Rusch (Ed.). *Competitive employment: Issues and strategies* (pp. 257–272). Baltimore: Paul H. Brookes.

Boles, S., Horner, R. H., & Bellamy, G. T. (1988). Implementing transition: Programs for supported living. In B. L. Ludlow, A. P. Turnbull, & R. Luckasson (Eds.), *Transition to Adult Life for People with Mental Retardation - Principles and Practices* (pp. 85–100). Baltimore: Paul H. Brookes.

Braddock, D. (1987). *Federal policy toward mental retardation and developmental disabilities*. Baltimore: Paul H. Brookes.

Braddock, D., & Fujiura, G. T. (1988). Federal foundations for transitions to adulthood. In B. L. Ludlow, A. P. Turnbull, & R. Luckasson (Eds.), *Transitions to adult life for people with mental retardation—principles and practices* (pp. 257–274). Baltimore: Paul H. Brookes.

Brown, L., Udvari-Solner, A., Frattura-Kampschroer, E., Davis, L., Ahlgren, C., Van Deventer, P., & Jorgensen, J. (1991). In L. H. Meyer, C. A. Peck, & L. Brown (Eds.), *Critical Issues in the Lives of People with Severe Disabilities* (pp. 195–218). Baltimore: Paul H. Brookes.

Buckley, J., & Bellamy, G. T. (1985). National survey of day and vocational programs for adults with severe disabilities: A 1984 profile. In P. Ferguson (ed.), *Issues in transition research: Economic and social outcomes* (pp. 1–12). Eugene, OR: Specialized Training Program, University of Oregon.

Conely, R. W., Noble, J. H., & Elder, J. K. (1986). Problems with the service system. In W. E. Kiernan & J. A. Stark (Eds.), *Pathways to Employment for Adults with Developmental Disabilities* (pp. 53–66). Baltimore: Paul H. Brookes.

Developmental Disabilities Act of 1984 (PL 98-527, 19 Oct. 1984), United States at Large 98, pp. 2662–2685.

Gerry, M. H., & Mirsky, A. J. (1992). Guiding principles for public policy on natural supports. In J. Nisbet (Ed.), *Natural Supports in School, at Work, and in the Community for People with Severe Disabilities* (pp. 341–346). Baltimore: Paul H. Brookes.

Heal, L. W., Hanley, J. I., & Novak, A. R. (1988). *Integration of developmentally disabled individuals into the community*. Baltimore: Paul H. Brookes.

Hill, M. L., Wehman, P. H., Kregel, J., Banks, P. D., & Metzler, H. M. D. (1987). Employment outcomes for people with moderate and severe disabilities: An eight-year longitudinal analysis of supported competitive employment. *The Journal of The Association for Persons with Severe Handicaps, 12,* 182–189.

Kennedy, C. H., Horner, R. H., & Newton, J. S. (1990). The social networks and activity patterns of adults with severe disabilities: A correlation analysis. *The Journal of The Association for Persons with Severe Handicaps, 15,* 86–90.

Kennedy, C. H., Horner, R. H., Newton, J. S., & Kanda, E. (1990). Measuring the activity patterns of adults with severe disabilities using the resident lifestyle inventory. *The Journal of The Association for Persons with Severe Handicaps, 15,* 79–85.

Kiernan, W. E., & Stark, J. A. (1986). *Pathways to Employment for Adults with Developmental Disabilities*. Baltimore: Paul H. Brookes.

Klien, J. (1992). Get me the hell out of here: Supporting people with disabilities to live in their own homes. In J. Nisbet (Ed.), *Natural Supports in School, at Work, and in the Community for People with Severe Disabilities* (pp. 277–340). Baltimore: Paul H. Brookes.

Lakin, K. C., Hill, B. K., Bruininks, R. H., & White, C. C. (1986). Residential options and future implications. In W. E. Kiernan & J. A. Stark (Eds.), *Pathways to Employment for Adults with Developmental Disabilities* (pp. 199–206). Baltimore: Paul H. Brookes.

Luckasson, R., Coulter, D. L., Polloway, E. A., Reiss, S., Schalock, R. L., Snell, M.E., Spitalnik, D. M., & Stark, J. A. (1992). *Mental retardation: definition, classification, and systems of support* (9th ed.). Washington, D.C.: American Association on Mental Retardation.

Mank, D. M., Rhodes, L. E., & Bellamy, G. T. (1986). Four supported employment alternatives. In W. E. Kiernan & J. A. Stark (Eds.), *Pathways to employment for adults with developmental disabilities* (pp. 139–154). Baltimore: Paul H. Brookes.

McDonnell, J., Nofs, D., Hardman, M., & Chambless, C. (1989). An analysis of the procedural components of supported employment programs associated with worker outcomes. *Journal of Applied Behavior Analysis, 4,* 417–428.

McDonnell, J., Wilcox, B., & Boles, S. M. (1986). Do we know enough to plan transition? A national survey of state agencies responsible for services to persons with severe handicaps, *The Journal of The Association for Persons with Severe Handicaps,* 11, 53–60.

Meyer, L. H., Peck, C. A., & Brown, L. (1991). *Critical Issues in the Lives of People with Severe Disabilities.* Baltimore: Paul H. Brookes.

Moon, M. S., Inge, K. J., Wehman, P., Brooke, V., & Barcus, J. M. (1990). *Helping persons with severe mental retardation get and keep employment: Supported employment issues and strategies.* Baltimore: Paul H. Brookes.

Nisbet, J., Clark, M., & Covert, S. (1991). Living it up! An analysis of research on community living. In L. H. Meyer, C. A. Peck, & L. Brown (Eds.), *Critical Issues in the Lives of People with Severe Disabilities* (pp. 115–144). Baltimore: Paul H. Brookes.

Noble, J. H., & Conely, R. W. (1987). Accumulating evidence on the benefits and costs of supported and transition employment for persons with severe disabilities. *The Journal of The Association for Persons with Severe Disabilities, 12,* 182–189.

O'Brien, J., & O'Brien, C. L. (1992). Members of each other: Perspectives on social support for people with severe disabilities. In J. Nisbet (Ed.), *Natural Supports in School, at Work, and in the Community for People with Severe Disabilities* (pp. 17–64). Baltimore: Paul H. Brookes.

Rhodes, L. E., & Valenta, L. (1985). Industry-based supported employment: An enclave approach. *The Journal of the Association for Persons with Severe Handicaps, 10,* 12–20.

Rusch, F. R. (1986). *Competitive employment issues and strategies.* Baltimore: Paul H. Brookes.

Rusch, F. R. (1990). *Supported employment: Models, methods, and issues.* Sycamore, IL: Sycamore Press.

Rusch, F. R., Chadsey-Rusch, J., & Johnson, J. R. (1991). Supported Employment: Emerging Opportunities for Employment Integration. In L. H. Meyer, C. A. Peck, & L. Brown (Eds.), *Critical Issues in the Lives of People with Severe Disabilities* (pp. 145–170). Baltimore: Paul H. Brookes.

Rusch, F. R., Destefano, L., Chadsey-Rusch, J., Phelps, L. A., & Szymanski, E. (1992). *Transition from school to adult life: Models, linkages, and policy.* Sycamore, IL: Sycamore Press.

Rusch, F. R., Johnson, J. R., & Hughes, C. (1990). Analysis of co-worker involvement in relation to level of disability versus placement approach among supported employees. *The Journal of The Association for Persons with Severe Disabilities, 15,* 32–39.

Sale, P., Revell, W. G., & Wehman, P. (1992). Achievements and challenges II: An analysis of 1990 supported employment expenditures. *The Journal of The Association of Persons with Severe Handicaps, 17,* 236–246.

Taylor, S. J., Biklen, D., & Knoll, J. (1987). *Community Integration for People with Severe Disabilities.* Baltimore: Paul H. Brookes.

The Association for Persons with Severe Handicaps (1987). *Policy statement for cessation of capital investment in segregated settings.* Seattle, WA: Author.

Thompson, L., Powers, G., & Houchard, B. (1992). The wage effects of supported employment. *The Journal of The Association for Persons with Severe Handicaps, 17*, 87–94.

Tines, J., Rusch, F. R., McCaughrin, W., & Conley, R. W. (1990). Benefit-cost analysis of supported employment in Illinois: A statewide evaluation. *American Journal on Mental Retardation, 95*, 55–67.

Vogelsberg, R. T. (1986). Competitive employment in Vermont. In F. R. Rusch (Ed.), *Competitive Employment Issues and Strategies* (pp. 35–50). Baltimore: Paul H. Brookes.

Wehman, P. (1981). *Competitive Employment: New Horizons for Severely Disabled Individuals.* Baltimore: Paul H. Brookes.

West, M., Revell, W. G., & Wehman, P. (1992). Achievement and challenges I: A five-year report on consumer and system outcomes from the Supported Employment initiative. *The Journal of The Association for Persons with Severe Handicaps, 17*, 227–235.

Chapter *10*

Programs for the Aging and Elderly

Advances in medical technology and social support have significantly increased the average lifespan of Americans (Rice & Feldman, 1985). For example, in 1981, women lived an average of 78.3 years. By the year 2050, the average longevity of women is expected to rise to 81.3 years (U.S. Bureau of Census, 1982). Similar patterns are seen for males whose expected lifespan is projected to increase from an average of 73.3 years to 75.1 years during the same period. The increased lifespan has occurred simultaneously with growth in the proportion of elderly individuals in the general population. The U. S. Senate Committee on Aging, American Assocation of Retired Persons, Federal Council on Aging, and the U. S. Administration on Aging (1991) reported that at the beginning of the 20th century less than 10 percent of the population was 55 or older. However, by 1989 this proportion had grown to 20 percent with at least 12.5 percent being at least 65.

The increasing number of elderly persons in our society also creates significant demands on the social and health service system. The U. S. Senate Special Committee on Aging et al. (1991) reported that, in 1989, there were approximately 6.9 elderly individuals who required long-term care. This number is expected to increase to 18 million by the year 2040. The "greying" of U. S. society has focused attention on the needs of aging and elderly people. State and federal governments face a significant challenge in developing health and social service programs that can adequately meet the needs of this group of citizens.

Researchers have documented similar demographic trends for persons with disabilities (Facter, 1993; Janicki & Wisiewski, 1985; Seltzer & Krauss, 1987; Seltzer, Krauss, Litchfield, & Modlish, 1989). For example, in the 1930s, persons with Down Syndrome lived an average of 11 years, the current average lifespan of this group of individuals is over 50 years (Eyman, Call, & White, 1989; Janicki et

WINDOW 10-1

Robert is a 64-year-old man with moderate mental retardation and is legally blind and deaf. During the last several years he has been having problems with his blood pressure and must eat a restricted diet. In spite of these problems he is still in good physical shape. Robert works in a sheltered workshop and lives in a group home with 6 other men who range in age from 23 to 45.

Robert's mother and father both died recently. He has had problems adjusting to this loss. He would spend holidays at their house and they would come to visit him at his home once a month or so. He still has contact with two of his brothers who live in another part of the state but he only sees them once or twice a year. Staff at the workshop and the group home say that he has been depressed, but seems to be working through his grief. The staff in the workshop and group home have been trying to keep him involved in lots of activities to keep his spirits up, but they also admit that they aren't exactly sure what to do to help him deal with his loss.

Robert still likes to work, but gets tired easily and needs to take more frequent breaks at work. Staff at the workshop and group home have discussed the possibility of reducing Robert's work schedule to let him become more involved in other activities or spend more time at home. They are exploring alternatives like the community senior center or finding the resources to allow Robert to engage in leisure activities that he likes. The problem is that they have never worked with someone Robert's age before, and the state agency has very few resources available to help people like him.

The state developmental disabilities agency has promised to try and find some resources to meet Robert's needs. They have also established a task force to study the needs of aging and elderly persons with disabilities like Robert. The agency recognizes that Robert and others like him should be allowed to retire. Unfortunately, the agency has no plan to allow this to happen.

al., 1985). The increase in the length of time that persons with disabilities live has created a significant policy dilemma for the community service system (Seltzer & Krauss, 1987). As discussed in Chapter 9, many state adult service agencies are struggling to develop programs that can support the inclusion of adults with disabilities in employment and other community settings. These agencies now face an equally pressing need to develop programs that can support older persons with disabilities.

Although the significant growth in the number of aging and elderly persons with disabilities was projected several decades ago, there has been surprisingly little effort to identify and develop appropriate service alternatives (Seltzer & Krauss, 1987). For example, in their 1984 survey of the state plans of the state Developmental Disabilities planning councils, Janicki, Ackerman, and Jacobsen (1985) found that 91 percent of the plans made no mention of older persons with disabilities. Those state councils which did address the issue focused solely on examining the demographic characteristics of this population.

A number of researchers and advocates have begun to grapple with issues surrounding aging and disabilities (c.f., Janicki & Wisiewski, 1985; Seltzer & Krauss, 1987; Thurman, 1986). This chapter will outline some of the issues surrounding the development of service programs for aging and elderly persons with disabilities, as well as the emerging principles upon which these efforts may be based.

Structure of Services for the Aging and Elderly

In 1987, Congress recognized the special needs of aging and elderly persons with disabilities through two actions. The first amended the Developmental Disabilities Act to appoint the administrator of the agency serving elderly people in each state to the Developmental Disabilities Council and require Councils to consider aging-related issues in developing their state plans. These amendments also created incentives for training and education for professionals working with persons with disabilities in the areas of gerontology and geriatric services. These outreach and support services were to be provided through the University Affiliated Programs (UAPs) previously authorized within the law.

The second legislative action amended the Older Americans Act to include provisions that recognize the needs of older persons with disabilities. These amendments were designed to promote collaboration and coordination between aging and developmental disability service agencies. Equally important, these amendments established the expectation that these agencies would design services to allow older persons with disabilities to participate in the full range of programs available to their peers without disabilities and to promote their inclusion in the mainstream of society.

Focus 1:

What is the current status of programs for aging and elderly persons with disabilities?

Research has suggested that there are substantial differences in aging and elderly people who live in community-based and institutional programs. For example, individuals who live in institutions demonstrate lower functioning levels (Krauss & Seltzer, 1986), experience greater declines in sensory, physical, and behavioral abilities than peers who live in community-based programs (Janicki & Jacobson, 1986), and do not continue to develop new skills and abilities as they age (Eyman & Arndt, 1982).

Hauber et al. (1985) also found that older persons with disabilities living in community-based alternatives were more likely to maintain relationships with family members and peers without disabilities than individuals who lived in institutional programs. In addition, individuals who were supported by community-based service programs had greater access to community activities and resources than individuals who lived in institutional programs. The authors concluded that the overall quality of life of older persons with disabilities being served by community-based programs was higher than their peers who lived in institutional settings.

The available studies suggest that the majority of aging and elderly people with disabilities currently live in community rather than institutional programs (Hauber, Rotegard, & Bruininks, 1985; Seltzer & Krauss, 1987). In a national survey of programs serving persons with disabilities, Hauber et al. (1985) found that over half (55.7 percent) of the 603 of the individuals in their sample who were 63 years or older lived in foster homes, 15.5 percent lived in group homes serving 15 or fewer individuals, 13.6 percent lived in personal care homes, 7.6 percent were served in nursing homes, 4.6

percent lived in large group homes serving between 16 and 63 residents, 2.8 percent were in boarding homes, and .2 percent lived in supervised apartments. Seltzer (1985) also suggested that up to 15 percent of older persons with disabilities who are in the community may live with parents or other family members.

Although most older persons with disabilities are being served in community-based service programs, it does not appear that the majority of agencies provide services that would meet the unique needs of this group of people. For example, Seltzer and Krauss (1987) found that less than half of community-based residential programs provided specialized retirement services for program participants. Those programs which did provide such support were more likely to have been established expressly by state agencies to meet the needs of this group of people. In short, the typical residential programs provided to persons with disabilities were not being responsive to the different needs of older program participants, and in fact the services that these individuals were provided did not differ significantly from their younger peers. Of the programs which did provide retirement services, 57.5 percent relied on generic senior centers available in the local community as the mechanism to provide support.

Seltzer and Krauss (1987) also examined the services provided to older persons with disabilities in day programs. They found that of the 135 programs responding to the survey, only 22.2 percent provide supplemental retirement programs to older participants. The majority of these day programs provide employment or employment training services to this group of people. In other words, aging and elderly people with disabilities were expected to continue to work or develop new work skills in spite of their advanced age. Results of the survey also showed that 67.8 percent of the community-based day treatment programs which did provide retirement services used generic senior centers in the local community to meet the needs of participants.

Although there is a paucity of research on the nature of service alternatives for aging and elderly persons with disabilities, it does appear that many of these individuals do live successfully in the community. However, the availability of specific age-related service options for older persons is extremely limited. In addition, the use of generic senior service programs to meet some of their support needs appears to be feasible. These studies point to the critical need to develop service options that will accommodate the diverse needs of older persons with disabilities.

Current Issues

> **Focus 2:**
>
> Describe the barriers to the development of effective service programs for older persons with disabilities.

While there is a general consensus about the need to develop appropriate service alternatives for older persons with disabilities, there are a number of issues which may impede immediate action by state and federal agencies. These issues include (1) the absence of a common definition of the term "elderly" for persons with disabilities, (2) competition for limited service dollars by elderly persons with disabilities with younger peers, (3) a lack of consensus over what constitutes age-appropriate services for older persons with disabilities, and (4) limited coordination between aging and disability service agencies. It is unlikely that significant progress can, or will be made in designing appropriate service support for this group of people until a coherent policy which directly addresses these issues is developed.

Definition of "Elderly" for Persons with Disabilities

A significant issue facing the development of appropriate services for older persons with disabilities is the absence of an acceptable definition of the term *elderly*. A number of definitions have emerged in recent years as our society begins to grapple with the "greying" of the general population. The problem is that who is considered "elderly" is determined by many different variables including chronological, biological, social, and psychological factors (Thurman, 1986).

Perhaps the most widely accepted standard in determining whether one is "elderly" is chronological age. Most Americans accept age 65 as the universal standard for designating someone as elderly. This age level has emerged as the standard primarily because it is when most Americans become eligible for full benefits provided by publically funded retirement, pension, and medical care programs for the elderly. This age standard was selected by Congress when the average lifespan of most Americans was much shorter. The intent of these programs was to provide support to persons, who because of diminishing health or functioning level, could not realistically support themselves (Berkowitz, 1988). Recently, political support for increasing the age of eligibility for such services has grown because of the rise in the average lifespan of Americans and the enormous costs of programs for the elderly.

Unlike their peers without disabilities, there is no universally accepted chronological age standard in determining when a person with disabilities is elderly. In general, authors have agreed that this age standard must be lower for persons with disabilities because they experience declines in functioning level and health much earlier than peers without disabilities (Janicki & Wisniewski, 1985; Seltzer & Krauss, 1987). However, the limited data available on expected lifespan of older persons with disabilities and the quality of their lives during their last years makes the establishment of such age standards difficult. In spite of these problems, support has grown for chronological age standards which identify people with disabilities between 55 and 64 years as "aging" and people over age 65 as "elderly" (Jacobsen, Sutton, & Jankicki, 1985; Seltzer & Krauss, 1987). However, these definitions have not been incorporated into the legislation or policies which govern services for persons with disabilities.

Competition for Limited Service Dollars

Although the amendments to the Developmental Disabilities Act and the Older Americans Act increased collaboration between aging and developmental disabilities agencies, these amendments did not authorize additional monies to create needed programs.

As pointed out in Chapter 9, adult service agencies nationally face a number of significant fiscal barriers to developing service programs that can support the participation of persons with disabilities in the community (Braddock, 1987). State agencies interested in developing age-specific service options for older program participants must either obtain additional funds from state legislatures or reallocate dollars from existing employment and residential service programs. This situation creates competition between the older persons and their younger peers for limited resources. Significant improvements in the care provided to older persons with disabilities is not likely to occur until funding for such programs is made available at the state and federal levels.

Age-Appropriate Services

For most people, retirement represents a significant transition in their lives. Time previously allocated to their job or career and raising a family is shifted toward other interests. However, the needs and desires of older people is extremely diverse and uniquely individual (Thurman, 1986). Consequently, determining what are appropriate services for aging and elderly persons with disabilities is a challenge. Many authors agree that the primary issue facing service agencies is whether programs for this group of people should focus on *habilitation* (i.e., the development of new skills) or on *maintenance* of existing capabilities. This debate reflects the incongruence between the traditional programmatic focus of the aging and developmental disabilities service agencies (Gettings, 1988). The developmental disabilities system is designed to promote continuous growth of the individual, whereas the aging system is more focused on maximizing the quality of life of the individual as their skills decline.

Throughout this text, we have argued that people with severe disabilities should have the opportunity to achieve certain outcomes including productivity, independence, and autonomy, access to community resources, and participation in a network of friends and acquaintances. We have also stressed that these outcomes remain stable across age levels and service programs. What changes is the way in which personal and structural supports are organized to allow each individual to achieve these outcomes. While much more research is needed, it is clear that service programs must be structured to address the unique age-related challenges that older persons with disabilities deal with on a day to day basis. Without this focus, older persons with disabilities will be caught in a system which seeks to "habilitate" them rather than let them age with dignity. What is needed is a consensus about the mission and purpose of service programs for this population. Cotten and Spirrison (1986) attempted to articulate the mission of such programs in their Bill of Rights for Elderly Persons with Mental Retardation (Table 10-1). The challenge facing both aging and disability agencies is how to develop program models which ensure that these rights are realized and protected.

Collaboration Between Aging and Disability Agencies

A final barrier to meeting the needs of older persons with disabilities is the lack of coordination between those agencies responsible for supporting elderly people in our communities and those agencies responsible for supporting persons with disabilities

TABLE 10-1   A Bill of Rights for the Elderly Person with Mental Retardation

1. The right to an adequate standard of living, economic security, and protective work.
2. The right to humane services designed to help them reach their fullest potential.
3. The right to live as interdependently as they are able in the community of their choice, in as normal a manner as possible.
4. The right to an array of services that is generally available to other elderly groups.
5. The right to choose to retire. In addition, the opportunity to retire "to something," rather than "from something."
6. The right to participate as a member of the community, having reciprocal interdependence.
7. The right to be considered a person and not merely "elderly" or "retarded."
8. The right to protected, personal well-being, and to a qualified guardian when required.
9. The right to be involved in setting one's goals and making one's decisions. The right to fail if necessary.
10. The right to a positive future, and having enough involvement with life to prevent a preoccupation with death.
11. The right to be romantic, not asexual.
12. The right to sufficient activity and attention to permit continued integrity of self, individual identity, and purpose.
13. The right to an interesting environment and life style, with availability of sufficient mobility to provide a variety of surroundings.
14. The right to live and die with dignity.

Source: Cotten, P. D., & Spirrison, C. L. (1986). The elderly mentally retarded developmentally disabled population: A challenge for the service delivery system. In S. J. Brody & B. E. Rugg (Eds.), *Aging and rehabilitation* (pp. 159–187). New York: Springer Publishing.

(Janicki et al., 1985; Ossofsky, 1988; Seltzer & Krauss, 1987; Sison & Cotten, 1989). From a systems perspective, neither the aging or disability agencies have the resources capable of meeting the needs of older persons with disabilities. Consequently, there is growing concern that aging and developmental disability agencies must begin to work cooperatively to meet the needs of this group of people.

Quirk and Aravanis (1988) have suggested that there is significant overlap in the missions of aging and developmental disability agencies. They suggest that collaboration is possible between these agencies in a number of areas including the development of cohesive systems of long-term care, access to adequate and affordable health care, employment opportunities for older workers, affordable housing options, ombudsman services for institutionalized older persons, adequate income maintenance programs, fostering informal support systems for family, friends, and neighbors, and protective and legal services.

The numerous areas of overlap in service delivery between the aging and developmental disability agencies raises a number of questions about the need for segregated program alternatives for older persons with disabilities. Currently, a significant proportion of those agencies providing retirement services to persons with disabilities rely on generic senior centers to meet participant needs (Seltzer & Krauss, 1987). Although there is a need for more program development, clearly integrated options are a practical alternative for older persons with disabilities.

Service Alternatives

> **Focus 3:**
>
> What factors currently shape the development of service programs for older persons with disabilities?

While our knowledge about the characteristics and needs of older persons with disabilities is limited, information on how to best organize service programs for this group of people is virtually nonexistent. Discussions about the structure of service programs for older persons with disabilities have focused on two main questions. First, should these programs be designed to serve only people identified as elderly or should they be designed to provide services with younger peers? Second, should programs be designed to only meet the needs of persons with disabilities or should they be designed to serve all elderly individuals? These two factors have driven the development of the existing array of service alternatives currently available for older persons with disabilities (Seltzer & Krauss, 1987). The matrix presented in Table 10-2 illustrates graphically the interaction between these two factors. As indicated in the Table, there are age-specific and age-general community-based programs, as well as age-specific and age-general institutional programs. Nationally, there are examples of employment, residential, and retirement programs which fit into each cell of the matrix. However, an increasing number of authors have argued for the benefits of age-integrated community-based service alternatives for older persons with disabilities (Seltzer et al., 1989; Wolfensberger, 1985).

Age-Segregated or Age-Integrated Programs

A critical decsion facing state agencies in the design of service programs for older persons is whether these programs should be age-segregated or age-integrated (Seltzer & Krauss, 1987). The development of age-segregated programs is based on the assumption that the needs of older people with disabilities are quite different from younger individuals. In fact, research has suggested while there is very little difference in the support needs of older persons with and without disabilities, there are differences in the service needs of older and younger persons with disabilities (Seltzer, 1985). In particular, older persons need access to more intense medical support and care. As individuals with disabilities grow older they are more likely to need immediate access to health facilities and/or ongoing nursing care. In response to this need, some states have developed community-based day and residential programs which include medical support as an integral part of the services provided to participants (Catapano, Levy, & Levy, 1985; Hauber et al., 1985; Seltzer & Krauss, 1987). In addition, older persons face a unique set of issues as they age, such as the death of friends and family members, and the frustration and depression associated with the loss of mental and physical abilities. Such events can have

TABLE 10-2:   Services for Aging and Elderly Persons with Disabilities

Factors	Community-Based	Institutional
Age-integrated	Persons with disabilities are served with persons who are younger in natural work, home, and community settings. Examples: Supported employment, Supported living	Persons with disabilities are served with persons who are younger in large congregate care facilities. Examples: State institutions, Intermediate Care Facilities for the Mentally Retarded, Group Homes, Day Treatment Programs
Age-segregated	Persons with disabilities are served with other aging or elderly individuals in natural work, home, and community settings. Examples: Generic Senior Centers, sheltered housing for the elderly, continuum-of-care communities.	Persons with disabilities are served with other aging or elderly individuals in large congregate care facilities. Examples: Nursing homes.

a substantial effect on the quality of life experienced by older people. Service programs must be structured in ways to assist elderly persons with disabilities in dealing with the emotional and psychological stresses associated with these transitions (Seltzer, 1985).

Age-integrated programs are the alternate approach to the provision of service support to older persons with disabilities. Research suggests that there are advantages to designing service programs that allow older persons to be a part of an age-integrated social networks (Hauber & Short-DeGraff, 1990; McMahon, 1987; Seefeldt, 1989). The interactions that these individuals have with younger peers are associated with higher levels of satisfaction, with quality of life, and with the development of multi-dimensional social networks which support participation in the community, enhanced self-concept, and improved self-confidence. Younger individuals also benefit from such relationships by developing a better understanding of the needs of older people. In addition, they may receive guidance in coping with their daily lives through the life experiences of older persons in their social network.

Another factor which will influence the debate over the development of age-integrated or age-segregated programs is individual choice. Persons with disabilities must have the same opportunities as persons without disabilities to choose the type of retirement option that best meets their needs. Ultimately, this choice must be based on the personal preferences of the individual, the level of natural support available from their social network, and the service options available within their community (Nisbet, 1992; Sarason et al., 1977). The opportunity to make such choices will allow older individuals with disabilities to age with dignity (Thurman, 1986).

Community-Based or Institutional Programs

The majority of elderly people without disabilities prefer retirement options which allow their continued participation in the community and view institutionalization as a dreaded last resort (Ansello, 1988). Improvements in home health care as well as other social support programs (e.g., friendly visitor, chore service, meals on wheels) allow an increasing number of elderly people to remain in their own homes. In addition, programs such as housing co-ops, accessory apartments within homes, sheltered housing, and continuum-of-care communities have provided elderly persons with a viable alternative to institutionalization in many states. Increasingly, the aging service network has begun to recognize the need to devise programs that will allow service to be brought to the individual and be fit to their individual needs rather than the individual being brought to the service (Orleans & Orleans, 1985; Zola, 1988). Such service alternatives allow elderly people to maintain critical relationships with families, friends, and neighbors.

This trend in aging services is consistent with the expanding emphasis in the service system on supported education, employment, and living options with disabilities. Although this concept has not been extensively applied to older persons with disabilities, it is consistent with the need to continue to foster the community participation of persons with disabilities across the age range. Given that research has consistently shown that community-based alternatives are superior to institutional programs in promoting personal development and overall quality of life (Hauber et al., 1985; Seltzer et al., 1987), the development of community-based service options for older persons with disabilities is necessary.

Conclusion

Practitioners and policymakers face significant challenges in meeting the needs of aging and elderly persons with disabilities. The increase in the average lifespan of people with disabilities has created a growing need for age-specific service alternatives. It is clear that current policies and programs do not adequately address the needs of these individuals. Confusion over how to best design service programs for aging and elderly persons is exasperated by a lack of clear definition of who is "elderly," competition for limited funds between programs for older persons and their younger peers, a lack of consensus over what constitutes age-appropriate services for older persons with disabilities, and a lack of coordination between aging and disability agencies at federal, state, and local levels. The challenge facing federal and state agencies is to develop service programs that are responsive to the unique needs of older persons with disabilities and maximize their participation in community life.

Focus Review

Focus 1: What is the current status of programs for aging and elderly persons with disabilities?

ajority of older persons with disabilities live in the community, but a signif-
ninority are still served in institutional programs.

is little differentiation between the types of services provided by residential
ty programs to older persons with disabilities and their younger peers.

programs do provide retirement services, a majority rely on generic senior
citizen centers to meet the needs of participants.

Focus 2: Describe the barriers to the development of effective service programs for older persons with disabilities.

- The absence of a common definition of the term *elderly* for persons with disabilities
- Competition for limited service dollars by elderly persons with disabilities with younger peers
- A lack of consensus over what constitutes age-appropriate services for older persons with disabilities
- Limited coordination between aging and disability service agencies

Focus 3: What factors currently shape the development of service programs for older persons with disabilities?

- Programs can be structured as age-segregated or age-integrated. Age-segregated programs have historically been more sensitive to the unique physical and psychological needs of older persons. Age-integrated programs foster the development of heterogeneous social networks which promote an high overall quality of life.
- Programs are provided in either institutional or community settings. Research strongly supports the superiority of community-based service alternatives for older persons with disabilities.

References

Ansello, E. F. (1988). The intersecting of aging and disabilities. *Educational Gerontology, 14*, 351–364.

Berkowitz, E. D. (1988). Social insurance for the disabled and elderly in historical perspective. *Educational Gerontology, 14*, 411–418.

Bradock, D. (1987). *Federal policy toward mental retardation and developmental disabilities*. Baltimore: Paul H. Brookes.

Catapano, P. M., Levy, J. M., & Levy, P. H. (1985). Day activity and vocational program services. In M. P. Janicki and H. M. Wisniewski (Eds.), *Aging and Developmental Disabilities: Issues and Approaches* (pp. 317–326). Baltimore, MD: Paul H. Brookes.

Cotten, P. D. & Spirrison, C. L. (1986). The elderly mentally retarded developmentally disabled population: A challenge for the service delivery system. In S. J. Brody and G. E. Tuff (Eds.), *Aging and Rehabilitation* (pp. 159–187). New York: Springer.

Eyman, R. K., & Arndt, S. (1982). Life-span development of institutional and community-based mentally retarded residents. *American Journal of Mental Deficiency, 86*, 342–350.

Eyman, R. K., Call, T. L., & White, J. F. (1989). Mortality of elderly mentally retarded persons in California. *The Journal of Applied Gerontology, 8*, 203–215.

Facter, A. R. (1993). Translating policy into practice. In E. Sutton, A. R. Facter, B. A. Hawkins, T. Heller, & G. B. Seltzer (Eds.), *Older adults with developmental disabilities: Optimizing choice and change* (pp. 257–276). Baltimore: Paul H. Brookes.

Gettings, R. M. (1988). Barrier to and opportunities for cooperation between the aging and development disabilities services delivery systems. *Educational Gerontology, 14*, 419–429.

Hauber, E. A., Rotegard, L. L., Bruininks, R. H. (1985). Characteristics of residential services for older/elderly mentally retarded persons. In M. P. Janicki and H. M. Wisniewski (Eds.), *Aging and Developmental Disabilities: Issues and Approaches* (pp. 327–350). Baltimore, MD: Paul H. Brookes.

Hauber, E. A., & Short-DeGraff, M. A. (1990). Intergenerational programming for an increasingly age-segregated society. *Activities, Adaptation and Aging, 14*, 35–49.

Jacobsen, J. W., Sutton, M. S., & Janicki, M. P. (1985). Demography and characteristics of aging and aged mentally retarded persons. In M. P. Janicki and H. M. Wisniewski (Eds.), *Aging and Developmental Disabilities: Issues and Approaches* (pp. 115–142). Baltimore, MD: Paul H. Brookes.

Janicki, M. P., Ackerman, L., & Jacobson, J. W. (1985). State development disabilities/aging and planning for an older developmental disabled population. *Mental Retardation, 23*, 296–301.

Janicki, M. P., & Jacobson, J. W. (1986). Generational trends in sensory, physical, and behavior abilities among older mentally retarded persons. *American Journal of Mental Deficiency, 90*, 490–500.

Janicki, M. P., & Wisniewski, H. M. (1985). *Aging and Developmental Disabilities: Issues and Approaches*. Baltimore, MD: Paul H. Brookes.

Krauss, M. W., & Seltzer, M. M. (1986). Comparison of elderly and adult mentally retarded persons in community and institutional settings. *American Journal of Mental Deficiency, 91*, 237–243.

McMahon, M. A. (1987). The value of intergenerational relationships. *Journal of Gerontological Nursing, 13*, 25–29.

National Center for Health Statistics (1982). Advance report on final mortality statistics, 1979. *NCHS Monthly Vital Statistics Report, 31*, (6, Supplement). Washington, DC.

Nisbet, J. (1992). *Natural Supports in School, at Work, and in the Community for People with Severe Disabilities*, Baltimore, MD: Paul H. Brookes.

Orleans, M., & Orleans, P. (1985). High and low technology - sustaining life at home. *International Journal of Technology Assessment in Health Care, 1*, 353–363.

Ossofsky, J. (1988). Connecting the networks: Aging and lifelong disabilities. *Educational Gerontology, 14*, 389–397.

Quirk, D. E. & Aravanis, S. C. (1988). State partnerships to enhance the quality of life of older Americans with lifelong disabilities. *Educational Gerontology, 14*, 431–438.

Rice, D. P. & Feldman, J. J. (1985). Living longer in the United States: Demographic changes and health needs of the elderly. In M. P. Janicki and H. M. Wisniewski (Eds.), *Aging and Developmental Disabilities: Issues and Approaches* (pp. 9–26). Baltimore, MD: Paul H. Brookes.

Sarason, S. B., Carroll, C., Maton, K., Cohen, S., & Lorentz, E. (1977). *Human Services and Resource Networks*. Cambridge, MA: Brookline Books.

Seefeldt, C. (1989). Intergenerational programs: Impact on attitudes. *Journal of Children in Contemporary Society, 20*, 185–194.

Seltzer, M. M. (1985). Informal supports for aging mental retarded persons. *American Journal of Mental Deficiency, 90*, 259–265.

Seltzer, M. M. & Krauss, M. W. (1987). *Aging and Mental Retardation: Extending the Continuum*. Washington, DC: American Association on Mental Retardation.

Seltzer, M. M., Krauss, M. W., Litchfield, L. C., & Modlish N. K. (1989). Utilization of aging network services by elderly persons with mental retardation. *The Gerontologist, 29*, 234–238.

Sison, G. F. P. & Cotten, P. D. (1989). The elderly mentally retarded person: Current perspectives and future Directions. *The Journal of Applied Gerontology, 8*, 151–167.

Thurman, E. (1986). Maintaining dignity in later years. In J. A. Summers (Ed.), *The Right to Grow Up: An Introduction to Adults with Devel-*

opmental Disabilities (pp. 91–118) Baltimore, MD: Paul H. Brookes.

U. S. Bureau of the Census (1982). Population estimates and projections. *Current Population Reports*, Series P-25, No. 922, October.

U. S. Senate Special Committee on Aging, American Association of Retired Persons, Federal Council on the Aging, and U. S. Administration on Aging. (1991). *Aging America: Trends and projections*. Washington, DC: Author.

Wolfensberger, W. (1985). An overview of social role valorization and some reflections on elderly mentally retarded persons. In M. P. Janicki and H. M. Wisniewski (Eds.), *Aging and Developmental Disabilities: Issues and Approaches* (pp. 61–76). Baltimore, MD: Paul H. Brookes.

Zola, I. K. (1988). Aging and disability: Toward a unifying agenda. *Educational Gerontology, 14*, 365–387.

Name Index

Subject Index